Capitalism, For and Against

Political philosophy and feminist theory have rarely examined in detail how capitalism affects the lives of women. Ann Cudd and Nancy Holmstrom take up opposing sides of the issue, debating whether capitalism is valuable as an ideal and whether, as an actually existing economic system, it is good for women. In a discussion covering a broad range of social and economic issues, including unequal pay, industrial reforms, and sweatshops, they examine how these and other issues relate to women and how to analyze effectively what constitutes "capitalism" and "women's interests." Each author also responds to the opposing arguments, providing a thorough debate of the topics covered. The resulting volume will interest a wide range of readers in philosophy, political theory, women's studies, and global affairs.

ANN E. CUDD is Professor of Philosophy and Associate Dean for Humanities, University of Kansas. She is the author of *Analyzing Oppression* (2006), and co-edited (with Anita Superson) *Theorizing Backlash* (2002) and (with Robin Andreason) *Feminist Theory* (2005).

NANCY HOLMSTROM is Professor Emerita and former Chair of Philosophy at Rutgers University Newark. She is the author of numerous articles on core topics in social philosophy and is the editor of *The Socialist Feminist Project: A Contemporary Reader in Theory and Politics* (2002).

Capitalism, For and Against

A Feminist Debate

Ann E. Cudd

and

Nancy Holmstrom

 CAMBRIDGE
UNIVERSITY PRESS

CAMBRIDGE UNIVERSITY PRESS
Cambridge, New York, Melbourne, Madrid, Cape Town, Singapore,
São Paulo, Delhi, Dubai, Tokyo, Mexico City

Cambridge University Press
The Edinburgh Building, Cambridge CB2 8RU, UK

Published in the United States of America by Cambridge University Press, New York

www.cambridge.org
Information on this title: www.cambridge.org/9780521114073

First published 2011

Printed in the United Kingdom at the University Press, Cambridge

A catalogue record for this publication is available from the British Library

Library of Congress Cataloguing in Publication data
Cudd, Ann E., 1959–
   Capitalism, For and Against : A Feminist Debate / Ann E. Cudd,
   Nancy Holmstrom.
      p.   cm
   Includes bibliographical references and index.
   ISBN 978-0-521-11407-3 – ISBN 978-0-521-13211-4 (pbk.)
   1. Capitalism–Social aspects.   2. Feminism.   I. Holmstrom, Nancy
   (Nancy Christina Louise), 1943–   II. Title.
   HB501.C875 2010
   330.12′2–dc22
   2010045709

ISBN 978-0-521-11407-3 Hardback
ISBN 978-0-521-13211-4 Paperback

Contents

Tables and figures

Acknowledgments

Our biggest debt of gratitude goes to Professor Louise Antony, first for organizing the panel at the American Philosophical Association convention in December 2006 on Feminism and Capitalism, for inviting us both to speak (and thus introducing us to each other), for her comments on our presentations, and then for supporting our book project at every point. Without Louise this book would not exist. We also thank our commentator on that panel Professor Christine Koggel for generous and helpful comments, as well as the audience of the session. Ann particularly thanks Almas Sayeed for her extended discussion of the papers after the session.

Louise subsequently persuaded us to pursue a publication venue for our debate, and this ultimately led us to propose the present book to Cambridge University Press. We are grateful to Hilary Gaskin, our editor, and several anonymous reviewers for their comments, criticism, and suggestions on our proposal and manuscript. In developing the proposal for the book we were helped greatly by the advice of Jay Hullitt, philosopher and publisher of Hackett Books, who, among other things, gave us the idea for our title. We thank Jeff Dean for his advice on the manuscript. Joe Braun helped with background research, and Matt Waldschlagel constructed the index for this book, and we thank them both.

Ann would like to thank Joe Braun, Pinfei Lu, audiences at Butler University, Bowling Green State University, and the Institute for Philosophy at National Tsing Hua University in

Taiwan, as well as her students in her Fall 2009 Philosophy of Social Science seminar for helpful discussions of portions of the book. She would also like to thank the University of Kansas for research support, as well as her colleagues in the Office of the Dean of the College of Liberal Arts and Sciences for covering for her when she was out of the office either working on this book, or hiking, or skiing in Colorado (they were never sure which). Most of all, Ann thanks her husband, Neal Becker, for help both intellectual and personal with this project.

Nancy would like to thank Gertrude Ezorsky, Sam Farber, Milton Fisk, and Richard Smith, who read her initial contribution in its entirety; Johanna Brenner for her ongoing political and personal support; and the participants in the Spring 2009 meeting of Socialist Feminist Philosophers in Action (SOFPHIA), who read a portion of the manuscript: Sandra Bartky, Sarah Begus, Ann Ferguson, Anna Gotlib, Jack Hammond, Don Hanover, Margaret McLaren, Marlisa Moschella, Mecke Nagel, Kathy Russell, Karsten Struhl, and, in particular, Jessica Kyle, who wrote extensive comments. Nancy would especially like to thank Richard for his loving support and for taking time away from his own work to help with hers. She looks forward to doing the same for him.

Finally, we would also like to thank one another for the extremely cooperative and productive working relationship we forged in spite of our disagreements.

Part I

1 For capitalism as a feminist ideal and reality

Ann E. Cudd

1 Introduction

A WOMAN BORN IN THE LATE SEVENTEENTH CENTURY in Europe had a life expectancy of less than thirty years.[1] She would have expected to bear seven children, and spend her days gathering wood and water, spinning yarn and making clothing, preparing food, and tending children. If she were born to a wealthy, aristocratic family she would have served mainly as a pawn in a diplomatic game between aristocratic families run by men and serving the interests of the oldest and most dominant among them. She did not look forward to any sort of political voice let alone power of her own unless she were one of the small handful of queens by birth. If she were born to a peasant family, she would have been illiterate. Much of her life was spent in hard labor and dirty, cramped conditions of life. She had little control over the timing or number of children she would bear, and she would likely bury most of her children before dying herself in childbirth.

My maternal grandmother was born in the late nineteenth century in the upper Midwest of the United States. She bore five children, four of whom lived until maturity, and she lived to be eighty years old in good health until her final days. When she was in her thirties, the Nineteenth Amendment to the US Constitution was ratified and she became eligible to vote in federal elections,

---

1 James C. Riley, *Rising Life Expectancy: A Global History* (New York: Cambridge University Press, 2001), 32–33. Life expectancy statistics for this period vary widely, but none are greater than thirty.

although she never lived to see a woman elected as governor or as a senator from her state. She graduated from high school and lived the hard working life of a farm wife, but her children were more educated, and her youngest daughter, my mother, was able to earn a Master's degree and have a professional career. While my grandmother was born in an age of horse-drawn vehicles, she lived to ride in cars, watch television, and have a phone in her home.

Today, a girl born in Europe or North America can expect to live into her eighties.[2] She will learn to read at an early age and grow up surrounded by ready access to information and entertainment. She will carry a phone in her pocket that she can use to communicate with virtually anyone on the planet. She will be able to choose when and whether to bear children, and the gender and sex of her intimate partners. With varying amounts of effort and good luck (depending on her race and class position at birth), she can live a professional life just like her brothers. She can participate fully in social and political life, with almost as good a chance of gaining real power as any man.

These massive changes in the lives of women and girls are due in large part to the development of capitalism, the now dominant economic system on the planet. Capitalism has been the incubator of ideas from technology to marketing, and morality to politics. In my contribution to this book, I will present the case for the claim that capitalism has been the main force in the advancement of women and of society more generally, and that it can continue to be a liberating force for women around the world. As convincing (or so I shall argue) as the historical case seems, though, there are reasons for skepticism about the positive value of capitalism in the contemporary world and going forward into the future. While the quality of life for women and girls in the middle and upper classes of North America and Europe is beyond question better on virtually any

---

2 Central Intelligence Agency of the United States, *CIA World Factbook*, Central Intelligence Agency, 2008, available at: www.cia.gov/library/publications/ the-world-factbook, accessed September 5, 2009. The 2008 *CIA World Factbook* reports life expectancies of 80.97 for the United States, 83.86 for Canada, 83.63 for Switzerland, and 84.23 for France.

measure than could ever have been imagined even by my grand-mother, women and girls in much of the global South live far lesser lives than their contemporaries in the global North.[3] Capitalism also clearly creates and sustains massive inequalities in wealth around the world and within wealthy societies. Although men are also the victims of global poverty and inequality, women are far more vulnerable to these twin ills. Women are also trafficked in greater numbers than are men, and this trafficking is motivated in part by greed and enabled by the great inequalities in wealth in the world. Women, as a group, remain dominated by men in all societies, with the possible exception of the Scandinavian countries, which have reined in the workings of capitalism through significant, democrat-ically implemented, government interventions in market and social life. These facts notwithstanding, I shall argue that women's best opportunity for liberation from both poverty and domination by men exists in the development of an enlightened capitalism.

Defining capitalism

A defense of capitalism must begin by clarifying the meaning of "capitalism" in order to classify societies, or possible societies, that fit under the term. To provide both a realistic assessment of the performance of capitalist societies and at the same time to look forward to a more enlightened form of capitalism, I seek an oper-ational definition of the term as it can be applied in the actual world to pick out economies that can properly be called "capital-ist." With this operational definition I will examine the empirical and theoretical case for capitalism as it has existed to this point in time. To create a reasonable hope for future improvements, how-ever, I will also offer a normative ideal of capitalism. Defining capitalism is thus both a normative and an explanatory task. It is also a political task, in the sense that the form of capitalism that I choose to define stakes out a territory to defend in practice against opposing forms that exist in practice.

3 By "Global South" I mean to denote poor and so-called developing societies, many of which are located in the southern hemisphere (sub-Saharan Africa, South America), but some of which lie in the southern parts of the northern hemisphere, including Central America and southern and eastern Asia.

The defining conditions of capitalism

Since economic activities have evolved greatly over human history, it makes sense to provide an operational definition that picks out capitalist economies as they have evolved. Capitalism is a term that was coined by Marx. By "capitalism" Marx meant an economic system whose core, defining feature is private ownership of the means of production, that is, of capital inputs to production:

> [Capitalism] can spring into life only when the owner of the means of production and subsistence meets in the market with the free laborer selling his labor-power. And this one historical condition comprises a world's history. Capital, therefore, announces from its first appearance a new epoch in the process of social production.[4]

Let us call this first feature of capitalism highlighted by Marx the *private ownership of capital condition*. Because ownership rights are defined within a community or a nation, economies are bordered by the boundary within which such rights obtain. I will refer to these bounded units as economies. Where private ownership of capital is possible, making very minimal assumptions of differences in individuals' preferences and/or initial distribution of capital inputs, along with their freedom to engage in voluntary exchanges (as entailed by their ownership rights), markets will develop, including markets for labor.[5] The feature on which Marx focused his moral critique of capitalism was production by free wage labor.[6] This definition served well to mark a line between the late Middle Ages in Europe, characterized by agricultural serf labor and a small landowning class, and the beginnings of industrial capitalism, where large numbers of workers freely contract

---

4 Robert Tucker (ed.), *Marx–Engels Reader*, 2nd edn. (New York: W. W. Norton, 1978), 339.

5 This is the basic idea of general equilibrium, a proof of which can be seen in just about any contemporary microeconomics textbook.

6 Philippe Van Parijs, *Real Freedom for All: What if Anything can Justify Capitalism?* (Oxford: Clarendon Press, 1995), 3. Van Parijs defines capitalism in a manner very similar to this: a system in which the bulk of a society's means of production is privately owned and people in some important sense own themselves.

their labor services with the small number of wealthy owners of capital. Let us call this the *free wage labor condition*.

There are a few problems with taking Marx's definition of capitalism as the operative definition, let alone the normative ideal. First, Marx's definition of capitalism is of a descriptive ideal type that no longer exists, if indeed it ever did. Taxation on capital, regulation of the use of capital, and outright government ownership of productive capacities restrict, to a greater or lesser degree, private ownership of capital in all countries of the world. Yet we would not want to say that capitalism therefore no longer exists. Second, in Marx's time, industrial production was the main form of production and material resources the major form of capital in economies that we would want to call capitalist, but that is no longer the case. "Means of production" specifically meant material, nonlabor inputs. To Marx, capitalist labor meant undifferentiated labor power. Now financial capital and human capital are much more prominent inputs into the production of value in the world. Third, in Marx's time the ownership of capital marked a sharp distinction between classes that no longer obtains. Today, most middle-class persons in the United States, for instance, are partial owners of a large number of firms through their retirement accounts and other forms of savings. Yet they are hardly the capitalists of Marx's imagination. Finally, Marx's definition fails to highlight the features of capitalism that make it most attractive, namely, the ability of markets to aggregate information about consumer preferences and the availability of, and demand for, capital, labor, and goods without the guidance of a central planner. Thus, if the definition is to fit both the historical and the contemporary cases of capitalism, the descriptive, operational definition of capitalism will have to be altered.

Harold Demsetz, a contemporary neoclassical economist, updates the simple Marxist definition of capitalism as follows: "an economy based on decentralized private ownership of resources and open markets."[7] Demsetz's definition speaks of "resources"

---

7 Harold Demsetz, *From Economic Man to Economic System: Essays on Human Behavior and the Institutions of Capitalism* (New York: Cambridge University Press, 2008), 81.

rather than means of production, which allows for financial capital and highly differentiated human capital, and adds the elements of "decentralization" and "open markets." Both of these ideas imply that governments do not control centrally what is made or consumed, but rather what is determined by the uncoordinated private decisions of individuals who are free to contract to buy or sell their labor, capital, goods, and services with each other with relative freedom from constraint by government. Let us call this the *decentralized open market condition*. Demsetz's definition is too spare, however, in that he leaves out the important aspect that Marx focused on: production of commodities. But commodities are at the heart of capitalism; we can defend capitalism partly because it produces them so well, and we can criticize capitalism for the ways that it makes us all too aware of how many material things we have. The definition also fails to elaborate the kinds of intervention and constraints that are permissible. Depending on how strictly we read the phrase "based on," Demsetz's definition still suffers from a defect similar to that of Marx because, as I stated earlier, the real world does not contain countries where private ownership of resources is complete nor is there a country where markets are completely free of any government intervention. If we read "based on" somewhat more loosely, we move in the direction of an operative definition of capitalism, which requires an economy relatively free of undue government intervention in markets or private ownership of resources.

What should count as undue government intervention for the sake of our operational definition? There are two levels on which we can ask this question. On the descriptive level we can ask: what are the limits of government intervention for the (descriptive) ideal type of capitalism? When is government intervention so great that an economy is better classified as socialist or centrally planned? On the normative level we can ask: what is the best, most enlightened form of capitalism? The descriptive ideal is the idealization of the economic model of capitalism as a market system, including the idealizations of the free market and free wage labor. There is no one measure of the descriptive ideal, but there are a few desiderata of such ideal types. Better descriptive ideal theories classify phenomena in ways that allow clear and useful distinctions between categories. Better descriptive theories make better predictions and are better able to make successful public policy recommendations (that is, ones that bring about their intended consequences). These are normatively loaded measures, to be sure. The descriptive ideal also assumes a set of background social conditions that constitute the ideas of property, free exchange, and free wage labor. Thus, even the descriptive ideal implies some normatively justified assumptions.[8]

One of these assumptions is that ownership and participation in markets is to be nondiscriminatory, in the sense of invidious discrimination against persons based on their attributed social group status, such as gender, race, sexual orientation, or national origin. The purely economic rationale for what I shall call the *nondiscrimination constraint* is that each individual is to be considered as a bundle of assets and preferences abstracted from other aspects of who they are because it is efficient. It is inefficient to treat individuals otherwise, since that would require every product or trade offer to be identified by an additional criterion other than its purely economic value; namely, by the attributive status (that is, the gender, race, etc.) of the individual who is offering the trade. This inefficiency is a transaction cost that need not be borne. Instead, individual assets are evaluated for the worth of those assets, regardless of who owns them. Their preferences define their utility functions, and the worth of their assets define their budget constraints. In the market, individuals are faceless, backgroundless utility functions, budget constraints, and production functions.

There is also a normative rationale for the nondiscrimination constraint, which is that if a person is not free to contract their labor or goods in the market with others based on the evaluation of their labor or goods, then they are not in reality free.

---

8 Ann E. Cudd, "How to Explain Oppression," *Philosophy of the Social Sciences* 35(1) (March 2005): 20–49. This article defends a set of theoretical desiderata for theories of irreducibly normative phenomena. Capitalism need not be modeled in this normative way, but the model of enlightened capitalism that I seek in my contribution to this book is such a normative model.

Rather, they are constrained by background features over which they have no control and with which they may not even identify themselves. Capitalism can meet the descriptive ideal of freedom, in the minimal sense of freedom from constraint, only by adhering to the nondiscrimination constraint. Now one might object that the sense of freedom that capitalism upholds requires one to be free to form preferences based on any form of bias or prejudice. I will address this deep concern in the final section of my contribution. For now I will rely on the historical, contingent fact that in contemporary capitalist societies the nondiscrimination constraint has become commonly accepted enough for government intervention to protect individuals from discrimination to be considered an appropriate form of interference in markets.[9]

The descriptive ideal of capitalism I will defend here is a system in which there are nondiscriminatory, legal protections of decentralized, private ownership of resources, cooperative, social production for all citizens, and free and open competitive markets for exchange of goods, labor, services, and material and financial capital. This definition implies the socially and governmentally sanctioned nature of the system. Laissez faire capitalism is an unrealizable ideal that could never exist in fact, because for capitalism to even exist, let alone prosper, property rights need definition by a legislative body and protection by a police force. If people do not have secure rights to things, they need not trade, since they can take, and when they have something, it can be just as easily taken away. Markets require trust and security, such as can be supplied only by a relatively complex social system of rights, trust, and protection.[10] Social, cooperative interaction is thus at the heart of the system, in both the creation of the

---

9 This is not to say that discrimination has ended, of course. There continues to be discrimination, but it is less explicit and has to be hidden from view on pain of legal and social sanctions.

10 Elizabeth Anderson, "Ethical Assumptions in Economic Theory: Some Lessons from the History of Credit and Bankruptcy," *Ethical Theory and Moral Practice* 7 (2004): 347–60. Anderson argues that capitalism has become less and less laissez faire, changing over time because of its own internal dynamic, which tends to increase everyone's preferences and expectations for rights and freedoms.

social, legal infrastructure that frames economic production and exchange, and in production and exchange in themselves. This definition emphasizes the competitive character of the system, which, as we shall see, has both positive and negative implications for human well-being. Capitalism is a form of cooperative competition, a set of socially accepted rules within which players seek their best advantage, as they see it. Its normative value as a social system will depend upon both the rules that delimit the game and the values by which its players define their best advantage. This definition does not specify how capitalism relates to the distribution of resources, since government or private charity can redistribute the outcome of production and exchange – but only to a point. Redistribution of goods that removes the ability or incentive for people to create firms and produce for exchange makes the system something other than and opposed to capitalism.

Recently Amartya Sen has suggested that "capitalism" has lost its meaningfulness because nearly all the countries of the world allow more or less private ownership of productive means, but also practice considerable government intervention in the market.[11] First, this is not entirely accurate, in the sense that there are a several economies that are quite isolated from global trade, either because they are failed states and so poor as to be unable to support a decent economy altogether (e.g., Mauritania, the Democratic Republic of Congo, or Chad), or because they are isolated politically and within their borders rule their populations strictly to disallow much large-scale private enterprise (Cuba, North Korea, Libya). Second, the term "capitalism" still wields a rhetorical force for both supporters and opponents that is worth exploring, even if most of the world is now capitalist. That is the point of this book. However, Sen is no doubt correct if he is taken to mean that the differences within capitalism are greater than the differences between at least some of the states that I would classify as capitalist, and some that do not meet that description.

---

11 Amartya Sen, "Capitalism Beyond the Crisis," *New York Times Review of Books*, March 26, 2009.

For example, there are states that are poorer than Libya, with its vast oil reserves, that are capitalist, such as Paraguay, and there are countries that are more restricted in basic negative freedoms (freedom of the press, assembly, religion) other than property rights as compared with Cuba that are capitalist, such as Singapore.[12] Therefore, I need to distinguish different kinds of capitalism in order to be more precise about what I am defending, and what is ancillary to capitalism and could be altered without losing the best features of capitalism.

Types of capitalism

The three defining conditions of capitalism: private ownership of capital; decentralized, open markets, and free wage labor; and the nondiscrimination constraint, imply a degree of government intervention to provide and protect, but not preclude the freedom of markets and exchange. That is, government intervention must frame markets without extinguishing them. We can identify a range of levels of government intervention in the ownership and control of resources and markets in the actual world. William Baumol, Robert Litan, and Carl Schramm identify four types of contemporary capitalism along these dimensions.[13] The first type is *state guided capitalism*, which is a national economic system in which the government decides which industries and firms will grow, but recognizes and enforces rights of property and contract, markets determine prices of goods and services and wages, and at least some small-scale activities are in private hands. While

---

12 This is not to say that Cuba respects freedom of the press or freedom of assembly, however. It is, in fact, impossible to find a country that severely restricts the right to private ownership of productive means that does not also severely restrict other negative liberties. See Amnesty International Report 2009, "State of the World's Human Rights," available at: http://thereport.amnesty.org/en/regions/americas/cuba, accessed August 1, 2009. For Singapore see Amnesty International Report 2009, "State of the World's Human Rights," available at: http://thereport.amnesty.org/en/regions/asia-pacific/singapore, accessed August 1, 2009.

13 William J. Baumol, Robert E. Litan, and Carl J. Schramm, *Good Capitalism, Bad Capitalism, and the Economics of Growth and Prosperity* (New Haven, CT: Yale University Press, 2007), ch. 4.

Baumol *et al.* focus on governmental control through banks and control of financial capital, governmental control and support of science and technology can also lead the way to a highly developed industrial capitalism. Megan Greene defines the "developmental state" as "a strong and proactive state that – armed with a meritocratic, efficient, and knowledgeable technocracy and institutions that provide it with highly embedded links to industry and society – imposes policies on the private sector that foster development."[14] Taiwan provides a paradigm example of such a developmental state through its sponsorship of science and technology in order to bring about rapid industrialization to achieve a level of economic development to rival the most highly developed economies. Other examples of state guided capitalist economies, or developmental states, include China, India, Singapore, South Korea, and Japan, the so-called "Asian tigers." This model for developing capitalist economies has proven to be highly effective in gaining the technological know-how and industrial infrastructure needed to develop a competitive, First World economy. However, these countries sacrifice some capitalist efficiencies that eventually lead to stagnation and recession until protectionist policies are gradually removed.

A second type of capitalism identified by Baumol *et al.* is *oligarchic capitalism*, nominally capitalist because there is private ownership of productive means. But in this kind of pseudo-capitalism markets are not exactly free; the government favors a particular elite or family with rules that make entrance into industries and markets difficult for outsiders. Hence, this pseudo-capitalism loses many of the advantages that capitalism is supposed to offer, according to economic theory, such as competitive efficiency (since there will be monopolies or at least monopolistic competition), and some of the incentives to innovation. It also forfeits any chance of offering the kind of political and social freedoms that capitalism is supposed to provide, such as free choice of occupation or the ability to work one's way out

14 J. Megan Greene, *The Origins of the Developmental State in Taiwan* (Cambridge, MA: Harvard University Press, 2008), 10.

of the working class. Finally, oligarchic capitalism institutionalizes inequality by family or group, not by merit or effort as the ideal, theoretical capitalism does. Examples of oligarchic capitalism include many states in Latin America and the former Soviet Union, oil exporting countries of the Middle East, and much of Africa. These countries tend to have the worst levels of inequality as measured by Gini coefficients, and are characterized by sluggish growth.[15] Because of the difficulties for outsiders to start official businesses, the informal economy grows, which creates its own inefficiencies and injustices as people are forced to evade the government and legal institutions to either produce or consume the products created.

A third kind of capitalism Baumol *et al.* call *big firm capitalism*, in which big firms dominate the economy, and where the originators of these firms have died or left the scene and the firms have passed into the ownership of institutional investors. This is a mature capitalist system in which a greater portion of the population owns shares in the major producers. Firms tend to be

---

15 A country's Gini coefficient is measured by the area under the Lorenz curve, which represents the proportion of total income in a country earned by percent of population (usually represented by households, so not sensitive to gender disadvantages within households), divided by the proportion of income for each percent of population under the assumption of perfect equality (i.e., 5% of population earn 5% of income, 50% earn 50%, 75% earn 75%, and so on). The resulting number ranges from 0 to 1, although it is sometimes multiplied by 100 so that the range is 0 to 100. The higher the number, the greater the inequality being represented. See http:// en.wikipedia.org/wiki/Gini_coefficient#Definition. Poor countries (those with low per capita GDP) generally have higher Gini indices, spread between 40 and 65, with extremes at 25 and 71, while rich countries generally have lower Gini indices (under 40). The lowest Gini coefficients (under 30) can be found in continental Europe. Overall, there is a clear negative correlation between Gini coefficient and GDP per capita, although the United States, Hong Kong, and Singapore are all rich and have high Gini coefficients. See also United Nations Human Development Report 2008, available at: http:// hdrstats.undp.org/indicators/147.html. While the Gini coefficient is the standard measure of economic inequality, it is problematic in that it measures income not wealth, it compares by household, not individual, and it only measures the reported income, missing income earned in underground activities.

large and include research and development programs in-house, ensuring that there are incremental, intentional improvements of the products from the perspective of the paying consumers. However, these firms introduce so-called principal–agent problems: the investors in the firms – the principals – have to rely on the advice of their agents – the managers of the firms – to make decisions on future research and investment. Yet what will be profit maximizing for individual managers may not maximize overall firm profits, which, however profit is defined, is the primary interest of the investors. Similar problems arise for consumers, who have to rely on the promises of the firms about the future performance of durable goods. Firms have an incentive to build in a degree of planned obsolescence in such goods in order to assure future sales.

The final form of capitalism that Baumol *et al.* describe and that they extol is what they call *entrepreneurial capitalism*. In this form of capitalism, there are a large number of persons – entrepreneurs – who seek to innovate and commercialize their innovations. Innovation, they argue, is the primary way that societies make material progress. This is because with a fixed set of technologies, there can be only so much improvement in the productivity of labor, and resources become ever more scarce as they are exploited in production. However, innovations allow new techniques and resources to be exploited; successful innovations are those that bring about great changes in the way that things are made, information is transmitted and managed, people are transported, and generally how life is lived.

Successful innovation offers the possibility of mega prizes of great wealth, as well as the psychic gains of being one's own boss and trying for the prize. This makes entrepreneurs the low cost innovators; they are the people who are willing to take the risks of having their investment in time and materials go to waste if their innovation does not succeed either technically or commercially, in return for the possibility of enormous payoffs. When a firm or a public social institution subsidizes innovation, it does so without promising the innovator the very large prize, and so those who would do it only for the large prize are not motivated to innovate through this institutional medium. Those who would innovate just for the joy of discovery would presumably not care much about the external motivations. More significantly, the innovator is likely to be in the best position to judge how good her or his idea is. This introduces a principal–agent problem,[16] in that only those who are less convinced of the value of their idea would choose to go down the institutional route to innovation where there is a choice. Hence, the best innovators are the most likely to become entrepreneurs, and are more likely to do so when they can go it alone.

Large firms can make innovation contagious. As an example Baumol *et al.* point to IBM computers, which, once they were introduced and became well known and available to a large number of consumers, created an ever increasing market for computers. This led to new firms like Apple and Dell, who produced innovations that enabled them to capture a larger and larger share of an increasing market for computers. While Apple competed through technical innovations in the capabilities and aesthetic appeal of the personal computer, Dell competed by its ability to customize the components of the computer to each consumer for a low price. What Baumol *et al.* point out is that capitalism is the only system in which we see such rapid and revolutionary technical innovation, the kind of innovation that can change the way in which we live in a very short period of time: "With rare exceptions, truly innovative entrepreneurs can only be found in capitalist economies, where the risk of doing something new – and spending time and money to make it happen – can be handsomely rewarded and the rewards safely kept."[17] Looking at the history of the twentieth century, for example, the only significant technical innovations made in noncapitalist

---

16 A principal–agent problem obtains when one person – the principal – hires another – the agent – to provide a service (or the principal sells the agent a good) that the principal has some expertise or privileged knowledge of (e.g., a physician), and hence the quality of the service (good) cannot be perfectly evaluated by the agent.

17 Baumol, Litan, and Schramm, *Good Capitalism, Bad Capitalism, and the Economics of Growth and Prosperity*, 87.

countries were in government-driven enterprises, mainly military defense. Confining innovation to such enterprises simply reduces the chances that wholly new kinds of technologies will be developed, since the number of areas on which governments will concentrate attention, even in a centrally-planned economy, is lower than in an economy driven by the variety of interests of private citizens. This is not to say that noncapitalist societies did not make improvements in technical efficiency; everyone knows that in fascist Italy the trains ran on time. But the kinds of technical improvements that tend to emerge from noncapitalist economies are of this type, and not the revolutionary type exemplified by the development of the locomotive, telephone, automobile, airplane, television, transistor, or personal computer.

Successful entrepreneurial economies embrace and encourage change. However, this then creates economic and social problems. The most obvious of these as I write this is the problem of financial crises which occur when investment overshoots the productive capacity of, or consumer demand for, an industry, creating an inflated nominal estimation of the real values of firms, which amounts to a financial bubble that can burst with the slightest pressure. Financial bubbles tend to accompany technological revolutions because many investors want to get in on the gains, but most of the companies are bound to fail. This leads to the boom and bust nature of financial markets. When finances are difficult to come by, consumption and production slows, workers are laid off, and people suffer from reduced expectations, reduced levels of consumption, and in some cases, poverty.

Workers under all forms of capitalism do well in terms of job security, benefits, and retirement as long as the industry in which they are working is doing well. But no industry lasts forever, and economies tend to undergo disruptive restructuring when the technology employed by these firms becomes obsolete because of the appearance of an effective competitor industry. In such circumstances, older workers suffer massive layoffs and reduced benefits. Younger workers typically have to relocate and possibly retool their skills in order to gain new employment. This is disruptive to neighborhoods and families, and can result in reduced consumption levels and lower levels of happiness. Inequality increases between workers in the affected industries and the owners and managers of unaffected firms. Thus, while capitalist economies are in general wealthier and have higher levels of personal income and consumption of goods, they also suffer from swings of boom and bust. These swings can be mitigated by government interventions, as the post-Depression capitalist economies have learned. A defensible capitalism must take such measures in order to avoid Depression-like catastrophe.

Opponents of capitalism

Given this variety of capitalist systems, what economic systems do not qualify as capitalist? Specifically, what are the rivals of capitalism against which I shall argue my case? The straw men against which I shall not aim my argument include systems that are based on slavery (legal or illegal), or bonded labor, nor those societies that are classified as failed states for their inability to rule according to settled law. I have two rhetorical opponents as I make my case for capitalism. The first is the socialist economy that was more or less envisioned by Marx as the successor economic epoch to capitalism. Just as there are many varieties of capitalism, there are many varieties of socialist economies, ranging from very democratic to totalitarian, and from collective ownership of almost everything to collective ownership only of large-scale production facilities and utilities. Indeed, defenders of both capitalism and socialism will want to claim some of the same societies (such as Sweden or Denmark) as prime examples of the success of their favored economic system. Thus, we need to come up with a fairly clear distinction in order not to be arguing past one another, disagreeing on peripheral features or extreme versions of our favored systems that we would not endorse, while agreeing on the best case versions but claiming them for our own side. The socialist opponent I will defend capitalism against is the centrally-planned, socialist economy typified by the Soviet Union or the People's Republic of China under Mao Zedong. Such societies violate the private ownership of capital condition, the free wage labor condition, and the decentralized, open market condition. The Swedish and Danish economies allow private ownership of productive means, and allow labor to contract freely (modulo immigration restrictions on foreign workers), but heavily tax wealth and redistribute income in a variety of ways. The ownership of all wealth is taxed, but the market is free and open to all. Thus, they meet my conditions of capitalist systems.

The second type of opponent for my argument is the social system that is based on social and religious tradition rather than universal ownership rights and relatively free markets. Traditional societies are those in which a person's work or social role is determined not by their own choice or preference, but by who and what they are; that is, by their gender, inherited class, caste, race, or ethnicity. Where women must stay within the home, their work is confined to domestic work or possibly also some piece work that can be done within the home. Such a system lacks the free and open competition that capitalism assumes and encourages; it violates the nondiscrimination constraint of capitalism. Examples include conservative Muslim, Buddhist, or Hindu societies, Taliban-controlled Afghanistan, and to some degree, although a lesser extent, many countries in Central Europe and Africa. Should my case for capitalism be stuck with some of these nonetheless? For example, the oil exporting Muslim economies that engage in massive global trade, or southeast Asian societies that engage in global sex tourism could be seen as capitalist because of their deep involvement with capitalist countries. Or countries such as Saudi Arabia and Oman can be described as oligarchic capitalism, although I did describe that form as pseudo-capitalism. I think that there are several reasons why they should not be classified as capitalist, although they do gain from trade with capitalist systems. They all violate the free wage labor condition by not allowing women to engage in most forms of labor. The last examples violate the condition on the private ownership of the means of production when the ruling family of the country is also the owner of the main resource for trade. Thus, like a socialist country, government effectively makes all the important economic decisions in the country.

The reader may be wondering whether my supposed alternatives to capitalism are also straw men. After all, the Soviet Union is dead, China is no longer communist, and no one interested in freedom or democracy would argue for the kind of communist totalitarianism of North Korea. Likewise, there must be very few who would hold out for the traditionalist regimes of Somalia or Afghanistan. But there surely are those who would argue in favor of the Cuban economic system, which is a tightly controlled socialist economy with little ownership of the means of production, but earns high scores on certain quality of life indicators like life expectancy and literacy. And there are others who would maintain that the traditionalism of societies like Saudi Arabia or Oman are worth preserving. So socialism and traditionalism are not straw men; they are full bodied enough to be worthy opponents, if only for the foil they provide against which the virtues of capitalism can be seen and the vices explored.

Assessing the counterfactual: alternatives to capitalism

Critics of capitalism complain that the hegemony of capitalism does not allow for a fair comparison of economic systems. Such critics may agree that the socialist and traditional societies I claim as my opponents are not worth saving, but there might be other possibilities were it not for the dominance of capitalism. What would Cuba have become without the dominating presence of the largest capitalist economy in the world some 60 miles (100 km) from its shores? I have compared capitalism with centrally-planned economies and with traditional economies. If capitalism were not now the hegemonic economic system on the planet, what would take its place and how would the system in place change the current situation?

To answer these questions, we want to know how another economic system would work if it were not interfered with by the workings of global capitalism. In order to make a strong empirical case for or against capitalism in the contemporary world, it is necessary to formulate the counterfactual that is being assumed: if not for this system, what would or could exist in the actual world?

To begin to answer this, recall the four definitional criteria of capitalism:

(1) private ownership of capital condition;
(2) free and open, decentralized market condition;
(3) free wage labor condition;
(4) nondiscrimination constraint.

In actually existing capitalism, none of these conditions holds perfectly. But the conditions must be at least regulative ideals for the system to be classified as capitalist. As mentioned earlier, an oligarchic capitalist system is not what I could characterize as capitalist because the nondiscrimination constraint and the free and open market condition do not hold. Another system that would violate a condition on capitalism – in this case condition (1) – is so-called market socialism, which exists when the major industries are owned by the government.[18] This system will depend on the distribution of political power to determine the distribution of economic goods; while it could result in more equal distributions of income, it could also lead to more economic inequality if the political process is not democratic. In that case market socialism would resemble oligarchic capitalism.

A system that ought not to be confused with market socialism is cooperatives, or worker ownership/control of firms. This is just a type of capitalism, and one that actually exists to some degree within capitalist systems in several forms: some are employee stock ownership plans, where the workers own but do not necessarily control the management decisions of the firms. Another is a cooperative in which employees make the management decisions as well as owning the firm. These types may also vary by the degree to which the shares are equal or not, and the openness of the firms to new cooperators. Since all of these forms of cooperative ownership and management are possible within typical legal structures of capitalism, I do not regard these as alternatives to capitalism, but as different forms of cooperative interaction within capitalism.

18 Jon Elster and Karl Ove Moene, *Alternatives to Capitalism* (Cambridge University Press, 1989), 26–28.

The free and open, decentralized market condition can be violated in two ways that are of interest here. We have already considered central planning, which is one way. Another violation is to have decentralized but highly controlled markets. If a specific elite within a country is granted an oligopoly on the industry without any nondiscriminatory rationale, then again this is a case of oligarchic capitalism, and thus not a true capitalist system.[19] However, most capitalist systems place some restrictions on free and open markets. For instance, where industries are protected from competition by tariffs or import restrictions, or assisted with export subsidies, markets in those industries are not free. This is very common in the world; there may be no country in the world that does not protect some industry, and most countries try to protect their agricultural producers. Most countries prevent weapons from being exported to at least some countries. The United States and many other countries attempt to prevent the importation of narcotics. The World Trade Organization (WTO), and its predecessor the General Agreement on Tariffs and Trade, were founded to restrict the number and types of such restrictions so that they would not result in "trade wars," where countries retaliate against each other's restrictions with new ones, resulting in an international system effectively closed to world trade. I will classify a country as capitalist if it attempts to limit the market restrictions to those restrictions that the WTO recognizes as legitimate protection of essential interests, and generally plays within the decisions taken by the WTO.[20] Alternatives to capitalism, then, will include countries that do not attempt to gain membership in, or abide by, the WTO, and prefer autarkic isolationism to international trade.

---

19 A nondiscriminatory rationale might be licensing restrictions, such as the requirement that one pass a medical board exam in order to be licensed to prescribe drugs, that are designed to protect consumers.

20 The WTO is essentially a dispute settlement mechanism, by which its members can monitor each other's trade policies to see that they live up to agreements made (typically to allow freer trade among the member countries) and to avoid discriminatory treatment of some of the WTO member states.

Capitalism and regulation

A further objection to the way I have carved up the economic world is that the way to distinguish capitalism from its alternatives must hinge on the amount of government intervention. If a country is highly governmentally regulated, the objection runs, then it is not capitalist, and if it is lightly regulated, then it is capitalist. Thus, Sweden and Denmark may be made to fall on the side of socialism rather than capitalism. But in my view this cuts things the wrong way, and lacks an empirical basis. As Adam Smith made clear at the beginnings of capitalism, and as I have argued in setting out the conditions of capitalism, some regulation is always essential for any form of law governed system of trade. There are no highly unregulated economies among the wealthy countries of the world, such as the United States, France, or Australia, even though these are paradigmatically capitalist. So (absence of) regulation *per se* cannot be the litmus test of capitalism; intensive regulation is neither foreign to nor intrinsic to capitalism.

Some sociologists, in fact, have argued that while capitalism has always involved some regulation, the degree of regulation of the most highly innovative and successful capitalist societies has grown to the point where we have a new kind of capitalism, which they call regulatory capitalism.[21] Deregulation, they argue, has been a myth; neoliberalism died with the Asian financial crisis. This regulatory regime is not all to the good, however. Capitalist enterprises constantly innovate, and one of the ways in which they innovate is in finding the means to get around regulation. This both creates wasted efforts and thwarts the point of regulation in many cases. The recent financial crisis that has gripped global capitalism, and UK and US capitalism first and most profoundly, resulted from a lack of regulation of new kinds of financial products that were designed to evade earlier regulations placed on banks, but not on other institutions that could effectively act as banks. At the time of writing it seems clear that

21 John Braithwaite, *Regulatory Capitalism* (Northampton: Edward Elgar, 2008).

many new regulations will be adopted to avoid these evasions, although new evasive maneuvers will not be far behind.

Regulation is the means by which capitalism attempts to fix itself. Regulations can be formed that create more or fewer opportunities to gain through evasion. The task of defenders of current capitalist systems, then, is to decide how to design regulations with this in mind. Regulation can be done privately or by government. To the degree that regulation is applied from outside the market and imposed by government, the less free are the markets, laborers, or owners of productive means. Regulations that are imposed most productively by government, I shall argue, are those that help to enshrine the conditions of capitalism in a society or internalize an externality (that is, make parties to the trade rather than outsiders bear the costs of the transaction). These will be part of any successful capitalist system. Thus, the normative ideal of capitalism will take up the question of what kind and how much regulation and government intervention to pursue.

The traditional normative justification of capitalism comes from liberal arguments for freedom. F. A. Hayek, for example, offered an argument for capitalism as against socialism on grounds of liberty.[22] More recently, Philippe Van Parijs has offered a left libertarian argument for capitalism on the ground that it maximizes freedom, in the sense of opportunity, subject to the constraints of a structure of rights which guarantee that everyone owns their own "self."[23] Not all the liberal justifications of capitalism are libertarian, however. Amartya Sen also defends capitalism in a limited sense as a matter of freedom, where freedom is understood to include a rich variety of support for individual autonomy.[24] This discussion points ahead to my defense of enlightened capitalism, which improves on the descriptive ideal type that I will use to categorize economies in order to analyze the descriptive case for capitalism. To improve on this descriptive ideal capitalism, I shall

22 F. A. Hayek, *The Road to Serfdom* (University of Chicago Press, 1944).
23 Van Parijs, *Real Freedom for All*.
24 Amartya Sen, *Development as Freedom* (New York: Random House, 1999).

describe the system that is entailed by these liberal arguments, given some suitable, feminist concept of freedom.[25]

Our project in this book is to view capitalism with feminist lenses in order to answer the question of whether capitalism is good for the world's women, in particular, but also for all persons in general. Women are the canaries in the mine of capitalism – more vulnerable to predation because of their acculturated propensity to caregiving and altruism. What would make an economic system good for women? Since feminists have been concerned with women's good, we can ask what are the feminist ideals by which an economic system ought to be evaluated?

Feminist ideals

Feminism is grounded in the desires for social equality and freedom, in the first instance for women vis-à-vis men, but also for all persons with respect to other social groupings. Women, after all, are members of most of these social groupings, and if it is an ideal for women to achieve social equality, then it is only consistent to hold social equality generally as an ideal. Anything else would be special pleading, hypocrisy, or downright irrationality. But that being said, feminists design ideals by attending to the inequalities, injustices, and lack of freedom from which women have suffered and continue to suffer. Women have never equaled men in wealth, political power, or the use of violence to achieve their ends. However, feminist anthropologists, historians, and sociologists have also attended to ways in which women in different societies or different social classes within the same society have resisted or wielded power in less obvious ways. It is important that feminist ideals seek to achieve greater formal and explicit

---

25 Nancy Hirschmann, *The Subject of Liberty: Toward a Feminist Theory of Freedom* (Princeton University Press, 2003). Hirschmann provides a feminist theory of freedom that I think is approximately right with its emphasis on freedom as freedom to choose one's life path and the cultural support for that freedom. Other useful feminist theories of freedom include Drucilla Cornell, *At the Heart of Freedom* (Princeton University Press, 2000); and Marilyn Friedman, *Autonomy, Gender, Politics* (New York: Oxford University Press, 2003).

power without losing sight of the informal ways that women gain and wield power; if tradeoffs are to be made between these, and I believe they are inevitable, they need to be made with conscious awareness of what those tradeoffs are.

Feminist political transformation

My main concern is to argue for capitalism as a feminist ideal for the future, by which I mean that capitalism initiated and continues to motivate a feminist political transformation of society from the oppressive patriarchy of the past to an enlightened freedom for women and men in the future. By feminist political transformation I mean a transformation of the formal and informal social structures of society that allows persons, regardless of sex, gender, race, or other attributed status, to freely and fully develop their personalities and capacities. Formal structures include laws, the structure of legal, civil, and religious offices, explicit institutional rules, and more or less explicit rules of etiquette and social comportment. Informal structures include norms and practices that are implicit but commonly known and relied upon in social interactions. There are multiple feminist theories, of course, and while all of them aim for such transformation, they may differ widely on what liberation looks like and how we can or should achieve that aim. The precise form of feminist transformation I endorse lies along liberal feminist lines that are largely implicit in the capitalist ideal for which I argue.

Some feminists, including my debate partner in this book, will no doubt reject the liberal feminist ideal that I seek on some deep level. However, there is much on which we can agree. Feminists agree that women of all races and classes have been oppressed as women vis-à-vis their male counterparts in the same relative social positions. We agree that sex and gender are largely socially constructed categories that hierarchically position women as subordinate to men. We agree that the division of labor and of consumption in all societies has benefited men vastly more than women both materially and in terms of status. We agree that women have been physically and sexually dominated by

men through economic, psychological, and violent force.[26] And
finally, we agree that these inequalities and injustices based on
sex and gender categories are unjust and ought to be condemned
and overcome. We disagree on the nature and kind of human
values that free and equal persons will endorse once these injustices are overcome. Nonetheless, we believe that this is enough
common ground on which to debate the question of whether
capitalism can serve as a feminist ideal. Our readers will have to
be the judge of whether our arguments for the efficacy of capitalism or socialism reach the ideals we endorse, and whether those
ideals, ultimately, are worth achieving.

Patriarchy, the anti-feminism

As a further specification of the opposition to the ideal of feminism, it will also be useful to define "patriarchy," which I take
to name both the ideology of institutionalized sexism or sexual
hierarchy, and the system itself. In patriarchy, (some) men control the major institutions of society and all women are legally
or practically subordinate to some men. As a social system, it is
"a system of interrelated social structures which allow men to
exploit women."[27] Traditional patriarchal societies combine gendered social and economic roles with religious rules and norms
for gendered behavior that keep women confined to the domestic sphere, and this allows men to control women's behavior and
the division of labor and goods within the family and within the
same religious or ethnic group. Patriarchy also exploits some
men for the benefit of others and involves stereotyped gender
roles that restrict most individuals of either sex in ways that harm
them. Young men are proscribed from having access to women
of the same class until they have earned enough of the medium

---

26 Of course, there will be some women who have more wealth and power
than some men. But on average, or comparing within social groupings, men
are better off than women in these various ways.

27 Sylvia Walby, *Patriarchy at Work* (Minneapolis, MN: University of Minnesota
Press, 1986), 51, quoted in April Gordon, *Transforming Capitalism and
Patriarchy: Gender and Development in Africa* (Boulder, CO: Lynne Rienner,
1996), 18.

of status (wealth or honor), and men from lower status families are also proscribed from having access to women seen as belonging to the higher classes. Since these rules clearly benefit men over women and impose invidious caste and class distinctions, I will assume that any feminist political transformation worthy of the name will demand the eradication of patriarchy.

It should be clear from the definition that patriarchy is a, at least partially, parallel (i.e., nonintersecting) system to any economic system, such as capitalism or socialism. Patriarchy does not preclude the existence of either socialism or capitalism. It remains to be shown, however, that capitalism does not entail patriarchy, and, more to the point, that capitalism provides no better home for patriarchy than does socialism. On the face of it, there seems to be no reason to think that capitalism would encourage patriarchy, since patriarchy constrains individuals from acting in ways a capitalist system encourages or emphasizes. That is because patriarchy is a communal or collectivist system, emphasizing the needs of the kin group or at least the patriarch over those of the individuals in the group. Capitalism is, perhaps notoriously among feminists, an individualist system, at least in theory. State guided or oligarchic capitalism varies from the theory, however, in emphasizing the needs of the state or the oligarchic family. So developing or pseudo-capitalism can give patriarchy a home when there is a great deal of government interference. Socialism, on the other hand, focuses on the communal group, and thus is similarly liable to be co-opted for patriarchal ends. Patriarchy is compatible with many, perhaps all, traditional cultures, though. Part of my argument, thus, will be to show that capitalism offers women a way out of patriarchal, traditional culture.

Capitalism has clearly in many ways helped women to free themselves from the bonds of tradition, home, and tribe, which I will demonstrate in section 2. In section 3, I explain why capitalism is so successful in expanding freedom. Then, in section 4, I examine and reject some of the most common critiques of capitalism. In section 5, I construct the strongest critique of capitalism from a feminist perspective and then offer my response to that critique. In the final section of this chapter I construct an ideal of an enlightened capitalism that I argue has much to offer to feminists. Although it has to be carefully constructed and controlled to maximize freedom, I will show that an enlightened capitalism can be constructed that would be a genuinely positive intervention, particularly for women.

2   The empirical case for capitalism as an actually existing system

Political philosophers often avoid empirical data and statistical analysis of that data, preferring to make normative arguments in a general and theoretical way. Philosophers even take pride in their unwillingness to consult data, as if that made their work more pure and deductively sound. This way of doing political philosophy is mistaken. Theoretical models can too easily be led down a completely irrelevant or erroneous path if they are not forced to face the tribunal of data regularly and rigorously. Take, for example, the literature on egalitarianism, which Elizabeth Anderson ridicules as not being able to be more embarrassing for progressives than if it had been secretly penned by conservatives.[28] By focusing only on theoretically possible, unequal, distributive outcomes, and taking only the most extreme claims of misfortune that could be imagined into account to build their theories, many of the most important of the theorists of egalitarianism construct theories that focus on the rich but bored playboy, the beach bum, and citizens with expensive religious ceremonies to perform. The resulting theories, Anderson argues, would penalize those who had legitimate complaints that their claim to equal democratic citizenship is overlooked in contemporary liberal, capitalist society: gays and lesbians, the disabled, and women, among others. If we begin from these actual problems with the world, then theories are less likely to go astray.

28 Elizabeth Anderson, "What is the Point of Equality?," *Ethics* 109(2) (January 1999): 287–337.

Economic theorists have also made the mistake of floating in the ethereal realm of theory without looking at the data, but it is perhaps less common for economists to do this because their discipline explicitly considers data about economies to be within the bailiwick of economists. One outrageous example in economics is the Laffer curve, which proposed that income tax revenues when graphed against the tax rate formed a kind of sideways parabolic curve, reaching its maximum at a certain point. Famously, the economist responsible first drew the curve on a napkin at a Washington cocktail party. The curve was taken to be proof that tax rates were too high, and the economist did not discourage this interpretation, basking in the glow of his sudden notoriety. Nor are these extremist theories confined to those that have practical application. The reader can no doubt fill in their own examples here, but a general formula for finding such theories is to ask oneself what the logical possibilities are for answering a question. If all the intuitively likely ones are taken, then choose the most unlikely, but still logically possible, option and run with it. Of course, this works particularly well when the empirical evidence is complicated and difficult to assess. But if we are to make any serious progress in political philosophy, we need to do our best to assess the data of the actual world when constructing and testing our theories. So I begin with an assessment of capitalism as it is in the actual world.

Comparing the quality of human life in different social systems

Assessing the record of capitalism requires us to propose criteria by which systems can be judged. How can we compare societies in order to judge whether human life is better in one society or another, or whether it is better for women's lives in one society rather than another? To compare we will have to make use of the kinds of broad comparisons for which we have some data. We can answer this question subjectively or objectively. Subjectively we can ask whether people are happier or at least less miserable, whether they find their life more fulfilling. Such happiness studies have become a major academic industry, and much good work is being done comparing happiness across societies and nations.[29] But we cannot get very far toward answering that question in the historical case with any scientific precision. We could look to the writings and other artifacts left by long ago generations to see whether people seemed happier then than now, but while we can find horrific tales or soaring narratives from the past, modern times give us comparably horrible and wonderful images. Jean Jacques Rousseau's *Discourse on the Origin of Inequality* imagines that human life was far happier and more carefree before the invention of private property (which itself was long before the advent of capitalism), but that is a myth of no greater verity than the Bible's story of the garden of Eden. Subjective welfare accounts of well-being suffer from many theoretical problems, but the empirical one that rules them out in this context is that there is no historical record of subjective welfare or utility that we can access.[30]

Objectively we can measure the quality of human life in many, competing ways. Rather than survey the many different ways and arguments for and against, I will propose a list of interests that humans have, and then investigate how we can go about measuring the degree to which these interests are served in the different societies that we will compare. In particular, I argue that humans have at least these minimal interests:

- life – other things being nearly equal, the longer the better;
- security from violence;
- a secure and plentiful source of good food and water;
- a safe and healthy abode;
- good health;
- family, friends, and a community;
- the opportunity to contribute to the well-being of one's community;

29 Ed Diener and Eunkook Suh (eds.), *Culture and Subjective Well Being* (Cambridge: MIT Press, 2000); R. Layard, *Happiness: Lessons from a New Science* (New York: Penguin Press, 2005).
30 Ann E. Cudd, "The Paradox of Liberal Feminism: Choice, Rationality and Oppression," in Amy Baehr (ed.), *Varieties of Feminist Liberalism* (Lanham, MD: Rowman & Littlefield, 2004), 37–61.

- freedom of movement, play, and conscience;
- a sense of basic dignity and respect in society;
- all of the above for their loved ones, particularly their children.[31]

Several of these interests point to other interests that persons are likely to have. The first one of these that comes to mind is an interest in education, which promotes the ability to contribute to community and allows one to make use of freedom of conscience, and perhaps others of these primary interests as well.

Each of these interests suggests measures for comparing societies by how well they secure the interests of their members. For the first, there is life expectancy at birth and at other points in the life span, or alternatively, mortality figures. For the second, there are crime rate statistics for various crimes. For the third, we could measure the average caloric intake and the average time consumed by securing food and water. And so forth. But things are neither as simple nor uncontroversial as this makes it sound. First, they are not simple because of the complexities of gathering and assessing the data. Since this is a work in empirical political philosophy, and not social science, I will not gather and produce this data myself, but rather rely on the best social science research available to solve these problems as best they can be solved. Second, they are controversial because the means by which the measure is taken could determine the answer to the question. One way it might do this is by emphasizing either quality or quantity of the good satisfying the interest. For example, one might argue that the quality of food or shelter is better in a pre-capitalist society. Or one might argue about whether the quality of community is better if the community is relatively closed, isolated, or homogeneous in some way.

In order to address the issues deeply but with a manageable scope, I will investigate only a few key ways of measuring the

---

31 This list is similar to Martha Nussbaum's capabilities list in *Women and Human Development* (Cambridge University Press, 2000), 78–80. I have stated the interests so as to more directly suggest how they can be measured and thus compared across societies.

performance of societies with respect to how well women fare in these fundamental interests. In particular, I will examine those statistics (where available) that have the greatest influence on the others; for example, longer life expectancy, lower fertility and child mortality, child labor and schooling rates by gender, measures of women's political and economic participation, and the most important overall indices of measures of well-being, the human development index and the gender-related index produced by the United Nations Development Programme (UNDP).

The historical case for capitalism

In this section I will construct the historical defense of capitalism from a feminist perspective. This consists in the empirical evidence for the claim that capitalism has brought about a massive improvement in life for human beings. Any such discussion has to begin with a discussion of life expectancy. Now one could argue that life expectancy measures only the quantity of life and not its quality. To be sure, the tradeoff between quality and quantity is important to consider on the margins of life and death, but not when we are talking about the two-and-a-half-fold increase in life expectancy that most countries of the world have experienced over the past two hundred years.[32] I will also consider the vast decreases in the number of children borne by women over that time and the corresponding decrease in infant mortality. In these life and health issues, quality versus quantity issues are swamped by the size of the quantity differences between capitalism and pre-capitalist societies. While there are clearly quality concerns about capitalist societies of various

32 Russell Waltz raised the objection that this claim leads to a form of the repugnant conclusion if a large enough increase in quantity of life is lexically ordered above increases in quality. Suppose that we extend life by that large enough amount but it is much more miserable, say barely worth living at all. Although this is worth considering in the abstract, I don't have to worry about this in the actual case. Quality of life has not been decreased much, if at all, and the additional length of life has led to intrinsic quality improvements because of the ability to experience the maturity of a second generation. I am not sure I would argue, however, that experiencing the maturity of a third generation would be as great a gain as this one.

types, the quantity differences between pre-modern and modern societies are too great to even be concerned about the more subtle differences.

Another controversial feature of these comparisons concerns the distribution of the goods that meet the interests within societies. If the distribution is highly unequal but the average enjoyment of goods is high, then the society may appear to be better on that measure than it should be. This is a serious concern, and to the extent that equality measures are available, we will have to examine those as well. However, as with the issues about quality, equality concerns are not likely to arise in the historical case because of the increases in equality, in terms of civil, political, and social rights and goods, a process begun during the era of capitalism.

There are several additional issues for the historical case. First, what are the proper points in time and space to compare in order to determine whether capitalism has improved human life? Second, how can we assess the causal claim that it was capitalism rather than some other difference(s) that accounts for the differences in outcomes? These are two related concerns. If we choose a time long before capitalism began and compare it with a contemporary capitalist society, then the claim that capitalism caused the change in measurements is harder to make. So we need to locate the approximate beginning of capitalism and choose a time period just before that.

If we take the accumulation of capital to be a necessary condition for the beginning of large-scale social production, then the historical beginnings of capitalism can be located in England in the seventeenth century with the enclosure of lands for sheep grazing, the elimination of feudal rights of peasants to work on lands, and the gradual accumulation of capital by merchants.[33] However, gains in per capita income due to capitalism required another century to appear. The real per capita income gains began first in England and Wales in the period 1783–1830, in Sweden

---

33 Maurice Dobb, *Studies in the Development of Capitalism*, rev. edn. (New York: International Publishers, 1963), chs. 5 and 6.

in 1868–90, in France in 1830–70, and in Japan in 1885–1905.[34] Shortly after each of these periods in each of these countries, life expectancy began what some have called the "health transition" or "takeoff:" England and Wales in 1871; Sweden in 1875; France in 1893; and Japan in 1923.[35] Although the exact gap between the dates of economic takeoff and life expectancy takeoff varies somewhat for each case, the proximity is highly suggestive.[36]

Rising life expectancy

A casual glance at a graph representing countries' life expectancy versus per capita income reveals a clear positive relation between the two, and this can be seen in historical graphs of this relation going back as far as one can find any data at all.[37] Figure 1.1 charts this relation for the United States over the past two centuries.[38]

It is very clear that humanity has made tremendous gains in life expectancy since 1800, and that we have also become vastly wealthier in much of the world. However, the actual relation

34 Richard A. Easterlin, "How Beneficent is the Market? A Look at the Modern History of Mortality," *European Review of Economic History*, 3 (1999): 257–94; W. W. Rostow, *The World Economy: History and Prospect* (Austin, TX: University of Texas Press, 1978).

35 Easterlin, "How Beneficent is the Market?"

36 Easterlin does not agree, and instead argues that the differences in these gaps show that economic growth is not closely related. He argues that if there were a tight relation between growth of income and growth in life expectancy then the gaps would be the same and small. However, I would argue that we should expect that the earliest gains in income would take the longest to create health gains. Furthermore, the degree to which each of these countries had large urban populations affects the timing of the longevity takeoff, since large urban populations lead to the spread of infectious disease.

37 The historical data are available in *Monitoring the World Economy 1820–1992*, OECD, Paris 1995; *The World Economy: A Millennial Perspective*, OECD Development Centre, Paris 2001; *The World Economy: Historical Statistics*, OECD Development Centre, Paris 2003. These have been compiled and reported in "Historical Statistics for the World Economy: 1–2003 AD" by Angus Maddison, available at: www.ggdc.net/maddison.

38 Gap Minder Foundation, "Gapminder World," available at: www.gapminder.org/gapminder-world/documentation/#gd004, accessed September 5, 2009.

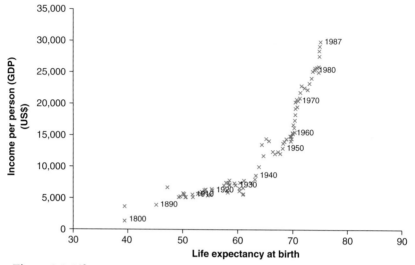

Figure 1.1 Life expectancy versus income (United States 1800–1987)

between life expectancy and income is more difficult to pin down, and uncovering the causal relation between life expectancy and capitalism is harder still. In this section I will review some of the main evidence and theories about these relationships. While it is clear that high income for individuals or countries is not required to make significant gains in life expectancy, I will argue that the advent of capitalism is causally linked to the truly impressive health transition that has occurred in the past two centuries.

Although my ultimate goal is to discover capitalism's relation to increased life expectancy, there can be no directly observable link because capitalism does not appear as a thing at a moment in time, but rather as a process that comes gradually into existence over time, and one that has a variety of neither necessary nor sufficient characteristics that may have different effects on health. One common and striking characteristic, however, is the growth in income in capitalist countries. Income and income growth, therefore, provide a proxy for the existence of capitalism: high income or high growth in income typically indicate that a county has a burgeoning capitalist system.

There are two ways in which this growth in income is causally related to improving health. First, wealth, which is typically correlated with income, enables individuals to buy food, better living conditions, education, and health care. Thus, with money one can learn how to, and afford to, prevent, treat, and cure disease. Wealthy countries can take on public health initiatives to provide clean water, medicines, sanitary facilities, education, and hospitals or other health care related centers. Second, higher incomes reduce poverty, which has a direct effect on the reduction of infant mortality, one of the two main contributions (the other being the decrease in infectious disease deaths) to the historical increase in life expectancy. Growth in income is also correlated with life expectancy through a third broad mechanism, which is that higher income countries typically also allow their citizens greater political and civil liberties, which tend to promote both gains in income and in life expectancy, largely through citizen demand for better sanitary conditions and health care.[39]

High income is not a necessary condition for improvements in life expectancy. There are some cases of a lower or higher than expected life expectancy for income, such as Japan and Sweden, which historically did better than their per capita incomes would have predicted, or the United States, which has consistently underachieved relative to its per capita income. Different countries have very different ways of achieving a health transition, and some of these are more or less costly than others. Two points stand out as most important for my argument. First, all of the health transitions in all countries have been achieved since capitalism began in some parts of the world. Thus, capitalism could be an important causal antecedent, and given the usefulness of wealth and income to achieving a health transition, the causal connection seems likely. Second, the two most common ways that these overachievers have made the health transition is through technical progress and female education and income.[40] Capitalism is related to both of these. Capitalist competition and the possibility of creating income and wealth from new products and services create incentives to make innovations. And the accumulation of

39 Riley, *Rising Life Expectancy*, 143.
40 Riley, *Rising Life Expectancy*, 137.

income and wealth that capitalism encourages creates the capital required to invest in education and equipment to make technical innovations. Capitalism has both direct and subtle indirect influences on female education. It provides incentives to invest in education, just as it does for males to be educated. But capitalism also, by providing an opportunity for an income independent of their male relatives, provides women with the ability to advocate for their education or to directly invest in their own and their daughters' education.

Richard Easterlin contends that neither rising income and wealth nor the development of capitalism brought about the health transition.[41] Rather, he argues, the main factor in extending life expectancy has been the control of infectious disease. This has come about not because of capitalist markets, but because of public health advances in controlling transmission of disease, scientific advances in understanding the causes and spread of disease, and more recently the development of vaccines and anti-microbial agents. Further, he argues, capitalist accumulation of wealth has not been needed for these advances; the economic takeoff and the health takeoff have been causally separate processes. His argument thus poses a serious threat to my thesis in this section, and so it bears careful scrutiny.

Easterlin rejects the idea that economic growth has been largely responsible for the health transition, and he tests a version of this hypothesis, the "McKeown hypothesis," which claims that the causal factor generating the health transition is specifically better nutrition from greater wealth and income.[42] Easterlin argues that if this hypothesis holds, then we should observe a tight connection between rising levels of income and rising life expectancy. There should be a short time lag between them, and the time lag should be approximately the same. But the data do not show this, rather they show that in England and Wales it took several decades for life expectancy gains to be made, while

41 Easterlin, "How Beneficent is the Market?," 257–94.
42 Easterlin, "How Beneficent is the Market?," 259. This hypothesis was put forward in Thomas McKeown, *The Modern Rise of Population* (New York: Academic Press, 1976).

in Sweden, for example, the gains came very quickly with the rising income that indicated the advent of capitalism in that country. Does this show what Easterlin wants to show, namely, that economic growth is not causally responsible for the historical health transition that has now been accomplished in much of the world? I think not. There are other relevant differences between the cases. England was highly urbanized, which created conditions for increased spread of infectious diseases, as Easterlin recognizes. But this means that there was a higher bar for the wealth effect to overcome, it does not mean that there was no wealth effect. Thus, I think his rejection of the McKeown hypothesis is premature. Furthermore, the fact that Sweden's transition to capitalism came later gave it an advantage in the sense that it could learn from techniques adopted in England to improve health. Easterlin's alternative hypothesis is that the introduction of smallpox vaccines accounted for the progress in life expectancy in both cases. But there are two things to note about this alternative that are relevant here. First, even if this is the main cause of the health transition, the wide availability of smallpox vaccines – their production and distribution, communication about their use and effectiveness, and the responsiveness of public health agents to the desire of citizens for them – must at least in part be due to the conditions created by capitalism, including greater wealth and income, higher levels of education, and increasing legal and public infrastructure. According to Jonathan Tucker, "a key breakthrough in the control of smallpox in industrialized countries was the invention of the icebox, which made it possible to refrigerate smallpox vaccine and thereby preserve its potency for long periods."[43] Second, citing smallpox vaccines alone ignores another major contributor to female life expectancy (the statistics he uses in his argument): falling fertility rates. Capitalism, I will argue, played a major role in encouraging and facilitating lower fertility rates, which in turn increased maternal and infant survival rates.

43 Jonathan B. Tucker, *Scourge: The Once and Future Threat of Smallpox* (New York: Atlantic Monthly Press, 2001).

To be fair, Easterlin considers whether capitalist markets effected the health transition through their drive to innovate. He considers both demand and supply side factors. Demand side factors would include increasing demand for health care, including immunizations, medicines, and health clinics, or health promoting environmental conditions, such as pure water, public education about health and hygiene, and sanitation. Supply side factors include the investments and innovations required for the technology changes, including the science of disease transmission and biomedical interventions. Easterlin argues that the health transition cannot be accounted for by market solutions reacting to demand for health care or improved life expectancy, because there are too many market failures for health care or public health improvements to be provided by the market effectively. Public health improvements are classic public goods, in that they are not rival (one person's enjoyment of the good does not rule out another's) or excludable (no one can be effectively excluded from enjoying the good if it exists for another), and it is well known that public goods are underprovided by the market. Furthermore, there are several principal–agent problems with health care, so that without government intervention there will be a tendency to provide poor or ineffective care. The improvements in public health and health care, he concludes, have all required government intervention to provide them. But this point does not rule out the claim that rising income and wealth were needed by governments to make the needed investments. Even supposing that the science and technical know-how existed for governments to take advantage of, the changes themselves were expensive.

For instance, among the major impediments to public health in the nineteenth century were dunghills and open sewers, which bred and spread (particularly by means of the flies that fed on them) infectious diseases. Dunghills consisted of both animal and human manure, and they were maintained as a source of fertilizer by people who sold and carted the manure to fields and gardens. As cities grew with increasing industrialization, so did the dunghills. Getting rid of the dunghills required not only the building of latrines or sewers, but also reducing the source of dung where possible. In the mid-nineteenth century trains began the transition away from horse transportation, but this was not concluded until well into the twentieth century when the bicycle and the automobile became common. The United Kingdom experienced a boom in railway lines between 1830 and 1840. By 1843, most major cities, towns, and villages in Britain were connected by rail.[44] This was but one of the many developments needed to rid cities of their dunghills – they could not just disappear when it was realized that they were a health problem, let alone a horrendous stench! Building latrines that avoided waterways, and later building closed sewers, removing garbage from cities, and building health clinics all likewise required massive capital investments requiring antecedent wealth accumulation. Easterlin cites the development of networks of local boards of health that could inspect and regulate the food and milk supply, and bacteriological laboratories for testing, as well as the production and distribution of vaccines, as all very important for the health transition.[45] These too require great expenditures of wealth on the part of societies, especially considering the opportunity costs of building the public health workforce. People had to be well off enough to have the education and the time to work on these activities that were not aimed at basic provision of food, shelter, and clothing. Thus, an accumulation of wealth, which in this era was made possible by capitalism, was required for the health transition, regardless of the fact that it had to be governments that channeled this wealth in order to bring about the health transition.

Likewise scientific advances require much wealth investment. Easterlin argues that scientific innovations do not require capitalist markets, rather they are due to factors internal to the evolution of science. He writes, "It is this sequence in the evolution of basic biomedical science – from epidemiological studies

44 P. J. G. Ransom, *The Victorian Railway and How it Evolved* (London: Heinemann, 1990), 79.
45 Easterlin, "How Beneficent is the Market?," 230–31.

to identification of causes and mechanisms – that principally explains, I believe, the chronology of advances in control of major infectious disease, not demand conditions."[46] But again he does not address the massive wealth accumulations necessary for this advance in biomedical science: the educational infrastructure; the laboratories; and the opportunity cost of spending one's time doing science rather than procuring food and shelter. No doubt government or other collective agents had to play a role in assuring that wealth was invested in these scientific advances, but the wealth had to exist to be so invested. It is no coincidence that biomedical science took great leaps forward during the period just subsequent to the economic takeoff of European and North American societies. At the same time, the health takeoff must in turn have furthered the accumulation of wealth in early capitalism. The two processes – growth of biomedical knowledge and growth of capital accumulation – could not have occurred separately. Furthermore, there is a great deal of positive evidence that capitalist firms invested in biological and chemical research in order to solve some of the pressing health problems of the day, including creating serums for diphtheria and other contagious diseases, and developing vaccines, pain killers, and cures for syphilis.[47]

This is not to deny Easterlin's conclusion, that "the history of mortality is testimony to the critical need for collective action."[48] The health transition in every country has required collective action, much of which is coordinated by government with the power to tax, to enforce regulations, and to supply education and health care. Private provision of any of these things is doomed to market failures and attendant waste and inefficiencies (including both undersupply of health care to the poor and, arguably, oversupply to the rich). Given these market inefficiencies, an enlightened capitalism will use the powers of government to provide

46 Easterlin, "How Beneficent is the Market?," 231–32.
47 Alfred D. Chandler Jr., "How High Technology Industries Transformed Work and Life Worldwide from the 1880s to the 1990s," *Capitalism and Society* 1(2) (2006), 1: 1–55.
48 Easterlin, "How Beneficent is the Market?," 288.

health care and regulation of public health through collective action, although this will also have the effect of losing some of the power of the market to reveal the desires of citizens for certain kinds of health goods. I will return to this when I discuss enlightened capitalism in the final section of my contribution.

Lower infant mortality and lower fertility

Rising life expectancy occurs in large part initially when infant mortality drops to low levels. Infant mortality remained high throughout the world (on the order of 20 to 30 percent of infants dying before their first birthday) until 1900.[49] Then sudden and rapid decline in Western countries: for example, France above 200 per 1,000 throughout the nineteenth century, which then dropped to 77 per 1,000 in 1930–2, and to 5 per 1,000 by 1997.[50] Babies are highly vulnerable to infections, particularly when they are not breastfed, and they easily become dehydrated from minor diarrheal illnesses. They also die during childbirth without special care, and prenatal care of pregnant women prevents dangerous premature births. "Milk pasteurization, sterile birthing, preventive health care for mothers and infants, and development of pediatric expertise lead among factors responsible for the ongoing decline of infant mortality."[51] In the twentieth century we have learned how to apply many of these lessons, but this too is highly correlated with income, both society-wide and individually.

The decline in infant mortality is especially important for women in three ways. First, women generally do not want to see their babies die. There simply cannot be a worse form of alienation from the product of one's labor. Second, one of the major causes of infant mortality decline is better care of mothers prior to, during, and after birth. Babies do better when their mothers are healthy and can breastfeed them, and obviously women have an independent interest in their own health. Third, when

49 Riley, *Rising Life Expectancy*, 185.
50 Riley, *Rising Life Expectancy*, 185.
51 Riley, *Rising Life Expectancy*, 186.

Table 1.1 Fertility transitions*

	1700s	1894–1900	1950	1970	2000
United States	7.04 (1800)	3.8	3.446	2.016	2.038
Japan		5.4	2.75	2.07	1.291
United Kingdom		3.5 (1900)	2.18	2.04	1.695
France	7.3–6.2 (1747)		2.726	2.31	1.8833
Russian Federation/ Soviet Union		7.1	2.85	2.03	1.298
China		5.5	6.22	4.86	1.7
India		5.8	5.9136	5.264	3.1132
Nigeria			6.9	6.9	5.845

* Statistics for 1950, 1970, and 2000 were taken from Gapminder.org, which was found using the UN data available at: http://data.un.org. Statistics for eighteenth-century France are for 1747 for lowest and highest socioeconomic classes reported in Rosny-Sous-Bois tax records from David R. Weir, "Family Income, Mortality, and Fertility on the Eve of the Demographic Transition: A Case Study of Rosny-Sous-Bois," *Journal of Economic History* 55(1995): 1–26, 15. The figure for the United States in the eighteenth century is for whites in 1800 as reported in M. Haines, "Fertility and Mortality in the United States," February 4, 2010, available at: http://eh.net/encyclopedia/article/haines. demography. All figures from the 1894–1900 column, unless otherwise noted, come from Gorän Therborn, *Between Sex and Power* (London: Routledge, 2004), 293. The UK figure comes from Joe Hicks and Grahame Allan, "A Century of Change: Trends in the UK Statistics since 1900," House of Commons Library Research Paper 99/111, 1999.

their babies live, women have fewer of them. If women have fewer babies, the women (and their babies) will be healthier, their life expectancy will increase, and they will be able to attend to other things in life, such as education of themselves and their children, and other productive, wealth increasing or community building activities. The decline in infant mortality, because of its concomitant effect on decreasing fertility, is perhaps the greatest improvement in women's lives in human history.[52] If it can be

52 Neil Cummins, "Marital Fertility and Wealth in Transition Era France, 1750–1850," Paris School of Economics Working Paper No. 2009–16, 2009.

shown that capitalism has played a role in bringing this about, then that is a strong historical case for capitalism as a positive development for women.

As with rising life expectancy, there is a strong correlation between rising income and lower fertility. Fertility statistics are difficult to come by historically, although they can be reconstructed for times when statistics were not officially kept but where there exist tax records or birth records. Table 1.1 records falling fertility rates over the period of the income transition for those countries that have experienced it (the United States, Japan, the United Kingdom, France, Russia, China). India is now beginning to make a serious fertility transition, though Nigeria has not yet done so.

Capitalism is causally related to the lowering of infant mortality and fertility in at least three ways. First, they are causally related in the same way as rising life expectancy: capitalism caused the initial accumulation of wealth needed to begin the lowering of infant mortality through public health and control and cure of infectious diseases. In addition to these health interventions, we must also add here the introduction of modern birth control methods, which first occurred in the nineteenth century with the development of the condom, and gave people greater control over their fertility.[53] Birth control is somewhat different from public health or vaccinations in being less subject to collective action problems, since it is not necessary that others should use birth control for one's own use of it to be effective. On the other hand, there are special problems generated by the fact that men must agree to use condoms, yet it is their female partners whose interests are most keenly and immediately affected by their use. (This problem does not arise with hormonal methods, as long as the woman has enough freedom to obtain them

Cummins investigates the correlation of rising wealth, lowering child mortality, and lower fertility rates in the crucial period of capitalist development in France.

53 Kathleen London, "The History of Birth Control," *Yale–New Haven Teachers Institute*, 6 (1982), published online at: www.yale.edu/ynhti/curriculum/units/1982/6, accessed August, 6 2009.

without her partner's consent.) Second, capitalism causes a lowering of demand for children on the part of both parents because of the way in which income and wealth are generated in capitalism. Third, capitalism gives women an opportunity to opt out of the traditional motherhood role by having fewer or even no children.

Let me expand on the latter two points. Harold Demsetz argues that capitalism causes fewer children because of the way that people tend to earn income and accumulate wealth, and the incentives this provides for people to have fewer children.[54] First, capitalism affected how wealth can be acquired and husbanded. With industrialization came an increasing legal structure to determine who owned what, as well as a reliable means to enforce these property rights. Reliable private property rights meant that work, enterprise, and luck could accumulate wealth without serious threat of theft or confiscation. Furthermore, decreasing agricultural work and the imposition of child labor laws in factories meant that children no longer contributed income to a family. Optimal family size dropped until the marginal (expected) costs of feeding, clothing, housing, and educating an additional child were equal to the marginal (expected) benefits to be obtained from that child. Thus, the emergence of capitalism and the concomitant development of liberal property rights served to impose penalties indirectly on those who had too many children. Demsetz writes, "The key to the declining rate of increase in total population lies in the decrease in family size, and the key to the decrease in family size lies in capitalism's effect on legislation."[55]

Demsetz rejects alternative hypotheses about why fertility declined in the West. He claims that the decrease in fertility is not due to modern birth control, since the decrease came before modern methods were available, and other methods had been known for a long time. This is not entirely accurate, since the rubber condom was introduced in 1840, and although there was a declining fertility rate in capitalist countries throughout the

---

54 Demsetz, *From Economic Man to Economic System*, ch. 4.
55 Demsetz, *From Economic Man to Economic System*, 55.

nineteenth century (see Table 1.1), large-scale declines in fertility (the fertility transition) did not occur until well into the twentieth century. Large-scale public population control initiatives, however, did not begin until 1877 with the Malthusian League in Britain, and the 1920s in America, when Margaret Sanger started the American Birth Control League, which later became Planned Parenthood.[56] Demsetz generally undervalues the contribution of women's demand for the control of fertility. Nonetheless, the timing of women's concerted action to control fertility is such that capitalism and liberalism more generally can be seen to have played an important causal role. Demsetz concludes that "Capitalism was involved [in freeing people from Malthus' population trap] in two ways: the upward trend in productivity it brought and the incentives it provided to keep family size in check."[57]

The standard demography literature on fertility decline offers three competing theories of the fertility decline in Europe, one of which is primarily economic and two of which are primarily sociological and cultural.[58] The primarily economic model is called the demographic transition model, and it portrays the fertility decline as a direct result of industrialization and increasing wealth. The move on the part of much of the population to urban environments as a result of industrialization caused children to be less beneficial to their families because they were no longer required to do the low skill farm work. Meanwhile, increasing wealth and demand for more skills caused parents to invest in schooling, which is costly and also takes children away from work. Thus, the fertility transition is caused by industrialization on this model. George Alter, in reviewing this literature, argues that the economic theory – the demographic transition

---

56 Planned Parenthood Federation of America, "History and Success," available at: www.plannedparenthood.org/about-us/who-we-are/history-and-successes.htm#Sanger, accessed September 5, 2009.

57 Demsetz, *From Economic Man to Economic System*, 61.

58 George Alter, "Theories of Fertility Decline: A Nonspecialist's Guide to the Debate," in John R. Gillis, Louise A. Tilly, and David Levine (eds.), *The European Experience of Declining Fertility, 1850–1970* (Cambridge, MA: Blackwell, 1992), 13–27.

model – is outdated, however. He points to the detailed historical accounts of the fertility transition in specific regions of Europe to show that the knowledge and acceptance of birth control follows from changes in intergenerational wealth flows on one account, and from sharing of knowledge and common social norms among people speaking the same language. This article commits a fallacy that is common in the literature on changes in noneconomic demographic trends in this period. It assumes that if income or wealth differences are not the direct cause, then there cannot be any economic cause. For example, a main reason for rejecting the demographic transition model is because the changes in fertility in localities in Europe followed more precisely the linguistic patterns of change than wealth patterns. But they seem here to be focusing too precisely on the dates and not enough on the large-scale socioeconomic changes occurring throughout. Even if one has to speak the same language as some others who have figured out birth control, that does not rule out the hypothesis that the economic situation gave people the motivation to change their family size. Neither the demographic transition model's nor Demsetz's argument for the motivational change is precluded by these detailed historical facts, which by themselves cannot explain the motivational change. Furthermore, as Alter recognizes, what the economic models have in their favor is that they can explain the fact that every society that has undergone a wealth takeoff has also undergone a fertility transition, as illustrated in Table 1.1.

Additional support for the economic model comes from considering specifically women's interests in fertility decline. Neither Alter nor Demsetz address women's motivations separately from men's, but the economic model that credits capitalism for the decline in fertility can be easily modified to take this into account. Demsetz notes that the opening of career opportunities for women would lead to lower family size through his argument, since the cost of an additional child preventing or inhibiting a woman from working would tend to lower family demand for an additional child. However, it undervalues the contribution of women's intentions to consider family size to be family or household decisions rather than at least in part due to individual decisions by women. It also misses some of the important counterforces if one does not consider how marital decisions may involve the competing interests of men and women. Women have interests in their own health and independence from children, in lowering their domestic labor burden, and in having less costly opportunities to gain education and outside employment. Men, as only indirect beneficiaries of the realization of these interests, have less interest in these benefits, and they have a clear interest in maintaining their dominance within the home and in the public sphere. This no doubt explains the greater resistance of men to birth control, and thus the delay between the health transition and the fertility transition in most countries.[59]

Changing quality of life under capitalism

The average quality of life for humans, particularly for women and children, has improved in the past hundred years, and many of the advances are causally related to capitalism. There are three categories of objective improvement of quality of life: material, moral, and political. Material improvements include physical changes in life and work, such as changes in the amount and strenuousness of physical labor, the availability of food, clean water, and decent shelter, the degree of violence suffered, as well as the disease burden. By moral advances I mean the degree to which human individuals are treated in a dignified and decent manner, as worthy of respect in their own right, and as responsible, autonomous self-owners. By political advances I mean the degree to which individuals have a voice in the government of their communities and nations. These three categories encompass the objective list of interests that I claim all humans have. While it is not possible to quantify or measure each of these categories, I can make some generalizations about the progress in quality of life over the past century. For virtually every interest, the quality of life has improved under capitalism.

59 In a speech before Congress in March 1905, President Teddy Roosevelt attacked birth control and the women who used it, charging that they

The most important material advances are the lengthening of the life span, the lowering of fertility, and the lowering of the child mortality rates; all of which I have already documented and tied to capitalism. Perhaps the next most important material advance is the shortening of the working day and working week. While in the Middle Ages people did not "work" many more hours than today, their working hours were largely constrained by the amount of light in the day and the patterns of seasonal agricultural work. When they were not working, however, people were often engaged in productive activities of one type or another. There was no clear distinction between work and leisure. Women, especially, were basically constantly working in childcare, home production of clothing, procuring water and fuel, and food preparation. With industrialization in the eighteenth and nineteenth centuries, paid work increased markedly, reaching a height of 3,150 hours per year in the United States in 1850.[60] But over the period of the development of capitalism, work hours have declined drastically. In the period between 1820 and 2001 hours worked in Japan dropped by 45%, by 40% in the United Kingdom, and by 20% in the United States.[61] In 2002, all employed workers in the United States averaged 1,815 hours per year, in the United Kingdom 1,707, in the Netherlands 1,340, and none of the OECD countries topped 2,000 hours per year.[62] The decline in working hours is due in part to the increased productivity of workers because of mechanization and other technological developments. It is also a result of the collective struggles

lacked morals, and urging all women to adhere to a strict sexual division of labor. Theodore Roosevelt, "Theodore Roosevelt on Motherhood and the Welfare of the State," *Population and Development Review* 13(1) (March 1987), 141–47.

60 Juliet Schor, *The Overworked American* (New York: Basic Books, 1992), 45.

61 Angus Maddison, "World Development and Outlook 1820–2030: Evidence Submitted to the House of Lords," February 20, 2005, available at: www.ggdc.net/maddison.

62 Organization for Economic Cooperation and Development, 2003, *OECD Employment Outlook, Statistical Annex*, 322, which includes thirty of the most developed countries in the world: Australia, Austria, Belgium, Canada, Czech Republic, Denmark, Finland, France, Germany, Greece, Hungary, Iceland, Ireland, Italy, Japan, Korea, Luxembourg, Mexico, the Netherlands,

by workers to decrease their hours through unionization and legal controls on the length of the working day.

Technological advances have not only lowered the paid working day, but have also improved the convenience and comfort of daily life. This may be true for women even more than for men, because women are typically responsible for domestic work. The invention and proliferation of household appliances has reduced the total amount of time needed to maintain a clean, healthy home, launder clothing, and prepare food. In the United States, the amount of time spent by all women declined from 46.8 to 29.3 hours per week during the twentieth century.[63] To some extent this understates the improvement in the quality of life, however. Homes are now larger than before, making them more comfortable and allowing greater privacy and space for leisure for individual household members. Also, women have consistently over time reported cleaning as their least favorite activity, and cooking and childcare as their most favorite domestic activities. Over this time period the proportion of time in these favored activities has increased.[64] Capitalism can be credited with the technological improvements that have led to these improvements in women's quality of life. But capitalism has also increased women's opportunity cost of working in the home, and thus creates incentives for both men and women to reduce the time women spend on household chores. Evidence for this point is that women who are not employed spend a much greater time doing unpaid domestic work than women who are employed. Unemployed women in Britain spend up to three times more hours cleaning and two times more preparing food as employed women.[65] Thus, capitalism has improved the quality of home life, making it cleaner,

New Zealand, Norway, Poland, Portugal, Slovak Republic, Spain, Sweden, Switzerland, Turkey, the United Kingdom, and the United States.

63 Valerie A. Ramey, "Time Spent in Home Production in Twentieth-Century United States: New Estimates from Old Data," *Journal of Economic History*, 69 (March 2009): 1–47; Elster and Moene, *Alternatives to Capitalism*.

64 Ramey, "Time Spent in Home Production in Twentieth-Century United States," 6–7.

65 Catherine Hakim, *Key Issues in Women's Work*, 2nd edn. (London: Glasshouse Press, 2004), 48.

more comfortable, and less time consuming to maintain and reproduce.

The past 150 years have brought enormous moral advances, if one takes the moral test of a society to be the degree to which individuals are treated with dignity and respect, regardless of their attributed status, that is, sex, race, ethnicity, or their religious, sexual, or gender identification. This is an admittedly liberal standard for moral progress; this treatise will have little to offer those who hold that collectives are of greater moral importance than individuals. In this time period legal slavery has ended throughout the world (with the exception of Mauritania, a traditionalist country). Legal racial apartheid and legal caste systems have ended. It is now commonplace to question the morality of racism, sexism, and even homophobia in much of the world. In the most developed capitalist economies, discrimination or segregation requires justification, and although those evils continue there are legal remedies in these countries for challenging them and demanding reparation.

Children are now treated in law as precious individuals in much of the world, and those countries where they are not are criticized. Although children work and have always worked throughout the world, since the early part of the twentieth century there has been a worldwide recognition of the harmful effects of too much and too dangerous work on children, coupled with a growing international consensus that such work should be stopped or reduced in time and strenuousness. How much and how dangerous work by children is acceptable in the world varies somewhat by country and by the age of the child. The United Nations Convention on the Rights of the Child (1989) and various conventions signed by member states of the International Labor Organization (ILO) set some international standards. Children below the age of 14 should not work in industrial establishments. No child should work in extremely dangerous, hazardous, illegal, or degrading (sex work) occupations. Children should not be forced to work under threat of bodily injury, or bonded into labor, or trafficked, or enslaved. Children should not be unable to take advantage of whatever education system their society provides because of their work.

Research on child labor has shown that it is largely the result of parental poverty, and that increasing parental income reduces or eliminates child labor and increases child educational levels. For countries undergoing industrialization, this has meant that child labor is widespread at the beginning, but as the country becomes wealthier, children are moved out of the labor force and into schools. As industrialization began in the eighteenth century in Britain, for instance, most of the children of the large class of poor and working-class persons labored for low wages, but by the 1870s there were only few child laborers at the margins of the economy.[66] So although capitalism initially increases child labor, as countries develop they become wealthy enough to support their children without having them labor. Adult workers in capitalism have a monetary incentive (in addition to a moral one) to reduce child labor to reduce the competition for jobs and raise wages. In democratic countries, then, adult workers who are able to care for their children without having the children earn a wage can pressure their governments to pass laws against child labor. Furthermore, in more technologically advanced societies, children become important human capital investments in their own right. Thus, there is an inbuilt incentive to educate them and help them become autonomous individuals. In an entrepreneurial society, creativity and the ability to innovate becomes even more valuable. Thus, as countries develop into entrepreneurial capitalist economies, we have every reason to expect that child labor falls and child educational and health investments rise.

Finally, the history of capitalism has coincided with a history of political advances for women and minorities. Women have gained the right to vote in every democracy in the world, although only in the past century and a half. This time period has coincided with increasing democracy and decreasing imperialism and colonialism. While capitalism is probably not to be credited too much with these advances, it is also not hostile to them. Women's entrance into the capitalist workforce, however,

---

66 Peter Kirby, *Child Labour in Britain, 1750–1870* (New York: Palgrave Macmillan, 2003), 4.

has helped them to make gains in representation in the world's democracies.

Contemporary capitalist societies versus noncapitalist societies

To this point, I have made the argument about actually existing capitalism in historical terms, that is, I have shown that capitalism created material, moral, and political advances. My historical purview has been from the mid-eighteenth century up until the late twentieth century, with only a few references to the current state of affairs. What about today or since there have been real alternatives to capitalism to bring about the health, moral, and well-being improvements through other forms of economic production? If we compare life expectancy versus per capita income for different countries in 2008, we get a graph similar to Figure 1.1, in which life expectancy correlates well with income. Figure 1.2 compares some of the main competitor economies with capitalist ones, and it is clear that the capitalist economies compare favorably in terms of life expectancy as well as per capita income with the others.

A similar graph can be produced by comparing fertility with per capita income across these countries for 2008 (Figure 1.3). While these graphs by themselves show only correlation, my earlier argument for the causal link between capitalism and increased life expectancy and lower fertility holds here as well.

There are other ways to demonstrate that life in contemporary capitalist countries is better than in noncapitalist ones. The Human Development Index (HDI) is a measurement and ranking system used by the UNDP to explore the level of development of each country and the world overall. There are three basic areas that the HDI tries to assess: a long, healthy life; education; and standard of living. The index itself is created by taking a weighted average of life expectancy at birth, literacy, school enrollment at the primary, secondary, and tertiary levels, and the natural logarithm of gross domestic product per capita, and then creating an index that ranges from 0 to 1, with 1 being the highest. Table 1.2 reports rankings, rather than raw scores. The Gender-related Development Index (GDI) takes account

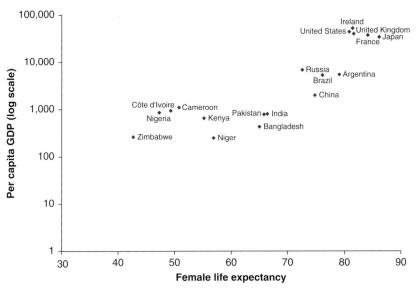

Figure 1.2 Female life expectancy versus per capita income

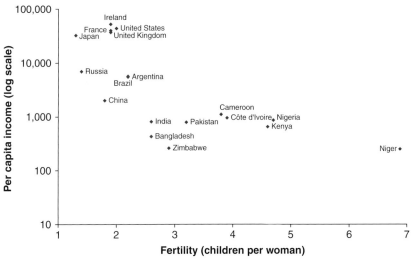

Figure 1.3 Fertility versus per capita income

of the same basic statistics as the HDI, but discounts the scores according to the gender inequalities in the statistics. The Gender Empowerment Measure (GEM) evaluates the degree to which women are advancing in political and economic forums, taking

Table 1.2 HDI, GDI, and GEM rankings 2008 update for selected countries*

Country	HDI rank	GDI rank	GEM rank
Norway[b]	2	3	1
Canada[b]	3	4	10
Sweden[b]	7	5	2
Japan[b]	8	13	54
Denmark[b]	13	11	4
United States[b]	15	16	15
United Kingdom[b]	21	10	14
Germany[b]	23	20	9
Republic of Korea (South Korea)[b]	25	26	64
Singapore[c]	28	26	16
Cuba[a]	48	49	26
Oman[c]	53	67	80
Saudi Arabia[c]	55	70	92
China[b]	94	73	57
India[b]	132	113	–
Sudan[c]	146	131	–
Senegal[c]	153	135	–
Niger[c]	174	155	–
Afghanistan[c]	–	–	–
Democratic Republic of Korea (North Korea)[a]	–	–	–
Somalia[c]	–	–	–

[a] Socialist countries.
[b] Capitalist countries.
[c] Traditionalist countries.
* UNDP, Human Development Reports 2009, available at: http://hdr.undp.org/en, accessed September 5, 2009.

into account female and male shares of parliamentary representation, female and male shares of positions as legislators, senior officials, managers, and technical and professional positions, and female and male estimated earned income.[67] According to the

67 UNDP, "Measuring Inequality: Gender-related Development Index (GDI) and Gender Empowerment Measure (GEM)," Human Development Reports

UNDP's own description of the two measures, "while the GDI focuses on expansion of capabilities, the GEM is concerned with the use of those capabilities to take advantage of the opportunities of life."[68] Table 1.2 reports the rankings of these three measures for selected countries, some capitalist and some from the opponents of capitalism.

As Table 1.2 makes clear, capitalist countries do better in terms of all three rankings. Cuba, a socialist country, does very well for its income level because of its excellent health and educational systems, but it should also be remembered that Cuba's human rights record is very poor in terms of the negative freedoms of assembly, free speech, and property rights.[69] The fact that many people are willing to risk their lives trying to flee its shores even today, more than fifty years after the revolution, is a clear sign that even good health care and education are not sufficient to secure a good human life for many. Japan does surprisingly poorly on the gender empowerment measure because of the way in which their form of state-guided capitalism has entrenched the patriarchy of feudal Japan; the case is similar for South Korea. Data is not available for some of these countries, which is, in itself, an indictment of their governments, which are either unable to collect the data or unwilling to share it with the United Nations. There is no capitalist country for which data is unavailable except India's record on the gender empowerment measure. A deeper look into the data indicates that the school enrollment rates are not well documented, but UNESCO estimates for these are comparatively poor, particularly at the tertiary level. India is, however, rapidly improving, and was, until the 1990s a socialist country. China likewise is lower than most capitalist countries, but is still under the shadows of a socialist government that

2007/2008, available at: http://hdr.undp.org/en/media/HDR_20072008_Tech_Note_1.pdf, accessed September 5, 2009.

68 UNDP, "Measuring Inequality: Gender-related Development Index (GDI) and Gender Empowerment Measure (GEM)," Human Development Reports 2007/2008, available at: http://hdr.undp.org/en/statistics/indices/gdi_gem, accessed September 5, 2009.

69 Amnesty International, "State of the World's Human Rights 2009".

allowed no market activity until the 1990s, and which still controls many more aspects of life than other capitalist countries.

One of the most trenchant critiques of contemporary capitalism is that it supports child labor. As I mentioned above, the number of children working has decreased since the nineteenth century, and recent decades have seen the development of child labor laws and international standards for child labor. Most countries have laws which roughly reflect these standards; however, laws in most countries exempt household and agricultural employment from these restrictions, providing a legal exemption for some child labor. Furthermore, in many poor countries child labor laws are entirely unenforced.

Approximately 250 million children between the ages of 5 and 14 are engaged in economic activity worldwide, and almost half of them work full time. (Age 14 is generally accepted as the cutoff age for a "child" worker.) Worldwide, about 75% of child labor is employed in agriculture, and just under 10% are engaged in production of nonagricultural commodities and related work. Most of the working children (61%) are in Asia, 32% are in Africa, and 7% in Latin America and the Caribbean. Africa has the highest labor participation rate of 41%, however, while in Asia it is 22%, Latin America 17%, and Oceania 29%. More boys than girls report working, but this is the result of excluding housework from the definition of labor used by the ILO. Approximately one-third of girls who do not attend school report that they must stay at home to do housework, often tending to other members of the family. If housework is included, it is likely that more girls work than boys (and, therefore, the estimates of the number of working children in the world should be increased).[70] Although the World Bank and other sources claim that there is no full-time child labor in North America and Europe, there are surely children working in agriculture, housework, and on the street as sex workers. Here, as in the rest of the world, statistics are

---

70 Peter Fallon and Zafiris Tzannatos, "Child Labor: Issues and Directions for the World Bank," The World Bank, 1998, available at: http://info.worldbank.org/etools/docs/library/76309/dc2002/proceedings/pdfpaper/module9pfzt.pdf.

difficult to come by and surely undercount the child laborers. But there is also a definitional issue in play here. What is counted as child labor by the ILO and UNICEF is what we might call the "bad" child labor, that is, labor that prevents children from going to school, or that is hazardous or dangerous. By this definition, perhaps it is true that child labor in North America and Europe approach zero. We must remain somewhat skeptical of these statistics, however. The United Farm Workers estimates that there are 800,000 agricultural laborers under the age of 18 in the United States.[71] Agricultural work is considered the second most hazardous occupation next to mining. Thus, I hold that there is, in fact, some child labor in the United States, even by the standards that the ILO sets for "child labor."

These statistics show that most work is domestic (meaning internal to the nation) production, not work done for international markets. In fact, the World Bank estimates that "probably less than 5% of child laborers are employed in export manufacturing or mining sectors, and only 1 to 2% are employed in export-oriented agriculture."[72] In some cases one might argue that it is still part of the global spread of capitalism, such as where the domestic industry competes with an internationally produced good, or where the industry or sector would not exist were it not for the opportunities of globalization. But much of the child labor is labor that would exist without the influences of global capitalism. The numbers of children working to produce goods for export markets is significant in absolute numbers, since any child labor is unfortunate. But it is not the result of global capitalism as much as it is of parental poverty. This suggests that the best way to end child labor is to increase parental income and wealth, which suggests that more capitalist development is the best route. Without such development, making child labor illegal is more likely to send it underground or into the illegal economy, since the children and their families must still make an income

71 Human Rights Watch, "Fingers to the Bone: United States Failure to Protect Child Farmworkers," 2000, section III, available at: www.hrw.org/en/reports/2000/06/02/fingers-bone-0.
72 Fallon and Tzannatos, "Child Labor," 1.

in order to live. Of course, massive charity would be useful in the meantime. Wealthy countries or individuals could pay poor parents to send their children to school, for example. Charity can be defended as a virtue or an imperfect duty, or it can be defended as an instrumentally rational way for the rich to prevent future instability and social unrest. The only sustainable long-term solution, however, is development of poor countries so that parents can earn incomes that allow them and their societies to invest in the education and health of their children. Capitalism creates an incentive for parents to do this by promising ways to achieve a higher income from education.

A common misperception in the literature on development and health outcomes is that if a positive public health outcome can now be achieved without accumulation of wealth and capital, then such development, and capitalism in particular, could not be causally responsible for improvements in health.[73] But this follows neither for the historical nor the contemporary case. I have just argued the historical case. Consider two contemporary examples of lifesaving and life improving medical advances. The development of anti-retroviral drugs to combat AIDS has been incredibly expensive, although today the drugs themselves are not expensive to make and they are being distributed in many developing countries for very low prices. These drugs are saving many lives. But clearly they would not exist at all were it not for the massive investments in capital and scientific expertise in academic settings in developed capitalist countries. Capitalism provided the wealth accumulation that made this possible, even while it was the collective action of government allocating funds for development of the drugs and global health organizations that made possible their delivery to poor, mainly noncapitalist countries. Another biomedical advance that promises to save or improve the health of many premature infants is the development of the actifier. Premature infants often have trouble learning to suckle, a task that requires

---

73 In addition to Easterlin, Janet Thomas, "Women and Capitalism: Oppression or Emancipation?," *Comparative Studies in Society and History* 30(3) (July 1988), 534–49 makes this argument.

a great deal of coordination of sucking, swallowing, and breathing muscles. The actifier is a simple, cheap device that provides instant feedback to the infant that teaches it to suckle properly, often in just a few sessions. Learning this coordination of muscles is the first step that infants need to take to bootstrap cognitive skills necessary for a successful and rich human life. It also allows infants to breastfeed, which is especially crucial in places where water quality is questionable and assaults against a child's immune system are likely to be many. This device will no doubt save many lives at low cost in developing countries. But its development has required a massive investment in science – the main developer of the device has a million dollar laboratory and many postdocs who work for him. And this accounting leaves out the many mis-steps and wrong turns that less successful innovations have taken. Any one successful biomedical device or drug comes from a large number of trials and errors, most of which are costly but never recover their cost directly.

Summary of the empirical case for capitalism

This section has argued that capitalism caused massive improvements in the quality of human life, taking into account the basic, common interests of humanity in general and women's particular interests. I began by stating the empirical case for the historical claim that the advent of capitalism started humanity on a path of improvement to the length and quality of life. Here I argued that capitalism helped to bring about dramatic changes in life expectancy, lengthening individual lives by one to even two additional generations on average in highly developed capitalist societies. Capitalism has also helped to lower infant mortality, through improvements in medical technology and health care for infants and pregnant women, and to lower the fertility rate from around seven per woman to two. This change in fertility has to be seen as the single greatest improvement in women's lives in history, and is the key to women's empowerment in all other social and political contexts. Capitalism has also improved the quality of human life materially by improving hygiene, comfort, and decreasing domestic labor for women, as well as decreasing work time overall for both men and women. Capitalism has also brought about or at least coincided with moral and political improvements. The most important of these has been the progress of liberal ideology, which espouses the fundamental moral importance of each individual as an autonomous being. Women's rights and empowerment have advanced markedly in liberal capitalist societies over the period of the development of capitalism.

I then argued the contemporary case for the claim that capitalist societies outperform noncapitalist ones on most of the essential bases of measurement of quality of life. Most capitalist societies have a longer life expectancy and lower fertility rate than most noncapitalist societies. Most capitalist societies perform better on the HDI, the GDI, and the GEM than most noncapitalist ones. The main counterexamples are Cuba, which is a country from which many of its citizens risk their lives to flee its shores, and China and India, which have only recently become capitalist systems after years of socialist central planning. I then discussed the horrible problem of child labor in the world, arguing that it is largely a domestic problem within countries, rather than a global capitalist issue, and that it is caused by parental poverty. I argued that these facts suggest that child labor has to be addressed by curing parental poverty, and that this is best achieved in a developed capitalist society.

In sum, the empirical case seems quite clearly to point toward capitalism as the best economic system that humans have developed. This is not to say that it is without its problems or critics, as I shall explore, and as my debate partner powerfully expounds. But before going on to explore those criticisms, it is important to see why capitalism has been so successful in bringing about vastly longer and better human lives than previous and current alternative economic systems, while continuing to explore how capitalism could be improved upon.

3   The theoretical explanation of capitalism's success

Why is capitalism so effective in bringing about these massive improvements in the quality of human life and human freedom?

The traditional defense of capitalism from Adam Smith to F. A. Hayek to Milton Friedman is that it provides both material prosperity and liberal freedom, and this defense provides a theoretical explanation of the connection of capitalism to prosperity and freedom. Capitalism provides material prosperity in two ways: by efficiently distributing goods through decentralized, open markets; and by giving individuals incentives to produce efficiently to provide additional goods for existing and new markets. There are four theoretical arguments that can be given for capitalism's success. The first and second of these arguments, that capitalist markets efficiently distribute goods and provide incentives to produce efficiently, can be analytically shown from an explanatory model of markets for consumption and production of goods. We can also show why the decentralized market system of capitalism is better than its centrally-planned socialist rivals at producing prosperity because of its efficient aggregation of information. The third, the explanation for why capitalism provides incentives to individuals to open new markets can also be given a theoretical argument that connects the nature of capitalism with rational behavior. Finally, we can connect the free, open, and nondiscriminatory markets of capitalism with its ability to provide for freedom using a normative model of freedom that has been articulated by political philosophers.

Economists have tried analytically to prove that free markets provide for economic efficiency and limited equity with an idealized model of free and open markets. Admittedly, the argument applies to the ideal of the perfectly competitive market, which bears only a passing resemblance to the capitalist market system I am defending. On the definition of capitalism that I am using in this book, a system is capitalist only if it provides nondiscriminatory, legal protections of decentralized, private ownership of resources; cooperative, social production for all citizens; and free and open competitive markets for exchange of goods, labor, services, and material and financial capital. This differs significantly from the perfectly competitive ideal with which economists work, but I will begin with the argument for optimality in that system and then work from there to answer the question of why capitalism is so effective at improving human life.

Competitive markets, economic efficiency, and equity

The concept of Pareto optimality, or efficiency as it is sometimes called, was invented by Vilfredo Pareto, an Italian economist at the turn of the nineteenth century, as a way of comparing states of affairs without making the interpersonal comparisons of utility required by utilitarianism.[74] Welfare economists avoid interpersonal comparisons of utility mainly because they claim that utility is essentially private. Thus, they avoid making claims about total or average utilities in society, fearing that they are meaningless sums. There are good normative reasons to avoid total utility as a way of comparing societies. This is well trodden ground for moral philosophers; I will rehearse just two arguments against utilitarianism that I find sufficiently persuasive. First, total utilitarianism suggests that the more utility seekers the better, leading to what Derek Parfit called the repugnant conclusion: that vast numbers of people with lives barely worth living is a better world than one with a small number of very happy people.[75] If we take average utility across all those persons to avoid this conclusion, then we are faced with the second problem, raised by John Rawls: that utilitarianism fails to take seriously the distinction between persons.[76] In other words, utilitarianism treats persons as mere utility generators that can be snapped together or taken apart like Lego pieces, and not as persons with distinct, impermeable boundaries. A human life is a series of projects that cannot be traded off at a moment for others' projects, yet average utilitarianism would suggest that one should engage in whatever activity raises utility at the moment (or in the long run),

---

74 See Julian Le Grand, "Equity versus Efficiency: The Elusive Trade-off," *Ethics* 100 (1990): 554–68 for a discussion of some problems with identifying Pareto optimality and efficiency. Vilfredo Pareto, *Manual of Political Economy* (New York: Austus M. Kelley, 1971), ch. 6.

75 Derek Parfit, *Reasons and Persons* (Oxford University Press, 1987), 388.

76 John Rawls, *A Theory of Justice* (Cambridge, MA: Harvard University Press, 1971), 27.

without regard to whose project it is. This sounds like another abhorrent conclusion, and one that is not compatible with either human rights or dignity. It seems particularly ill-suited to the task of defending capitalism from the perspective of feminism, since utilitarians are not typically concerned with the issue of preferences formed under conditions of oppression. I will not mount a full critique of utilitarianism, though, since whether or not it is the correct theory of morality, one could defend capitalism along lines similar to mine. In fact, it might be argued that if we need not take distributional concerns directly into consideration, the argument for capitalism would be even easier to make. I will not pursue the project of defending capitalism as a positive feminist transformation from the perspective of total or average utility.

The welfare economist is still concerned about utility or welfare without having to sum it across persons, however. Pareto optimality characterizes a distribution of goods when no trades could be made to make anyone better off without making anyone else worse off. The Pareto criterion has three advantages over maximization of total or average utility for a theory of justice. First, one can determine which states are Pareto optimal without making interpersonal comparisons of utility. All that matters for judgments about Pareto optimality are individuals' own preferences for different social states. Second, Pareto optimality is a weaker criterion than maximization of total or average utility, and unlike those criteria does not generally provide a unique ideal distribution. Since many different distributions may satisfy Pareto optimality, holding Pareto optimality to be a criterion of justice need not imply that one holds a welfarist conception of justice; Pareto optimality can be a necessary criterion of justice in a view that takes other, nonwelfarist criteria to be equally necessary.[77] Third, since economists avoid making explicitly ethical judgments, Pareto optimality and related criteria are the only bases by which welfare economists could make comparative

---

77 I am using "welfarist" in the sense of Amartya Sen. See *On Ethics and Economics* (Oxford: Blackwell, 1987), which refers to theories that take the justice or goodness of a society to be completely determined by the utilities of the individuals in it.

social policy judgments.[78] Since Pareto optimal states are typically not unique given a set of goods, there is still plenty of work left for the ethicists and the politicians in making policy.

Welfare economics has made remarkable progress with these weak criteria, however. The two most important results of welfare economics concern an idealized model of a market called the perfectly competitive market (PCM). PCMs are characterized by the following conditions:

C1 Resources are privately owned and privately consumed.

C2 Force and fraud does not exist.

C3 There are many buyers and sellers, and entry and exit to the market is free, so that no one can act unilaterally, or collusively, to affect prices.

C4 Transactions (e.g., publicizing or gathering information about goods for exchange, shipping, preparation for consumption) are costless.

C5 Individuals' utility functions are stable, monotonic (which means that if any amount of a good ever raises an individual's utility, no greater amount of the good would lower the utility), and reflect transitive preference orderings.

C6 There are no externalities, that is, all costs and benefits of producing or consuming a good are borne by the owner of the good.

C7 No transactions take place out of equilibrium.[79]

Of course, the PCM model abstracts from reality in each of these conditions. The condition that goods are privately owned and consumed insures that no one takes another's interest as her or his own; each acts in her or his own self-interest. This condition seems to imply that not only altruism, but also, perhaps more importantly, envy, is ruled out as a motivation for individual actions. Amartya Sen has shown that, in fact, the important efficiency results of the PCM can be derived without

---

78 An example of a welfare economist using Pareto optimality as a normative criterion is Gordon Tullock, "Inheritance Justified," *Journal of Law and Economics* 13 (1970): 465–74.

79 These criteria are redundant to some extent. In particular, C1, C3, C4, C5 would be sufficient to characterize the PCM, properly understood. I add the others just to make the conditions clear.

assuming any particular motivations lie behind the preferences, and even allowing for moral values and commitments to play a role in determining individuals' preferences.[80] The requirement that utility functions be monotonic is pretty accurate for most goods, especially when there is a resale market. But it is well documented that individuals' preferences often fail to be transitive.[81] There are externalities in almost every economic activity, and in the world these give rise to free riding, public goods, political posturing, and lawsuits. Ideally, a society might be able to internalize many of them, but there will always be some externalities. Mill found that he could not say that any action was completely self-regarding, and instead argued that living in a liberal society requires individuals to put up with some states of affairs that one finds offensive, that is to say, externalities of others' behaviors.[82] Finally, C7 requires that everyone knows what equilibrium prices are, and that any price below the equilibrium price would be rejected by the seller, any price above would be rejected by the buyer. But clearly this kind of knowledge is not available, even though the Internet, eBay, and Craig's List makes the idealization more realistic for many markets and many individuals.

The other three conditions of the PCM rule out strategic behavior, or acting in ways to bluff or confuse the other individuals in the market. By prohibiting force and fraud from playing a role, the PCM rules out taking the market to be a larger game, in which illicit, extra-market behavior is figured in as a possible strategy, one with great risks and great potential rewards, to be considered in the light of rational self-interest. If transactions were costly, then there might be an advantage in delaying or hiding information so that some advantageous trades would not be made. Finally, the condition that no one can affect prices rules

---

80 Amartya Sen, "Markets and Freedoms," *Oxford Economic Papers* 45 (October 1993): 519–41.

81 See Richard Thaler, "Psychology of Choice and the Assumptions of Economics," in Alvin Roth (ed.), *Laboratory Experimentation in Economics* (Cambridge University Press, 1987), 99–130, for a review of experimental evidence of violations of economic assumptions about human behavior.

82 J. S. Mill, *On Liberty* (London: Longman, Roberts & Green, 1859), ch. 4.

out monopolies and oligopolies, so that there is no incentive for individuals to cooperate in small coalitions; in the PCM it is each person for her- or himself.

In the PCM, individuals trade until all trades that are mutually agreeable to the buyer and the seller have been made, since trades are costless, they can get something they want better by trading, and they have no fraud to worry about. The first fundamental theorem of welfare economics tells us that in the PCM, individuals seeking their own interests will reach a Pareto optimal outcome:[83]

WE1 In the PCM the outcome of free trade is Pareto optimal.

This can be shown informally by supposing that the outcome is not Pareto optimal. Then there is at least one person who can be made better off without making another worse off. Suppose that person is Ed and he could be made better off by trading two of his oranges to Evelyn for one of her apples, a trade that would not make her worse off. Then (provided that there are no externalities) by making the trade they make a Pareto improvement, that is, they increase someone's utility without decreasing anyone else's, and neither will see any reason not to.[84] If there are any other potential Pareto improvements then they are made as well, by the same kind of argument. If not, then there is no way to make anyone better off without making another worse off, that is, the situation is Pareto optimal. Pareto optimal states are those in which the distribution of goods is as effectively used to raise total welfare as it can be, and in the PCM it is done without forcibly taking anything from anyone. There are many such outcomes that we would not call just, in particular, if the starting point for trade was unfair or coercive. Still, there is a connection to justice for anyone who thinks that liberty is one component of it: WE1 implies that Pareto optimality is a byproduct of the PCM, in which force and fraud, as well as government coercion, is absent.[85]

---

83 Sen, *On Ethics and Economics*, ch. 2.
84 Recall that there are no transaction costs, so that if a person is indifferent to a trade there is no sense in which he would prefer not to trade; we shall suppose that in these cases the indifferent party makes the trade.
85 But see, Allan Gibbard, "What's Morally Special About Free Exchange?," in E. F. Paul, F. D. Miller, Jr., and J. Paul (eds.), *Ethics and Economics* (Oxford

The second fundamental theorem of welfare economics extends the significance of Pareto optimality for concerns of justice:

WE2 Any Pareto optimal outcome can be achieved through the PCM from some initial allocation of goods.

In other words, if one chooses a particular Pareto optimal allocation, say for reasons of equity, it could be reached through free trade from some particular initial allocation, which can be arrived at through lump-sum taxes and forced transfers. Beginning from a fair initial allocation of goods, the PCM allows agents to come to a new allocation, which everyone likes even better, through freely entered trades, and this maximizes the social welfare that can be achieved given the starting point. Since WE2 allows that any Pareto optimal end-state allocation could have been brought about through the liberty of the free market, welfare economists take it that Pareto optimality is at least a weak criterion of justice, justifying the market as the only just allocative mechanism. As Hal Varian writes, "the interesting result of welfare economics is that we can relate an end-state principle of justice – maximum 'social welfare' – to an allocative procedure – the market mechanism."[86] This fact has often been used, controversially, to justify the free market in the real world. It is controversial mainly because although it is one thing to say that any Pareto optimal outcome *could be* achieved, it is another to argue that either some Pareto optimal outcome *is* achieved, let alone that the most *fair or just* one is achieved in the actual world. The only way to achieve a different outcome is for the distribution of goods to be changed, but such re-distributions are politically infeasible.

The view of many welfare economists is that since Pareto optimality can be had without sacrificing equity or other distributional concerns, then it would be foolish not to take it. Who could complain about a Pareto improvement? This seems to be a powerful appeal, but it faces several key objections. First, the argument for Pareto optimality as providing for equity from WE2 does not

University Press, 1985), 20–29, for a criticism of the notion that free exchange is even *prima facie* a good thing.

86 Hal R. Varian, "Distributive Justice, Welfare Economics, and the Theory of Fairness," *Philosophy and Public Affairs* 4 (1974–75): 223–47.

extend beyond the confines of the PCM. In the real world the conditions of the PCM do not exist, and neither WE1 nor WE2 hold. The two most significant of the abstractions from reality are the existence of externalities and the assumption that there are no transaction costs, in particular, that information gathering is costless. The existence of externalities means that there will be beneficial trades that are not made, and costs imposed on persons who are not party to trades.[87] The classic examples of externalities are the guiding light from lighthouses and pollution. Lighthouses provide a valuable service to ship navigators, for which they would be willing to pay if that were the only way that they could use it. But the beam of light that the lighthouse sends is free for all who see its beam to consume, so naturally, shippers will try to consume it without paying for it. Knowing this, few would want to construct lighthouses in a private free market, since they will bring about financial loss for most of them.[88] Hence, there will be an undersupply of lighthouses in the free market. In just the opposite way, too much pollution will be produced. Firms who pollute a river, for example, are able to let their waste, which would otherwise be costly to dispose of, run downstream freely, where it becomes someone else's cost. The firm then can sell its product without considering that cost, and the consumers of the product will consume it without having to pay that cost. Since some of the consumers would not pay the higher cost which includes waste disposal, more of the product, and hence more of the pollution, is created than there would be if the waste disposal cost were internalized. The result of externalities is that the free market does not lead to Pareto optimality. Provided that there are enough shippers who would pay

87 The Coase theorem shows that some of these trades could be made given precisely enough defined property rights. However, this requires governments to be able to assign and monitor property rights in unmanageable ways, such as assigning property rights to clean air. This method of internalizing the externalities can also create incentives to pollute in order to be paid not to do so.

88 Building a lighthouse is rational whenever the expected value of the lighthouse is less than the expected cost of the lighthouse. For a large and profitable enough shipping company that would be the case for some locations.

something for it, if they could prevent any nonpayer from consuming it, a lighthouse could be constructed which would make all of them better off without making anyone else worse off. And provided that the pollution is costly enough to the downstream neighbors, if they could prevent the firm from freely using the river, a level of pollution that reflects the costs and benefits to all could be chosen. But since there are externalities in the world, and some of them cannot be internalized, the link between the freedom of the PCM and Pareto optimality is broken.[89] What is more, there is no proof that Pareto optimality can always be had without sacrificing equity, since WE2 does not hold in the presence of externalities.

The ubiquity of externalities implies a role for government intervention in the free market in order to reach an efficient outcome. Government can tax the users of lighthouses so that enough of them are supplied; government can tax the polluters so that they have an incentive to create less pollution. But this governmental solution brings with it problems of its own. First, since governments are made up of agents whose incentives are distinct from those of the government or population as a whole, the agents in charge of determining the taxes may seek their own interests or opinions. They might value lighthouses or pollution differently from the population as a whole, and thus also cause an under- or oversupply. They might take side payments (bribes or other favors) from polluters or lighthouse users to change the incentive structures. Second, even if they were willing to honestly represent the interests of the whole, they might not be able to accurately determine the optimal number of lighthouses or level of pollution. In the PCM the optimal level does not have to be determined separately from the outcome – the process leads

---

89 It is not quite a unanimous opinion in the economics literature that externalities harm third parties, that is, persons who are not party to trades. However, the argument that externalities are harmless depends on the assumption that costs of making voluntary agreements are completely uniform across the market, and this is clearly violated in the world. See James M. Buchanan, "The Relevance of Pareto Optimality," *Journal of Conflict Resolution* 6 (1962): 341–54; esp. 349.

"as if by an invisible hand" to the optimal outcome without anyone having to gather any information or make any judgments other than seeking their own self-interest.

However, the basic argument strategy for WE1 still holds in relatively free and open markets where the goods are excludable and externalities can be internalized. Many of the goods (cars, trains, toilets, televisions) that have made our lives better over the past 150 years are no doubt of this type. And many of the goods that are not of this type (education, sewers, streets, vaccinations) have been provided by governments because of these recognized market failures, in part because of their link to marketable goods. That WE2 is less robust to the problem of externalities should be no surprise, since capitalism has not greatly reduced economic inequalities over time, nor does it have any edge over centrally-planned economies in this regard. The basic lesson I take from welfare economics is that capitalism is highly efficient, and is made even more so by the right kinds of government interventions to internalize externalities where that can be done. This in part explains the success of capitalism in terms of its ability to generate increases in wealth and well-being. Welfare economics also suggests that capitalist economies could be more equitable than they are in practice, but that requires a re-distribution of goods that may or may not be politically viable.

Capitalist markets as aggregators of information

Capitalist markets can also be defended on grounds that they are efficient aggregators of information, in particular, information about preferences, costs, and benefits. Rather than needing someone to figure out who wants or needs what and what is the least costly way to fill the need, markets cause the resources to flow to fill consumer demands. They are in effect analog generators of answers to the question: what is the optimal distribution of goods, resources, capital, and labor given the current distribution of rights over these items, and a right to trade freely with perfect information about the availability of offers for sale and bids to buy? As I noted in the previous section, the PCM brings about a Pareto optimal result, that is, a distribution of these goods that cannot be improved upon for any one person without making another worse off. But as I also noted, there are many heroic assumptions being made by this model, particularly with regard to the information available. The kinds of information include not only the offers and bids, but also the quality of the goods and the availability of other substitutes for them. This information is not costless to gather or to disseminate in practice.

At an earlier time in the development of economic theory, economists thought that information could be treated like just another good that would be traded and have an equilibrium price in the market. However, information turns out not to be like just any other good. Like some other goods, information is not what economists call "rival," that is, one person having it does not rule out others having it. But it is also subject to manipulation in ways that other nonrival goods are not. Information is subject to a principal–agent problem: the one who has the information can appear to share it, while in fact be conveying that information in ways that shade or hide the truth. Consider the saying that "if you go to a surgeon, you are likely to get a recommendation for surgery." In this case, surgeons make a living from performing surgery, and it is what they know best as the treatment of disease. Their advice is not going to be from an "all things considered" perspective, but from a particular one with a particular subjective interest. Exchanging information is typically clouded with these kinds of biases, which create special problems for markets for information.

Information is asymmetrically distributed and having information allows one to extract what economists call "rents," that is, profits that are beyond what one could expect to achieve in the PCM. In the past forty years, much of the economic literature on markets has focused on ways that information failures and inequities can lead to inefficiencies, that is, failures to achieve Pareto outcomes, and to serious inequities that favor those who can manipulate information. In a survey of the results of information economics, Joseph Stiglitz, an economist who won a Nobel Prize for his contributions to this literature, explains the types of information asymmetries that the literature has explored.[90] Moral hazard problems arise when someone insures against a bad outcome and then does not take as much care not to bring that bad outcome about. Principal–agent problems occur when the agent, who is selling a good or service to the principal, has an incentive to shade or hide information from the principal in order to sell that good or service for a higher price. Adverse selection problems arise when products differ in quality and the owner of the product has privately held information about that quality. In insurance markets, the ones who buy insurance are likely to be the ones who are most prone to the catastrophe being insured against, and if this is privately known information, the sellers of insurance will have to charge a higher price than they would if the information were openly known; in markets for used cars, the ones selling the cars are the ones who know which cars are lemons, and this results in a general mistrust of all used cars. Although these information problems are not specific to capitalist markets – they can arise in any kind of interaction that takes the form of exchange – these problems have serious consequences for the adequacy of a model that abstracts away from information asymmetries, such as the PCM. As with externalities, information asymmetries imply that government intervention can lead to Pareto improvements by offering to improve or certify information. In the case of health insurance, the inevitable failures in insurance markets lead many to argue that private insurance will inevitably cost more and deliver less health care than socially provided health care which covers everyone regardless of their health status.

Information asymmetries raise problems for not only WE1, the claim that Pareto optimality results from the market without external interventions, but also for WE2, the claim that equity and efficiency can be aligned given a fair starting point. Stiglitz gives several examples of inequities that are generated by

---

90 Joseph Stiglitz, "The Contributions of the Economics of Information to Twentieth Century Economics," *The Quarterly Journal of Economics* 115(4) (November 2000): 1441–78.

information asymmetries. For instance, a richer person is better able to work for low wages initially, contingent on a performance bonus once his or her high ability is revealed, a richer person is better able to absorb losses or post collateral, and so internalizes more of the consequences of his or her actions, and a richer person is better able to post a bond – as a kind of hostage – to mitigate the scope for opportunism.[91] He concludes that the "results of information economics show forcefully that the long-standing hypothesis that economies with imperfect information would be similar to economies with perfect information – at least so long as the degree of information imperfection was not too large – has no theoretical basis."[92]

Given these problems, can it reasonably be claimed that capitalism has any advantages over socialism with respect to aggregating information? Yes, we can still make this case, but now it has to be argued by showing that information problems are even worse for central planners or bureaucrats (even if they are employed by a democratically elected government). Let us begin by considering what sort of information the bureaucrats need to gather in order to make economic decisions. This information includes individuals' needs, wants, tastes, abilities, physical condition, and talents; manufacturers' input needs and output quantity and quality; and other potential techniques for manufacturing. There are no doubt many other things that need to be known, but this list will suffice for the points I want to make.

There are four reasons to think that a decentralized market system will be better than a centrally-planned distribution system in terms of the flow of information. First, the bureaucrats still have the same problems of information asymmetries, and the individuals and manufacturers will still have different incentives to reveal or conceal information from the bureaucrats. The asymmetries arise from many sources, including the separateness

91 Stiglitz, "The Contributions of the Economics of Information to Twentieth Century Economics," 1469.
92 Stiglitz, "The Contributions of the Economics of Information to Twentieth Century Economics," 1470.

of persons and beliefs, and the differences in interests, biases, influences, knowledge, and learning ability. The problems that arise for some markets in a market-based system potentially arise for all distributive schemes in a centrally-planned system.

Second, decentralized markets save effort and expense in gathering the available information. While central planners have to pay someone to count or assess the information, decentralized markets do this, as I said before, as a kind of analog device. The information may not be in digital form, but it is effectively utilized by consumers and firms nonetheless. In those markets where government intervention is necessary because of asymmetries, the intervention can be targeted to gather only the information needed to correct the inefficiency or inequity that arises. Thus, government interventions can be less costly and more narrowly targeted in a decentralized market.

Third, it must also be recognized that introducing bureaucrats brings new informational asymmetries. The person who regulates and enforces policies has their own set of incentives and beliefs, and in order to use their information to make decisions, she or he has to communicate them to others. Because that person is an individual with biases, interests, and beliefs, she or he will frame this information in ways that support her or his own case for a decision. But that raises new principal–agent problems, where the bureaucrat is the agent and the people, the government, or just the bureaucrat's boss is the principal. Furthermore, if she or he has to ask consumers, citizens, and manufacturers for information, then another layer of principal–agent problems arise. Unless we think that somehow these multiple principal–agent problems will cancel each other out (and I can think of no reason to think that), then central planning seems to multiply informational asymmetries.

Fourth, and perhaps most fundamental, is that we have to ask the question of what the bureaucrats are to count if there are no prices. A price system allocates goods according to who has the most willingness to pay for those goods. That system has its problems (which I will explore in a later section), but it offers a feasible, tractable solution to the distribution problem. It is tractable precisely because it need not be assessed explicitly; the solution arises implicitly within the market system. What alternatives could a central planning system choose? The problem has to be specified more precisely. Given the (technically) possible goods and services that could be provided with the available resources, what should be produced, how much, and how will it be distributed? The problem requires assessing the possible goods and services, the available resources, and the possible alternative distribution outcomes. Central planning seems attractive because it begins from a principle of distributive justice and answers the contribution and production questions in light of that. For instance, utilitarian central planners will distribute, as well as produce and require contribution from individuals, according to what maximizes utility. These planners will then require information about individuals' utility functions. But other than through a decentralized market process, it is difficult to see how information about utility functions could be gained. Would we need a survey of every human being asking them to assess and compare every possible good and every possible task? The mind boggles at the almost limitless information required here. Furthermore, people would have incentives not to reveal their preferences in every case. Perhaps more plausibly, a Marxist central planner distributes and produces by the maxim: "to each according to his need, from each according to his ability." For this central planner the bureaucrat has to assess needs and abilities. Needs could be assessed by nutritionists, psychologists, and sociologists who assess the requirements for a decent human life and the material goods required to attain them. Abilities could perhaps be assessed by educators and psychologists who could, like the guardians imagined by Plato, tote up the abilities of each citizen and put them in the proper school for their ability level. But three problems arise for this scenario when compared with the decentralized market alternative. First, once again, there would be an incentive for people not to honestly reveal, or to even conceal, their true needs and abilities. In other words, such a system creates incentives to game the system, and training people not to do this is at least very costly in material and freedom terms, if not altogether impossible. The second is the problem of stagnation, or lack of incentive to innovate or change. Finally, there is total lack of freedom that would ensue if the central planner assigned each person their labor contribution and distribution of goods based on an external assessment of their needs and capacities. I turn now to these issues, incentive to innovate and freedom, in the next two subsections.

Capitalism, production efficiency, and innovation

The second explanation for capitalism's success in bringing about massive increases in the quality of human life comes from the incentives that it provides for producers to create marginally better and cheaper goods. The productive aspect of capitalism is widely acknowledged, of course, but it is worth rehearsing the explanation for how capitalism creates productive efficiency. According to standard neoclassical economic theory, firms in competitive industries will produce until their marginal cost equals their marginal revenue, that is, until the cost of the last item they produce is equal to the amount for which they can sell it. This also implies that if someone can find a cheaper way to produce a good, they will be able to sell more goods, and generate more profits (although according to the theory, when the market is fully saturated, there are no "economic profits," just normal returns to capital and labor). Thus, firms have incentives to produce goods ever more cheaply and in greater quantities. One might object that this is actually the problem with capitalism – it is too efficient. And this objection is made in two forms. First, in the quest to cheapen production, labor will be paid less and less. This is the immiseration objection. Second, goods will be produced that no one really needs – call this the junkyard objection.

The immiseration objection claims that there is a "race to the bottom" for labor, in that capital will seek out ever cheaper labor to hire and this will cause laborers to compete by accepting lower and lower wages. The argument depends on the assumption that there is a large supply of unemployed and interchangeable labor that can be tapped at will, and that capital can flow freely to exploit these laborers. These conditions do not hold precisely in practice, though it is at the heart of the feminist objection to capitalism that women and children are often exploited in this way. It is surely true that labor will seek out the best wages available within other constraints that one's way of life imposes. Capital has to compete for labor with other firms, and so the going wage will depend on what other firms exist, as well as on what other options a society offers persons who are unable or unwilling to work for the wages offered. The better the outside option, then the better position labor has to bargain for higher wages. But likewise, the more mobile capital is, the better able it will be to seek out workers in different places whose outside options are worse and demands for wages are lower. Those unemployed laborers who are out there willing to accept the low wages are, after all, presumably better off when they earn the low wages than they were when they earned nothing. So it is not possible to say analytically how this works out; it has to be empirically determined. The real moral question then is this: does capitalism improve the available options to the most vulnerable women and children? One of the key findings of international trade economists is that when a new international firm enters a developing market, wages as a whole rise in the region.[93] This suggests that more capitalist trade and production increases wages. In some cases, governments will intervene to artificially lower wages and raise the level of production in ways that a free market would not support, say by outlawing unions or breaking strikes. Although this no doubt happens in many places in the world, it is the result of political and social oppression by governments, and hardly to be blamed on the capitalist system *per se*. An analogy would be blaming the political oppression of communist leaders on the socialist economic system. Any economic system will leave open the possibility for unscrupulous

---

93 Drusilla K. Brown, Alan Deardorff, and Robert Stern, "The Effects of Multinational Production on Wages and Working Conditions in Developing Countries," in Robert E. Baldwin and L. Alan Winters (eds.), *Challenges to Globalization: Analyzing the Economics* (University of Chicago Press, 2004), 279–330.

but powerful leaders to exploit the system and oppress people. On the other hand, governments may also interact in ways that raise wages, such as by giving the companies tax breaks or other incentives to locate in the country. Whether they govern socialist or capitalist systems, governments need to be responsive to the people; they can create much good or much harm regardless of the economic system they oversee.

The junkyard objection holds that capitalism creates a lot of useless junk, which messes up the planet and creates materialistic, soulless people and cultures.[94] I am sympathetic to this concern, and I will discuss the related critique of commodity fetishism at greater length in the next section. But I want to respond to the objection by distinguishing two forms that the junkyard objection can take, one which is serious but can be answered by a properly enlightened capitalism, and the other which I think can be rejected. First, the environmental worry arises because many goods create negative externalities upon obsolescence. These externalities can be to some degree internalized through taxes for recycling and clean-up of the goods after they have been discarded. By taxing the consumer for the clean-up, the true social cost of the good is revealed in the price, and there will be fewer produced and sold. Meanwhile more resources will be channeled into reusing and recycling efforts. There will be incentives for firms to make cleaner, more cheaply recycled goods, and for other firms to specialize in reusing the goods in other ways. In short, much can be done through the market mechanism in concert with laws and regulations that prevent the costs of negative externalities from being borne by persons not party to trades. Second, the junkyard objection is also in part an aesthetic objection, and I have less sympathy for this. People typically think it is other people who have too much stuff, not themselves. But part of what it is to be a liberal is to tolerate the imposition of the unappealing or offensive behavior and ways of life of others, in return for their toleration of one's own. After all, one person's junkyard is another's collection.

---

94 Elster and Moene, *Alternatives to Capitalism*, 8.

More importantly than its productive efficiency, though, as I argued in describing entrepreneurial capitalism, under the right conditions capitalism provides incentives to innovate and solve problems in completely new ways. True innovation involves risk taking, since by definition innovation means trying something completely new that goes beyond expectations and may be ridiculed or ignored. To bring about this sort of risk taking from a critical mass of people to ensure a series of successful innovations, there need to be incentives. Capitalism provides the possibility of great wealth as an incentive. Other systems might provide other incentives, such as honors or status, but these are less tangible, and arguably less effective in bringing forth large numbers of risk takers. Furthermore, somewhat successful innovations or innovations that prove to be small improvements can bring at least a partial prize.

Two objections may be raised to entrepreneurial capitalism: first, that it creates greater inequalities of wealth; and, second, that it leads to instability when firms become obsolete because of new innovations. I will address each one in turn. First, it is important to note that although wealth inequalities are very high in entrepreneurial capitalist countries, those countries do not have the highest income inequalities currently. The highest income inequalities, as mentioned earlier, are in very poor countries, such as Namibia or Sierra Leone. Most developed capitalist countries have much lower Gini coefficients. However, among capitalist countries, the highest Gini coefficients are in the United States, Singapore, and Hong Kong, which are among the most friendly places to entrepreneurial activity. Second, wealth inequalities are very great indeed when one takes into account the Bill Gates and J. K Rowlings of the world, but these are very few individuals, whose great wealth hardly makes anyone else worse off. Indeed, if they make philanthropic gestures like the Bill and Melinda Gates Foundation has, they make a great contribution to the well-being of the poor in the world through the use of their wealth. Considering household wealth on average within countries and between countries, it is within countries, that is, within the various economic systems, that wealth inequalities are highest.[95] This suggests that political power, whatever its source, is a large part of the cause of differential income and wealth levels in a society, and insofar as that is a problem, it requires a political solution. Finally, although wealth inequalities can create social instability, poverty is really the underlying difficulty. If capitalist development provides a solution to poverty, as I have argued, then it attacks the root of many of the problems (poor health, inadequate education, unemployment) that lead to social instability and human misery.

Entrepreneurial capitalism creates its own sort of instability when new technology is introduced and firms that capitalize on that new technology replace firms that are unable to switch from old technology. When the old firms are in the process of going out of business, laying off workers, idling manufacturing plants, and still producing commodities that are no longer wanted, the system is inefficient in a static sense, in that it is not making optimal use of the existing resources or allocating them in a Pareto efficient manner. Another sense of efficiency, dynamic efficiency, is the optimal creation of new goods and services.[96] New kinds of goods, production techniques, and services obviate the need to spend resources on older technologies and provide better means to achieve our ends. Personal computers have obviated the need for typewriters, and provided much improved ways of recording, reproducing, and analyzing information, communicating, and a wide variety of other tasks that typewriters could not do or did very poorly. (I can still recall the smell of the mimeograph machine that would allow me to make forty or fifty copies of a document before it had to be retyped.) Entrepreneurial capitalism, by promoting innovation, fosters dynamic efficiency.

Capitalist markets and freedom

Freedom is the ultimate appeal of capitalism. The early proponents of capitalism, such as Adam Smith, as well as more

---

95 James B. Davies, Susanna Sandström, Anthony Shorrocks, and Edward N. Wolff, "Estimating the Level and Distribution of Global Household Wealth," UN–Wider, Research Paper No. 2007/77, 2007.

96 Elster and Moene, *Alternatives to Capitalism*, 5.

recent defenders, including economists from such diverse political motivations as Milton Friedman and Amartya Sen, have all defended capitalism on this ground. While efficiency and the ability to raise living standards is an important reason to maintain free markets, and an aspect of the freedom that Sen extols, the freedoms provided by capitalism are intrinsically valuable and partially constitutive of freedom. As Sen argues, regardless of the efficiencies of the market, "the more immediate case for the freedom of market transaction lies in the basic importance of that freedom itself."[97] While securing this freedom is straightforward and simple for middle and upper class men of the First World, for women and others oppressed by traditional norms of their cultures, the freedom to transact in the marketplace can be liberating on a far wider scale. Thus, I will argue as well that capitalism enhances women's freedom.

The free market system of capitalism enhances freedom in three ways. Traditionally freedom of exchange has been seen as a basic form of individual freedom, with which it would be wrong to interfere, and in this sense is a basic, negative freedom like the freedom of speech, assembly, the press, or conscience. Gerald Gaus, a liberal defender of the morality of markets, summarizes the liberal case for freedom in capitalism: "classical liberalism embraces market relations because (but not, of course, only because) they (1) are essentially free, (2) respect the actual choices of individuals, and (3) legitimately express different individuals' rational decisions about the proper choice between competing ends, goods, and values."[98] Market freedom is necessary to respect individuals as free choosers and designers of their own "experiments in living," as Mill famously puts it.[99] Free markets also have positive aspects, however, in providing opportunities by increasing persons' material wealth in order to choose things that they value. Another aspect of the positive freedom

97 Sen, *Development as Freedom*, 112.
98 Gerald F. Gaus, "Backwards into the Future: Neorepublicanism as a Postsocialist Critique of Market Society," *Social Philosophy and Policy*, 20 (Winter 2003): 59–91, 61.
99 Mill, *On Liberty*, ch. 4.

that markets promote is the freedom of persons to develop their autonomy as decision makers, and to find opportunities to escape from oppressive traditional roles. Markets also promote a third, more controversial, sense of freedom in that they allow persons to interact in mutually beneficial ways even when they do not know each other or have any other traditional reason to care about the other. I call this sense of freedom "social freedom." In each of these ways – negative, positive, and social – markets have much, and in some cases even more, to offer to women, as women have been more confined by traditional roles to a con-strained family life, deprived of a fair distribution of benefits and burdens of family life, and treated as second-class citizens in their communities. While capitalism has already, as we have seen, brought great advances in the realm of negative and positive liberties, capitalism's ability to destruct the old and create new forms of community offer a vision of freedom that is yet to be fulfilled. In what follows I will explore each of the three senses of freedom to see how capitalism is related to its realization.

Negative freedom is the freedom not to be interfered with, and a list of such freedoms typically includes civil and political freedoms, but also the economic freedoms to engage in market transactions and to use or benefit from one's legitimately owned property. These latter two – the freedom to exchange and the freedom to use or benefit from one's property – are two of the hallmarks of capitalism as I have defined it in terms of the private ownership of capital, free wage labor, and free market condi-tions. I also added the freedom from discrimination constraint, which is another aspect of negative freedom. Capitalist systems, whether any of the forms discussed at the beginning of my con-tribution or the enlightened form that I defend, do place some constraints on trade. Taxation by government to provide public goods that the market does not efficiently provide or to internal-ize negative externalities that traders would otherwise ignore to the detriment of bystanders places legitimate constraints on trade. So, too, do reasonable restrictions on trade designed to certify the quality of some goods. But capitalism by definition defends the basic freedom to open or close a business, to contract one's labor with the highest bidder, and to exchange goods without attending to the social status of the trading partners. Negative freedoms for the serf, the bonded laborer, or the slave would be freedom to leave the master – to not be impeded, whether by custom or law – to freely engage in wage labor. The nondiscrimination constraint also comprises this freedom; it is the freedom not to be constrained by features about one that are fixed at birth and that have nothing to do with one's talents or abilities.

As Sen explains, there are four ways in which free markets are needed now to uphold negative freedom or, put another way, to resist tyranny and enslavement.[100] First, they allow persons to escape the bonds of traditional labor bondage by being able to seek wage employment away from traditional bosses. In many rural areas people farm land for traditional landowners, and markets for labor allow them to escape this bondage. This is the freedom capitalism offers that Marx recognized as an improvement over feudalism, where serfs had no choice in their place or way of life. Second, the communism of Eastern Europe and the former Soviet Union, and still existing in North Korea and Cuba, denied the freedoms to engage in exchange or choose where one lives. That these freedoms are now less abridged makes it no less important to recognize that they are important negative freedoms that capitalism upholds. Third, free markets help to liberate children from bonded labor. Children in parts of South Asia are particularly susceptible to being placed in bondage to higher caste men, who put them to work making carpets or bricks for a very small pittance paid to their parents. The main reason for child labor is parental poverty. Where parents can earn more by their labor, they send their children to school. Even if the parents are still too poor or shortsighted or lack schools, if the children can earn wages by their labor, then they can do better than they do in bondage, where they have no income and no ability to resist harsh, violent treatment. Fourth, market employment for women is crucially important for their economic independence and for getting a better deal in intra-household distributions.

100 Sen, *Development as Freedom*, ch. 5

Outside employment gives women opportunities that are not directly tied to their menfolk. It makes them able to bargain for a better share of the family wealth and income, but also for less of the burden of chores, or enables them to pay others to do some of the work. The opportunity to work in the same kinds of jobs as men eventually wears away gender distinctions, or makes those distinctions less confining and more equal in terms of status. In this way, enlarging women's negative freedom also tends toward enlarging their positive freedom.

Positive freedom is defined in two different ways: either as simply the positive supports that individual persons need in order to live a life with enough good choices to deserve the name freedom, or as also including the internal qualities of character that allow persons to be autonomous or self-lawmakers. The two are connected in that persons are typically unable to develop their capacities to plan their lives or live according to principles if they do not have enough to eat, or they have to worry about their physical health and security, or if they have not had an adequate education. Positive freedom in the sense of auton-omy recognizes that completely unconstrained behavior is not necessarily action motivated by desires that are one's own. And positive freedom in the sense of social supports recognizes that without the wherewithal (material and psychological) to act on one's own desires, there can be no freedom. Sen refers to these as the process and opportunity aspects of freedom.[101] In this book I do not take a stand on which is *the* proper sense of positive freedom; both are clearly desirable as described. Instead, I argue that both senses of positive freedom are supported in capital-ism, though not necessarily guaranteed. In the first sense, capit-alism supports, but does not guarantee, the ability of persons to secure their own livelihood and material well-being. As we have seen, capitalism has increased life expectancy, improved health, and decreased fertility and child mortality on average. Increasing wealth is also correlated with increasing educational levels, and decreased fertility is correlated specifically with increasing female

101 Sen, "Markets and Freedoms."

education.[102] Capitalism, as a highly cooperative and social form of production, requires socially coordinated and regulated efforts. Thus, capitalism is clearly a form of social provision in design as well as in outcome. Capitalism does not guarantee that any given individual will develop or exercise autonomy, but rather supplies external supports for autonomy by offering opportunities to plan and to raise one's level of material well-being. In particular, capitalism does not guarantee that persons will develop autonomous desires, and in some ways may be seen as encouraging nonautonomous or what Kant would have called heteronomous desires, a point I will return to in section 6.

The most important objection against capitalism, however, is that it enables gross inequalities in wealth and income. When these inequalities also entail absolute impoverishment, so that persons do not have the ability to choose between decent ways of life, then this is clearly a failure. But capitalism raises the overall level of material wealth in a society, and so allows for the possibility of addressing such abject poverty. The fact that market interactions lead to inequalities is not, in itself, a denial of freedom. But it does pose the possibility of inequalities in power that can lead to positive and social unfreedoms, and indeed this is borne out in the actual world in many ways. Perhaps the worst sort is where wealth buys political influence in a nominally democratic country.

Before leaving the topic of inequality, however, it is important to point out that capitalism is not alone in supporting gross inequalities, but the way in which it does so is acceptable where it is not in other systems. North Korea, a socialist totalitarian system, creates gross inequalities of wealth through political power that controls resources. The leader and his minions live in vast wealth while much of the population teeters on the brink of famine. The communist systems of the Soviet Union and China were also notorious for the vast consumption and indulgence of their leaders compared with the average citizen, and notoriously one

102 P. N. Mari Bhat, "Returning a Favor: Reciprocity Between Female Education and Fertility in India," *World Development* 30(10) (October 2002), 1791–803. While most studies focus on showing that increasing female education lowers fertility, this article shows that the causal arrow points both ways.

had to be a party member in the Soviet Union in order to own a car. Traditional societies are no better; the patriarchs of many such societies are rich while the young and the less powerful labor for far less. But in each of these cases the wealth comes not through productive effort, but rather through political control, and in some cases through inheritance. While the leader of North Korea is in charge simply by virtue of being the son of the previous leader, the richest capitalists in the world were not born to the previous generation of the wealthiest. It is true that Bill Gates and Warren Buffet were born to upper-middle-class families, but their vast wealth was earned through innovation, skills, and talents, and not through inheritance. This is not to say that inequality in wealth is not a problem, nor to say that opportunities to achieve great wealth are fairly distributed in capitalism. They are not, and that is a serious moral issue. But it is to say that socialist and traditional societies have at least equally difficult problems to address in terms of inequality in wealth and power. In the final section of my contribution, I will argue that an enlightened capitalism must do better to address inequalities that either amount to absolute poverty or cause political and social inequalities that deny freedom. It is also important to note, however, that inequality that does not rule out good options for life does not seriously interfere with individual positive freedom, in either sense of the term. One need not live in the best of all possible worlds, after all, in order to be free enough to pursue one's own projects.

Positive freedom as autonomy requires that one is not manipulated by the social structure under which one lives. One's desires must be one's own and one's beliefs must be rationally generated for one's actions to be entirely autonomous. Isaiah Berlin, who draws the distinction between negative and positive freedom in this latter way, ultimately rejects the idea of positive freedom because, he argues, to posit a breach of positive freedom one would have to impose desires on individuals that they do not acknowledge.[103] For governments to attempt to guarantee

103 Isaiah Berlin, "Two Concepts of Liberty," in Henry Hardy (ed.), *Liberty* (Oxford University Press, 2002).

positive freedom, then, they would have to posit a good for their citizens and entice them to seek it, that is, in Rousseau's famous phrase, to force their citizens to be free. Berlin, as a liberal, argues that freedom requires merely imposing no impediments to individuals' given preferences. Positive freedom, Berlin concludes, insinuates a totalitarian menace.

Although Berlin's is a commonly cited libertarian line of argument that is often aligned with defenders of capitalism, I want to argue that Berlin's distinction between positive and negative freedom is drawn incorrectly, and that positive freedom in the sense of autonomy is not hostile to capitalism. It is especially important for women and other oppressed groups to attend to internal, psychological impediments to freedom that are generated by social constraints on what they can do and be. Negative and positive freedom cannot be easily separated for two reasons. First, a persistent lack of negative freedom for a social group harms the individuals of that group psychologically, causing them to lack positive freedom. Second, even though the idea that a government might posit an individual's good for her raises the specter of totalitarianism, that fact does not vitiate the claim that an individual's freedom can be compromised by a lack of vision of viable alternative options. A person can lack freedom without there being a clear way for the person to attain freedom in the future. Violations of negative freedom turn out to result in deeper harms that slide over into the kinds of harms that violations of positive freedom entail.

This is particularly the case for victims of oppression, and particularly for women.[104] Women are often convinced by many different social norms, expectations, and incentives to live within constraints that similarly placed (in terms of race, class, culture, and time period) men need not consider. This sort of internally constrained vision, whether it is because of false consciousness,

---

104 In *Analyzing Oppression* (New York: Oxford University Press, 2006), I discuss psychological forces of oppression and their effects on oppressed groups in detail. An important discussion of how psychological oppression affects women can be found in Sandra Bartky, *Femininity and Domination: Studies in the Phenomenology of Oppression* (New York: Routledge, 1990).

shame, stereotype, or trauma, is the kind of violation of their positive freedom that should most concern feminists. Capitalism, by providing an option outside kin and traditional community norms for independence and social power, can allow women the wherewithal to escape these constraints. Even if a particular woman does not choose to work outside the home or compete in the marketplace as an entrepreneur, the fact that women have this option under capitalism increases the freedom of all women. Enlarging the set of things that women are seen as capable of can reduce the sense that women have that they are inferior, and this can increase their confidence in a wider set of social circumstances. It puts the lie to the idea that women are incapable, and helps women to stand up to ill-treatment and violence.

While many philosophers recognize negative and positive freedoms in quite similar ways, a third concept of freedom has been proposed by different philosophers in quite different ways. Quentin Skinner's third concept of liberty is the lack of an ongoing threat to one's freedom of thought and expression.[105] Skinner argues that this requires the existence of a noncoercive government or absence of a threat of domination by one. This form, however, is reducible to negative freedom from interference by government, insofar as it refers to legitimate forms of coercion. A legitimate government may legitimately apply coercive measures to assure the good of the whole or the protection of others who have a rightful claim to such protection, provided that the measures are, in Thomas Scanlon's terms, something that no reasonable person could reject. Skinner clearly does not mean to rule that out, but rather to rule out coercion that is wrongful. Yet this is already covered under the concept of negative freedom; one is not free in the negative sense if one is coercively dominated by one's government. However, it goes too far to suggest that one is not free if one is threatened by domination of a coercive government. In this sense Skinner's third concept of freedom is similar

---

105 Quentin Skinner, "A Third Concept of Liberty," *Proceedings of the British Academy* 117 (2002): 237–68.

to Philip Pettit's view of freedom as nondomination. Both are mistaken to take the (implied) ability to pose a threat to be the same thing as a coercive threat.

If freedom in this third sense is compromised by even the threat of coercion or domination, then the free market is not free in this sense. But both Skinner and Pettit claim too much for a concept of freedom. As Gaus argues, it fails to distinguish between power to and power over.[106] Wealth gives one the power to afford many trades, but it does not give one the ability to exercise power over another by forcing a person to make a trade she or he does not want, and thereby limit that person's liberty. While the classical liberal claims that market transactions are free as long as there is no force, fraud, or coercive threat, Pettit denies this with an argument that freedom requires nondomination, and one dominates another if one has the ability to exercise power over another (including by means of financial clout, technical advantage, or political power). To avoid domination, he argues, one has to have anti-power. Rule of law gives anti-power. Gaus argues that Pettit's view is profoundly anti-market because the market will inevitably lead to unequal wealth and income, and this would always involves domination on Pettit's understanding, since greater success would allow one to potentially exercise power over another. Thus, the market is full of relations of domination – everyone except Bill Gates is dominated, after all, on this analysis. Furthermore, since equals have equal ability to attack each other, if we all had equal power to achieve our ends, we would all be unfree. Such an analysis trivializes the concept of domination. If Skinner or Pettit are understood to simply mean that freedom requires that there is no active threat or active domination, then this requirement can be seen as entailed already by negative freedom, since an active threat or domination is a direct constraint of one's basic civil, political, and property rights. If Skinner or Pettit are taken to mean that there can be no potential threat, however, then their concept of freedom falls prey to this triviality objection. And insofar as these concepts

106 Gaus, "Backwards into the Future."

are positive, that is, perhaps requiring social supports for individuals to be able to fully participate in social cooperation, they are reducible to positive freedom.

Berlin discussed and rejected a third sense of freedom that he finds in the claims of colonial oppressed persons, and which emerged in the writings of philosophers writing about colonial oppression, such as Jean-Paul Sartre and Frantz Fanon. Freeing oneself from oppression requires negative freedoms in the form of freedom of protest, and positive freedom. In progressive hands, "negative freedom is the capacity to destabilize identities and interrupt norms."[107] This form of freedom, defended as well in Cynthia Willett's *Irony in the Age of Empire*, is the desire for sociality and belonging within one's group, and recognition of one's social group and its distinctive values and norms from outsiders. She calls this third form of freedom, "solidarity." Willett's third freedom as solidarity requires something more than those two concepts, though. In particular, it requires the existence of social bonds that tie the individuals beyond their ability to resist and set themselves free. I want to resist the notion that this is a form of freedom, regardless of how good social bonds might feel. For they are the very forces of unfreedom in many cases. Bonds of solidarity both enable and constrain. The first, enabling, is indeed freedom, but the second, constraint, is not; it is the dark, exclusionary side of solidarity. Willett does not embrace any particular terms on which social solidarity might be forged. Cornel West's appeal to nuclear family norms as form of third freedom raises her suspicions. She writes, "West's appeal to the virtues of sacrifice may not subjugate women to patriarchal control, but it doesn't sound like the battle cry for liberation that we might desire."[108] But her suspicions here raise for me the question of why, then, she would align social bonds with freedom. If concepts of freedom proceed from sources of anxiety, I cannot think of anything that produces more anxiety than the requirement

107 Cynthia Willett, *Irony in the Age of Empire: Comic Perspectives on Democracy and Freedom* (Bloomington, IN: Indiana University Press, 2008).
108 Willett, *Irony in the Age of Empire*, 60.

that I follow the norms of some particular community, without any opportunity to opt out of that community.

In my view we want freedom to pursue or reject social bonds – not to be dominated or threatened with constraints by others who would prevent our ability to pursue or imagine them. This is most important for members of social groups that have been oppressed for generations, as women have been. Such persons have a constrained vision of what is possible for them, and need to be able to see beyond these constraints that have been erected by others, but reinforced internally. Nonetheless, a third form of freedom can emerge under the right circumstances, namely the social conditions which allow and support individual autonomy for each person, which I call "social freedom." Social freedom transcends positive freedom by considering the needs of each, not just of individuals one at a time. Autonomy requires an absence of oppressive social constraints that prevent free self-development. Systematic violence, economic discrimination and segregation, social shaming, and vicious stereotyping are among the most autonomy-defeating forces. Social freedom poses a collective obligation to provide for the education of the next generation, not because they are "our children," as if we own them or they are our personal, genetic or property-inheriting legacy, but because children are at that stage where they need to be taught to develop their capacities if they are to be autonomous adults. Mill argued for this on the utilitarian grounds that more and higher quality pleasure is created that way.[109] Other moral and political theories can generate this obligation as well. For example, a contractarian can argue that by educating children in this way we provide more and better opportunities for cooperation for mutual advantage. A Kantian can simply argue that it is the only way to treat children as ends in themselves. Social freedom can be described as the Rawlsian union of social unions, which he argues arises in the society that is structured by his

109 Wendy Donner, "John Stuart Mill on Education and Democracy," in Nadia Urbinati and Alex Zakaras (eds.), *J. S. Mill's Political Thought* (New York: Cambridge University Press, 2007), 250–75.

two principles of justice, and involves each taking pleasure in the achievements, the flourishing, of others. I take it that this is true of the society of free persons, which is not only free of current oppressions, but whose members seek to free all persons from oppression. For in such a society the individuals are able to seek their own good with good will toward others as well. They seek to encourage diversity and enhance the freedom of others. They take pleasure in and identify with the accomplishments of others. And further, they come to see their own freedom as connected to that of the others.

Capitalism supports social freedom, but, as with positive freedom, does not guarantee it. That would be too much to ask of an economic system alone. As I have argued elsewhere, capitalism embraces the positive aspects of competition.[110] Competition in capitalism is valuable because it allows many different persons to succeed at least in part. For businesses to be profitable there must be consumers to buy their products, and for there to be consumers to buy products, there must be a large sector of the population that earns enough through their labor to consume, and a significant number who can invest and create new opportunities for work. Capitalism thrives where the situation is more like what game theorists call a cooperative competition; that is, the players of the game have interests that are partly shared and partly opposed. The optimal and equilibrium outcome arises when each pursues a strategy that both maximizes their outcome, but also leads to the others being better off, as WE1 suggests. This contrasts sharply with the situation of either the zero-sum game, where there is only one winner and all the others are losers, or worse, a game in which, when each of the players pursues their own best strategies, a socially suboptimal outcome arises (such as in the Prisoner's Dilemma).

This optimism about capitalism and its role in raising the sights of women is as applicable in poor, developing countries as it is in rich, First World ones. As Sen has argued, freedom is both

---

110 Ann E. Cudd, "Sporting Metaphors: Competition and the Ethos of Capitalism," *Journal of the Philosophy of Sport* 34 (May 2007): 52–67.

constitutive of development seen in a progressive light, but also instrumental toward that form of development. Development as he understands it requires making human lives better on a variety of levels that he calls "capabilities." Included among these capabilities are the abilities that I have listed as the interests of persons, and as the requirements of autonomy. Not only are negative and positive freedoms constitutive of development, though. Social freedom arises from the development of these freedoms as well. Capitalism is not the only route to development, but development seems, empirically, not to be complete without opening up markets to relatively free trade. Sen illustrates this by pointing to the development in China, which moved to a market-oriented economy in 1991.[111] While pre-reform China pursued basic education and health care for all, it lacked democratic freedoms, and this meant less responsiveness to famine and social crises. China suffered an enormous famine, in which 30 million people died, during the Great Leap Forward of 1958–61. Sen credits democracy with preventing any famine in India since independence in 1947. The development of capitalist markets has raised the overall level of income in China, however, to the point where it is unlikely to suffer another such catastrophe, despite the lack of democracy.

Capitalist enterprise can be seen to be working in this positive sum way in the work of Grameen Danone, a spinoff social business of the Grameen Bank in partnership with the French yogurt company, Danone. This company produces low cost, nutritious yogurt in Bangladesh using small, local factories and distributing the yogurt with a network of sellers, "yogurt ladies," who pedal the yogurt in the surrounding villages. In his final training speech to these women before their initial sales, the Danone representative offered these words of encouragement that sum up very well the idea of the positive sum aspects of capitalist trade:

> When you sell a cup of Shokti Doi, you are doing many good things. You are earning some money for yourself and your family. You are providing good nutrition for children. You are

111 Sen, *Development as Freedom*, 42–43.

making jobs for farmers who sell us the milk. You are making jobs for workers in our factory. And you are helping to develop the business. If we are successful here in Bogra, we will build another factory somewhere else in Bangladesh. Then another and another.[112]

Now it is true that this sort of business is one that is designed to solve a social problem, and while it needs to break even, it need not make a profit that provides a dividend to investors. These investors take the social benefit to be their adequate return to capital. But this illustrates how businesses can be positive sum, while existing within a competitive market. In this case the business meets a need, fills a demand that is often overlooked by companies that seek only to meet the demand of wealthier consumers, and in doing so satisfies the desires of the producers, distributors, and consumers. Of course, people sometimes desire things that are not good for them, and satisfying such desires is not necessarily socially or even individually good. Because capitalism is good at satisfying the desires of so many, it is objected that capitalism harms people by giving them too much of a good thing. For instance, the consumption of sugary sodas has created an epidemic of obesity in the United States.[113] Some such desires need to be thwarted rather than catered to, and it is reasonable for government to take measures to do so. But the best way to preserve freedom, in either the negative or positive sense, is to provide information so that people choose not to consume what is bad for them. That makes products disappear from the market without having to use the blunt and expensive instruments of legal prohibition.

Notwithstanding this strong case for capitalism, in its reality as well as an ideal system, however, there remains room for controversy. In my view, these critiques of capitalism are largely mistaken, but some of them are importantly mistaken in ways from which we can learn and build a better capitalist system. In

---

112 Muhammad Yunus, *Creating a World Without Poverty* (New York: Public Affairs, 2007), 151.

113 William H. Dietz, "Sugar-sweetened Beverages, Milk Intake, and Obesity in Children and Adolescents," *The Journal of Pediatrics* 148 (February 2006): 152–54.

section 4 I will examine one direction from which the critique of capitalism comes, namely, feminist critiques of the actually existing capitalist system. In section 5 I will examine what I believe to be the deepest and most powerful critique of capitalism, inspired by a variety of Marxist and feminist thoughts about the kinds of people that some forms of capitalism encourage us to be.

4   Feminist critiques of capitalism

Despite the progress of women toward achieving rights and freedoms in the two centuries of capitalism, many feminists argue that capitalism has been, and will continue to be, destructive of feminist ends. Feminist critiques of capitalism can be divided into two major types: material and psychological. Both types can be traced to Marx's rich and nuanced critique of capitalism, although feminists have appropriated and elaborated Marx's theories through the lens of gender to create unique, radical feminist critiques of capitalism. One feminist critique grows from and extends Marx's concept of exploitation, claiming that capitalism exploits women.[114] A second feminist material critique of capitalism is that it requires and reinforces the distinction between public and private, and this distinction itself oppresses women. The third feminist material critique of capitalism is that it creates, maintains, and exacerbates existing inequalities. The psychological critiques of capitalism stem from the dual processes of false consciousness and adaptive preference formation. Marx criticized capitalism for promoting commodity fetishism, which includes both a misunderstanding and a misevaluation of our social world. The feminist appropriation of this critique also argues that persons in capitalism misunderstand and misevaluate the world in particularly sexist ways. In this section I will articulate and respond to these specifically feminist critiques of capitalism.

114 Zillah Eisenstein, "Developing a Theory of Capitalist Patriarchy," *Capitalist Patriarchy and the Case for Socialist Feminism* (New York: Monthly Review Press, 1979); Heidi Hartmann, "The Unhappy Marriage of Marxism and

Capitalism and exploitation

Exploitation on Marx's theory occurs when those who create value are deprived of it by others through some coercive means.[115] According to the Marxist analysis, through their labor workers create surplus value, which is appropriated by the capitalist.[116] This appropriation is coercive because workers lack the market power to command an equivalent value in exchange for the fruits of their labor.[117] Capitalists take advantage of the unfair bargaining position of workers that comes as a result of their relative poverty compared with capitalists, and thereby coerce them into giving up a great share of the surplus created by the interaction of the workers' labor power and the capitalists' capital. Thus, there is a vicious cycle of disadvantage and exploitation in capitalism. Marx argued further that the workers' class disadvantage was necessary for the capital accumulation required by capitalist industry. Without a reserve army of the unemployed there would be no ability to accumulate profits from the surplus labor of the workers.

Similarly, feminists argue, men appropriate the surplus value of women's domestic, sexual, and psychic labor, thereby exploiting women. In addition, women are exploited by capitalism under these patriarchal conditions both as workers and as women

Feminism: Toward a More Progressive Union," in Lydia Sargent (ed.), *Women and Revolution* (Cambridge: South End Press, 1981), 1–41.

115 I do not want to argue, however, that this is the best account of the harm of exploitation, particularly as women suffer from it. Ruth Sample, *Exploitation: What it is and Why it's Wrong* (Lanham, MD: Rowman & Littlefield, 2003) provides a better account of exploitation as degradation. However, the more limited Marxian sense in which I use the term is better suited to a critique of *capitalism*.

116 Karl Marx, "Wage Labor," *Economic and Philosophic Manuscripts of 1844*, trans. Martin Mulligan (Moscow: Progress Publishers, 1959).

117 On Marx's view, this appropriation is coercive because workers create all the surplus value through their labor. This is necessitated by the labor theory of value, on which all value is created by labor. But the labor theory of value is a now discredited economic theory, and so I will not rely on it in my analysis of exploitation. However, I can still see that exploitation can be coercive using the concepts of market and bargaining power, as I explain in the text.

because women's wage labor is exploited by capitalists through the even further disadvantage they have in the market due to their gender disadvantage. Occupational segregation forces women to crowd into less well paid jobs, keeping the supply of workers high and the pay low in these occupations.[118] Furthermore, women are discriminated against in the labor market and suffer from sexual harassment when they are hired, further dimming their opportunities to get and keep good work. Finally, women's greater time investment in unpaid domestic and community care work leads to a lesser investment in human capital for paid work. Thus, radical feminists argue, capitalism enables or encourages the exploitation of workers and of women, and so feminism and capitalism are incompatible.

The exploitation charge *as a critique of capitalism* dissolves under scrutiny, however. The critique accurately assesses women's condition as generally exploited in capitalist society, but it fails to accurately assess the cause of this exploitation. To make this argument I need to make two distinctions. First, we need to note that exploitation can be harmless advantage-taking or it can be a kind of moral harm.[119] Exploitation, understood in the Marxist sense, is morally permissible when a surplus is created by the interaction of two agents and they share that surplus (thus exploiting their relationship) or one voluntarily, without coercion, permits the other to enjoy the entire surplus.[120] There need be nothing wrong with surplus going to one member of the relationship if

---

118 Barbara Bergmann, *The Economic Emergence of Women*, 2nd edn. (New York: Palgrave Macmillan, 2005).

119 John Roemer, *Free to Lose* (Cambridge, MA: Harvard University Press, 1988).

120 There are liberal conceptions of exploitation, as well. Robert Goodin, "Exploiting a Situation and Exploiting a Person," in Andrew Reeve (ed.), *Modern Theories of Exploitation* (London: Sage, 1987), understands exploitation as taking advantage of vulnerable others. Alan Wertheimer, *Exploitation* (Princeton University Press, 1996), understands exploitation as a transaction in which one person takes unfair advantage of another. Wertheimer's account is compatible with my claim that exploitation is wrong when it takes advantage of an unfair or oppressive situation. Goodin's account is to me overly expansive in that it includes too much if the vulnerability is not the result of unfairness or oppression. Finally, Ruth Sample, *Exploitation: What*

that is voluntarily agreed upon. Exploitation is morally unaccept-able when one party takes more than their agreed share of the surplus or coerces the other into relinquishing it, or permits back-ground coercive conditions to force the other into relinquishing the surplus. Second, workers need not be exploited under capit-alism if there are no coercive background conditions. The surplus that a worker creates is the marginal product of her or his labor. If that worker is not coerced by background conditions of pov-erty or inequality, then she or he is just as able to demand her or his share of this surplus as the owner of the capital inputs to pro-duction. Although a lone worker against a large firm or colluding employers does not have equal market power, there is nothing in the theory of capitalism to require that workers go it alone, that capital be controlled by one agent, let alone that collusion among employers be permitted. These, again, are background conditions that are subject to control by the political and legal systems. The question of whether this is unjust exploitation becomes, then, the question of whether the background conditions are unjust. If they are, then the injustice of the exploitation may be blamed on the background conditions.

Patriarchy creates coercive background conditions for women, and thus patriarchy, not capitalism, is to blame for women's exploitation under capitalism. Women are exploited under cap-italism because they are forced by gendered expectations of women's place into segregated spaces. In the home, gendered expectations about what women ought to do causes them to devote more time and energy to caring activities. Not only are women expected to be the main source of childcare and domestic labor in the home, they are also the psychic caregivers, coord-inating social, spiritual, and emotional efforts for families. Their

---

it is and Why it's Wrong, offers an account of exploitation as degradation, or failure to treat persons in a way appropriate to their value. This account, too, is more expansive than mine, since that would include ways of treating people badly that do not involve transactions. However, her account would not include the harmless forms of exploitation that I discuss as exploitative, which for her is always wrong, and it would include the forms I claim are harmful as exploitation.

doing this explains the exploitation of women qua women in capitalism. The best evidence for this claim is that women in other economic systems are also exploited. For example, in the Soviet Union women were exploited for their domestic and sexual labor despite living under a noncapitalist economic system.[121] I do not mean to say that there is no economic or material component to women's condition. Women are stuck in these roles in part for material and economic reasons; they do not have enough bargaining power within heterosexual relationships generally to escape these roles. If women are able to gain an economic foothold, as is possible in an enlightened capitalism that eschews discrimination and gender segregation, then they can begin to work their way into better bargaining positions in their homes. And with better bargaining outcomes in their domestic lives, women can do better in the capitalist economy. Thus, capitalism does not provide an easy escape route, but it does point in the direction of escape from patriarchy.

It will be objected that wealth inequality and poverty are background conditions created by capitalism that cause exploitation. I have already presented a great deal of evidence to suggest that the poverty claim is false. Capitalism makes persons wealthier, not poorer. Virtually no one denies that income and wealth rise in countries when they become more involved in capitalist markets and develop industry and trade. Capitalist markets and firms create opportunities for interactions that improve the wealth of both sides of a trade; otherwise the interaction would not occur, at least not as sanctioned by capitalism, as defined by the private ownership, free and open markets, and free wage labor conditions. Although corrupt government may steal or alter property rights and so impoverish some of its citizens, this is not the fault of capitalism but of corruption! Capitalism does arguably create inequalities, although it does not create them everywhere. But it is certainly an implication of the conditions

---

121 Francine du Plessix Gray, *Soviet Women: Walking the Tightrope* (New York: Doubleday, 1989); Olga Voronina, "Soviet Patriarchy Past and Present," trans. Nicole Svobodny and Maude Meisel, *Hypatia* 8 (1993): 97–111.

of capitalism that inequality will occur, provided that there is an initial inequality in resources and no or little social redistribution by government. Since persons differ in their talents and skills, at a minimum there will be inequalities in the resulting income and wealth derived from capitalist interaction. Inequality creates the possibility of exploitation because those who have lesser endowments may be more desperate to make a trade than those with greater endowments. But is this the morally unacceptable form of exploitation? The answer depends on whether the exploitation involves coercion. But it involves coercion only if there is absolute poverty. Thus, it is only the combination of poverty and inequality that create a problematic form of exploitation. Insofar as capitalism helps to remedy poverty, then, it tends to lessen the morally unacceptable forms of exploitation.

The public–private divide

The second Marxist derived feminist argument critiques the public–private divide and its implications for women. The argument is that capitalism requires that workers be cared for in the private sphere so that they may freely contract their labor in the public sphere. This entails that there will be a private sphere. But this sphere is the one in which women are coerced to perform unpaid labor and are subject to abuse and violence. Furthermore, women are entrapped by their more onerous labor in the private sphere, giving men a greater opportunity to dominate the public sphere. Thus, men are the leaders in politics, the market, and other social institutions which structure the forms and outcomes of people's daily lives both in the public and private sphere. By endorsing and supporting this private sphere, capitalism oppresses women.

As with the exploitation critique, however, this critique of the public–private dichotomy turns out on scrutiny to be a critique not of capitalism but of patriarchy. Again the Soviet Union provides a good counterexample, although most contemporary noncapitalist societies would as well (witness Iran, Saudi Arabia, sub-Saharan African countries). In each case men control or dominate politics, the economic, and religious institutions, forming a public–private dichotomy that functions similarly to that in capitalist countries. Capitalism, once again, capitalizes on the patriarchal forms that it finds, but does not cause them. An enlightened capitalism which eschews discrimination and segregation will provide a better way to bridge the public–private divide in both directions, for men to contribute more in the private sphere as women contribute more in the public sphere.

Inequality under capitalism

A third feminist critique of capitalism is that it creates gross economic inequality. Socialist and post-colonial feminists formulate this critique both internally to capitalist economies and as a critique of global capitalism. Feminists charge that capitalism grossly enriches the rich and impoverishes the poor, and that women are predominately poor and thus especially harmed by capitalism. Economic inequality causes political and social inequality as well, and thus multiplies the injustice of the inequality.

The charge that capitalism exacerbates inequality stands as the most serious, material critique of capitalism. It is not a specifically feminist critique, although combined with the recognition of patriarchy in the background it generates the claim that inequality harms women even more than men. Unlike the other two critiques I have just examined, however, inequality in the morally problematic sense clearly is caused by capitalism. But there are two caveats to make about this critique that defuse it as an argument for the claim that capitalism and feminism or feminist political transformation are incompatible. First, inequality is a particular problem for women under capitalism because of patriarchy. If men did not dominate women in the public sphere and exploit them in the private sphere, capitalist-engendered inequality would not differentiate by gender. Of course, that does not absolve capitalism, nor does it make capitalism of no interest to feminism. Feminists aim for social structures that allow all persons, regardless of sex, gender, race or other attributed status, to freely and fully develop their personalities and capacities. The second caveat is that inequality is not always or necessarily morally problematic. Hayek argued that inequality is an inevitable consequence of freedom and difference.[122] However, if inequalities do not prevent persons from freely and fully developing their abilities and capacities, then they are not in themselves morally problematic. To hold that inequality in itself is problematic is a manifestation of envy, and a system ought not be constrained by the envious yearnings of some individuals.

Most capitalist societies that currently exist do harbor gross inequalities, but this does not entail that capitalism, ideally construed, necessarily causes gross inequality. In another work, I argued that capitalism can be shown to be compatible with the provision of social services, such as a welfare minimum, which would prevent gross inequalities within a society.[123] I argued for this claim by showing that the justification of capitalist property rights itself rests on the right to a minimum standard of living. As Jeremy Waldron argued, the "recognition [of such a right] is part and parcel of the justification of property."[124] The entitlement theory justification of private property rights, stemming from Locke, begins with the claim that the fruits of the earth are our common legacy, and then justifies individual appropriation from that common legacy on the grounds that each person has a right to draw sustenance from the world in some way or other. Locke carefully denies that all the natural resources were simply up for grabs for the first or most efficient appropriator, and introduces the famous proviso that there be "enough and as good left for others."[125] If, after the initial appropriation of the natural resources, all things come into the world already owned, as Nozick argued, there seems to be no way for the person who has

122 F. A. Hayek, *The Constitution of Liberty* (University of Chicago Press, 1978), ch. 6.

123 Cudd, *Analyzing Oppression*, ch. 5. Van Parijs, *Real Freedom for All*, offers an extended argument for this claim from left-libertarian principles.

124 Jeremy Waldron, "Property Rights and Welfare Distribution," in R. G. Frey and Christopher Wellman (eds.), *A Companion to Applied Ethics* (Malden, MA: Blackwell, 2003), 38–49, 47.

125 John Locke, *Second Treatise of Government*, C. B. Macpherson (ed.) (Indianapolis, IN: Hackett, 1980), ch. 7.

no ownership rights over resources to gain sustenance.[126] That would condemn to starvation all (at least infant and toddler) children who are not cared for by others who will share their wealth. Since that contradicts the notion that everyone has a right to gain sustenance from the world, some welfare minimum is required by the very justification of property. More generally, if the economy effectively prevents any persons from making a living because they have no marketable skills and no usable capital, then again the right to gain sustenance from the world would entail that they should be guaranteed a welfare minimum. Thus, a justifiable capitalist society must provide sustenance for all who cannot, for whatever reason, provide it for themselves. Taxation at reasonable levels for the sake of meeting this goal is compatible with, even required by, the very justification of the ownership of private property. The only remaining step in the argument is to show that providing a welfare minimum does not contradict the ability to accumulate capital enough to enable production. But this is clearly not the case; capital could be accumulated by many owners of stock in any one firm, as now exists in many firms and industries, large and small.[127] Hence, I conclude that ideal capitalism actually requires the amelioration of gross, morally problematic, inequality.

Moreover, capitalism helps to combat some of the most egregious causes of gross inequality, in particular those that may be attributed to patriarchal traditions. It is a standard argument in neoclassical economic theory that there can be no advantage for firms to discriminate against workers, let alone consumers, for reasons other than their productivity as workers and the wages or prices they ask for. Therefore, in a world in which force is prohibited, capitalism provides a way out of traditional social roles for women. Now one might argue again that given the existence

126 Robert Nozick, *Anarchy, State, and Utopia* (New York: Basic Books, 1974), 160.
127 William Greider in *The Soul of Capitalism: Opening Paths to a Moral Economy* (New York: Simon & Schuster, 2003), considers several possible forms of ownership of productive means that are decentralized and democratic, such as employee stock ownership plans or worker cooperatives.

of patriarchal traditions that discriminate against women there could be reason for firms to acquiesce in this. For example, if men command most of the wealth and will refuse to buy from a firm that hires women, then the firm is all but forced to discriminate against the women.[128] But the descriptive ideal of capitalism would prescribe against that, since such a situation entails inefficiencies in production. Furthermore, noncapitalist systems would likewise face this problem, yet would not motivate or perhaps even tolerate changes in discriminatory preferences as capitalism does.[129]

Summarizing, I have argued that the feminist material critiques of capitalism, with the exception of the inequality critique, fail as critiques of capitalism and are best seen as critiques of patriarchy. Inequality that is great enough to be morally problematic in itself (and not because it was caused by coercion), while a problematic feature of existing capitalist societies, is not a necessary feature of ideal capitalism. An enlightened capitalism that is consistent with feminist political transformation will have to eliminate morally problematic inequalities, but it will have means to do so by eliminating discrimination and segregation, as well as motivating changes in preferences for trade and cooperation across race, gender, and ethnic boundaries.

Psychological harms of capitalism

The second form of feminist critique of capitalism charges that even ideal capitalism is inevitably tied to patriarchy. Therefore, patriarchy cannot be overcome without overcoming capitalism. Feminists have argued that ideal capitalism is inherently patriarchal because it is based on masculinist and gendered premises

128 Adrian M. S. Piper, "Higher Order Discrimination," in Amelie Oksenberg Rorty (ed.), *Identity, Character, and Morality* (Cambridge, MA: MIT Press, 2000), 285–309, names this sort of discrimination "higher order discrimination."

129 Actual, living capitalism, however, can be seen to hold out some hope that this problem is not completely self-sealing. That is, capitalism has proven in reality to fight against patriarchal traditions, motivating women to leave their prescribed places to work for wages and thereby improve their standard of living and that of their families.

that inevitably subordinate women.[130] Primary among these gendered premises are the assumptions of independent, autonomous, unencumbered selves who can freely interact in the market. Feminists argue that capitalism fosters and glorifies independence and does not reward care, nor honor dependence, which are necessary and inevitable features of human life, and have been relegated to the sphere of women.[131] Women are acculturated to be the caregivers and often provide care as unpaid labor. But since this labor is not honored or supported, women are less honored and supported than men. Furthermore, dependency is held as dishonorable, yet women, as childbearers and primary childcare providers, require more support even when they are healthy adults, since they are responsible for the material well-being of two or more humans. The root of the problem is that the argument for capitalism assumes a notion of freedom that is itself gendered in that it privileges freedom from interference by others as opposed to positive supports for relationships and capabilities. Thus, the argument justifies capitalism insofar as it supports such negative freedom, and requires that when the two kinds of freedom conflict, freedom from interference be maintained at the expense of support of autonomy.

We can analyze this critique as charging that capitalism causes two distinctive but related types of psychological harms – one cognitive and one affective – that especially affect women. First, the ideology of capitalism creates a particular kind of false beliefs – false consciousness – that reinforce patriarchy. Second, capitalism deforms persons' desires so that they come to prefer and choose the domination of men over women. Together these critiques are similar to Marx's critique of capitalism that he called

---

130 Gordon, *Transforming Capitalism and Patriarchy*, 23. Gordon is elaborating on what she sees as standard feminist concerns with capitalism, although she does not endorse them herself. J. K. Gibson-Graham, *The End of Capitalism (as we knew it): A Feminist Critique of Political Economy* (Cambridge, MA: Blackwell, 1996), 8: capitalism "is the phallus or master term within a system of social differentiation." Their critique seems more aimed at the ideology of capitalism than the system itself.
131 Eva Feder Kittay, *Love's Labor* (New York: Routledge, 1999).

commodity fetishism. Viewing it through this critique of commodity fetishism can help us to see just how capitalism and patriarchy are alleged to be intertwined.

Marx leveled the false consciousness critique against capitalism in his discussion of commodity fetishism.[132] A fetish is an object of unnatural attraction whose meaning is symbolic rather than literal. Our understanding of commodities constitutes a fetish according to Marx because of our confusion of the use values of things and exchange values of (those things qua) commodities. Capitalism and capitalist ideology, Marx argued, confuses people about the nature of their work and productive relations. They fixate on the exchange values of goods and the exchange value of labor, rather than on the needs that those goods satisfy or the relations among persons that their production promotes.[133] People come to confuse the social relations among them for relations among the commodities they exchange. Since in capitalism production and distribution of commodities is guided by market exchange, social relations between persons are determined by the exchange relations among things. Persons tend to overlook the social and coercive aspect of production of goods in capitalism, seeing them as ahistorical, unchanging facts of human existence rather than as a social construction determined by political forces that are controlled by capitalists. The ideology of individualism is reinforced by this sense that individuals' actions are determined only by the physical or natural limits of existence, and not by socially constructed institutions that benefit capitalists.

132 Karl Marx, "The Fetishism of the Commodity and its Secret," *Capital: Vol. I*, trans. Samuel Moore and Edward Aveling (Moscow: Progress Publishers, 1887), Book I, ch. 1, section 4.

133 This "fixation" on exchange value is seen as the major theoretical advance of modern economics, of course. While modern price theory does a better job of explaining how prices of things are related, it makes otiose such questions as how much labor is expended to fulfill this or that need, and how is the amount of labor a person performs related to their ability to satisfy their needs? Neoclassical economic theory thus takes itself to be answering quite different questions than those Marx (and the classical economists before him) thought important to raise. An effective theory of justice, it seems to me, must be able to ask and answer both sorts of questions.

Implied in his discussion of commodities is the critique of desire or preference formation in capitalism, as well. Since in capitalism persons tend to confuse the value of things for their exchange values, our desire for them is determined not by their use value but by their exchange value.[134] Thus, our desires are deformed by the confusion of real value and price. This deformation of preference is manifested in seeking more commodities than we need to satisfy our material needs. Shopping becomes an activity desired in itself. We compete with our neighbors and friends for the latest styles, valuing them more for what they say about us than what we can do with the commodity, and we toss out those commodities that, while still useful, no longer portray us in the right way.

The feminist psychological critique of capitalism may be elaborated in similar terms. In reality women and men are of equal worth and dignity; it is no more reasonable or natural to see women as objects of men's sexual gratification than it is to view men as objects for women. Women's caregiving work is crucially important in the human economy, but it is also no more reasonable to see this as women's "proper place" than it is as men's place. Human life invariably includes periods of dependence and of responsibility for the care of dependants, and thus dependence itself is no reason for disvaluing human beings. But capitalism, which encourages us to allocate effort and goods according to the exchange values of labor and commodities, causes us to disvalue labor that is unpaid or low paid. Further, we disvalue those who perform unpaid or low paid labor. Finally, we disvalue those who cannot perform paid labor, and that means we disvalue the elderly, the infirm, and children.[135] Thus, capitalism causes us to misunderstand the degree and role of dependence and interdependence, as well as the contribution that caregiving makes

134 Thorstein Veblen's concepts of pecuniary emulation and conspicuous consumption describe similar ways capitalism deforms desires. See Veblen, *The Theory of the Leisure Class* (Boston, MA: Houghton Mifflin, 1973).

135 In Iris Young's terms, such persons suffer "marginalization," which is one of her five forms of oppression. Iris Marion Young, *Justice and the Politics of Difference* (Princeton University Press, 1990), ch. 5.

in human life. And, hence, since women are more likely to be caregivers and to be dependent as adults, they are believed to be inferior to men.

Prostitution, pornography, and surrogacy prompt another analysis in terms of false consciousness and deformed desires. Women's sexual labor and reproductive labor are exchanged on the market and so become commodities rather than essential aspects of human bodily integrity or of the self.[136] Women and men become confused about what women's bodies are and they are instead viewed in terms of the exchange relations that can be engaged in with or by them. As the market for them expands, women's bodies are twice fetishized: once as sexual (or reproductive) object and again as another commodity for exchange. Thus, feminists can show that commodity fetishism reinforces capitalism and patriarchy together.

My first response to these objections is again to look to the background patriarchy for the problems and argue that capitalism could be reformed to eliminate them. Clearly, pre-capitalist and parallel patriarchal beliefs and institutions play an important role in forming the beliefs and desires in question. But this response is not entirely adequate in this case.[137] For commodification and commodity fetishism are caused by capitalism. The background patriarchy explains why *women's* sexuality and *women's* reproductive and caregiving labor is commodified. But two problems remain for the feminist defender of even enlightened capitalism. First, women's caregiving labor is not commodified in living capitalism, and that is at least part of the problem. That it is not commodified is, again, due to patriarchy. But suppose it were commodified. Economic theory predicts that it would not

136 Elizabeth Anderson develops this critique of the commoditization of women's reproductive labor through commercial surrogacy in "Is Women's Labor a Commodity?," *Philosophy and Public Affairs* 19 (Winter 1990): 71–92.

137 Similarly, Marx's critique of capitalism in terms of exploitation and inequality can be countered by showing that with the proper starting points and fair legal framework, these problems can be overcome in a free market system. But Marx's critique of capitalism in terms of commodity fetishism, it seems to me, still holds. This form of false consciousness and adaptive preference formation is internal to the capitalist or free market system.

be adequately provided, either in terms of quantity or quality, in the market. Caregiving has many positive externalities, such as the value to the economy and the society of physically and mentally healthy persons. Since these externalities cannot be internalized by those who would be paid for providing them, the service would be underprovided in the market. Furthermore, caring labor provides some essentially unquantifiable goods. As Gasper and van Staveren note, "caring labor produces more than just goods and services: it simultaneously generates and cherishes a set of values – interpersonal values of belonging and sharing."[138] In other words, we would lose something of value (though not exchange value) if care were completely commodified. Second, suppose that ideal capitalism were to eliminate patriarchy and the sexual and reproductive labor of both sexes were commodified. It is not clear that this is the feminist future we hope for.

In my estimation, commodity fetishism – enacted through these dual processes of false consciousness and adaptive preference formation – is the most serious obstacle to the compatibility of feminist political transformation and ideal capitalism. To see why this is so, however, we need to decide what morally and politically speaking is wrong with the distorted beliefs and desires caused by false consciousness and adaptive preference formation, and how we can tell whether beliefs and desires are distorted in ways that are morally and politically wrong.

Deformed preferences, false consciousness, and how to detect them

Adaptive preferences are preferences formed by awareness of one's available (feasible) options, but without one's control or awareness of how that affects the preferences.[139] Persons tend to become content with whatever they see as their lot in life, regardless of whether they would choose that life if they were presented with other options. Adaptive preference formation

---

138 Des Gasper and Irene van Staveren, "Development as Freedom – And as What Else?," *Feminist Economics* 9 (July/November 2003): 137–61.
139 Jon Elster, *Sour Grapes* (Cambridge University Press, 1983).

as such is normatively neutral, but it opens the possibility for manipulation or coercion. When preference formation mechanisms utilize and reinforce oppression, then they are no longer neutral. Normatively bad preferences may be called deformed preferences or deformed desires.[140] One mechanism of adaptive preference formation is the habituation of preference.[141] Girls and women are encouraged by multiple sources to think of the kind of work that oppresses them as the work that they ought, by nature, by sentiment, and even by God, to do. Women become habituated to doing women's work, as they do it daily and see women on all sides doing it. All of these sources have powerful effects on emotions, making it likely that women's preferences will favor their oppressive work activities. It's not that they will prefer oppression to justice, or subordination to equality, rather they will prefer the kinds of social roles that tend to subordinate them, make them less able to choose, or give them fewer choices to make. Another mechanism of adaptive preference at work for women in patriarchy is systematic social denigration of options.[142] When options are generally viewed in society as bad or inappropriate or otherwise wrong, persons tend not to choose them. Conditions of oppression often include condemnation of some morally permissible choices, either for everyone (e.g., homosexuality) or for only some (girls don't do math). A third form of adaptive preference formation mechanism that is relevant here is restriction of options, or the sour grapes phenomenon, in which an individual comes to prefer an option

---

140   The term "deformed desires" is used by Anita Superson, "Deformed Desires and Informed Desire Tests," *Hypatia* 20 (Fall 2005): 109–26. Other important treatments of adaptive preference or deformed preference include Elster, *Sour Grapes*; Amartya Sen, "Gender Inequality and Theories of Justice," in Martha Nussbaum and Jonathon Glover (eds.), *Women, Culture, and Development* (New York: Oxford University Press, 1995); and Bina Agarwal, "Bargaining and Gender Relations: Within and Beyond the Household," *Feminist Economics*, 3 (1997): 1–51.

141   Cass Sunstein, *The Partial Constitution* (Cambridge, MA: Harvard University Press, 1993).

142   John D. Walker, "Liberalism, Consent, and the Problem of Adaptive Preferences," *Social Theory and Practice* 21 (Fall, 1995): 457–71.

because she or he is prevented by outside forces from choosing another option that she or he would, absent that restriction, prefer. For example, if women think that they cannot be political leaders, then they may come to see political life as unappealing. If the conditions causing these adaptive preferences are oppressive conditions, then these deformed preferences must be criticized.

Desires are formed in a social context that makes the desired objects or states meaningful to the one who desires them. Not all adaptive preferences are bad for the agent, since they do allow the agent to get more welfare from her or his feasible set of options. If the agent cannot change the feasible set of options by her- or himself, it is better she or he should adapt her or his preferences to what is feasible. Those adaptations that are made to adjust to unjust conditions of material deprivation or psychological harm consequent on social group membership are oppressive and, therefore, contrary to freedom. If one's preferences adapt to oppressive circumstances, then one's desires turn away from goods and even needs that, absent those conditions, one would want.[143] Deformed desires cause oppressed persons to see their conditions of oppression as the limits within which they *want* to live. Feminists argue that women desire conditions that oppress them. For example, women in patriarchal cultures may prefer sexual subordination or a subordinate place in a home in which

---

143 I have argued in *Analyzing Oppression*, ch. 5, that women often face incentives through the social structure to choose ways of life that will further their oppression. The example that I used to illustrate this was a couple deciding on how to allocate unpaid and paid labor between them, and I argued that the gender wage gap (or any of a number of other structural incentives) would make it rational, from a total household perspective at least, for the wife to do the unpaid domestic labor and the husband to do the paid market labor. But, given the exit options that this choice would give each of the spouses, the woman's power to control resources and outcomes in the marriage and in bargaining over goods would be seriously reduced. Hence, the oppressive conditions that give rise to the choices would then tend to be reinforced by those choices. Yet to make an opposite choice might require a degree of power in the marriage that was already precluded by the relative bargaining positions of men and women. Women prefer housework against this background of oppression.

there is a male breadwinner.[144] Such preferences or the desires that generate them thwart feminist political transformation.

False consciousness is a belief formation process that creates beliefs that are unjustified and that are formed under conditions of oppression which support the maintenance of the oppression. To label a belief a matter of false consciousness, then, is to challenge it on three grounds: (1) its justification; (2) its origin; and (3) its implications for oppressive social relations. While a belief being false must count against it, one might object that neither the origins of a belief nor its implications matter. Indeed, to argue that the origins count against a belief seems to commit the genetic fallacy. I argue that both certain origins for, and implications of, beliefs give us good reason to reject them as beliefs that are relevant to political theorizing or policy formation.

First, we have reasons to be suspicious of them because of their implications. False consciousness generates beliefs that are generally held by members of both the groups whose dominance and whose subordination they justify. The beliefs are thus held to be both true and relevant to justification of a hierarchy or some social institution. This suggests one way of criticizing the beliefs, then: if they justify involuntary dominance and subordination, then the beliefs must entail the claim that those conditions are right or good. But if we believe that those conditions are not good, we derive a contradiction. Hence, the beliefs either do not imply the justification of subordination and domination or they are false. Either way we have reason to reject the beliefs as inputs to normative political theory.

We also have reason to be suspicious about the truth of the belief because of its origin. With false consciousness-generated beliefs, the dominant group of society – at least some members of that group – has the most incentive and ability to mold common social beliefs. False consciousness has a special place in the maintenance of oppression because when the oppressed themselves believe false things, which support their place in the social hierarchy, they have an additional reason not to resist

144 Bartky, *Femininity and Domination*.

their oppression or not to even recognize it. For oppression is *undeserved* harm, and false consciousness causes the oppressed to believe that their place is deserved.

In modern capitalist society those who benefit from false consciousness own the media and the companies that employ people, and run the schools that educate people; in socialist societies they are the political elite who have power over the media, employment, and education; in traditional societies they run the religious institutions, including schools, and the tribal councils. They have the power to shape opinion. While some members of the dominant group are passive receptors of the beliefs, some seek to construct and perpetuate these ideological beliefs through their greater ability to shape public opinion. In other words, they are just making this stuff up – they have no justification for the beliefs that help them maintain their dominant position. Now, the fact that a belief is widely shared is in some instances reason for holding that belief to be true. This is particularly true when those who hold the belief have reason to critically analyze it, such as is the case with scientific beliefs among scientists. A belief that upholds the status quo and its being widely believed gives persons who benefit from the status quo the power to promulgate that belief, they cannot, however, receive any cognitive credit from that widespread agreement. Indeed, it is at least as likely that the belief is false, for if the belief were true, one would expect scientific evidence and theoretical arguments to be displayed. Beliefs we have no more reason to hold to be true than false are not very credible.

Commodity fetishism is false consciousness insofar as it produces unjustified beliefs that support the status quo in capitalism and are generated by the oppressive conditions of capitalism. Commodity fetishism involves adaptive preference formation, as well, insofar as the false beliefs engendered reinforce values through habituation, denigration of options, and restrictions of some persons' feasible sets. As I discussed above, there are clearly oppressive conditions in living capitalism, against a background of patriarchy (not to mention white supremacy and other forms of oppression not under discussion in this chapter). Women's caring labor is not given its due and women's bodies and sexual and reproductive labor are commodified under capitalist patriarchy. However, absent patriarchy, which the descriptive ideal of capitalism recommends against, widespread commodification in itself would not lead to oppression, and hence would not fulfill the conditions of false consciousness.

Deformed preferences and false consciousness are not only unjustified, but they are also insidious because they are hidden from the individuals who harbor them. They are hidden by the same social forces that introduce and reinforce them. Uncovering or detecting them requires the kind of deconstructive, social analysis that can reveal the interests and oppressive social structures that benefit from their existence. Then the unjustified beliefs can be shown to be false by scientific or economic investigation, and finally the values that these false beliefs support can be questioned and, perhaps, re-evaluated.[145]

5   Fetishism

The fetishism of tradition

Tradition is another sort of fetish, and is thus a source of adaptive preference and false consciousness. Tradition can be defined as the set of beliefs and values, rituals, and practices, formal and informal, explicit and implicit, which are held by and constitute a culture. Because tradition constitutes social meaning, though, it is the vehicle by which oppressive beliefs and desires are formed. By traditional culture I mean a culture in which most of the social roles and relationships are determined by traditional rules and norms, and a person's place is determined by these rules according to their status at birth, and not by merit, desert, or personal preference. Oppressive beliefs are those according to which some persons are judged to be of lower worth because of their group membership. Oppressive beliefs in traditional cultures

---

145 Deformed desires may stick to individuals more than false beliefs, however, because of the way that desire is tied up with emotion and bodily states. On this point see Bartky, *Femininity and Domination*, ch. 4.

come about largely through a different kind of false conscious-ness than that which we find in capitalism. Traditional cultures exist within capitalist societies, although they do not find capit-alism to be a very friendly home, for reasons I will explore in the next section.

Andrew Kernohan explains how traditions can give rise to per-vasive oppressive beliefs in his discussion of what he terms "cul-tural oppression."[146] Our beliefs about value come to us largely via our culture. That is, we learn them as small children from our parents and other significant adults, who in turn learned them from their parents and others, and so forth. This is the adaptive preference mechanism of habituation. Traditional cul-tures habituate people to evaluate each other according to their given status. We rarely have reason to question the values we are given, and traditional cultures often enforce them on pain of ostracism or violence. The background beliefs we have are the shared meanings of our culture, and they allow us to formulate the beliefs and desires against which some of these beliefs and desires can be understood and questioned.

Another way we learn values from our culture is through the status that is accorded to various occupations. In traditional cul-tures, religious leaders are the highest status persons in the cul-ture. Religious traditions that keep women out of the priesthood, the clergy, or the rabbinate, etc. and thereby keep them from some of the highest status occupations of that culture teach us that women are less worthy than men. While traditional cultures also assign status to mothers, this is often the only form of status recognition available to women. But since there are many moth-ers and few religious leaders, motherhood is granted some respect and honor, but not authority, and the respect and honor are inferior to that available to men. Since traditional cultures trans-mit values through traditions that individuals find unavoidable, those values often include unequally valuing persons according to the social group to which they are seen as belonging.

---

146 Andrew Kernohan, *Liberalism, Equality, and Cultural Oppression* (Cambridge University Press, 1998), see ch. 1.

Thai Buddhism, for example, constructs distinctions through its assertion that everyone must repay the karmic debt accumulated in past lives with suffering in this life. This in turn justifies the mistreatment of some social groups, since it can be said that their members are members of those groups in order to repay their karmic debt. In Thailand this is a convenient way for brothel owners and pimps to keep their prostitutes in line. Such beliefs encourage girls who are sex slaves to turn inward, as they realize that they must have committed terrible sins in a past life to deserve their enslavement and abuse. Their religion urges them to accept this suffering, to come to terms with it, and to reconcile themselves to their fate.[147]

Religion is an important force for constructing and justifying family life and the roles of women and men within the family. Marriage is, in most cultures, a religious event first, and only secondarily a civil status. Marriage vows in Christianity require women to "honor and obey" their husbands, while not requiring the obedience of husbands to wives. Muslim rules for women and men are also asymmetric and unequal, giving men the dominant status in public affairs. In Judaism, in all but the Reformed sect, women and men are likewise prescribed separate roles, and women are unable to serve as rabbis. No major religion of the world, in all of its branches, treats men and women equally. Moreover, religions construct genders and sexuality, and exaggerate the distinction between the sexes. Religions typically forbid homosexual unions, and the power of religion to enforce this restriction can be seen in the current debate in the United States over gay marriage.

Feminists have discussed a number of examples of typical ways that women's preferences have been molded by traditional patriarchal cultures. One example is the *marianismo* woman, the counterpart of the *machismo* man, who believes that women are morally and spiritually superior, but that women should be submissive to men and that their superiority lies in their self-denial

---

147 Kevin Bales, *Disposable People: New Slavery in the Global Economy* (Berkeley, CA: University of California Press, 1999), 62.

and self-sacrifice.[148] Thus, *marianismo* women prefer their men to have more of what they want rather than the women's own (first order) preferences to be satisfied. Another example is African women who force their daughters to undergo genital surgery because they think that it makes them more beautiful and more acceptable to men who might otherwise choose not to marry them. In both cases the women have desires that, when satisfied, help to maintain the oppressive structures that caused them to have those desires.

In traditional cultures, religious institutions dominate and determine status, distribution of goods and labor, and other personal and collective rights. The religion as it is locally understood also prescribes norms about what one can do and be, whether one can be seen without shame in public, and to whom one must subordinate oneself.[149] In dominating every material and psychological aspect of life, religions have the power to determine that a culture will be just or oppressive, at least adequately prosperous or desperately poor, egalitarian or hierarchical. Yet even when a traditional culture is oppressive, poor, and hierarchical, the favored group does well enough to want to maintain its position through its manipulation of the religion, and thus can be very stable and difficult to dislodge.

What are the dangers to women of traditional culture? Materially, women are worse off in traditional, noncapitalist cultures in terms of their maternal mortality, in addition to higher fertility:

> As of 1983 one estimate suggests that about 500,000 women died each year in childbirth, 494,000 in developing countries.

---

148 Evelyn P. Stevens, "Marianismo: The Other Face of Machismo in Latin America," in Anne Minas (ed.), *Gender Basics: Feminist Perspectives on Women and Men* (Belmont, CA: Wadsworth, 1993).

149 I don't wish to get into a debate about whether some local understanding of a religion is a "true" or authentic interpretation of a religion. Since religions are all artifacts, there is no reason to think of some interpretations as made up while others are real or true. Religions differ greatly on how women are treated, and some progressive religions have developed to eliminate sexism from their origins in some more fundamentalist type.

The highest rates occurred in Africa (70 per 10,000 births in Western Africa) and Southern Asia (65 per 10,000). Continued high fertility, with its age and parity hazards, the low status of women in some developing countries, and the continuing use of untrained or poorly trained birth attendants seem to be the leading factors behind these levels.[150]

These countries are also poor, and some are becoming capitalist (such as India), but still harbor the strictures of tradition, where women are considered to be lesser beings, fed less, educated less, and not allowed the freedom of movement that men are.[151]

Women in traditional societies also have much lower incomes than in capitalist, nontraditional ones, and lower incomes relative to men.[152] As Table 1.2 showed, the GDI for traditional countries is much worse than for capitalist ones. Women are less likely to be politically powerful (although there are some exceptions, such as Benazir Bhutto, who came to power in Pakistan after her father's assassination). As we have explored in section 2, women in traditional societies have higher fertility rates and lower life expectancy. It is not too much of a stretch to say that generally speaking, life for women in traditional societies is nasty, brutish, and short.

As a bar to materially beneficial norms and practices that nonetheless reinforces and reproduces itself, tradition constitutes a fetish. Tradition itself is an object of unnatural attraction which causes false beliefs about the relations among and values of persons. Saying that some practice is "tradition" is enough to justify it to members of traditional cultures, no matter how heinous, strange, or irrational it seems from the outside of the culture. While the details of the argument differ for different cultures, there are commonalities. First, traditional cultures are dominated by religion. God and the religious hierarchy are

150 Riley, *Rising Life Expectancy*, 115.
151 Nussbaum, *Women and Human Development*. Nussbaum writes here about Indian women who cannot leave their homes because of the norms of how widows must live, on pain of social ostracism and violence.
152 Human Development Reports 2007/2008, Statistical Update 2008.

paradigm examples of fetishes. Through them things and persons are evaluated in light of their religious values rather than for the real human needs they serve. Second, women's social roles are severely limited in traditional cultures, making them prime candidates for sour grapes type deformed preferences. Women, who are prohibited from holding the rank of priest (mullah, rabbi, etc.) are evaluated as lesser. In many traditional religious cultures women are regarded as unclean or at least as religiously inferior. This evaluation flows over into all aspects of life. The belief in the relevant god and the fundamentalist interpretation of the sacred religious text justifies and reinforces these evaluations. Since these beliefs are false (for all we know), formed under oppressive conditions, and reinforce oppression, they constitute false consciousness.[153] Therefore, feminist political transformation demands the overthrow of traditional culture.

Freedom from fetishism

Many cultures today stand at a crossroads, where they may continue with traditional, religiously infused cultures or allow capitalism to change their cultures beyond a point of return. Capitalism forms this sort of watershed for many traditional cultures because it introduces belief and desire forming mechanisms that disrupt those that constitute the fetish of tradition, and because it introduces its own form of fetishism of commodities that can take the place of the traditional one. Capitalism offers not only a new way of transacting, but also a different way of seeing the world. Post-colonial feminists and socialist feminists resist the influx of

---

153 Would it be possible to separate the background patriarchy from the religion that forms the foundation of traditional cultures, as I argued in the case of capitalism and patriarchy? Would this be a feminist political transformation? Martha Nussbaum has argued for the positive, feminist value of Reformed Judaism, in which there are no distinctions drawn between men and women, and homosexual marriage is permitted. But this does not qualify as a traditional culture because status and options are not determined by birth status. Anyone who undertakes the study and relevant practice can become a rabbi, for example. It does seem compatible with either democratic socialism or capitalism, but surely not an economy determined by religious leaders.

global capital, giving as critiques those I discussed earlier in this section. Some also defend traditional cultures as not seriously patriarchal, but since traditional cultures introduce patriarchal fetishistic thinking, I maintain that they are seriously degrading for women. I have dismissed most of the material critiques of ideal capitalism as misaimed or mistaken. The remaining one, inequality, is not readily comparable to the inequality of status in traditional cultures. The psychological critique in terms of commodity fetishism has been shown to be a general, not gendered, critique. The critique of tradition as a fetish, however, is a gendered critique, and feminist political transformation requires that traditional culture be overthrown.

In spite of the drawback of commodity fetishism, capitalism offers mechanisms for overthrowing tradition, with its attendant form of fetishism, and a path to the end of patriarchy. First, materially capitalism subverts traditional forms of deformed desires and false consciousness by offering options that expand the feasible set of opportunities for women. By offering jobs and wages to women, capitalism offers women an opportunity for activities outside the home and for income that opens other doors. In some developing countries, mainly those where men's human capital is relatively low as well, women will immediately compete with men for equal wages. This gives women greater bargaining power within families and communities, and thus a greater ability to resist violence and exploitation by men of their community. Capitalism also offers the option for women to become entrepreneurs and thus their own bosses. The Grameen Bank and its many offshoot social enterprises provide concrete evidence that this is a real option for women in the developing world.

Second, the capitalist ideology of individual rights can be adopted by women and disrupt the traditional gender ideology.[154] Recall that ideal capitalism derives its prime justification from the maximization of individual liberty. Capitalism helps to break down patriarchal and sexist norms and practices of traditional cultures. A good example of this is the common traditional resistance

---

154 Gordon, *Transforming Capitalism and Patriarchy*.

to contraception and the forbidding of abortion. Capitalism directly provides incentives to fight against this by making children less valuable as uneducated, unskilled laborers and more valuable when educated and raised to adulthood before going into paid employment. By first making practices materially better, capitalism can help to change norms to endorse those practices. Capitalism also indirectly incentivizes small families by improving income, and thus health outcomes of infants and children, as I argued in section 2. However, even in capitalist societies women and men must struggle against the forces of tradition to preserve women's rights to reproductive and bodily autonomy. The ideology of individualism which capitalism reinforces and relies upon helps women and men to see women as valuable in themselves, and not only for the subordinated social roles that they fulfill. At the very least they are consumers who have their own preferences and tastes that the market attempts to satisfy. But capitalism is also part of the liberal worldview that values individuals and individual autonomy above all else. Once the ideology of individual rights becomes widely known and discussed, the false beliefs about the inferiority of women can be challenged and countered, and this in turn challenges their evaluation as inferior.

Third, capitalism, in promoting free market exchange, promotes the idea of mutual advantage. Adam Smith's notion of the invisible hand is one original formulation of this idea. In capitalism, suitably monitored and constrained, each person pursues their own advantage and the advantage of the group arises. Another formulation of the idea of mutual advantage comes from the game theoretic idea of a positive-sum game, in which all the players may gain at the same time. In playing by the rules within a suitably constrained and monitored system, each one can strive to achieve without depriving others. Mutual advantage opposes the notion that women (or lower caste persons) should sacrifice their own interests for the sake of others without any expectation of benefit.[155] In this way, capitalism enshrines the idea of equality in the market exchange itself.

155 David Gauthier, *Morals by Agreement* (Oxford University Press, 1986).

Finally, capitalism promotes innovation, and as a path to technical innovation, science. Science offers a means for critical analysis of beliefs, and hence a way to uncover and debunk false consciousness.[156] In the quest for a creative, innovative workforce, ideal firms seek out highly educated individuals and individuals from widely varying backgrounds. If a society is to support such innovation, it will need to support the education of individuals from all walks of life in order to maximize the potential for finding the uniquely creative individuals who will invent new technologies and new forms of life. But a necessary byproduct of such broadly distributed education will be the creation of critical thinking individuals who question the fetishes of the current generation. In this way, capitalism creates the conditions for trenchant critiques of capitalist fetishes.

By contrast, there is no internally generated path away from fetishism from traditional cultures. Tradition opposes science and upholds its fetishes self-consciously. Although there are critical traditions within orthodox cultures, such as the Jesuits in Catholicism, or Talmudic interpretation of Orthodox Judaism, there are strict boundaries within which the critiques can work, and these boundaries uphold the very fetishes of the culture. These critical traditions are also closed to women, and so are particularly resistant to feminist transformation.

Traditional, fundamentalist, and orthodox subcultures within capitalist (and socialist) societies continue to compete for men's and women's minds. It may be objected that confronting traditional culture with capitalism will generate a backlash against women and development that will do more harm than good. Although I have to admit that there seems to be some truth to this objection, at least in the short to medium term, there are

---

156 Helen Longino, *Science as Social Knowledge: Values and Objectivity in Scientific Inquiry* (Princeton University Press, 1989). Longino shows how science can achieve objectivity procedurally through openness to criticism. Because capitalism essentially involves a similar kind of openness to competition, it is a similar constant evaluation and sifting of ideas. Although not in the service of truth, it seems to me that true beliefs may be a happy byproduct of the competition of ideas.

two responses to be made. First, it seems likely that any feminist political transformation will be resisted by traditional cultures, whether they are capitalist or socialist. The rise of the Church in the former Soviet Union reveals that socialism did little to overcome the tendency of religion and tradition to reassert itself in the wake of progressive change. Second, to give up in the face of this objection is to give in to the forces of superstition and injustice. Rather than giving up, feminists should attempt smaller steps that build bridges and gradually change their cultures in positive ways. Again, the Grameen Bank provides an example of how small steps toward capitalist empowerment can gradually make large changes in some women's lives, and perhaps eventually also change their cultures.

6 Enlightened capitalism: a feminist capitalist manifesto

My defense of capitalism as a feminist political transformation depends on the assessment of capitalism as it is and has been in the world, as well as how it might be. In this concluding section I propose an enlightened capitalism that is feminist and liberal. The task before me is to collect together the ways in which the practice of capitalism falls short of its ideal, and propose remedies which are consistent with the ideal of capitalism and what makes capitalism successful in practice, as well as promoting feminist desires to end sexism and oppression generally. But I will also propose extensions of the ideals and values that capitalism embodies which lead to either greater material success, or to even more positive feminist transformation.

Recall the defining conditions of the descriptive ideal of capitalism:

(1) private ownership of capital condition;
(2) free and open, decentralized market condition;
(3) free wage labor condition;
(4) nondiscrimination constraint.

As I argued in section 3, since the justification of capitalism depends on the maximization of freedom subject to the constraint of self-ownership, ideal capitalism requires the eradication of discrimination practices that oppress individuals as members of social groups. This can be shown simply through the argument against discrimination by any factor that is not relevant to marginal productivity, since such discrimination creates inefficiencies and thereby fails to maximize individual freedom. Thus, the nondiscrimination constraint, although violated in practice, is justifiable internally within the ideal of capitalism. We thus have an argument from freedom for using government to enforce this constraint.

An enlightened capitalism not only ought to enforce nondiscrimination, for the same reasons it ought to discourage workforce segregation. Only when all persons, regardless of their attributed status, can participate freely in market interactions are those markets free and also efficiently exploiting the talents of all individuals. Thus, enlightened capitalism will also avoid segregation, and use government to provide incentives to integrate the workplace. This is especially important for women because we have found that even when discrimination is overcome, segregation remains a key force in the economic subordination of women.[157] And so enlightened capitalism works to reduce discrimination against women, integrate women and men, and all races and ethnicities in the workforce.

Although its reliance on markets promotes freedom, growth, and efficiency, as I explained in section 3, there are many examples of market failures in real capitalist economies, such as information asymmetries and externalities. In such cases, an enlightened capitalism will protect itself from the problems that arise by seeking, where possible, to internalize the externalities, or by collectively providing the good or service that is underprovided by market mechanisms. Thus, an enlightened capitalism will provide public health care and education, as well as defense and a police force, and will seek mechanisms to collectively reduce pollution.

In the section "Inequality under capitalism," I argued that ideal capitalism must eliminate the gross inequality among individuals,

---

157 Bergmann, *The Economic Emergence of Women.*

based on the argument from self-ownership for private property rights. That is, the only defensible forms of capitalism are those that provide individuals with enough goods to enable them to survive at a decent standard of living. But there may be a tendency among the better off to reduce the level of what is considered decent. The amelioration of inequality, when that entails improvements in the capacities of individuals to better participate in market interaction, can also be defended on the grounds of improving mutual advantage. Schooling that enables as broad a portion of the population as possible to become innovators and critical thinkers will improve the benefits of market interaction for all. Thus, enlightened capitalism will provide the means for all children to be able to participate in market interactions, and for all qualified students to continue their education at higher and higher levels.

We have seen that the best form of capitalism in material terms is an entrepreneurial capitalism that provides incentives for innovation and competition. Innovations change our lives unpredictably, but can sometimes massively improve our lives. We often think of innovations as pushing the edge of technology using the latest scientific discoveries, requiring enormous investment, and extremely costly for the first generation of users. From our example of Grameen Bank and its offshoot companies, we can see that innovation can occur in many dimensions, and that businesses can be designed to meet many different social needs while maintaining profitability in a capitalist system. Since many niches exist in catering to less well off and lower status individuals, an enlightened entrepreneurial capitalism will create incentives and eliminate obstacles to such businesses. This means providing legal and financial means of making small loans at affordable rates, as well as capitalizing high technology enterprises.

At the same time, entrepreneurial capitalism is subject to financial bubbles and social disruption when old technologies (and their firms and its workers) are replaced, and they suddenly lose their value in the market. Since this creates financial instability and can lead to financial collapse and panic, as well as social disruption and psychological harm, an enlightened capitalism will take measures to prevent overspeculation, to save for such inevitable catastrophes, and to re-stimulate new economic activity when collapse occurs.

A major force in restraining capitalism in the United States and Europe has been unions that allow workers to take advantage of collective bargaining with capitalists. An enlightened capitalism will preserve and even promote the ability of workers to form unions. There are two reasons for this. First, unions can help to promote greater equality between workers and managers. If managers have to bargain with all workers as one, they will be in a weak position to be able to extract all the profits generated by their firm; they will be forced to share to some degree. Promoting equality is advantageous for a capitalist society for the reasons I have previously enumerated: it is instrumental in bringing about maximum participation in the market, and it promotes mutual advantage, which is also morally good. Second, collective bargaining of workers with large capitalist firms promotes a fair competitive bargaining situation. A large firm that is the only employer in an area for a large group of workers is monopsonistic, and thus able to bargain for less than competitive wages. A reasonable remedy for this market failure is for the workers to be able to form an equally unified bargaining position.

By promoting and embodying the ideology of individual rights, ideal capitalism opposes oppression. An enlightened capitalism will self-consciously exploit this connection of individualism and opposing oppression. Furthermore, it will seek not to align itself with individuals or groups that oppose individual rights in order to preserve the ideological connection, and also to promote the ideal of mutual advantage on which capitalism thrives. By institutionalizing mutual advantage through the logic of voluntary exchange, ideal capitalism promotes the idea that no one is to be expected to sacrifice their interests with no expectation of benefit. As an opponent of oppression, enlightened capitalism quite naturally aligns itself with feminist political transformation.

The main remaining problem with ideal capitalism that may particularly concern feminists is the crisis of care created by the underprovision of care if caring labor is fully commodified.[158] I have two responses to this. First, if women provide less care, men might take up the slack and provide more. This would be beneficial to everyone if it should come to pass, since men would get the intangible benefits of greater intimacy, sharing, and community that come from caring labor. For one thing, it would engender changes in norms of masculinity that constitute patriarchy and condone violence. Yet it is also possible that men will not choose to participate in this gift economy, and neither will women. Commodity fetishism presses against seeing benefits or values that are not exchange values. On the other hand, paid care work will have to be done, and government will have to correct for the market failures due to the undervaluation of caring labor in the market. Those who perform care for decent wages, then, may come to see it as having intrinsic value. In capitalism good ideas and values that run counter to particular instances of commodity fetishism will have a forum. We will continue to support science, critical thinking, and sources of creativity such as humanistic thinking because it is efficient and freedom producing. Thus, there is a path, one that is internally generated by ideal capitalism, which leads to an enlightened future of caring individuals, in spite of the force of commodity fetishism. The crisis of care is a serious worry, but the greater worry is that under traditional and capitalist patriarchy, there is no crisis of care because women are coerced into providing it for free.

Enlightened capitalism would be a feminist future because it would treat men and women as individuals who are valuable in themselves. It would not tolerate discrimination and would promote integration of people from different walks of life. It would tend to break down ideologies of tradition that subordinate women to men, or some groups of men and women to other groups because of ancient ideas of status and birth. It would promote positive freedoms, by providing health care, education, and a welfare minimum for those whose abilities and goods do not

158 Nancy Folbre, *The Invisible Heart: Economics and Family Values* (New York: New Press, 2002).

allow them to earn it in the marketplace. Enlightened capitalism would also promote social freedom because it adheres to an ideal of competition within the rules which allows interactions to be to the mutual advantage of all. Enlightened capitalism is thus not only compatible with feminism, but arguably the most positive feminist political transformation that we can imagine.

Part II

2   Against capitalism as theory and as reality

Nancy Holmstrom

1   Introduction

Current crisis

WHEN WE STARTED ON THIS PROJECT IN 2006, capitalism seemed to be bigger and stronger than at any point in history. It was truly a global system, fulfilling – for better or worse – Karl Marx's description in *The Communist Manifesto* of 1848: "The need of a constantly expanding market for its products chases the bourgeoisie over the whole surface of the globe. It must nestle everywhere, settle everywhere, establish connexions everywhere … In one word, it creates a world after its own image."[1]

The fall of communism in the Soviet Union in 1989 led market enthusiasts to proclaim that liberal capitalism was "the end of history."[2] The free market approach to capitalism had been hegemonic in the United States for over a quarter of a century, President Ronald Reagan having declared in 1981 that "Government is not the solution to our problem; it is the problem." Although the dot.com boom of the late 1990s was over, there was the new housing boom. A financial crisis had exploded in Asia a decade before, but the West had weathered the storm, and it only confirmed the experts' conviction that the Keynesian approach of mixing government spending with the market, more

1 *The Communist Manifesto*, in Robert C. Tucker (ed.), *Marx–Engels Reader*, 2nd edn. (New York: W. W. Norton, 1978), 476f.
2 Francis Fukuyama, "The End of History," *National Interest*, Summer 1989.

typical in Asia, was bad for the economy. Whatever its validity, Keynesianism was defeated politically. The European model of capitalism, sometimes called social welfare capitalism because of its extensive government spending on social services (or branded as "socialism" by adherents of the free market), was under heavy pressure due to global competition with the more market-oriented approach of the Americans, known as neoliberalism. This was true throughout the developing world as well, as international agencies like the World Bank insisted that as a precondition for loans, countries must cut public spending. Although some critics pointed to fundamental problems in the system,[3] and some protested against the effects of the free market model on the working class and the poor throughout the world, this was undoubtedly a triumphalist period for capitalism. Margaret Thatcher, the UK Prime Minister during the 1980s, famously declared "there is no alternative," repeating it so often that the doctrine became known simply as TINA.

How very different today! Indeed, it would be difficult to overstate how different the economic landscape looks in 2009. The *biggest financial institutions in the world failed*. They have survived only with massive government, that is, taxpayer, assistance (but never called "welfare"). Blue chip stocks fell in value to less than a dollar. Nobel Prize winning economist, Paul Krugman, described recent economic numbers from around the world as "terrifying," writing, "Let's not mince words: This looks an awful lot like the beginning of a second Great Depression."[4] Some have managed to stay rich or become even richer through the crisis ("spinning gold out of other people's misery," in the words of playwright Wallace Shawn),[5] but most people throughout the world are

---

3 Robert Brenner, for example, pointed to a steady decline in the real economy since 1973, calling it "the long downturn." See, *The Economics of Global Turbulence* (New York: Verso, 2006). Aside from Marxists like Brenner, very few foresaw the current crisis. An exception was Nouriel Roubini in a speech to the International Monetary Fund in 2006. See, Stephen Mihm, "Dr. Doom," *New York Times*, August 15, 2008.

4 Paul Krugman column, *New York Times*, January 5, 2009, 21.

5 Interview on *Democracy Now*, Pacifica Radio, November 17, 2009.

suffering.[6] Most mainstream economists and the press advocate some variant of Keynesianism as the only way to prevent "Great Depression II" and to managing capitalist economies beyond our immediate crisis (although academic economists remain resistant to questioning the fundamentals of their free market theory).[7] The majority debate in the public sphere concerns *how much* and *where* to put the government aid and *how much government control* there should be over it. The February 16, 2009 cover of *Newsweek* magazine proclaimed, "We are all socialists now," meaning simply that everyone favored more government involvement in the economy, that is, Keynesianism, and in April 2009 the widely respected Rasmussen Poll showed that only 53 percent of Americans say capitalism is better than socialism[8] – a particularly striking figure in a country which has no socialist or even labor party and where liberal capitalists are considered the "left." Some people are even saying that Karl Marx's thought is more relevant today than it was at the time when he wrote.[9] The

---

6 On the same day the *New York Times* reported that bonuses for employees at financial companies on Wall St. were the sixth largest on record and on the opposite page was an article by Rebecca Cathcart entitled "Burden of Debt Weighed on Family in Murder-Suicide," January 29, 2009, 1 and 18. The same divide into winners and losers is happening on a global level; there is a virtual epidemic of suicide among impoverished Indian peasants, 200,000 since 1997. Vandana Shiva, "Why are Indian Farmers Committing Suicide and How Can We Stop This Tragedy?," available at: Voltairenet.org, May 23, 2009. On September 11, 2009 the *New York Times* reported that the 30,000 employees of Goldman Sachs were on track to earn an average of $700,000 this year. Alex Berenson, "A Year After a Cataclysm, Little Change on Wall St," 1.

7 Patricia Cohen, "Ivory Tower Unswayed by Crashing Economy," *New York Times*, March 5, 2009, C1.

8 Rasmussen Poll, April 2009, available at: www.rasmussenreports.com.

9 The cover of *Courier International*, No. 924, July 17–23, 2008 was entitled "Marx, le retour," with abstracts from articles published in *The New York Review of Books*, *The Financial Times* and elsewhere. In March 2009 an article by Mark Steele in the British newspaper *The Independent*, "So Karl Marx Was Right After All," reported that most newspapers have had articles on him in their business pages and he was on the front page of *The Times*. More startling is that in 1997 before the crisis, *The New Yorker* issue devoted to "the next" of everything in the twenty-first century had an article describing Marx as "the next thinker." John Cassidy, "The Return of Karl Marx," October 20, 1997.

question implicit in these reactions is whether our current crisis is simply a crisis of the financial sector, or of neoliberal capitalism generally, or is it, most fundamentally, a crisis of capitalism?

I cannot predict how things will look when you are reading these words. Will capitalism have managed to stabilize itself, and the preceding paragraph sound like hysterical ranting? If it stabilizes itself, on what basis will it have done so? Since the crisis is global, how would Keynesianism be applied beyond the nation-state? Will it work? if so, for how long? Will the crisis be resolved only through an even bigger crisis, with a massive restructuring and shakeout of low profit firms and a lowering of wages – which is what happened in Asia after their recent crisis? Who will have paid, in other words, for the crisis? (Talk of a *"jobless recovery"* gives us a hint as to who will pay.) Or will the crisis be ongoing, and with what political, economic, and personal effects on people throughout the world? Or will it be resolved, but then reappear? And if so, what other alternatives will be proposed, either within capitalism, or going beyond? Or, by the time you read this, could the whole economy have been re-configured, as were the economies of Eastern Europe in just a few years? In their case, of course, the change was toward capitalism, but their story illustrates *just how rapid social economic transformation can be* when conditions are right.

At the very minimum, we can conclude from this crisis that the economics experts at the highest levels of the US government, universities and financial institutions – the so-called "best and the brightest" – did not know what they were talking about and that capitalism has shown itself to be what critics have always said it is: a highly volatile, crisis-ridden system with devastating effects on the most vulnerable. But today this is exponentially more true as the economic problems of the United States spin around the globe with untold consequences for the globe itself; poor countries that had nothing to do with the causes of the crisis are seeing their economies shrink.[10] The many trillions of

10 Edmund L. Andrews, "Report Projects a Worldwide Economic Slide," *New York Times*, March 9, 2009, B1.

dollars spent to aid financial institutions also put the lie to the claim that "there just isn't enough money" that was used to justify lack of public spending on health care, education, and other public goods needed by the majority, particularly the most vulnerable. It is now completely transparent that the real question is *how resources are distributed and who gets to decide this.*

What does all this imply regarding whether or not capitalism is good for women? That is our concern in this book: to examine capitalism *from a feminist point of view,* that is, to examine it with a special concern for the interests of women. As there is no one feminist perspective on capitalism (or almost anything else), a case has to be made. However, I am taking as a premise that feminists should be concerned with ending the oppression of women whatever the causes, be they sexism, racism or economic, or some combination difficult to disentangle. A feminism concerned only with ending the oppression of women *based on gender* would be a very limited version, far from the emancipatory vision at its core. Positions on capitalism among feminists range from apparent indifference since they ignore it, to support for capitalism with various degrees of criticism, to opposition. Indifference is not a responsible position given the enormous and ever-increasing impact of the system in which we all live on all domains of our lives, even the most intimate.[11] Instead, a feminist position on capitalism should be based on whether or not capitalism is good for women. Since capitalism is not the same in all times and places, and moreover is constantly changing, we cannot limit our inquiry to any particular form in which it is realized. To see the possibilities capitalism might have to offer, we have to examine both its ideals, on the one hand, and the

11 See Arlie Hochschild's *The Managed Heart: Commercialization of Human Feeling,* 2nd edn. (Berkeley, CA: University of California Press, 2003); *The Commercialization of Intimate Life* (Berkeley, CA: University of California Press, 2003); Rachel P. Maines, *The Technology of Orgasm: "Hysteria," the Vibrator, and Women's Sexual Satisfaction* (Baltimore, MD: Johns Hopkins University Press, 1999). One theorist describes capitalism as "the most totalizing system the world has ever known," Ellen Meiksins Wood, *Democracy Against Capitalism: Renewing Historical Materialism* (New York: Cambridge University Press, 1995), 2.

fundamental structure and tendencies inherent in capitalism in all its manifestations, on the other hand. Many of its abstract ideals are very attractive, so in theory capitalism has much to recommend itself for all individuals, including women. As an historical reality also, capitalism has tendencies that are liberatory for women. However, other fundamental features and tendencies are arguably at odds with these liberatory aspects. So, ultimately, the question of whether capitalism is good for women has to rest on capitalism as *an actually existing, historically evolving political economic system, not just a logically possible system. To focus on capitalism as an idea – without powerful arguments to show that it is also feasible – would be to make an apologia for capitalism.*[12] In any case, a political/economic system cannot be willed into existence. It comes into existence through a complicated social historical process of evolution and/or revolution, and its nature depends both on how it came into being and what it is replacing. Thus, while an examination of an abstract model, or what can be called the ideal or optimal version of a political economic system, has some value, this value is quite limited.

Therefore, my principal concern in this debate will be on whether capitalism as an actually existing system is good for women. We will find, however, that there is no simple yes or no answer to this question; it depends on how we answer these crucial sub-questions: compared with what?; which women?; with respect to what aspects of their lives?; in what time frame? I will argue in what follows that while capitalism creates favorable possibilities for women it also puts limits on these possibilities. Overall, I contend, the respects in which capitalism can be said to be good for women are more limited than those in which they are bad. Women do not

12 See Charles Mills, "'Ideal Theory' as Ideology," in Peggy DesAutels and Margaret Urban Walker (eds.), *Moral Psychology* (Lanham MD: Rowman & Littlefield, 2004). For a general philosophical argument for the importance of situating and evaluating abstract norms in the real world, see Louise Antony, "Naturalized Epistemology, Morality and the Real World," *Canadian Journal of Philosophy* 26 (2000): 103–37; as applied to questions of justice and poor women, see Onora O'Neill, "Justice, Gender and International Boundaries," in Martha C. Nussbaum and Amartya Sen (eds.), *The Quality of Life* (New York: Oxford University Press, 1993).

tend to be the "winners" in the brutally competitive system which is capitalism; indeed, they are among the poorest and most vulnerable people on earth, particularly dependent on public goods. Therefore, feminists truly committed to women's well-being – dare I say "women's liberation"? – should oppose capitalism.

Basic definitions

"Capitalism"

What exactly is capitalism? Not only has capitalism as a system evolved and taken various forms at different times and places, but theories of capitalism – regarding what it is, and what it could be and should be – have also evolved and they vary today as well. Sometimes it is not entirely clear just what its proponents mean by it. However, we need a minimal working definition to proceed and readers need to be aware of how I understand the concept. Common to almost all definitions of capitalism are the following: (1) the bulk (or the most important segments) of the means of production are privately owned; (2) wage labor is the most important form of labor; (3) production is primarily for a market rather than directly for the needs of the producers; and (4) the point of production is to maximize profit. Despite (3) and (4), it is alleged – most famously in Adam Smith's "invisible hand" argument – that selfish pursuit of individual profit is, in fact, the best way to satisfy the social good.[13] The validity of this claim will be a central issue in our debate.

To clarify further the meaning of private ownership it is important to distinguish "private property" from "personal property," which is individual property simply for one's own use. A society could have personal property but collective ownership of the means of production. With collective or common property, for example, public parks, every individual has a right to use the park; hence, common property involves an individual right to property just as private property does. The difference between the two forms of individual right to property is that, by definition, common property is not exclusive; no one has the right to exclude others from

13 Adam Smith, *The Wealth of Nations* (New York: Modern Library, 1937).

using the park. In contrast, if the land were privately owned by a resort, the owners could exclude everyone else from using it. Hence, private property – which can be small scale or truly vast in scale – is essentially a right of exclusion. In capitalism, the owners of the means of production have the exclusive right to decide what to produce, and where and how to produce it.

This definition of capitalism allows for significant differences among capitalist societies with respect to government's role in the economy. As I have already mentioned, the specific form that any given capitalist economy takes is a function of many things, not only during its existence, but how it developed (evolution or revolution) and the specific history, class structure, and culture of the social formation from which it developed. In theory, a society could be purely laissez faire (free market), with no state intervention in the economy. (It is important to note, however, that even in such a hypothetical system a state, with its monopoly of force, would be necessary to *uphold* private ownership. Hence. government plays an essential role in *all* economic systems.[14]) No society in history has ever fitted this abstract free market model (nor could it, I will argue), but some come closer than others. The United States, for example, has public education, roads, sanitation systems, etc. However, it is the only developed country in the world that does not have government-funded universal health care but leaves health to the market. Not only do many governments provide more social welfare than the United States, but in many capitalist countries the government owns banks, railways and airlines, radio and TV stations, and it directs much investment. For example, scholars have shown that government direction of investment was crucial in developing the economies of the so-called "Asian Tigers."[15] Capitalist societies have gone

---

14 A conceivable exception would be communistic anarchism, without private property, but an adequate discussion of this alternative is not possible here.

15 Chalmers Johnson, *Miti and the Japanese Miracle* (Stanford University Press, 1982); Alice Amsden, *Escape from Empire: The Developing World's Journey Through Heaven and Hell* (Cambridge, MA: MIT Press, 2007); *The Rise of "the Rest": Challenges to the West from Late Industrializing Countries* (Oxford University Press, 2001).

through cycles of government regulation and de-regulation. In the United States, many industries were de-regulated in the past few decades, including the banking industry in 1999 thus allowing new financial "products" like derivatives that contributed to the collapse of the industry. It is likely that we will see a turn back to regulation in the coming period. Some writers refer to societies based on private property but with greater state ownership and direction of investment as "social welfare capitalist" or "state capitalist," but this variant is nevertheless capitalist as long as our criteria above are met (private ownership of the most important means of production, wage labor, most production for profit). At times the fundamental long-term goal of maximizing profit is best served by government taking over a particular industry – temporarily or permanently – and sometimes popular pressure wrests more support from the government. President Obama recently described health care reform as "not only a moral imperative but a fiscal imperative." Automakers in the United States may be wishing that instead of employer-based health care, our government provided health care as this would reduce their costs and make them more competitive. To call societies socialist just because the state plays this kind of role in the economy is to mistake the abstract model for reality and to misunderstand the nature of capitalism.

"Women's interests"

Before we can address whether such a system is best for women, some methodological difficulties must be addressed. How can one judge what's good for women? We can say, initially, that what's good for women is what advances their interests, but what are their interests? Is there even such a thing as "women's interests"? How do we judge them? Does it depend simply on their preferences? The most abstract concern, coming from postmodern thinkers, is that women's well-being is not an objective matter of fact, but depends on interpretation and language. What this means is not entirely clear. If the claim is interpreted in a very strong way, then no evaluations are possible and thus the feminist enterprise is doomed. However, we can recognize that facts are not transparent, that language and interpretation are inevitable, without giving up. If we are talking about the interests of particular women, then we must include how they perceive and evaluate their interests, what they do and what they say. This involves language, certainly, but language is not an abstract structure separate from real women, but rather it is how women explain how they perceive things, and why they do what they do. Thus, language and interpretation do not pose an insuperable epistemological barrier to ascertaining women's interests, but is simply one of the best ways we have for ascertaining them.[16]

A related objection that would derail our efforts here is that each woman's identity is too complicated to make any judgments about what she wants or needs. In addition to being a woman, she has a class, a nationality, a race/ethnic group, a sexuality, marital status, health status, etc. It is naive, some claim, to make any inference from her social location in this nexus of social groups to her interests and identity. But this would be to give up all social science and history. Reliable inferences about interests and identity must be based on as much information as we can get, without reducing anyone's identity to only one dimension, and, of course, they are subject to counterevidence, like any scientific claim. But if we know anything, we know that social location – being a man or a woman, rich or poor, Afghani or Swedish – is "causally relevant" to the experiences she or he will have. And *these experiences, in turn, are causally relevant to identity.*[17]

On a somewhat less abstract level: when we try to judge what conditions are good or bad for women, we often seem to be caught in a dilemma. On the one hand, to ignore women's subjective

16 Joan Scott, *Gender and the Politics of History* (New York: Columbia University Press, 1988); Louise Tilly, "Gender, Women's History and Social History," *Pasato e Presente* (1989): 20–21, cited in Eleni Varikas, "Gender, Experience and Subjectivity: The Tilly–Scott Disagreement," *New Left Review* 211 (May/June, 1995), 89–101.

17 Paula M. L. Moya, "Post-Modernism, 'Realism,' and the Politics of Identity: Cherríe Moraga and Chicana Feminism," in M. Jacqui Alexander and Chandra Talpade Mohanty (eds.), *Feminist Genealogies, Colonial Legacies, Democratic Futures* (New York: Routledge, 1997).

satisfactions or preferences seems arrogant and runs a high risk
of bias. Who are we to second guess what a woman says she
wants? How can someone else know what she wants better than
she does? On the other hand, to rely only on preferences ignores
the reality of adaptive preferences (the "sour grapes" phenomenon) and gives up all chance of an objective assessment of people's lives. A fascinating book, *The Good Women of China: Hidden
Voices*, by Xinran[18] illustrates the problem of relying on felt satisfaction as a measure of women's condition. In the final chapter
the author introduces us to women living in a remote area in
the most extreme poverty the author had ever seen, in complete ignorance of the outside world, in ill-health, and in total
subjugation to all the men of their community. The women are
property, breeding machines, whose existence is justified only
by their utility. Yet as striking as the awful conditions of their
lives is the fact that of all the women we meet in the book, they
are the only ones who told her they were happy. The author
reports how deeply shaken she was by her visit. This example
illustrates the fact that felt satisfaction and objective well-being
are not necessarily correlated, nor is domination always perceived; a happy slave is possible. There are objective matters of
fact regarding human health and capacities and freedom and,
therefore, the extent to which particular practices enhance or
limit them. Independent of any subjective (dis)satisfaction, we
know the dreadful physical effects on women of very early mar-
riages and multiple children, for example. It makes sense, therefore, to say that it is in women's interest to end these practices.
Though felt satisfaction and preferences cannot be ignored, if we
stop there, we lose the opportunity for any moral and political
assessment. At a minimum, as John Stuart Mill implied, satisfactions and preferences formed in total ignorance of alternatives
or in disbelief that any alternatives are possible should not be
the standard. Given the high risk of bias, however, we should
approach these judgments with as much information as possible
and with considerable care and humility.

18 Xinran, *The Good Women of China: Hidden Voices* (New York: Anchor, 2003).

Gender interests: strategic and practical

On the premise therefore that we can – and must – speak of how capitalism affects women, let us explore further the concept of women's interests; a highly contested concept.[19] Using the concept in an unqualified way seems to imply that despite the many diverse causes of women's subordination and the extreme differences among women, that there exists a homogeneity of interests for all women. This, however, is definitely problematic. Maxine Molyneux, a comparative sociologist specializing in developing countries, suggests that we speak instead of gender interests, which she defines as the general interests women (or men) have in common by virtue of "their social positioning through gender attributes" – which can take many forms. She distinguishes between what she calls *strategic gender interests* and *practical gender interests*,[20] a distinction that is particularly useful for comparing how women fare in different societies and how they themselves are likely to assess their situation. It also helps to illuminate why women sometimes seem to acquiesce to arrangements that would appear, at least to outsiders, to be against their interests.

Strategic gender interests are those goals that are in fact necessary for women's liberation. Legal equality, reproductive freedom, dismantling of the sexual division of labor disrupt the institutions that reproduce women's subordination, and, hence, there will be

---

19 See Anna G. Jónasdóttir, "On the Concept of Interest, Women's Interests, and the Limitations of Interest Theory," in Kathleen Jones and Anna G. Jónasdóttir (eds.), *The Political Interests of Gender Revisited: Developing Theory and Research with a Feminist Face* (London: Sage, 2009), 33–65.

20 Maxine Molyneux, "Mobilization Without Emancipation? Women's Interests, State and Revolution," *Feminist Studies* 11(2) (1985): 227–54; a shorter version "Conceptualizing Women's Interests," is reprinted in Nancy Holmstrom (ed.), *The Socialist-Feminist Project* (New York: Monthly Review Press, 2002). Molyneux's distinction has been extremely influential and also critiqued, for example, by Ann Ferguson, who conceptualizes strategic as "re-visionary" gender interests and practical gender interests as needs, "Empowerment, Development and Women's Liberation," in Kathleen Jones and Anna Jónasdóttir (eds.), *The Political Interests of Gender Revisited* (Manchester University Press, 2009).

no liberation of women unless they are achieved. These are the kinds of strategic goals usually identified as feminist goals, that feminists claim to be in women's objective interest – and they are.

But women have other interests based on their immediate needs that do not challenge the existing gender order, but instead, that arise from that gender order. Molyneux calls these *practical gender interests*. For example, since women everywhere are primarily responsible for the care of children and households, women have special interests in protecting them. Molyneux notes that it is such practical, rather than strategic, gender interests that women are most likely to identify as their interests and to act in defense of, for example, in bread riots that women have engaged in throughout history. Women will also prioritize them over strategic gender interests if they perceive a conflict. Note that practical gender interests are decidedly not universal to all women since they overlap with class interests. Marie Antoinette did not need to riot for bread.

2   Capitalism in theory: ideals and limits

On property, ownership, and freedom

Primary virtues

With these clarifications of the key concepts we now turn to examining whether or not capitalism is best for women. Keeping in mind the caveats I have offered about abstract models of political/economic systems, our focus in this section will be on capitalism *in theory*, its ideals, and, as I will argue, its limits. Proponents of capitalism often equate capitalism with modernity and see it as the vehicle for realizing the values of the modern (Western) world: liberty, equality, and fraternity (or solidarity in gender neutral terms). But when focusing specifically on capitalism as an economic system they most often cite two values on its behalf over all alternative systems: greater efficiency at producing material well-being and greater freedom. Related to the second is the alleged tendency of capitalism toward equality of individuals.

This would seem to have particular importance for women and will be discussed in some detail in the latter part of this chapter. The two primary values of efficiency and freedom are connected in that well-being enhances freedom, but independently of this capitalism is alleged to be essentially freer than all alternatives. Many think that capitalism is also a just society, but the principal argument that it is *more just than alternatives* rests on the claim that it is more free (this is the theory that calls itself libertarianism), so by addressing freedom, I will be addressing the latter claim regarding its justice indirectly.[21] Other possible values of a political economic system, such as material equality and community, are seldom professed by capitalism so will not be discussed in this section. If I can succeed in showing that capitalism does not realize its own most important professed values, my critique will be that much stronger.

Whether capitalism provides more material well-being than alternatives is largely an empirical question, not an abstract one, and hence will be addressed at length in section 3 on capitalism *in reality*. Here I will just say that this question is more complicated than is apparent from most discussions. To evaluate it there are many issues to keep in mind. First, we have to recognize that what counts as efficient or inefficient (wasteful) depends on what one is trying to achieve; in short, *efficiency does not exist in and of itself*, but is always relative to our goals. Political/economic systems are likely to be efficient and wasteful in different ways given their different goals and structures, so we have to decide which of our goals are most important and how to balance them. Only once we decide this can we judge the efficiency of a given

---

21 Other defenses of capitalism as just tend to rest on the denial of any viable alternatives to capitalism, not that it is in principle more just than all other possibilities. John Rawls' theory of justice, for example, defends abstract principles of justice, not any particular economic system. Hence, if capitalism met his principles of justice better than any alternative, as he seemed to believe, then it would be just, but if in fact a different system fitted them better, that other system would be most just: *A Theory of Justice* (Cambridge, MA: Harvard University Press, 1971). Friedrich A. Von Hayek even warns against attempting to defend capitalism on the grounds of justice: *The Fatal Conceit* (University of Chicago Press, 1988).

economic system or policy in achieving them. A goal of maximum output per hour is likely to yield a different judgment of
efficiency than a goal of maximum health and happiness. Hence,
efficiency should not be simply conflated with maximization of
output as is so often done. We also have to consider how material well-being is distributed in a society, not simply the absolute
amount, and we have to be sure that all the dimensions of material well-being are included, not simply material goods. A certain
amount of unemployment and underemployment are highly efficient from a capitalist point of view and therefore inherent in
all capitalist societies; indeed, economists talk of a "natural" level
of unemployment, "currently thought to be 4.8 [percent] in the
United States."[22] But unemployment– now *officially* 10.2 percent –
is highly wasteful from a human and social point of view.[23] Our
evaluation of efficiency must always be sure to include the long
run, not just the short run, whether we are considering the efficiency of a product, method, or policy. This is also true for a mode
of production, as it is possible that a particular feature of a system
is a virtue at one stage of history and not another. I will argue that
this is true of capitalism's tendency to growth. Finally, and perhaps most important, we have to be sure to consider all genuine
alternatives. When these considerations are kept in mind, we will
see in section 3 that capitalism is not in fact more efficient at producing material well-being in all its dimensions for the majority
of people in the long run than all alternatives to capitalism. A pol-
itical/economic system that was genuinely democratic, economically as well as politically, would do better for *all* its members,
particularly the more vulnerable members of society, like women
and children, the elderly, and the disabled.

Freedom has been the object of dreams and struggle throughout the ages by individuals and groups, large and small, and it

---

22 Paul Krugman, "How Did Economists Get It So Wrong?," *New York Times Magazine*, September 6, 2009, 38.
23 The rate is 17.5 percent if it includes discouraged workers and the under-
    employed. The official rate among Black Americans is 15 percent. David
    Leonhardt, "Jobless Rate Hits 10.2%, with More Underemployed," *New York Times*, November 7, 2009, 1.

has many dimensions and degrees. Whether capitalism provides more freedom than all alternatives must ultimately be answered at the level of reality, not simply ideals and abstract models. However, in order to assess whether a given political economic system provides more or less freedom than another, we have to be clear as to just what freedom is, what conditions enhance it or limit it, and for whom. These are the kinds of questions we will address in this section on capitalism *in theory*. Women have sought liberation as individuals and in organized groups for eons; in fact, Orlando Patterson has argued that women played a crucial role in the origin of personal freedom.[24] So, if capitalism does indeed provide more freedom than alternatives, this would be an enormously important point for feminists in favor of capitalism as the best system for women.

Political freedom and democracy

One important dimension of freedom for which people have struggled, and millions of people around the globe are still deprived of, is political freedom. Capitalism is usually discussed as if all capitalist societies were political democracies; hence, free from a political point of view with each citizen enjoying basic political rights and liberties, with elections, an independent judiciary, and a multi-party system. Indeed, the phrase "a free society" is often used as equivalent to capitalism as when the United States is called the leader of the "free world," though its allies include dictatorships (their actual criterion being freedom *of the market*, not political freedom). It is true that representative systems of government came into existence with the rise of capitalism, and many theorists see a special affinity between political democracy and capitalism. Even Marx agreed. Nevertheless, the connection was hardly automatic. At the beginning of capitalism, only large landowners, a very small percentage of the population, had the vote; property qualifications for male voters were not removed in all of the United States until the middle of the nineteenth

---

24 Orlando Patterson, *Freedom in the Making of Western Culture* (New York: Basic Books, 1991).

century, while women have had the vote for less than a hundred years. Each extension of political rights was won only after long and intense struggle. African Americans were effectively denied the right to vote in the Southern United States until the Civil Rights movement won the Voting Rights Act of 1965, and their struggles continue today over such issues as felon disenfranchisement and voter ID. In the modern period the fact is that capitalist economies have existed with a variety of forms of government, from representative democracies like those of the United States and Western Europe, to dictatorships like Nazi Germany or most Latin American countries throughout the twentieth century.

Milton Friedman, a principal theorist of free market capitalism, contends that political democracy and freedom can exist only in a capitalist economy.[25] However, one of the "purest," that is, most free market forms of capitalism existed in Chile under the Pinochet dictatorship that the United States helped bring to power, overthrowing the democratically elected socialist government of Salvador Allende. Ironically, given Friedman's claim, Pinochet acted under the guidance of followers of Friedman known as the Chicago School of economists. Today, in China we find an increasingly capitalist economy co-existing with a Communist political system. Leaving aside the special case of China, I see no way of denying that these other dictatorships were capitalist societies except by some question-begging definition of capitalism that restricts it to political democracies. Dictatorships cannot be declared to be noncapitalist simply because of greater government involvement in society, since, as already discussed, capitalist democracies also vary a great deal as to the amount of government intervention in the economy, both in terms of ownership, investment, and social welfare. Thus, capitalism is demonstrably not *sufficient* for political democracy and has not been shown to be *necessary*. Of the many dimensions of freedom, the only freedom that is *definitional* of capitalism, and therefore part of *all* capitalist societies, is market freedom: the freedom to buy

---

25 Milton Friedman, *Capitalism and Freedom* (University of Chicago Press, 1962).

and sell what one likes, especially labor, to contract as one likes, without needing anyone else's permission (though this too is subject to some restrictions in every capitalist society). Nevertheless, for purposes of this discussion of freedom and capitalism, I will restrict myself to the idealized version of capitalism which is politically democratic, that is, free from a political point of view.

The democracy characteristic of capitalism is, however, quite limited. The literal meaning of "democracy" is "rule by the people" and admits of degrees along two dimensions: how many are included in "the people" and how much they get to rule over. Although democracy within capitalism has gradually, with struggle, become more inclusive, the range of issues over which the voters have power is extremely limited, however, as it is restricted to the political sphere.[26] The best one can do is vote for a viable candidate and *hope* that he or she institutes the economic policies one prefers. Ellen Meiksins Wood has made the case that with the rise of capitalism political democracy simultaneously became possible and greatly de-valued. The reason is that in capitalism the "economic" and the "political" become separate for the first time, and real social power rests in the economy rather than the state.[27] The most crucial decisions affecting us all are made by capitalists who were never elected. Wood contrasts democracy in its original meaning as it existed in Athens in the third century BC with democracy as it was re-conceived in the last couple of centuries, particularly in the United States. Although Athens is credited as the birthplace of democracy in standard Western accounts, contemporary

---

26 Marx and Engels famously argued that political power reflects economic power, hence, governments in capitalist societies were no more than "executive committees of the bourgeoisie."

27 Ellen Meiksins Wood, *Peasant-Citizen and Slave: The Foundations of Athenian Democracy* (London: Verso, 1988), and "The Demos Versus 'We, the People': from Ancient to Modern Conceptions of Citizenship," in Wood, *Democracy Against Capitalism*, 204–37. C. B. Macpherson focuses on how the system of political parties prevented universal suffrage from resulting in the domination by the numerically more numerous working class, as opponents of universal suffrage had feared. See *The Life and Times of Liberal Democracy* (Oxford University Press, 1978), 64ff.

sensitivity to the importance of slavery and the domination of women in Athens has resulted in less attention being paid to the unique character of its democracy. Wood argues that its peasant citizens, based in the deme (village), were a social formation never seen before or since. Democracy – rule by the people – was understood by all to be a constitution in which, as Aristotle put it, "'the free-born and poor control the government – being at the same time a majority'" as distinct from oligarchy, in which "'the rich and better-born control the government – being at the same time a minority.'"[28] That peasants and shoemakers should have more political influence than the rich, who had the leisure to contemplate goodness and engage in politics, was anathema to thinkers like Plato and Aristotle who were explicitly and unapologetically anti-democratic. With the demise of Athens, democracy disappeared from the historical stage for over two thousand years.

In the early days of capitalism it was still possible to echo publicly Plato's sentiment that people without property who worked with their hands were unfit to be full citizens. However, this became increasingly difficult, especially in the founding days of the United States with its politically active citizenry, its experience of being a colony, and of fighting a revolution against the British crown. The constitutional debates carried out in the *Federalist Papers* reveal how fearful the Founding Fathers were of Athenian-style democracy, which they equated with mob rule, and how they advocated instead a republic modeled on Rome. But given the political climate of the time, "they had to reject the ancient democracy not in the name of an opposing ideal, not in the name of oligarchy, but in the name of democracy itself." Although the Federalists had contrasted democracy to their preferred model of the Roman republic, they ended up christening their model "representative democracy," a novel conception Wood describes as, "the *populus* or *demos* with rights of citizenship but governed by an aristocracy."[29] (It goes without saying

28 Aristotle, *Politics 1290b*, quoted in Wood, *Democracy Against Capitalism*, 220.
29 Wood, *Democracy Against Capitalism*, 224–25.

that this aristocracy was understood to be exclusively white and male.)

It is important to see that the issue is not simply one of size, nor of representation as such. Some form of representative system would likely be required with a large population, but a representative system need not be opposed to democracy in its original literal sense. The two could be combined (especially in the days of the Internet). Imagine a representative system of government in which (1) the representatives earned the average of those they represented and (2) they were subject to immediate recall. Just these features were part of the Paris Commune of 1870, which Marx called the first workers' government.[30] But the motivation of the Founders and hence their particular conception of that representation was opposite to that of the Communards. As Madison opined in *Federalist No. 10*, the advantages of an extensive representative system were that the views of a great many ordinary men would have to go through a small "medium of a chosen body of citizens," and Hamilton, in *Federalist No. 35*, echoing Plato on the unsuitability of mechanics and such for political rule, considered "merchants ... the natural representatives of all these classes of the community."[31] Today, the general understanding of democracy around the globe as it developed from this foundation is even further from its original literal meaning of rule by the people and instead has become associated with the ideas and institutions of limited government. The role of ordinary people is a passive one, to enjoy its benefits simply as independent individuals. So while the political freedoms of limited government are certainly very important, just how much actual freedom and power they give to people depends on the social structure of which they are part. In capitalist democracies, where political democracy is compatible with the rule of the rich, their value is distinctly limited.

30 Karl Marx, *The Civil War in France*, in Tucker (ed.), *Marx–Engels Reader*. These were also features of the workers' councils that sprang up during the Russian Revolution and the Hungarian Revolt of 1956.
31 Wood, *Democracy Against Capitalism*, 215–16.

Political freedom is also much less than is touted. That there was no freedom of speech in the Soviet Union was transparent; anyone who criticized the official government line, for example, who described the Soviet presence in Afghanistan during the 1980s as an "invasion," was arrested or sent to a mental institution. In the United States we are free to criticize government policy without fear of these consequences. Yet as Noam Chomsky has documented, it is a striking fact that during the Vietnam War the word "invasion" was not used by the mainstream media. Journalists learn to censor themselves. Those who take a more radical perspective are effectively marginalized.[32] A clear example from academia is the economics profession in the United States where critics of the reigning free market ideology are found in only a handful of universities. And note that these criticisms come *from within a framework supportive of capitalism*; more radical perspectives that challenge the system of capitalism are simply beyond the pale of what is considered rational discussion.[33] The domination of the political sphere by business is clear in the current discussions – or nondiscussion – of health care reform. Despite polls showing that a clear majority of physicians, nurses, and the general public favor a single payer plan (also known as improved Medicare for all), the Senate Finance Committee discussing the issue ruled it "off the table." (The committee Chair, Senator Max Baucus, is one of the largest recipients of donations from pharmaceutical companies.) When physicians and other advocates stood up at a hearing to ask why it was off the table, they were removed by Capitol police.[34] It is not only the dependence of politicians on campaign donations by which business interests exercise their domination of politics. In the age of agile, mobile capital, liberal politicians throughout the country

---

32 Edward S. Herman and Noam Chomsky, *Manufacturing Consent: The Political Economy of the Mass Media* (New York: Pantheon, 2002); Robert McChesney, *Rich Media, Poor Democracy: Communication Politics in Dubious Times* (Champaign, IL: University of Illinois Press, 1999).

33 Cohen, "Ivory Tower Unswayed by Crashing Economy," C1.

34 www.Common Dreams.org, accessed May 6, 2009.

have dropped their support for public social programs for fear of losing business abroad.

Our discussion above of the limitations of democracy within capitalism brings out a crucial aspect of freedom that is omitted from most discussions of freedom that focus exclusively on the freedom of individuals. Individualism is completely appropriate in the context of the metaphysical question of whether or not human beings have free will. It is also a crucial aspect of the social political question of whether a society provides freedom for its people. It is not, however, the whole story. The analysis of the concept of freedom that I will offer below is applicable both to individuals and to groups. For individuals have, or lack, freedom not only *as individuals*, but *as members of collectivities*. Therefore, the fact that in capitalism there is no economic democracy, that is, working-class people do not get to decide directly where society's resources should be invested, nor do they decide it indirectly via the political process since government is dominated by the rich, entails that the majority in capitalism lack freedom in this crucial respect.[35] Since women tend to be clustered at the bottom of the economic ladder, this is especially true of them; and women higher up the ladder are still underrepresented relative to men of their class in the centers of economic and political power. (Further implications of the limits of the individualistic model of freedom prevalent in capitalism will be explored at a later point.)

Let us turn now to freedom in a general and abstract sense. Some supporters of capitalism, like economists Friedrich Hayek and Milton Friedman and philosopher Robert Nozick, argue that the more pure (free market) a capitalist society is, that is, the less government is involved in the economy, the more free it is *overall*, not only from a political point of view. Though conceding that great inequalities exist, such theorists claim that capitalism is

---

35 While some writers talk of personal autonomy versus political autonomy, this is not exhaustive, as the economy is rendered invisible, perceived as natural background conditions. Other writers use the terms civic freedom or democratic freedom, but these do not clearly bring in the economy either.

characterized by equality of opportunity, rather than results, and that freedom has a higher value than equality. As already discussed, this perspective has been very influential in the last few decades in the United States. But this is not the only view among supporters of capitalism. Others argue that fewer inequalities would make for a more ideal form of capitalism, defending this position on various grounds: the greater economic and social stability of such a society, the greater happiness and/or freedom for the majority or in terms of its greater justice. In the next section we will examine these claims and consider their relevance to the question of whether capitalism is good for women.[36]

Freedom, private property, and self-ownership

As discussed, common to all definitions of capitalism is that the bulk of the means of production is privately owned. Those who own are a small minority of the population, while the majority of people own nothing. Radical critics of capitalism contend that this inequality of property entails lack of power and freedom for the majority and allows the former to live off the labor of the latter.[37] Defenders of capitalism leave vague the question of how numerous are the owners of the means of production, seeing it as not essential to the definition of capitalism, but many theorists insist that individuals in capitalist societies do all own something,

---

36 I focus more on Nozick in this section since he rests his case entirely on freedom, while Hayek and Friedman and indeed the majority of so-called libertarians mix in utilitarian considerations which Nozick explicitly eschews. I am saving the empirical issues for the "In reality" section.

37 In *The Communist Manifesto* Marx and Engels say:

You are horrified at our intending to do away with private property. But ... private property is already done away with for nine-tenths of the population; its existence for the few is solely due to its non-existence in the hands of those nine-tenths. You reproach us, therefore, with intending to do away with a form of property, the necessary condition for whose existence is the non-existence of any property for the immense majority of society. (*The Communist Manifesto*, in Tucker (ed.), *Marx–Engels Reader*, 486)

This inequality of property and power is the basis for the twin evils of capitalism as they see it: exploitation and alienation, the precise analysis of which is not necessary here.

viz. themselves.[38] And they see this as the foundation of freedom. The notion of "propriety in one's person," or self-ownership, is very old and has resonance not only among defenders of capitalism but among many of its critics, including feminists, so it is worth pausing to explore just what it means, how it connects to freedom, and whether it should be part of any theory committed to a better society, particularly one that is better for women.

Self-ownership: history and import of the concept

Do individuals own themselves and what exactly does this mean? The concept is a complicated and contested one with an interesting and illuminating history. To appreciate its connections to private property, and the debates surrounding it then and now, a historical detour is warranted. The concept of "self-propriety" was first articulated in the seventeenth century in England; a revolutionary period when feudalism was giving way to capitalism,[39] common land was being enclosed thereby depriving ordinary people of their hereditary rights to the commons, small property owners were contending with the rising capitalists, and wage labor was becoming the dominant form of labor as they lost all other means of subsistence.[40] King Charles I had his head cut off for raising taxes for military ventures without the approval of Parliament. The slave trade was thriving. Moderates and radicals were united in the struggle against the monarchists, but there were deep differences between them and differences among the radicals as well. Those who called themselves the True Levellers,

---

38 Robert Nozick, *Anarchy, State, and Utopia* (New York: Basic Books, 1974); Philippe Van Parijs, *Real Freedom for All: What if Anything can Justify Capitalism?* (Oxford: Clarendon Press, 1995), 3.

39 This transition is called "primitive accumulation" by Marx, referring to the process by which the necessary conditions of capitalism were established: on the one hand there must be "the owners of money ... and on the other hand, free laborers ... free in a double sense: legally free and free of any means of production of their own; primitive accumulation is ... nothing else but the historical process of divorcing the producer from the means of production." *Capital: Vol. I,* in Tucker (ed.), *Marx–Engels Reader,* 432.

40 See Karl Polanyi, *The Great Transformation* (Boston, MA: Beacon Press, 1957).

also known as the Diggers,[41] were the most radical of the radicals. They supported universal male suffrage and protested not only against tyrannical laws but also against private property, seeing the enclosure movement (the forcible privatization of what had been common land) as theft. As their leader, Gerrard Winstanley, proclaimed: "In the beginning of time, the great creator Reason made the Earth to be a common treasury, to preserve beasts, birds, fishes and man, the lord that was to govern this creation … And the reason is this, every single man, male and female, is a perfect creature of himself, and the same spirit that made the globe dwells in man to govern the globe."[42] It is not clear whether their idea that each individual was "a perfect creature of himself" should be expressed in terms of self-ownership, but, if so, it had a radically different meaning from the way others understood the concept. For the Diggers believed that no one had the right to own another person's labor, "neither take hire nor give hire."[43] The natural rights they proclaimed were both individual and communal; each individual had a right to partake from this common treasury, but not to exclude others. Enclosure of land into private property by some individuals made everyone else "servants and slaves" they said, proclaiming that "those that buy and sell land, and are landlords, have got it either by oppression or murder or theft";[44] hence, private property has no moral validity. True liberty was incompatible with private property; until the earth is "free and common for all, to work together and eat together,"[45] they proclaimed, England would not be a free land.[46]

41 They were called the Diggers because in 1649 they undertook to peaceably "dig up, manure and sow corn upon George Hill in Surrey" (and other commons land around the country) on which they intended to work and live collectively. Similar actions have been undertaken in recent years by landless peasant movements in Latin America, particularly the Landless Peasants Movement (MST) in Brazil.

42 Gerrard Winstanley, *Winstanley: "The Law of Freedom" and Other Writings*, Christopher Hill (ed.) (Harmondsworth: Penguin Classics, 1973), 77.

43 *Winstanley: "The Law of Freedom,"* 89.

44 *Winstanley: "The Law of Freedom,"* 85.

45 *Winstanley: "The Law of Freedom,"* 89.

46 The best history of the radical ideas and movements of this period is Christopher Hill's *The World Turned Upside Down* (Harmondsworth: Penguin

The more moderate and better known radicals of the period were the Levellers, such as Richard Overton, who wrote *An Arrow Against All Tyrants* in 1646 from prison. He began by saying "To every individuall in nature, is given an individuall property by nature, not to be invaded or usurped by any: for every one as he is himself, so he hath a selfe propriety, else he could not be himself … No man hath power over my rights and liberties, and I over no man's." He went on to say, "Every man by nature being a King, Priest and Prophet in his owne naturall circuite and compasse, whereof no second may partake, but by deputation, commission, and *free consent*" (my emphasis).[47] The gender ambiguity in the above is clarified by Leveller leader John Lilbourne's statement, "Every particular and individual man and woman that ever breathed … are and were by nature equal and alike in power, dignity, authority and majesty."[48] The Levellers supported a broader franchise than the moderates, but far from universal male suffrage. Unlike the Diggers, they took "self-propriety" to entail a right to private (not merely personal) property as essential to freedom, and they accepted wage labor. But the property they supported was a limited property and they railed against the "greedy usurpers" who wanted more. Thus, the concept of self-propriety was used by the radicals to express a belief in people's natural freedom and natural right against tyranny, though the Levellers and the Diggers disagreed as to whether this included an individual right to (limited) private property.

The concepts of self-propriety and legitimate rule requiring free consent were picked up – appropriated, one could say – by the social contract theorists. Thomas Hobbes used the premise to

---

Classics, 1972). Peter Linebaugh's *The Magna Carta Manifesto* (Berkeley, CA: University of California Press, 2008) traces the history of struggles for rights to the commons from the thirteenth to the twenty-first century, making a powerful case that economic rights are essential to political freedom.

47 *The Levellers in the English Revolution*, G. E. Aylmer (ed.) (London: Thames & Hudson, 1975), 68f.

48 Elizabeth Potter, "Locke's Epistemology and Women's Struggles," in Bat-Ami Bar On (ed.), *Modern Engendering: Critical Feminist Readings in Modern Western Philosophy* (Albany: SUNY Press, 1994), 31.

argue in *Leviathan* in favor of an absolute form of government, and John Locke's *Second Treatise of Government* of 1690 offered a defense of limited government based on a right to unlimited private property. Locke's *Treatise* is usually seen as a reply to Robert Filmer, who defended absolute monarchy, and to Thomas Hobbes.[49] But other scholars of the period have argued persuasively that Locke is equally or primarily concerned with responding to the radicals, indeed, that the radicals set the terms of the debate.[50] I focus on Locke because his theory is foundational for our system of limited government resting on the right to unlimited property.[51]

As a social contract theorist Locke sets out to justify his preferred form of government by arguing that it would arise from agreement (contract) among free, equal, and rational individuals in a state of nature. His theory is particularly powerful in that it purports to demonstrate that free, equal, and rational people would *freely consent to loss of freedom and equality*. In his lengthy chapter on property, Locke makes some momentous moves: from a right to common property to a right to limited property to a right to unlimited private property – which property is then taken as a reason and as a basis for a government. Until there are large accumulations of wealth, he says, there is no need of government.[52] Starting from the premise (almost word for word from radical texts) that God has given the Earth, its fruits and its beasts, to humankind in common, he remarks that

---

49 Despite Hobbes' enduring philosophical importance, scholars have shown that Filmer, an influential figure at the time, is the more likely target of Locke's criticism of absolute government. Locke's *First Treatise* is devoted to refuting Filmer's defense of absolute monarchy on biblical grounds, and in the opening chapter of *The Second* he pointedly distinguishes political power from patriarchal power which Filmer conflates.

50 Ellen Meiksins Wood and Neal Wood, *A Trumpet of Sedition* (New York University Press, 1997); Hill, *The World Turned Upside Down*; C. B. Macpherson, *The Political Theory of Possessive Individualism* (Oxford University Press, 1964).

51 Some, for example, Carole Pateman, have argued that this is simply because Hobbes' theory is more naked in its analysis of the power relations inherent in a market system.

52 "The equality of a simple poor way of living, confining their desires within the narrow bounds of each man's small property, made few controversies,

some have wondered how then private property could be justified. In response, he first makes the valid point that individuals
must be able to appropriate some of it for their own use or they
would starve. Furthermore, he writes: "every man has a *property* in his own person; this nobody has any right to but himself.
The *labor* of his body, and the *work* of his hands, we may say, are
properly his. Whatsoever then he removes out of the state that
nature hath provided, and left it in, he hath mixed his labor with,
and joined to it something that is his own, and thereby makes
it his *property*." But he adds the explicit limit that there must be
"enough, and as good, left in common for others,"[53] on top of
what would appear to be the implicit limit in the "mixing one's
labor principle" (how much, after all, can one mix one's labor
with?). He goes on to state an additional limit to the right of individual property that it must be put to some use before it spoils.

Thus far then, Locke has justified a right to very limited private
property. But these limits disappear one by one as he progresses
through the chapter. Elaborating on the idea that an individual
has a right to what he has mixed his labor with, Locke says,
"Thus the grass my horse has bit; the turfs my servant has cut;
and the ore I have digged in any place, where I have a right to
them in common with others, become my *property* ... the labor
that was mine, *fixed* my *property* in them." So "he" has as much
right to the product of his servant's labor, as to that of his own
labor or his horse's. But why doesn't the servant have the right to
the product of his own labor, a right Locke has just enunciated?
The only answer is that Locke understands the premise that each
person has a property in his person and therefore in his labor
to entail a right to sell that property. The person who buys the
labor then has a right to the product of that labor ("my" servant,
"my" horse, "my" turf). Here Locke simply assumes that the
"property" in one's person should be conceived of as an alienable

and so no need of many laws to decide them, or variety of officers to superin-
tend the process, or look after the execution of justice, where there were but
few trespasses, and few offenders." John Locke, *Second Treatise of Government*,
C. B Macpherson (ed.). (Indianapolis, IN: Hackett Publishing, 1980), 57.
53 Locke, *Second Treatise of Government*, 19.

commodity. This assumption *transforms ownership to nonownership for those who sell their labor*. As wage labor was becoming dominant, and the more radical Levellers also accepted wage labor, he could presume that his readers would share this assumption. In this passage we can also see a move from a right to property based on labor to a right to property based on the productive *use* of labor by its owner.[54] Since there is no limit to how many "servants" (the seventeenth-century term for wage earner) one can employ, the right to wage labor erases, on the theoretical level, one implicit limit to the right to private property, and in actual history, leads to the concentration of property.

The "no spoilage" limit disappears from Locke's justification of property because of what he calls the "tacit" and voluntary agreement to introduce money, which does not spoil. "And as different degrees of industry were apt to give men possessions in different proportions, so this *invention of money* gave them the opportunity to continue and enlarge them."[55] Thus, although Locke stated at the beginning of the *Treatise* that men (sic.) are naturally equal, now he contends that natural differences in "industry" will result in unequal property. (Quite different from the Diggers' story of murder and theft as its origin![56]) And this allegedly all happens by consent. The very limited private property which Locke has justified early in the chapter has become considerably less limited. It is not yet unlimited, though, as long as "there must be enough and as good left in common for others."

While this last limit on the right to private property is never explicitly rejected, it disappears. Locke seems to believe it remains in spirit, however, as can be adduced from his claim that:

---

54 Ellen Meiksins Wood, "the activity of labour and all its attendant virtues are attributes of the master ... It is a short step from here to the eclipse of labour altogether by the economic activity of the capitalist," *Democracy Against Capitalism*, 157–58.

55 Locke, *Second Treatise of Government*, 29.

56 Karl Marx agreed, referring to accounts like Locke's as "childish idylls ... In actual history it is notorious that conquest, enslavement, robbery, murder, briefly force, play the great part." *Capital: Vol. I*, in Tucker (ed.), *Marx–Engels Reader*, 432.

he who appropriates land to himself by his labor, does not lessen, but increase the common stock of mankind: for the provisions serving to the support of human life, produced by one acre of inclosed and cultivated land, are (to speak much within compass) ten times more than those which are yielded by one acre of land of an equal richness lying waste in common. And therefore he that incloses land, and has a greater plenty of conveniences of life from ten acres, than he could have from an hundred left in nature, may truly be said to give ninety acres to mankind.[57]

Thus. starting from a premise of *self-ownership*, Locke's theory justifies a right *to unlimited private property*. Purely in a state of nature some people would acquire large accumulations of property which would then generate the need for a government to protect it. This is the foundation for the kind of limited government that he defends. Since the purpose of government, as he says repeatedly, is the protection of property, it would be a contradiction to suppose that those with property had not explicitly consented to government. And if the government fails to fulfill its side of the contract, citizens have a right to revolt. This is the politically liberatory aspect of his philosophy which is rightly celebrated.

On the other hand, those without property cannot be said to have *explicitly* consented to government, Locke says, but only *tacitly*, like visitors from foreign countries, and hence they are not to be full citizens of civil society.[58] Then what is left in his theory, one might ask, of the original freedom of the majority?

---

57 Locke, *Second Treatise of Government*, 23–24.
58 Section 119–22. In some of his other writings, Locke is more explicit in his view that those without property do not have the requisite rationality for this responsibility, though it is unclear whether he thinks this is by nature or due to the circumstances of their lives. He proposes that any unemployed person (female or male) without property over the age of three years of age (!) should be made to work. C. B. Macpherson, *The Political Theory of Possessive Individualism: Hobbes to Locke* (Oxford University Press, 1962), 222–38; Nancy Hirschmann has a thorough discussion of this issue in *Gender, Class and Freedom in Modern Political Theory* (Princeton University Press, 2008), 80–106.

The answer lies in his assumption that those who make the laws do so for everyone's best interests. The majority *subject to law* but *without the right to make law* can still be said to be free, in his view, since "that ill deserves the name of confinement which hedges us in only from bogs and precipices."[59] A happy conclusion for all, in Locke's eyes, but far from freedom as most of us would understand it.

It should be pointed out that Locke's rationale for abandoning his "enough and as good left in common for others" limit on the right to private property functioned as an important justification for taking the land of Native Americans and the Aborigines of Australia and that, moreover, it does not actually satisfy his condition. First, he assumes, as do contemporary defenders of capitalism, that the only alternative to private property is land left to waste in common, whereas common land may be developed as productively as enclosed and private land. Second, greater productivity does not automatically mean that people will have their needs met, as defenders of capitalism imply in their focus on the productivity of the capitalist system. The crucial question is whether they have *access* to what is produced – and this depends on the system of property and rights in place. As Amartya Sen has pointed out, millions of people have died in famines not because there was not enough food; the problem was that they had neither land to produce the food themselves nor the money they needed to buy it in a market system.[60] This point is particularly apparent today as the United Nations reports that the number of people who are hungry has reached 1 billion,[61] and we see food riots around the world caused *not by lack of food* but because of loss of access to land and because of price increases. This is not the result of less food or more hungry mouths coming onto the market, but of the free market policies of recent decades which imposed austerity measures and pushed technology that

59 Section 57.
60 Amartya Sen, *Poverty and Famines* (Oxford: Clarendon Press, 1981) and other writings.
61 Geoffrey Lean, "Year of the Hungry: 1,000,000,000 Afflicted," *The Independent*, December 28, 2008.

was biased against small farmers.[62] Hunger worldwide has been exacerbated recently by the desire of the wealthy of the world to burn for fuel what could be food.

Where do women fit into this story? What did the debates about property in early capitalism imply with respect to women and their rights and interests? And what does this suggest about capitalism and women's interests? Though I have been using the gender neutral language typical of political theory, it would be ahistorical to assume that all our writers intended their principles to apply universally. The Levellers did advocate equal civil liberties for everyone regardless of sex, or wealth, or employment status, a very radical position at the time, and Leveller women were very active as preachers, traders, petitioners, and protestors to Parliament.[63] Nevertheless, the Levellers did not demand political rights for women for the same reason that they did not include servants or those accepting charity in the franchise. Wives' dependence on their husbands, servants' dependence on their masters (employers), and the dependence on charity of the impoverished caused each group to lose the natural freedom Levellers believed all human beings had by birth. Their political rights were presumed to be transferred to their husbands or masters.[64] The Diggers supported universal male suffrage, the most radical position at the time, not to be realized

---

62 Bio-technical innovations applied to agriculture in the developing world in the 1960s were dubbed the "Green Revolution" and had the explicit aim of forestalling a "Red Revolution" as the head of USAID explained. See John Perkins, *Geopolitics and the Green Revolution: Wheat, Genes and the Cold War* (New York: Oxford University Press, 1997). Though output grew during this period, so did hunger (with the exception of China); while it exported food in the 1960s, Africa now imports 25 percent of its food. See Raj Patel, *Stuffed and Starved* (Brooklyn, NY: Melville House Publishing, 2008) and Eric Holt-Gimenez, Raj Patel, and Annie Shattuck, *Food Rebellions! Crisis and the Hunger for Justice* (Oakland, CA: Food First Books, 2009); Raj Patel, Eric Holt-Gimenez, and Annie Shattuck, "Ending Africa's Hunger," *The Nation*, September 21, 2009; Walden Bello, *The Food Wars* (London: Verso, 2009).

63 Patricia Higgins, "The Reactions of Women, with Special Reference to Women Petitioners," in B. Manning (ed.), *Politics, Religion and the English Civil War* (New York: St Martin's Press, 1973).

64 Macpherson, *The Life and Times of Liberal Democracy*, 143–46, 296.

for more than three centuries, but they did not think to extend it to women, though it is not clear why since they expressly said that male and female were "perfect creatures of himself" with the capacity of Reason. As for Locke, one can infer that women were not included among the individuals who are said to be naturally equal. For he says that in marriage "the last determination, i.e. the rule … naturally falls to the man's share, as *the abler and the stronger.*"[65] Despite this, he contends that "the conjugal society [as he calls marriage], is made *by a voluntary compact between man and woman*"[66] which exists in a state of nature. But there is an inconsistency here that rests on the meaning of freedom. If women were equal to men and could acquire property, why would they agree to become subordinate to a man and lose all rights to property, even what they had before marriage? On the other hand, if they are not equal and need the support and protection of a man, is the conjugal contract really based on their voluntary consent? Unlike Hobbes, Locke distinguishes between agreement based on superior force and genuine consent, so it is hard to see how the "conjugal contract" between unequals could be said to be an example of genuine consent. Thus, in Locke's story all women, like landless men, freely agree to unfreedom, both in an imagined state of nature and in civil society.

An interesting alternative perspective on women's rights in marriage is provided by Locke's contemporary, Mary Astell, who pointed out his inconsistency: "if Absolute Sovereignty be not necessary in a State, how comes it to be so in a Family? Or if in a Family why not in a State? … If all Men are born free, how is it that all Women are born slaves?"[67] Today we would infer from her acute rhetorical question that absolute sovereignty is not justified either in the family or the state but, interestingly, Astell eliminated Locke's inconsistency in the opposite direction. Combining

65 Macpherson, *The Life and Times of Liberal Democracy*, 44.
66 Macpherson, *The Life and Times of Liberal Democracy*, 43.
67 Mary Astell, "Some Reflections Upon Marriage," in *Women and Men Political Theorists: Enlightened Conversations*, Kristin Waters (ed.) (Malden, MA: Blackwell, 2000), 48.

radical feminism with religious and political conservatism, she argued that there was no right to rebel in either case; absolute monarchy was founded on God's will and if a woman chose to marry then she chose to obey her husband even if he was stupid and cruel (analogously, she says, if someone agrees to work for a pig farmer, then they are obliged to shovel pig manure). Her radical feminism is reflected in her low opinion of most men and her consequent advice to women not to marry but instead to seek a community of like-minded women. Thus, both in its more conservative and more liberal versions, classical liberal theory defended a property form and marriage based on that form that necessarily put limits on women's rights and freedom. As we will see, this has changed in some respects and not in others. Would it be possible to rewrite his story to allow for equality between men and women as today's liberal feminists would like to do? No, for as Lorenne Clark explains, "One of Locke's major objectives was to provide the theoretical basis for the absolute right of the male to pass his property to his rightful heirs."[68]

Returning to the notions of self-ownership and freedom, we can see how dramatically different Locke's conception was from that of the Diggers and Levellers. The specific kind of freedom associated with capitalism came into existence and was theorized in the context of a struggle against broader more radical visions of freedom. Against these visions, Locke promotes a *limited* kind of freedom – freedom from arbitrary rule by a monarch – for a *limited* class of individuals – large landowners – and *subordination for the majority in the name of freedom*. All women are among the subordinated majority. The discrepancy between the words and the reality behind Locke's theory is revealed even more blatantly by his involvement in the slave trade, which played so prominent a part

68 Lorenne M. G. Clark, "Women and Locke: Who Owns the Apples in the Garden of Eden?," in Clark and Lynda Lange (eds.), *The Sexism of Social and Political Philosophy* (University of Toronto Press, 1979), 27. The father's right to pass his property to *whomever he wished* persisted in English law until 1939. See also Carole Pateman, *The Sexual Contract* (Stanford University Press, 1988) for a powerful argument that the social contract is a sexual contract and Hirschmann, *Gender, Class, and Freedom in Modern Political Theory*.

in the rise of capitalism.[69] Although there was no chance in that historical period for the radical democratic forces to prevail, their alternative visions make clear the limitations of Locke's view of freedom, and are especially important today when it is possible – even necessary, I will argue – to realize the most radical visions.

Self-ownership: the contemporary debates

Whatever its historical genesis, is the notion of self-ownership a useful one for liberatory purposes? What sort of conception of a person is implicit in the notion – and is it even coherent? Certainly ownership of self or body, and by extension one's labor, is rather different from owning other things. I can lose, sell, or destroy my house, my car, or my stocks without losing, selling, or destroying myself or my body. If what I own is small enough, I can forget it on the bus! The point is that owner and owned are distinct. On the other hand, if it even makes sense to say you lose your body or your self, then you are lost too. If you destroy your self or body totally, you are destroyed along with it. If, on the other hand, you *sell* your body or your labor, there is still you – but you go with it. What's done to it is done to you; if it is damaged you are damaged. And it is the new owner who gains its use value, all its creative potentials, while the seller necessarily loses them. In this unique and peculiar case where owner and owned are one and the same, the ownership conception seems to many critics to introduce a radical split within the person. Alienability, arguably, implies alienation, a separation from self. On the other hand, however, critics might say that this split is only metaphoric. In reality if one sells one's labor one is selling oneself, even if the sale is subject to temporal and other

---

69 Combining philosophical argumentation and historical documentation, Charles Mills demonstrates that social contract theory is also a theory of racial contract: *The Racial Contract* (Ithaca, NY: Cornell University Press, 1997). Karl Marx writes of the transition of feudalism to capitalism, "the veiled slavery of the wage workers in Europe needed, for its pedestal, slavery pure and simple in the new world," *Capital: Vol. I*, in Tucker (ed.), *Marx–Engels Reader*, 760; Eric Williams gives a detailed account of this relationship in *Capitalism and Slavery* (New York: Capricorn, 1966).

restrictions. It is these differences between self-ownership and ordinary ownership and the moral concerns that accompany the differences that lead many to put limits on it, or to conceive it in a radically different way from the Lockean conception – or to reject the notion entirely.

Contemporary political philosophers in the liberal and analytic tradition, including some critics of capitalism sympathetic to Marxism, are divided over the idea that each person has property in her or his person and what moral and political conclusions would follow if they do. Feminists have engaged in similar debates regarding the meaning, utility, and implications of the idea of self-ownership, seeing the question as an especially salient one for women. Though the debates are quite parallel, it is striking how little interchange there is between the two. Robert Nozick, like Locke, made self-ownership a key premise of his philosophy believing that it justified a right to unlimited private property even if, unlike Locke, this meant that others would starve. While Nozick is an extreme economic conservative, some liberal and left philosophers also accept the premise of self-ownership, but they interpret it more weakly or in other ways try to forestall Nozick's extreme conclusion. There has been much discussion of whether this is possible,[70] and whether Marx accepted the premise of self-ownership.[71] Feminists, naturally, have debated the question with specific reference to its implications for women. Many believe the notion of each individual having property in her or his person is critically important for women because they see it as the basis of each individual woman's rights over her body.[72] Thus, they see it as the necessary ground for the right to free expression of sexuality and the right to abortion. Jennifer

70 G. A. Cohen, *Self-Ownership, Freedom and Equality* (Cambridge University Press, 1995); Van Parijs, *Real Freedom for All*; Richard J. Arneson, "Lockean Self-Ownership: Towards a Demolition," *Political Studies* XXXIX (1991): 36–54.

71 Paul Warren, "Self-Ownership, Reciprocity, and Exploitation, or Why Marxists Shouldn't Be Afraid of Robert Nozick," *Canadian Journal of Philosophy* 24 (1994): 33–56; Nancy Holmstrom, "Review of *Self-Ownership, Freedom and Equality*," *Philosophical Review* 106 (October 1997): 583–86.

72 Donna Dickensen supports contract theory for feminists in *Property, Women and Politics* (New Brunswick, NJ: Rutgers University Press, 1997); Jennifer

Church, for example, treats a woman's rights over her body as immediately following from the "fundamental fact that it is hers," which she takes to be equivalent to saying that she owns her body or that she has property in her body. Some liberal feminists believe that self-ownership also entails a right to sell the use of one's body for sexual services or for procreation,[73] on the grounds that since one owns it, one should be able to do with it what one likes. To deny this, they contend, would be to deny the individual her sexual autonomy. Most feminists disagree with this inference; they believe that even though one owns one's body, it is not like all other property and in particular should not be sold.[74] (Similar arguments occur regarding whether we should have the right to sell our bodily organs.) Margaret Jane Radin, a noted legal theorist of property, argues that certain things should not be available for sale within a market system. After considering prostitution, baby-selling, and commercial surrogacy, she concludes that because of their importance for personhood, the latter two should not be permitted. While sympathetic to the view that sexual services should not be commodities either, she argues that in our present world of economic and gender inequality, to ban prostitution would be worse for poor women than to allow it. However, she advocates various legal restrictions to reduce its inherent exploitation.

On the other side of this debate, Carole Pateman[75] is strongly critical of the very concept of self-ownership, denouncing it as

Church, "Ownership and the Body," in Diana Tietjens Meyers (ed.), *Feminists Rethink the Self* (Boulder, CO: Westview, 1997).

73 Janet Radcliffe Richards, *The Sceptical Feminist: A Philosophical Inquiry* (Harmondsworth: Penguin, 1980); Karen Lehrman, *The Lipstick Proviso: Women, Sex and Power in the Real World* (New York: Doubleday, 1997).

74 Margaret Jane Radin, "Market Inalienability," *Harvard Law Review* 100 (1987): 1849–937; Church, "Ownership and the Body." Elizabeth Anderson argues that neither sexual services nor women's (procreative) labor are appropriately thought of as economic goods because to do so would violate other human goods: "The Ethical Limitations of the Market," *Economics and Philosophy* 6 (1990): 179–205; "Is Women's Labor a Commodity?," *Philosophy and Public Affairs* 19 (Winter, 1990): 71–92.

75 Carole Pateman, *The Sexual Contract*. See Carole Pateman and Charles Mills, *Contract and Domination* (Cambridge: Polity, 2007) for further discussion and debate over the utility of contract theory for liberatory purposes.

inherently masculine, individualistic, and capitalist. Selves and bodies are inseparable and bodies are sexually differentiated. Thus, a woman cannot simply sell her body, or sexual or pro-creative "services," without also selling her self. Pateman makes the same point about the sale of labor power, a concept she calls a political fiction. However, she contends that prostitution is dif-ferent from and worse than wage labor, even poorly paid and subordinate forms, in that ordinary labor can be replaced by machines, but in prostitution what the customer buys is the dir-ect use of *a woman* for sexual purposes. In commercial surrogacy, a woman conceives, carries, and bears a child but has contracted to give it to the man whose semen has been implanted in her. To call her the "surrogate" mother and to give all rights over the child – who has for nine months literally been a part of her-self, only gradually becoming an "other" being – to the father, reveals fully the classical patriarchal and capitalist nature of this arrangement. To make a part of a woman's body, her uterus, and her labor, into property that a man can contract to buy and then claim the product of these, the baby, as properly his is the ultim-ate form of exploitation and alienation. In sum, Pateman believes it is deeply mistaken for feminists to try to use the language of ownership and contract for their ends, as the "power and genius of contract ... proclaims that a contract of subordination is (sex-ual) freedom."[76]

Socialist feminist Rosalind Petchesky has a distinct and inter-esting position. While agreeing that self-ownership is very important for women, and does not entail the right to sell one's body, she casts her position in a more general discussion of the many meanings of property and ownership. Arguing that both sides to the feminist debate about self-ownership accept a nar-row Lockean interpretation, she seeks to restore the historically earlier understandings of the concept found in the Diggers and Levellers, as discussed above, and current elsewhere around the world. She cites examples of people claiming their "self-propriety"

---

76 Pateman, *The Sexual Contract*, 200. She expands her critique to the "global racial–sexual contract" in Pateman and Mills.

to assert their rights against state harassment and their freedom to be sexual as far back as the seventeenth century. This assertion of inalienable personal autonomy was not entirely individualistic, she argues, as many radicals of the time did not make a sharp distinction between self and community. She also cites examples from parts of the world where they use a word translated as "own" which really means "has responsibility for," and which does not imply that one has exclusive rights over, especially not the right to sell. In our own society, too, she notes examples of mixed property forms, of rights and relationships that lie between private and common property such as "coops, condominiums, residents-only parks and beaches, guardianships and foster care."[77]

Given that people of varying political persuasions use the concept of self-ownership, but interpret it so differently and draw such radically different political conclusions from it, self-ownership does not seem to me to be a helpful way of expressing the moral and political ideas that its users intend by it. All want to claim that individuals have some basic moral rights over their bodies. That is, each individual should be free to do what she or he likes (within certain constraints) with her or his body. The debate is over whether these rights include the right to alienate it, that is, to sell it, to profit from it as one can with any commodity in a capitalist system.[78] If one does not accept this implication, it is not clear what is added by saying that one *owns* one's body. The moral questions regarding what rights one has over one's body should

77 Rosalind Pollack Petchesky, "The Body as Property: A Feminist Re-vision," in Faye D. Ginsburg and Rayna Rapp (eds.), *Conceiving the New World Order: The Global Politics of Reproduction* (Berkeley, CA: University of California Press, 1995). Petchesky's attempt to recast this right of individual control to the earlier notions of ownership is particularly tricky since some of these were committed to common property and opposed to private property. She tries to address this by arguing that these thinkers would not have made a sharp distinction between self and community. More needs to be said.

78 One approach to this debate is to distinguish two kinds of ownership: control ownership and income ownership. One can have a right to control something, and to that extent own it, but not necessarily to have a right to dispose of it and make income from it. See John Christman, *The Myth*

be debated on their own without connecting them to the notions of property and ownership. Given the ubiquity of the market system and the dominance of private property, connecting the question of rights to ownership and property tends to pre-judge the moral debate. Granted, there are broader meanings of ownership, as Petchesky argues and I have discussed above, but as the concept has developed, in current usage ownership is *contrasted* to relationships such as responsibility and caretaking that in some cultures are called ownership. For example, we expressly deny that parents "own" their children, even if granting them many rights over their children, and many people concerned about the environment would be sympathetic to Marx's comment that:

> From the standpoint of a higher socio-economic formation [i.e., socialism or communism], the private property of individuals in the earth will appear just as absurd as the private property of one man in other men. Even an entire society, a nation, or all simultaneously existing societies taken together, are not owners of the earth, they are simply its possessors, its beneficiaries, and have to bequeath it in an improved state to succeeding generations.[79]

We should recognize that women have special reasons for claiming a right of control over their bodies, but we do not need to describe this in terms of ownership. While this does not resolve the feminist debates as to whether there are moral or political limits to this right, for example, regarding prostitution or "surrogacy," it separates them from the distracting idea of ownership.[80]

Thus, the contention that in capitalism everyone owns something, viz. themselves, cannot be sustained. Nor can we say that self-ownership is *foundational to* freedom and rights, because they

---

of Ownership: Toward an Egalitarian Theory of Ownership (New York: Oxford University Press, 1994). This distinction was customary historically in property law. Cheyney Ryan argues that ownership involves a "bundle of rights" that do not always go together: see, "Yours, Mine and Ours: Property Rights and Individual Liberty," *Ethics* 87 (1977): 126–41.

79 Marx, *Capital: Vol. III* (New York: International Publishers, 1967), 776.

80 Ann Ferguson pointed out the need for this clarification.

come down to the same thing. The question of whether in capitalist societies each individual owns something, viz. her or his
self or body, is simply the question of whether capitalism provides basic liberties and rights, control over self and body, for
all individuals. *In theory* the answer is yes, though as discussed
above, *in fact* not all capitalist societies do, since not all are politically democratic – and even those that are democratic do not
always grant women control over their bodies. Ireland and Chile,
for example, deny women the right to abortion even in cases of
rape. Throughout history women have been denied their rights,
and have struggled for the freedom to act as they wish. The first
wave women's movement was primarily for the freedom to vote,
but the second wave movement was called the women's "liberation" movement. Given the centrality of freedom to women, we
need to clarify exactly what it means before we can address how
much freedom capitalism offers to women.

Freedom/unfreedom in the abstract

> The words "liberty" and "freedom" are slippery and change
> their meaning over time… one man's liberty can be another
> man's slavery. (Christopher Hill[81])
>
> Security of property! Behold in a few words the definition of
> English liberty! (Mary Wollstonecraft[82])
>
> Freedom is clothes and fire and food for the trampled multi-
> tude. (Percy Bysshe Shelley[83])
>
> I want the same thing that I did thirty years ago when I
> joined the Civil Rights movement and twenty years ago when
> I joined the women's movement, came out, and felt more alive
> than I ever dreamed possible: freedom. (Barbara Smith[84])

So what is freedom exactly? Now that we have detached the
notion of freedom from self-ownership, we need to clarify the

---

81 Christopher Hill, *Liberty Against the Law* (London: Verso, 1996), 243 and 19.
82 Mary Wollstonecraft, *Works*, quoted in Hill, *Liberty Against the Law*, 242.
83 Percy Bysshe Shelley, *The Mask of Anarchy*, quoted in Paul Foot, "Poetry of
    Protest," *Socialist Review* 55 (July–August 1992): 18–20.
84 Barbara Smith, *The Truth That Never Hurts*, quoted in Robin D. G. Kelley,
    Freedom Dreams (Boston, MA: Beacon Press, 2002), 136.

concept. What are we to make of the above very disparate statements about freedom which, as Orlando Patterson has said, is "unchallenged as ... the supreme value of the Western world."[85] Certainly, there are different interpretations of freedom, debated throughout the centuries, which have different implications for our question of whether people are freer in capitalism than in alternative systems. This, therefore, is a political as well as a philosophical debate. (Some conceptions of freedom are so narrow that they would rule out the very question.) Who are the people who are or are not free, and in what respects are they free or unfree? For freedom comes in many *dimensions* and *degrees*, and so does lack of freedom. We need an analysis of the concept of freedom which can illuminate the controversies, how freedom can be different and also the same, as expressed in our quotations above. This is what I shall try to offer here.

Obviously one person can be free and another not, and, indeed, as Christopher Hill points out above, one person's freedom, for example, to own slaves, entails the lack of freedom of others. Just as obviously, we can be free to do one thing and not another. Also, but perhaps less obviously, we can be free to do a particular thing in one respect and not in another. More precisely, to say one is free is to say one is free *from* an obstacle preventing one from doing something; one is unfree *to do* something because an obstacle prevents one from doing it.[86] Thus, one can be free to do something with respect to one obstacle and unfree to do it with respect to another. The obstacles preventing one from doing something may be physical or may involve persons in some significant way. So someone might be free to go into a particular restaurant because no physical obstacle prevents her or him from doing so, but unfree because it is a "whites only"

85 Patterson, *Freedom in the Making of Western Culture*, ix.

86 My account here follows Gerald C. MacCallum Jr., "Negative and Positive Freedom," *Philosophical Review* 76 (1967), 312–34; Gertrude Ezorsky, *Freedom in the Workplace?* (Ithaca, NY: Cornell University Press, 2007); several articles by G. A. Cohen, especially those collected in *History, Labour and Freedom* (Oxford University Press 1988); Jeffrey Reiman, "Exploitation, Force and the Moral Assessment of Capitalism: Thoughts on Roemer and Cohen," *Philosophy and Public Affairs* 16 (Winter 1987): 3–41; David Zimmerman,

restaurant in the segregated South and she or he is not white. The law, backed up by force, is the obstacle to her or him entering the restaurant. The civil rights movement removed this obstacle, thereby expanding the freedom of African Americans. The law then became an obstacle to the restaurant owner's desire to exclude them. Prior to the US Supreme Court's 1973 decision in *Roe* v. *Wade*, which the women's movement was crucial in securing, a woman was not free to get an abortion because the law forbade it. After that she would be free with respect to the law. However, government is not the only source of lack of freedom. A woman might still be unfree to get an abortion if she were poor because the Hyde Amendment of 1977, upheld by the Supreme Court in 1980, denied the use of federal funds for an abortion. In this case, lack of money is the obstacle.[87] Neither the law nor lack of money is what prevents most gays and lesbians from displaying physical affection in public, but rather negative social attitudes which could result in harassment, violence, and even death. The prevalence of violence against women, particularly rape, is an important obstacle to women moving about as freely in their daily lives as men. Their reasonable fear leads them to curtail their actions, and if they do not and something happens, then they are blamed.[88]

"Coercive Wage Offers," *Philosophy and Public Affairs* 10 (1981): 121–45; Nancy Holmstrom, "Free Will and a Marxist Concept of Natural Wants," *Philosophical Forum* 6 (1975): 423–45 and "Firming Up Soft Determinism," *The Personalist* 58 (1977): 39–51. Though the preceding were not written from an explicitly feminist perspective, I am gratified that they accord for the most part with Nancy Hirschmann, *The Subject of Liberty: Toward A Feminist Theory of Freedom* (Princeton University Press, 2003).

87 John Rawls is among those who deny that lack of money is a limitation on freedom, though he says it may affect the "worth" of someone's liberty: *A Theory of Justice*, 204. Philip Pettit, *A Theory of Freedom: From the Psychology to the Politics of Agency* (New York: Oxford University Press, 2001), groups poverty with "natural limits" on freedom such as "disability and illness," 130 and argues that it is always worse to restrict people's freedom to overcome the limits posed by "the natural order or the ways things are socially organized," 132.

88 I am thinking particularly of a widespread reaction to the case of the young woman who was jogging in New York's Central Park after dark who was gang-raped and almost killed.

This analysis of what it means to be free might seem to stress so-called negative liberty (freedom from interference) at the expense of positive liberty (freedom to do ...),[89] but this is misleading. As Gerald MacCallum explained more than forty years ago, there really is no difference between kinds of freedom; any claim about freedom involves both aspects.[90] Some writers, for example, John Gray and Nancy Hirschmann,[91] have stressed, correctly, that there are not only constraining conditions to our actions, but also enabling ones and both need attention in an analysis of what it is to be free. I take this important point to be included in the above analysis since the absence of positive supports can be a decided obstacle preventing one from doing something. (We will see examples of this below.) As Rhonda Copelon, the attorney opposing the Hyde Amendment before the Supreme Court argued, our "choices are shaped, facilitated or denied by social conditions ... to protect a 'right to choose' without assuring the social conditions necessary to foster an autonomous choice provides equality of opportunity in form but not in fact."[92] Similarly, the absence of constraining conditions is an enabling condition. The analysis of freedom I am presenting, which combines the positive and negative, is quite compatible with a stress on the positive. Indeed, this would make sense since

89 Isaiah Berlin understood the concept of "positive liberty" to mean more than this, but I prefer this simpler conception. "Two Concepts of Liberty," in Henry Hardy (ed.), *Liberty* (Oxford University Press, 2002).

90 MacCallum, "Negative and Positive Freedom," says that with regard to individual freedom to act, "such freedom is thus always *of* something (an agent or agents), *from* something, *to* do, not do, become, or not become something; it is a triadic relation ... [If any] of these terms is missing ... it should be only because the reference is thought to be understood from the context."

91 John Gray, "On Positive and Negative Liberty," *Political Studies* 28 (1980): 507–26, argues that MacCallum is biased toward negative freedom because he cites only constraining conditions; Nancy Hirschmann, *The Subject of Liberty*, stresses both, as I do, but interprets the distinction between negative and positive freedom as a distinction between external and internal factors that constrain or enable us, rather than simply freedom free from and freedom to.

92 Rhonda Copelon, "From Privacy to Autonomy: The Conditions for Sexual and Reproductive Freedom," in Marlene Gerber Fried (ed.), *From Abortion to*

the reason one wants to be *free from* obstacles is *in order to be free to* do things one wants to do. Liberation *from something* is necessary for liberation *for something*. Recognition of this moves us toward a conception of the fullest kind of freedom as self-determination or autonomy in both personal and political terms.[93]

Some philosophers have restrictive views about the kinds of obstacles that can limit someone's freedom. One particularly narrow view is that someone is unfree only when another person physically restrains them from doing something (some even say it must be intentional); others take a broader view and allow that if a person is threatened if she or he doesn't do something, then that person is coerced into doing it and hence is not free. While the latter view is broader than the former, both are narrower than the obstacle view of freedom presented above because they require that persons be causes of the lack of freedom.[94] Hence, as Gertrude Ezorsky explains, they cannot explain how a person *becomes free* to do something when some physical obstacle is removed.[95] For example, "when they moved the car blocking her way, she was free to drive down the street"; this implies she was not free to drive before they moved it. So persons are not the only obstacles to freedom.

Other philosophers put moral restrictions on what counts as limiting someone's freedom. Robert Nozick, for example, contends that other people's actions that limit someone's opportunities do not thereby limit his or her *freedom* as long as they had the *moral right* to act as they did.[96] Thus, in the above example, if the person had the moral right to park his or her car in a way that blocked my car, this would not limit my freedom to drive

Reproductive Freedom: Transforming a Movement (Boston, MA: South End Press, 1990), 38f.

93 There is a very extensive literature on autonomy as well as freedom with different understandings of their relationship.

94 This literature is vast so I would just refer interested readers to the sources found in the works I have cited elsewhere.

95 Ezorsky, *Freedom in the Workplace?*, 12.

96 Nozick, *Anarchy, State, and Utopia*, 55, 178–82. Hayek, too, has a moralized understanding of freedom. See John Gray, "Hayek on Liberty, Rights and Justice," *Ethics* 92 (October 1981): 73–84.

down the block. Since this seems patently false, one might wonder why he would define freedom so narrowly. Other examples suggest an explanation. "When she got a higher-paying job, she was finally free to take a vacation," implies that she was not free to take a vacation before that. "Until discrimination in private employment became illegal, women and Black Americans were not free to work in many businesses," implies that discrimination limited their freedom. Since Nozick believes that employers have the moral right to pay so little that their employees can never take a vacation, and that private employers have the right to discriminate if they want, it would follow on his analysis of freedom that low pay and discrimination do not limit the freedom of the employees in these examples. But again, this is patently false. Nozick seems driven to this very restrictive definition of freedom because to allow that the ordinary workings of capitalism[97] limit people's freedom would create a problem for his claim that capitalism is the morally best economic system *because it is the most free*.[98] Whatever the explanation, it is unacceptable. As G. A. Cohen observes, this "moralized" concept of freedom would entail the absurd conclusion that "if a criminal's imprisonment is morally justified, he is then not forced to be in prison,"[99] quite rightly calling this an "abuse of the language of freedom."

So let us assume that obstacles to someone acting freely may be physical or may "significantly involve persons" regardless of whether or not those persons have the right to act as they do. Now someone can limit another person's freedom in various ways, not only by direct physical force or by coercion. Certain kinds of proposals or offers can also prevent someone from acting freely. "Forcing offers" is Gertrude Ezorsky's apt characterization of cases

97 In the second example it is the "libertarian" or free market version of capitalism that restricts freedom, rather than capitalism *per se*.

98 Some writers on freedom take existing property relations as the natural background conditions against which we judge freedom of action. This clearly is biased toward capitalism as it prevents us from even asking whether another system of property relations might provide more freedom.

99 Cohen, *History, Labour and Freedom*, 256. Reiman, "Exploitation, Force, and the Moral Assessment of Capitalism" also shows that Nozick's argument is circular.

like that of an employer's offer of a dangerous and low paid job to someone whose only alternative is starvation for herself and her family. In such a case the worker could say, "I had no choice; I was forced to take the job."[100] When all the choices are terrible, freedom of choice *among them* does not mean freedom overall. Not only individuals, but social institutions, organized and maintained by people, may also limit someone's freedom. This can be missed if we focus just on individuals. Two such examples from the United States of particular relevance to women are the absence of adequate childcare and the absence of universal medical care. One woman may be prevented from taking a job she would like by the absence of childcare;[101] another woman may stay in a dangerous low paid job she hates, even accepting worse conditions, because she needs the company's health insurance for her sick child. Choices discussed above about whether or not to have an abortion provide other examples. Laws restricting abortion may leave a pregnant woman no choice but to have a child, while on the other hand, the absence of social supports like childcare, medical care, etc. may lead another pregnant woman to have an abortion because she feels she cannot afford to provide a good life for a child she would love to have. In all these cases, people make rational choices, and hence are free to that very minimal degree, but are nonetheless forced to do what they do. As Jeffrey Reiman has said, "structural force can operate through free choice."[102]

Internal obstacles

Thus far, all the examples of obstacles preventing someone from doing something have been "external' to the person. An

---

100 Ezorsky, *Freedom in the Workplace?*, 29ff. There is a large literature on the concepts of threats, coercion, offers, coercive offers by, among others, Robert Nozick, Harry Frankfurt, Roger Wertheimer, Hillel Steiner, Virginia Held, and David Zimmerman.

101 Gendered expectations regarding women's roles within heterosexual relationships may also contribute to this decision, but this is not the primary explanation as single and lesbian mothers face exactly the same obstacle.

102 Reiman, "Exploitation, Force, and the Moral Assessment of Capitalism," 15.

adequate account of freedom I will argue would allow that the obstacles limiting someone's freedom could also be *internal* to the person.[103] As just discussed, if a woman is prevented from getting a job because the law discriminates against women, or because she has no childcare, or because the men in her family will beat her up, she is not free to work. However, suppose a woman is prevented from getting a job because she has a mental illness or an addiction, or suppose she feels that it is wrong for a woman to work outside the home, or wants to accommodate her husband who wants her at home, or suppose she believes (falsely) that she is incompetent, or suppose she is afraid to travel to a job because she has been traumatized by violence? Such feelings and beliefs are widespread among women due to sexism. If there is no external obstacle preventing someone from going out to work, as in the above cases, is she simply *unable to work*, or is she also *unfree*? Many thinkers would say that she is unable to work, but she is not unfree. However, by the same reasoning used above, this seems an unreasonable restriction on what can cause someone to be unfree. The varied internal constraints mentioned above, many of which are related to sexism, can be very powerful obstacles to acting freely. As feminists from Mary Wollstonecraft and John Stuart Mill to today have stressed, women have been acculturated not only to conform to gendered expectations but *to want to do so*. Now suppose that due to cultural shifts or through her involvement in political activism, or through support groups, or psychotherapy, her beliefs and her feelings change such that she becomes able to work. We could also say that she becomes *free* to work. It follows that she was *unfree* until these internal obstacles were removed.[104] The constraining emotions, habits, and beliefs of the past that prevented her from working have been replaced by enabling ones. This analysis accords with our common understanding that such processes and changes can be liberating, as

---

103 Holmstrom, "Free Will and a Marxist Concept of Natural Wants," and "Firming Up Soft Determinism"; Hirschmann, *The Subject of Liberty*; Pettit, *Theory of Freedom*.

104 This follows Gertrude Ezorsky's argument for the obstacle view of freedom though she does not extend it to internal obstacles. It can be difficult

when it is said that the cultural changes and political movements of the 1960s and 1970s were immensely liberating for women, or that psychotherapy can liberate us from our "hang-ups" or "blocks." This is why the women's liberation movement of this period organized consciousness-raising groups for women as well as rallies and lobbies to change laws and policies, and why there are support groups for survivors of domestic violence and rape. The problem of internal obstacles to freedom, stemming from oppression, is not limited to women. As Terry Eagleton says, "The most efficient oppressor is the one who persuades his underlings to love, desire and identify with his power ... any practice of political emancipation thus involves that most difficult of all forms of liberation, freeing ourselves from ourselves."[105]

Tests of the analysis

We started our discussion of the concept of freedom with some statements suggesting that freedom means different things to different people. And this is certainly true. For one person freedom might mean escape from a dictatorship, for another freedom is being able to openly express her or his sexuality, for another freedom is having enough to eat every day. Though such expressions are sometimes more literary than literal, they express something profoundly important. Can the unified analysis of the concept of freedom I have offered accommodate these differences? I think it can. Recall the quotation from Barbara Smith: "I want the same thing that I did thirty years ago when I joined the Civil Rights movement and twenty years ago when I joined the women's movement, came out, and felt more alive than I ever dreamed possible: freedom."[106] According to our analysis, a person can be

---

to separate the internal obstacles from the external when the internal are responses to sexism, as Margaret McLaren stressed to me. Certainly, the external obstacles should be eliminated but it is possible sometimes to eliminate the internal on their own.

105 Terry Eagleton, *Ideology* (London: Verso, 1991), xiv. Hirschmann, *The Subject of Liberty*, explores the many dimensions of how this takes place, arguing that our very selves are constructed through gendered expectations.

106 Barbara Smith, *The Truth That Never Hurts*, quoted in Kelley, *Freedom Dreams*, 136.

free with respect to one obstacle and not to another; for other people the situation may be reversed or they may face overwhelming obstacles in every direction. Barbara Smith's statement reflects the fact that different obstacles constrained her in different respects; in order to achieve her *single goal* – freedom as a whole person – she had to struggle to remove one set of obstacles after another.

On the other hand, what statements suggesting *differences* in the meaning of freedom express most fundamentally is that different people will experience different things either as the *most salient obstacle* to their freedom, or as the *most salient condition enabling them* to do what they want. A person who does not have enough to eat is not free to do much of anything regardless of the laws or social mores of their society. Food is freedom to the starving because it is the most salient enabling condition for them. For a person who cannot walk, freedom will be a wheelchair, elevators, and curb cut-outs. For a middle-class, able-bodied person living in a dictatorship, freedom will be getting away from that government. Someone living in a market society who wants to buy a book and has the money to buy it but the government forbids its sale will find this particularly galling. "One man's freedom is another man's slavery" is literally true in that the freedom of one person to own slaves entails that others are slaves; in exactly the same way, the freedom of an employer to discriminate in hiring is the lack of freedom of others to work.

Our unified theory of freedom can also accommodate historian Christopher Hill's statement that freedom changes its meaning over time. Though not literally true as he would undoubtedly acknowledge, his statement reflects the fact that different obstacles are the focus of struggle at different historical junctures and for different groups. The change in "meaning" may also reflect the fact that different groups have hegemony of expression at different times. In the seventeenth century freedom was associated with private property for landowners who had to fight against the monarchy and feudal restrictions. But while landowners certainly had hegemony of expression, many others expressed themselves too and private property was not all that "freedom" meant even then. Indeed, freedom was "a continuing theme" for Gerrard Winstanley, the most famous Digger, who attacked private property in the name of freedom, arguing that private property was an obstacle to freedom for all – which required communal property.[107] In the 1960s and 1970s, the words "freedom" and "liberation" were associated particularly with movements for *national* liberation against colonial domination, and this was extended to the black liberation movement and then the women's liberation movement. At that historical juncture, colonial domination, and racist and sexist power structures, were seen as the primary obstacles to freedom in the eyes of the millions who suffered under them.

As we will see in section 3, the examples discussed earlier of lack of freedom are not simply hypothetical. Particularly relevant to an evaluation of capitalism are the external obstacles. Even in the United States, the richest country in the history of the world, people are often forced to take or keep jobs, or sometimes forced to decline jobs, because of threats and because they face terrible alternatives due to the absence of socially provided necessary goods. As documented by Human Rights Watch, some workers in the United States live in conditions close to indentured servitude. Several US Supreme Court decisions have reinforced the imbalance of power that creates this lack of freedom, most importantly, the denial that individuals have economic and social rights, and the 1915 decision which allows employers to fire workers for any reason they choose. Though this power has been weakened somewhat over the years, nonunion employees are still subject to this power (known as "employment at will") unless they can show that they were fired for very specific discriminatory reasons.[108] In some capitalist societies around the globe, workers have won more job protection, but in the poorer capitalist countries, people live with even less freedom due to more dire choices.

---

107 Hill, *Liberty Against the Law*, 276. *The Law of Freedom* was Winstanley's most famous work.

108 See the useful appendix on twentieth-century US labor laws in Ezorsky, *Freedom in the Workplace?*

A more ideal capitalism?

To what extent could capitalism be re-organized so that the inequalities of wealth and power that limit the freedom of the majority are removed or overcome? This has been the dream of liberals committed to genuine equality of opportunity for *all* members of society starting with John Stuart Mill.[109] Recall that on the above analysis of freedom, to say someone is unfree is not to say that she or he has literally no choice whatsoever. The obstacles preventing one from doing something are seldom as severe as that. Indeed, unless one is physically restrained to such a degree that there is no possibility of fighting back, there is always some choice. And the choices may be perfectly rational. So it is not whether someone has or does not have choices, nor simply the number of choices, but rather *the nature of the choices* that is critical in determining the *degree to which someone is free*. Our question then is to what extent can capitalism be reformed in order that so many crucial choices people make are not simply the best of a very bad lot, made in pain to avoid worse pain? In theory, capitalism could certainly be freer for most people than it is. In theory, some of the obstacles to freedom discussed above could be removed. Then people's choices could be different. If there were universal childcare, a mother would not be prevented from getting a job by the need to care for children. If there were universal medical care, no one would have to take or stay in a terrible job just because they needed the health insurance. If there were adequate subsidies for all children, no woman would have to have an abortion because she was unable to provide a decent life for her child. If the law did not allow employers to fire someone almost at will, a power that legal theorist Morris Cohen likens to absolute monarchy,[110] then a worker would be free to

---

109 See his *Principles of Political Economy with Some of their Applications to Social Philosophy* excerpted in C. B Macpherson (ed.), *Property: Mainstream and Critical Positions* (University of Toronto Press, 1978) and the critique by Macpherson in *The Life and Times of Liberal Democracy*.

110 Morris Cohen, "Property and Sovereignty," in Macpherson (ed.), *Property: Mainstream and Critical Positions*, 173.

protest unsafe conditions. Many capitalist societies, most notably the Scandinavian countries, have gone some way in removing these obstacles to freedom. Could these reforms be extended to our own society and to all other capitalist societies? Could they be extended even further? And how can such reforms be shown to be compatible with capitalism as a theory?

In theory

These reforms can be shown to be compatible with philosophical theories in support of capitalism in several ways. One line of argument is that although in capitalism individuals have the right to own the bulk of the means of production, the very justification of this right to property assumes that there is a general right to subsistence and therefore a claim on that property. Recall that Locke starts out his argument for private property by arguing that everyone has a right to partake of the resources of the world for their sustenance. He initially puts limits on how much any individual can appropriate, saying there must be as much and as good left in common for others. Though he later drops this limit and supports a right to unlimited private property, the spirit of the limit on the right to individual appropriation remains in his claim that the greater productivity of private cultivated property can be said to give back more to mankind than if it were not privately appropriated. Though I have argued that this happy assumption does not actually meet his condition, because greater productivity does not necessarily mean that all are provided for, it can be the basis for a claim for a social minimum that stays close to this theoretical framework. Every individual has some right to the resources of the world, so if the system of property, laws, and their own abilities do not allow them to appropriate it on their own it should be provided for them.[111] And, indeed,

---

111 One finds this argument in Jeremy Waldron, *The Right to Private Property* (New York: Oxford University Press, 1988). It is also Van Parijs' (*Real Freedom for All*) argument for a guaranteed individual income. Whether this minimum takes the form of a guaranteed income or extensive public goods is a further issue. Supporters of the former ("left libertarians") argue that it gives more freedom of choice. Support for the latter comes from Elizabeth

Locke himself insisted on a right to basic sustenance for all from the surpluses of others more fortunate.[112]

Another way to justify a reformed capitalism would be to challenge Nozick's argument for the minimal state, a "night watchman" state that provides only military and police protection. Everything else he maintains must be provided by the market and if not, then too bad. Most critiques of Nozick focus on the minimal nature of his conception of government's role, arguing for a more positive and extensive role for government, and that is certainly how capitalist societies have developed. However, it is interesting to look at the minimal state from the other side: why even this much government? In the minimal state government has the monopoly on the means of violence (and is actually a very extensive state in terms of the share of the tax budget devoted to military and policing functions in the United States). Some find even this role for government to be too much; picture the radical right-wing individualist anarchist with guns prepared to take on any threat. Nozick addresses this perspective but argues that a state would likely, or at least could, have come about from an anarchic state of nature without anyone intending it or trying to bring it about. In his story, an invisible-hand story, self-interested individuals would "back into a state" through their need for protection against transgressors. They form protective associations; one gradually becomes dominant and becomes a *de facto* state.

A more plausible story would acknowledge that people have needs for protection against manifold insecurities of life, not only

Anderson's argument that "freedom of exit is no substitute for the loss of voice … Some forms of freedom can be secured only through institutions of voice established over goods to which public access is guaranteed … There is a value … in collectively taking a stand on what goods the community regards as so important that it would be a disgrace to let any of its members fall short of them." "Ethical Limitations of the Market," in Charles K. Wilber (ed.), *Economics, Ethics and Public Policy* (Lanham, MD: Rowman & Littlefield, 1998), 236 and 239.

112 Locke, *First Treatise of Government*, section 42 quoted in Virginia Held, "John Locke on Robert Nozick," *Social Research* 43 (Spring 1976): 169–95, 173. As Held shows, this means that Robert Nozick cannot claim to be following Locke. If one reads Locke's policy prescriptions, however, one can see how terribly meager this minimum was.

intentional threats to our well-being from aggressors. The classical liberal picture of Locke and Nozick of naturally independent individuals who come together by agreement is a deeply implausible one. As feminists have stressed, building on communitarian and Marxist analyses, human beings are interdependent creatures, by nature and in all societies. Nor are they only self-interested. We start out totally dependent on others, particularly our mothers, for a significant period and can become so again at any point throughout our lives. As Carole Pateman remarked, if people actually lived as the social contractarians describe, they would be the last generation.[113] Even at the height of our health and strength, we need the cooperation of others to satisfy our needs. Contrary to the Robinson Crusoe fables popular in the early days of capitalism,[114] human beings, like those primates closest to us, have always lived in some sort of society, in families and larger communal groups, with a division of labor.[115] If a state were to have evolved out of associations, these associations would likely have had aims much broader than protecting people and property and punishing aggression against them. Hence, the functions of the state would also be broader. Would every individual need and want this kind of protection? Perhaps not; no more than our gun-toting individualist who rejects the need for the military and police protection that is part of Nozick's minimal state. But this is just a story – like Nozick's. Is it a story that is compatible with capitalist theory? Yes, though it involves a modification of the individualist model dominant in liberalism. One can see something more like this picture in John Rawls' conception of society as a cooperative venture for mutual advantage.

113 Pateman, *The Sexual Contract*, 49.

114 The Robinson Crusoe story actually illustrates the reverse of the usual moral drawn from it. Crusoe is shipwrecked from a slave-trading ship, sets up bookkeeping accounts, and establishes a master–servant relationship with the only other human he encounters. Thus, he replicates the society from which he comes, rather than some "state of nature."

115 According to researchers, primates closest to us even have a morality. See Frans De Waal, *Good Natured: The Origins of Right and Wrong in Humans and Other Animals* (Cambridge, MA: Harvard University Press, 1996).

At a philosophical level, then, there is no inconsistency in supporting a form of capitalism that provides at least minimal welfare for its citizens – and, indeed, despite the popularity of the free market model in recent decades in the United States, most defenders of capitalism defend a model of capitalism with some welfare provisions, from middle-of-the-road liberals in the United States to supporters of more extensive social welfare as found in most European countries. Without directly challenging capitalism a number of theorists, such as Amartya Sen, Peter Singer, and Thomas Pogge, have argued strongly for extending our moral duties beyond national borders to the people of the world.[116] As Onora O'Neill eloquently puts it, poor women throughout the world "not only raise children in poverty, they raise crops and do ill-paid and insecure work whose rewards fluctuate to the beat of distant economic forces." An *international* economic system, but only *national* systems of taxation and social supports, further subordinates them to forces beyond their control.[117] So arguments can be made from within the liberal tradition for a more humane form of capitalism.

In history

But these changes in capitalism will not come about, if they ever do, simply by moral argument, however persuasive. In actual history, the broadening of government functions in capitalist societies to include such things as public education, unemployment insurance, national health care (in some countries) were the result of many causes. Chief among these were the manifest failures of capitalism, particularly after the Great Depression, and the movements of working people, often influenced by communists and socialists, who were demanding these changes – or much more radical change. The Russian Revolution was even

---

116 Probably the most relevant of Sen's many works is *Development as Freedom* (New York: Alfred A. Knopf, 1999); among Singer's works, see especially, *The Life You Can Save: Acting Now to End World Poverty* (New York: Random House, 2009); Thomas Pogge, *World Poverty and Human Rights: Cosmopolitan Responsibilities and Reforms* (Cambridge: Polity, 2002).
117 O'Neill, "Justice, Gender and International Boundaries," 303.

more frightening to leaders of the capitalist world than fascism, despite the fact that the Soviet Union was allied in the Second World War with the United States and Great Britain against Germany, Italy, and Japan. "If you provide not for the poor, they will provide for themselves" was the anxious thought expressed in support of what was known as "poor relief" from the earliest days of capitalism.[118] One can see both the moral and the pragmatic strains of thought in the famous speech by Franklin Delano Roosevelt toward the end of the Second World War in which he enunciated the idea of an economic Bill of Rights:

> We cannot be content, no matter how high that general standard of living may be, if some fraction of our people – whether it be one-third or one-fifth or one-tenth – is ill-fed, ill-clothed, ill-housed, and insecure … The Republic had its beginning, and grew to its present strength, under the protection of certain inalienable political rights … As our nation has grown in size and stature, however – as our industrial economy expanded – these political rights proved inadequate to assure us equality in the pursuit of happiness … *People who are hungry and out of a job are the stuff of which dictatorships are made.* (my emphasis)

He then lists elements of a necessary second Bill of Rights such as the right to a job, housing, and adequate medical care, and concludes, "America's own rightful place in the world depends in large part upon how fully these and similar rights have been carried into practice for our citizens."[119]

Though the specific rights enunciated above were not won by Americans, whatever gains working people throughout the world won from capitalism in this period were everywhere the result of their hard struggle. Moral arguments played a supportive role at most. The stronger and more radical the movements, the more gains they made. After the Second World War, powerful left-wing mass movements in Europe threatened radical changes and forced the governments to provide some social supports.

118 Hill, "Editor's Introduction," *Winstanley*, 22.
119 *The Public Papers and Addresses of Franklin D. Roosevelt: Vol. XII*, Samuel Rosenman (ed.) (New York: Harper, 1950), 40–42.

Though the United States never had as large or as radical movements as Europe did, it is clear that here, too, it was movements
of the poor and working class, often led by socialists of all stripes,
which succeeded in winning whatever social supports Americans
have. Mass unemployment, and its consequent suffering, was not
enough; there had been depressions in the nineteenth century
that led to protests, but these protests were met only with repres-
sion. By the 1930s, however, the increased size of the industrial
working class and their willingness to take militant illegal actions
like sit-down strikes, forceful resistance to evictions, and riots –
leading in some cities to what observers called virtual class war –
combined with international developments, was what made
their protests more successful.[120]

The welfare measures at the heart of the New Deal, like social
security and unemployment insurance, expand the freedom
of the recipients. Legislation like the Fair Labor Standards Act
proposed by Roosevelt in 1937, which set a minimum wage,
limits on overtime, and prohibited child labor, and later, anti-
discrimination laws, can be justified on the same grounds. While,
on the one hand, they are restrictions on freedom (the freedom
of exchange), as opponents of the legislation argued vigorously,
on the other hand, such laws expand greatly the freedom of the
many people who benefit from them. Labor unions, which were
so crucial to winning these gains in every country, expand the
collective freedom of those involved in that they allow them to
struggle for and to achieve gains they could never win on their
own, as well as adding to the freedom of all those who benefit
whether they contributed or not. If freedom is a primary value,
one should want to maximize it,[121] even though this entails some

---

120 Frances Fox Piven and Richard A. Cloward, *Poor Peoples' Movements: Why
They Succeed and How They Fail* (New York: Random House, 1979); Irving
Bernstein, *The Lean Years: A History of the American Worker, 1920–1933*
(Baltimore, MD: Penguin, 1970); *The Turbulent Years: A History of the American
Worker, 1933–1941* (Boston, MA: Houghton Mifflin, 1971); Art Preis, *Labor's
Giant Step: 20 Years of the CIO* (New York: Pioneer Publishers, 1964).

121 By maximizing freedom I mean creating conditions in which more people
are subject to fewer kinds of constraints. Nozick rejects the argument for

limits on freedom of exchange (just as prohibiting slavery put limits on the freedom to buy and sell human beings). In 1948 the United Nations adopted the Universal Declaration of Human Rights, Article 25 of which states "Everyone has the right to a standard of living adequate for the health and well-being of himself and of his family, including food, clothing, housing and medical care and necessary social services, and the right to security in the event of unemployment, sickness, disability, widowhood, old age." The United States, however, has never ratified this declaration because it has never committed itself to the idea that people's basic material necessities are a *right* rather than a privilege or a hard-fought political gain.

Economists less trusting of the free market, most notably John Maynard Keynes and his followers, believe that it is necessary for government to intervene in the economy to "save capitalism from itself." The market is volatile, prey to bubbles and busts, and cannot be counted on to regulate itself. Alan Greenspan, who as Chairman of the Federal Reserve had led the deregulation of the US economy, admitted as much when he said that "the whole intellectual edifice" had collapsed in the financial crisis of 2008. Just as Keynes argued in his day, suddenly virtually all mainstream economists today are arguing for the necessity of government spending to stimulate the economy, whether it takes the form of investment in technology, roads, or education or outright gifts to business.[122] In fact, despite fierce opposition to social welfare by

maximizing freedom because he is committed to what he calls "moral side constraints," holding that it is always wrong to restrict individual liberty even if it would expand liberty. But this seems irrational. Moreover, he does not stick to this position in every case. Acknowledging the loss of freedoms that common people enjoyed before the transformation of commons land into private property (e.g., the freedom to hunt and to gather), he dismisses this on the grounds that a system of private property provides so much material benefit for people. But this is a consequentialist argument justifying the restriction of individual liberties in favor of greater welfare that is inconsistent with his notion of moral side constraints. Cheyney Ryan makes this point in "Yours, Mine and Ours: Property Rights and Individual Liberty," 126–41, 139.

122 Most of these economists were free marketeers until fall 2008. For example, Lawrence Summers, President Obama's economics advisor, played a

many sectors of the capitalist class in Roosevelt's day and now in our own, hardly any capitalists want the government to stay out of the economy completely. They want the government to pay for infrastructure, for environmental damages due to private enterprise, and for subsidies (known as "corporate welfare" to critics), including government bailouts of failed businesses, as we have seen so spectacularly since the fall of 2008. The latter was the bulk of the "stimulus packages" of both presidents Bush and Obama. Such corporate welfare ordinarily amounts to $100 billion or so, but the recent bank bailouts amount to $2.5 trillion.[123] While philosophers like Nozick can be pure free marketeers, the opposition to government intervention of most actual capitalists is very selective; they want government action that serves their interests and they have the power to ensure this. So truly laissez faire capitalism is a utopian ideology; it has never existed and never will.

How ideal? The inevitability and importance of extreme inequalities

But just how far from laissez faire in the direction of greater equality could capitalism go? (I am asking a purely theoretical question now, not about what kinds of changes are actually achievable in capitalism today.) And is this not just better than what we have, but rather the best that humankind can do? As capitalism is a global system, the problems cannot be solved merely by changes within nations, so one would have to imagine a global social welfare system, international labor laws, and so on. But for simplicity of exposition I will focus on individual

central role in deregulating financial institutions, allowing deposit banks to move into speculative investments previously barred by the Glass–Steagall Act.

123 Nancy Folbre, "Welfare for Bankers," *The New York Times Economix Blog*, April 20, 2009 points out the moral double standard applied to bankers and welfare mothers: "The top executives of banks bailed out this year – about 600 guys – received an estimated $1.6 billion in bonuses in 2007. That's a little over a third of what 1.6 million families got in cash from TANF [Temporary Assistance to Needy Families] that year." See http://economix. blogs.nytimes.com/2009/04/20/welfare-for-bankers.

societies, particularly the United States.[124] Reforms like the basic welfare provisions discussed above lift the floor, so to speak, so that the choices people face are not so dire. If people know they will not starve, this gives them more freedom to act. But lifting the floor does not thereby lower the ceiling; a society could still be as unequal, or more so, than one with no floor. While there have been huge controversies historically, and again today, over a very minimal, and declining, minimum wage, the idea of a *maximum* salary or a cap on income or wealth has never even been on the table in the United States[125] – although the wealth of today's wealthiest individuals exceeds that of many nations. (Not to mention the wealth of corporations which have the status of persons under US law.) Inequality is greater now than at any point in history, both globally and within the United States with *two-thirds* of income gains during 2002–7 going to *the top 1 percent*.[126] Even if the bottom of the economic pyramid were raised, can anyone seriously claim that democracy is compatible with such inequality?

Furthermore, the kinds of inequalities inherent in capitalism should be morally problematic for capitalist theory's emphasis on the individual and its supposed commitment to equality of all. To appreciate why, it is important to recognize, first of all, that only a small part of the inequality can be explained as the result of choices individuals have made. Hence, it cannot be said to be "their own fault." Individuals do not choose the single most important determinants of where they end up materially, viz. where their parents are located in the social economic hierarchy of the globe or of their own society, as a recent World Bank study

---

124 For the best summary account of how the US economy works, see Jonathan Teller-Elsberg, Nancy Folbre, and James Heintz, *Field Guide to the U.S. Economy: A Compact and Irreverent Guide to Economic Life in America* (New York: New Press, 2006).

125 An exception, ironically, is found in colonial laws limiting wages and forbidding organization. Actually, there were laws limiting income in the colonial period – but they only applied to *people earning a wage*! Piven and Cloward, *Poor Peoples' Movements*, 102.

126 Bob Herbert, "Safety Nets for the Rich," *New York Times*, October 20, 2009.

shows.[127] Nor do they choose the personal qualities (still less the luck) that make it possible for some individuals to be the exceptions to this rule.[128]

Material inequalities, moreover, are also inequalities of power and freedom and general well-being. The connection between general well-being and material goods seems so obvious that it is not necessary to elaborate except to point out, first, that it can literally be a matter of life and death, and, second, that material inequalities are correlated with other problems usually perceived as unrelated, such as domestic violence for example. Feminists have stressed that this problem is not confined to particular groups, but is found everywhere. But while true, this is misleading because research shows that domestic violence is seven times as likely to occur in low income than in high income households.[129] This should not be surprising when we consider the stress that financial problems bring to families. As for freedom, the more money individuals have, the more freedom they have to act in every area of their lives. And the more money individuals have, the more power they have to influence what happens in society. Though everyone is equal before the law, clearly an individual accused of a crime who depends on a public defender with a huge volume of cases does not have an equal chance in court to that of someone who has the money to buy the services of an entire law firm. Though political offices and legislation are forbidden by law to be bought and sold in a political democracy, the fact that it takes millions, even hundreds of millions of dollars to run

127 Branko Milanovic, "Global Inequality of Opportunity: How Much of Your Income is Determined by Birth?," World Bank Report, February 2009, concludes that these two variables determine 80 percent of variability in income. "Thus globally speaking, the role of effort or luck in improving one's incomes position, cannot be large," 1.

128 These two points are a foundation for Rawls' theory of justice according to which socioeconomic inequalities need to be justified. What socioeconomic system he thinks would best meet his principles of justice is not so clear.

129 Amy Farmer, Jill Tiefenthaler, and Amandine Sambira, "The Availability and Distribution of Services for Victims of Domestic Violence in the US," available at www.waltoncollege.uark.edu/lab/AFarmer/services%20 RR%202004.doc.

for political office brings our system very close to this. This is all connected to the fact discussed earlier that real social power in capitalism resides in the economy not in the government. What is produced, how it is produced, where it is produced, are decisions made by the owners of private property (subject only to minimal government restrictions regarding health and safety). The power of the vast majority of individuals who do not own the means of production to influence the crucial decisions in society is therefore very limited. The bailout (some use the word "rescue" and others "theft") of the banks by the governments of the major capitalist powers in the fall of 2008 at the cost of trillions of dollars after decades of starving the public sector because there "wasn't enough money" should make this clear to anyone. To what extent could these inequalities of wealth and power be reduced in capitalism? To some extent, certainly; not all capitalist societies are as unequal as the United States. But even if the degree of inequality varies, capitalism remains an inherently unequal system materially, politically, and with respect to the freedom that different groups enjoy. This explains why Walden Bello and many others in the global justice movement oppose what might be called global social democracy; even though it would obviously be better than the current form of global capitalism, it is not their moral and political ideal.[130] Only in an egalitarian society would political freedom and democracy be maximized in that everyone would have the right to participate in collective decision-making on an equal basis on economic as well as political issues.

That capitalism is inherently unequal has implications for internal obstacles to freedom as well. If human nature is not fixed, but rather evolves and takes different forms in different social structures, and different places within those structures,[131] if society actually "constructs the choosing subject" in Nancy

---

130 Walden Bello, "Reforming the WTO is the Wrong Agenda," in Kevin Danaher and Roger Burbach (eds.), *Globalize This! Ten Ways to Democratize the World Economy* (Monroe, ME: Common Courage, 2000), and other writings.

131 Nancy Holmstrom, "A Marxist Theory of Women's Nature," *Ethics* 94 (April 1984): 456–73; "Humankind(s)," *Biology, Behavior and Society, Canadian Journal of Philosophy* suppl. vol. 20 (1994): 69–105.

Hirschmann's words,[132] then a hierarchical society will produce people who reflect this hierarchy. The groups with power control not only the means of production, but the psychic means of reproduction, from educational institutions to the media. But most fundamentally, the hierarchical structure, the social relations of power, appear natural and, therefore, inevitable and right (except in times of crisis and transition). Those born wealthy who receive every possible advantage tend to have the strongest sense of entitlement; "he was born on third and thought he hit a triple" is often very apt. That women do the bulk of caring labor on top of all other labor they do, that poor and working-class people work hard for little reward, while others have wealth and power that kings would envy, is seen as "just the way things are." In capitalist society today, with an ideology of individual meritocracy, no legal barriers to individual advancement based on race or sex, and the high achievements of certain individuals from oppressed backgrounds, the explanation and justification of inequality has changed from those given in the past. It is less often claimed today that the poor are immoral and lazy and more often claimed that they are unintelligent or come from dysfunctional cultures. Poverty is perceived by many as a "natural" limitation like illness and disability,[133] and yet at the same time the majority of Americans have the illusion that everyone can make it if they only try hard enough.[134] Thus, poor and working-class people, and women and racial minorities, tend to internalize their oppression and blame themselves when they do not succeed in improving their lot in life. This greatly increases their suffering and further limits their freedom[135] as they will be unable even to

---

132 Hirschmann, *The Subject of Liberty*.
133 Pettit, *A Theory of Freedom*, refers to "the natural limitations imposed by disability, illness, poverty and the like," 130. In fact, poverty is purely a social limitation and social conditions often cause or exacerbate illness and disability. (Some theorists have a social analysis of disability as well.)
134 Everett Carl Ladd and Karlyn H. Bowman, *Attitudes Toward Economic Inequality* (Washington, DC: AEI Press, 1998).
135 Jonathan Kozol, *Savage Inequalities* (New York: Crown Publications, 1992); Richard Sennett and Jonathan Cobb, *The Hidden Injuries of Class* (New York: W. W. Norton, 1993).

imagine a better life for themselves, or think they are entitled to one. Dorothy Allison, author of *Bastard Out of Carolina* and *Trash*, says that more important to her deepest psychic life than being a victim of incest and childhood violence or being a lesbian was being born poor in a society that despises the poor.[136]

This internalized oppression that afflicts most poor and working-class people profoundly affects the form of human nature that is realized in capitalist societies. Capitalism provides opportunities for individual self-development possible in few if any earlier societies. The United States, without as long a history of entrenched class privileges as most societies, and with its multiculturalism, is particularly open in this respect. But at the same time capitalism limits the possibilities for the development of most individuals' capacities. A moving illustration is provided in the film and musical *Billy Elliot* about a gifted young boy in a mining town in northern England during the coal miners' strike of 1982, which had been called to resist Margaret Thatcher's determination to crush the National Union of Mineworkers and the national coal industry in favor of cheaper imports. Billy's gift for dance, combined with luck and the support of family and community, enable him to develop the talent that gives him such joy. But Thatcher succeeded in destroying the union and mining communities throughout the country. While Billy had an exceptional gift for dance, he was not unique in having talent; almost everyone has talents and capacities that have little opportunity for development. The Suzuki method of teaching violin is based on this belief and succeeds in having almost every child taught by their method playing Vivaldi by the time they leave elementary school. Only a society that was fairly egalitarian would eliminate these internal barriers to freedom and self-expression, as all groups in society would be involved on an equal basis in the institutions that shape them. Only in such a society that allowed

---

136 Dorothy Allison, "A Question of Class," *Trash: Short Stories* (Ithaca, NY: Firebrand Books, 1988) reprinted in Holmstrom (ed.), *The Socialist-Feminist Project*. If she were black instead of white her race would likely be as or more salient, as she describes how determinedly poor whites of the South held on to their racism; at least they could feel they were better than some other people.

for both personal and political autonomy would freedom as self-realization be possible.

Thus, if the material supports provided by government in many developed capitalist countries could be expanded further, this would increase the freedom and well-being of those who benefit, and opponents of capitalism certainly support such reforms. But the question remains as to just how extensive could one envisage such changes within capitalism to be (leaving aside the question of whether they could be achieved). Just *how* free, *how* ideal, could a capitalist society be? If everyone were guaranteed food, shelter, medical care, and all other necessities, this would free people from the need to take dangerous low paid jobs. But, in fact, if such guarantees were generous enough, they would free people from the need to work at all. That seems to me to be problematic for capitalism even in theory. While the current unemployment rates are particularly high, capitalist societies always have unemployment; in fact, economists talk about an "ideal" rate of unemployment in the United States as being 4.8 percent. This counts as full employment for the capitalist system even though millions of people who want to work would be unable to find a job, and if unemployment drops below this, financial and government elites take steps to restore it. The reason unemployment must be maintained within all capitalist societies is because the threat of unemployment provides a downward pressure on wages and allows for expanding the workforce when and where needed. (This may be why the government has not addressed our current crisis by providing jobs, which would seem a logical thing to do since it would not only directly help those needing work but also the economy, as the employed would have money to spend.) How could this be addressed in our ideal version of capitalism? If the guarantees provided by such a system were generous enough so that many people would choose not to work, capitalists would not have the workers they need, or they would have to greatly increase worker compensation to get them to work, which would put them at a competitive disadvantage to capitalists in less generous countries. On the other hand, if, as is more likely, the supports were kept minimal enough so that almost everyone who could work would choose to do so, then the fundamental lack of freedom for the majority in capitalism is still there.

The most basic inequality

> When I give food to the poor, they call me a saint. When I ask why the poor have no food, they call me a communist. (Dom Helder Camara, Brazilian Liberation theologian)

Charity is good, and a capitalist society with welfare minimums would be even better. But it would still not provide genuine equality of power, opportunity, and freedom for all. The problem is the basic structure of wealth and power in capitalism which means a fundamental lack of freedom for the majority. This is what is missed by liberals who want a capitalist system with genuine equality of opportunity and freedom for all. Liberal theorists worry about the power of the state to limit freedom more than about private power because, they say, the state has the monopoly on the means of coercion, and because, unlike private powers, the state provides no exit.[137] But these differences are more apparent than real. Labor in capitalism is free in two senses, as Marx explained. Unlike slavery and serfdom, workers in capitalism are legally free to work for anyone, or for no one. This gives them the "exit" from *any particular* private power. But they are also *free of* the means of production. This makes them economically dependent, with no choice but to sell their capacity to labor to someone else – not to any particular person, but to some owner of means of production. By selling their labor to someone, they thereby put themselves under that person's control (or more likely, the control of a giant corporation), acting not on their own will but that of the owner who has distinct, maybe antagonistic, ends. Selling their labor is like temporarily selling *themselves* in that respect. They are free to do so or not, but the structure of ownership and control of the

---

137 For example, Pettit, *A Theory of Freedom*, 155. As discussed earlier, "libertarians" do not even allow that private economic power limits freedom at all.

means of subsistence makes them *not* free *not* to. There is no exit. Hence, at its foundation, capitalism is a system of "forced labor – no matter how much it may appear to result from free contractual agreement."[138] The owners determine what is produced, how much, and in how many hours of work. And with today's technology, which allows employers to monitor everything their employees do and say, they have more complete control over the labor process than slave owners had over the labor of their slaves.

This is true in any system where the producers do not possess the means of production and appropriation. Consider other examples. Slavery is a system of private ownership of the means of production where people are among the means of production. By definition, slavery involves forced labor. Individuals with sufficient economic means had the power and the legal right to apply direct physical force to other individuals to make them work for them. Here the coercion is individual, direct, and intentional.[139] In feudal societies the force was less ever present and direct than in slavery, but the relation between peasants and their lord was clearly one of domination. Although peasants possessed their means of subsistence within the communal setting, sometimes individually, sometimes collectively, and directly controlled their own labor process, they were required by law, backed up by brute force, either to work part of the time for their lords, or to give them some of the products of their labor. In most cases, the threat was sufficient to force the producers to do the lords' will. In the bureaucratic systems that existed in the Soviet Union, China, etc. for much of the twentieth century, the means of production nominally belonged to all the people whose power was vested in the state. But the bureaucracy, collectively, owned the state, that is, it had exclusive monopoly control of the means of production. This compelled workers to work for the bureaucracy because

---

138 Karl Marx, *Capital: Vol. III*, 819.
139 As will be discussed later, slavery can exist without legal ownership but with control through violence.

they had no access to the means of production/subsistence except through the bureaucracy.

In all three of the above systems, slavery, feudalism, and the bureaucratic system, the coercion is extra-economic. Now consider a different kind of unfree labor, that of indentured servitude, which is not an economic system in itself, but an economic relationship that has existed within other systems including capitalism.[140] It lies between slavery and free labor in that the worker agrees to work for someone else under conditions set by them, usually very arduous and brutal, for some specified period of time, typically seven years. Given that the choice is starvation or close to it (why else would anyone agree to such a contract?),[141] the worker has no choice but to agree.[142] It is an example of what we have earlier called a "forcing offer." No direct force is necessary; the force comes from the distribution of economic resources. The difference between indentured servitude and the free labor of capitalism is only a matter of the degree of unfreedom. For some people in capitalist societies, the choices are equally dire; the difference between indentured servitude and wage labor is mostly a matter of the duration of the contract. Fortunately, the choices are not nearly so dire for most people in developed capitalist societies. Some people can survive by begging or stealing, or they succeed against the odds at opening small businesses, or after retirement from years of working in well-paid jobs. But the majority of those without access to the means of production and subsistence are "compelled by social conditions" to work for others. This is why Marx refers to private property as "the power to subjugate the labor of others."

140 Some have argued that capitalism necessarily articulates with forms of unfree labor such as slave, convict, indentured, and contract labor. See Robert Miles, *Capitalism and Unfree Labor: Anomaly or Necessity?* (London: Tavistock, 1987).

141 For this reason Nozick would allow that someone should have the right to sell themselves into slavery. See *Anarchy, State and Utopia*, 133.

142 In reality there is often not even this appearance of freedom since it is often a parent who contracts with a master for a child's labor which makes it more like short-term slavery.

Feminists who have argued that marriage has not been a free choice for most women use similar notions of unfreedom,[143] as do feminists who argue against prostitution and (so-called) surrogate motherhood. It is not necessarily particular individuals who directly force other individuals to be surrogate mothers or prostitutes, but it is the inequality of their "bargaining positions" that allows others to take advantage of some women's position (economic and/or psychological) to secure an agreement that harms them. The social and economic context of the choice makes it not a genuinely free choice. And she cannot sell her "sexual services" without selling her body and herself. If those examples are acknowledged by all feminists as unfree, it should be recognized that the same is true of women (or men) who do less controversial work. Women are clustered at the bottom of the economic ladder in all societies and sometimes sex work may in fact be the best of the available alternatives.[144]

The only way to eliminate the force inherent in all these economic systems is to create a system in which the producers themselves control the means of production. Only if the producers are also the owners are they not dependent on and subordinate to the owners. A possible objection to this conclusion is that on the analysis of freedom I have offered, force would be inherent in *any* economic system, including this one. Since, so the objection would go, I argued that physical conditions as well as people can be obstacles to freedom, then even in an economic system where the producers were the owners, people would not be completely free but would be forced to work to satisfy their physical needs.

143 For example, Pateman, *The Sexual Contract*; Nicole-Claude Mathieu, "When Yielding is Not Consenting," *Gender Issues* 10 (1990): 3–49.
144 Jo Bindman of Anti-Slavery International argues against the criminalization of prostitution. "[Should we] take away their power to choose this occupation, maybe condemning them to worse conditions in another field?" "An International Perspective on Slavery in the Sex Industry," in Holmstrom (ed.), *The Socialist-Feminist Project*, 209–10. *Cf.* Hirschmann, *The Subject of Liberty*, for very sensitive discussions of the social and economic conditions in which so many women's choices are made, or Barbara Ehrenreich, *Nickel and Dimed: On (Not) Getting By in America* (New York: Metropolitan Books, 2001), for concrete work examples.

Plato and Aristotle used this idea to argue against democracy; anyone who was tied to physical necessity through their need to work for a living was thereby unsuited to participate in politics.[145] As a reply to this objection, I would refer to Marx's treatment of the issue. In the realm of physical necessity, which he says would exist in every economic system:

> Freedom can only consist of socialized man, the associated producers, rationally regulating their interchange with Nature, bringing it under their common control, instead of being ruled by it as by the blind forces of Nature; and achieving this with the least expenditure of energy and under conditions most favorable to, and worthy of their human nature. But it nonetheless remains a realm of necessity. Beyond it begins that development of human energy which is an end in itself, the true realm of freedom, which, however, can blossom forth only with the realm of necessity as its basis. The shortening of the working day is its basic prerequisite.[146]

Thus, in a system where the producers control the means of production, they are not forced to work for anyone else, as there is no separate class of owners who live off their labor. The producers themselves would decide what to produce, and how much of it, and how to balance leisure time and material goods. Though external conditions create the need to work, their goals, desires, values, and beliefs also determine both the nature of their work and its duration. Hence, a system where people's need to work arises simply from features of the natural world does not involve domination by others. No one else, no other group has power *over them*, and, hence, they are not unfree in that crucial way. Moreover, being able to make their own decisions regarding work within the limits set by physical necessity, they would be likely to organize work in more satisfying ways and to reduce the working day, thereby expanding "the true realm of freedom."

145 See Wood, *Democracy Against Capitalism*, 221.
146 Tucker (ed.), *Marx–Engels Reader*, 441. Tucker dubs this section "The Realm of Necessity and the Realm of Freedom." For Plato and Aristotle being constrained by material necessity, having to work for a living, is inconsistent with political freedom.

Interestingly, this realm would include labor as Marx conceived it; in fact, he says, "really free labor, e.g., composing, is at the same time precisely the most damned seriousness, the most intense exertion."[147] Marx's conception of freedom and work is echoed by psychologist Mihaly Csikszentmihalyi, who developed the concept of "flow," an optimal experience of intense concentration, challenge, and pleasure that can be found as often in work (under the right conditions) as in leisure.[148]

Freedom, self-realization, and alienation

It is only a fortunate few among us in capitalist societies for whom their primary work, that is, what they get paid to do, has this quality of freedom, allowing for occasional "flow" experiences. It is not unreasonable to expect more at this stage of history. The liberal philosophy of capitalist societies promises individuals the opportunity to develop themselves (to pursue happiness in his or her own unique way), and compared with previous societies this promise was definitely fulfilled in most respects. However, capitalist society has built-in barriers to the fulfillment of the promise of self-realization that is implicit in this freedom and, indeed, in some ways things have gone backward. The truly astounding growth in the productivity of labor under capitalism, which massively reduces the time it takes to produce the necessities of life, could mean greater freedom and satisfaction for all. This has not happened because the producers are not the owners in capitalist society (the producers are separated or alienated from the means of production), and the owners' purpose in developing technology is not to expand freedom but to increase profits.[149] Since labor power is a commodity in capitalism, capitalists quite

---

147 Karl Marx, *Grundrisse*, trans. Martin Nicolaus (Harmondsworth: Penguin, 1973), 611.

148 Mihaly Csikszentmihalyi, *Flow: The Psychology of Optimal Experience* (New York: Harper & Row, 1990).

149 In the chapter "Machinery and Modern Industry" in *Capital* Marx quotes John Stuart Mill who says, "It is questionable if all the mechanical inventions yet made have lightened the day's toil of any human being," and comments jokingly in a footnote that Mill should have said "of any human

naturally want to cheapen it like any of the other commodities they need to buy and utilize to maximum effect. The result is that individuals are undeveloped by capitalism in crucial ways. Consider the fact that most people spend most of their waking adult lives at work. (Given its importance to our lives, indeed, its importance to *who we are*, as one of the principal institutions that shape us, it is striking how little attention it is given in liberal theory.) Certainly, not everyone can be a composer, as in Marx's example above, and there is much routine work that needs to be done in any society. But it can be done in more or less fulfilling ways. Any worthwhile work can be satisfying when people decide to do it and how to do it; doing it together then can constitute what Robert Paul Wolff called productive community.[150] Instead, work has become less fulfilling for most people under capitalism. This is not the inevitable result of industrialization. In capitalist countries, as soon as someone enters the door of a factory or office, they lose whatever basic rights they have in the society at large, even freedom of speech; workplaces are essentially "managerial dictatorships."[151] As employees, they are under the control of their employers who have the power and the right to decide what kind of work their employees do, for what purposes, and at what pace, with little or no room for individual

being not fed by other people's labor," 371. That profit is the motor force behind technological development can be seen by the atypical absence of development we see in some technologies. Sewing machines have changed hardly at all in a hundred years because women have been available here and abroad to do the work so cheaply that capitalists had no motivation to reduce labor time.

150 Robert Paul Wolff, *The Poverty of Liberalism* (Cambridge, MA: Harvard University Press, 1968).

151 The First Amendment states that *"Congress* shall make no law abridging freedom of speech," and the due process clause of the Fourteenth Amendment, which applies the Bill of Rights to the states, provides that "No *state* shall ... deprive any person of life, liberty, or property, without due process of law" (emphasis added). But these do not forbid *private employers* from firing workers for exercising their right to free speech and assembly. (For an argument that the Thirteenth Amendment ought to be interpreted so as to protect speech at the workplace, see James Gray Pope, Peter Kellman, and Ed Bruno, "Free Labor Today," *New Labor Forum* (Spring 2007): 8–18.)

decisions and creative initiative. (More highly skilled and highly paid employees, of course, are given more room.) This inevitable feature of capitalism entails alienation, a central moral flaw of the system.[152] Alienation has different interpretations, but for our purposes we can say that workers are alienated from their work when they are powerless in their work, find their work meaningless, and are estranged from their own selves and from others in their work.

The degrading of work began before industrialization. Since the advent of capitalism jobs have been divided into narrower and narrower tasks in pursuit of efficiency and profit, exemplified by Adam Smith's famous example of pin making being divided into eighteen distinct operations and then assigning each task to a different worker; instead of making pins, a worker straightened wires all day.[153] "The knowledge, judgment and the will, which, though in ever so small a degree, are practiced by the independent peasant or handicraftsman ... these faculties are required only for the workshop as a whole."[154] Since the capitalist owns this collective mechanism, its productive powers "appear to be the productive powers of capital." Workers become "crippled monstrosities."[155] With machinery the process was greatly intensified. "The separation of the intellectual powers of production from the manual labor, and the conversion of those powers into the might of capital over labor, is ... finally completed by modern industry."[156] The worker becomes an appendage of the machine. This process was carried further by so-called "scientific management," which made the worker into a machine. First developed by Frederick Taylor and his followers in the late nineteenth century and subsequently applied to many more kinds of jobs, this approach uses time and motion studies of the labor process to

---

152 Much the same criticisms can be made of the bureaucratic Soviet system and for the same reason, viz. that the producers were not those who controlled production.
153 Smith, *The Wealth of Nations*, 4–5.
154 Marx, *Capital: Vol. I*, 361f.
155 Marx, *Capital: Vol. I*, 360.
156 Marx, *Capital: Vol. I*, 423.

calculate the exact motions necessary to get the most output in the shortest time, and then imposes on the workers precisely this one way of doing each task. All individual freedom and choice is removed from the labor process. The reason why this is an inherent feature of capitalism is that labor is the only input to production whose contribution is hard to calculate in advance. To calculate the input of each worker – and to increase it as much as possible – is essential to capitalists, and the only way they can do it is via greater control over the labor process since it is assumed that workers and owners have contrary interests. Taylor had recognized that the problem of getting the maximum output from the worker (what he called "a fair day's work") was stymied by the fact that although he was foreman, "the combined knowledge and skill of the workmen who were under him was certainly ten times as great as his own"[157] – and this is what he set out to change. The key to scientific management was its second principle: "All possible brain work should be removed from the shop and centered in the planning or laying-out department."[158] The result: labor that was less skilled and therefore cheaper.

This is not a thing of the past. Though some of us are lucky enough to do work where creativity is prized, this is a small minority.[159] Millions of people still work in factories (though many have moved from the developed to the developing world), others work in low-level service jobs, many in isolated situations like home health aides, and many in call centers which have been likened to present-day "Satanic mills."[160] Offices and professional jobs have been subjected to the same processes, as documented by Harry Braverman's magisterial *Labor and Monopoly*

157 Quoted in Harry Braverman, *Labor and Monopoly Capital: The Degradation of Work in the Twentieth Century* (New York: Monthly Review, 1974), 102
158 Braverman, *Labor and Monopoly Capital*, 113.
159 See the Bureau of Labor Statistics, *Occupational Outlook Handbook*, 2010–11 edition, and the *Career Guide to Industries*, 2010–11 edition. As an economist friend put it, "the shit jobs are just overwhelming."
160 Peter Bain and Phil Taylor, "Entrapped by the 'Electronic Panopticon'? Workers Resistance in the Call Centre," *New Technology, Work and Employment* 15 (2000): 2–18.

Capital,[161] and other works like Barbara Garson's *All the Livelong Day: The Meaning and Demeaning of Routine Work* and *The Electronic Workshop: How Computers Are Transforming the Office of the Future into the Factory of the Past*. Like the pin maker who becomes a straightener of wire, or the skilled worker who becomes a reader of dials, a professional social worker becomes a clerical worker whose job is reduced to specific tasks, calculated in tenths of minutes – "authorize funeral and burial expenses," "issue lost or stolen check" – which can then be done by a high school graduate – or by no worker at all. We have all gotten used to talking to machines and taking care of business on line that used to be done for us. The same approach has been applied to professional jobs like doctors, lawyers, engineers, estate planners, and stockbrokers. "Expert systems" have been devised to do their jobs – not quite as well but good enough so that the system needs fewer experts. In the catch-all category of service work, which includes so many women, often it is emotions that are controlled, or at least the outward appearance of emotion.[162] While some highly skilled workers will always be needed, increasingly capitalism has learned how to package that creativity.[163] In the 1970s, the alienation of American blue-collar workers resulting in sabotage and wildcat strikes was in the news and there was talk of more humane ways to organize work, such as the (short-lived) Volvo team approach.[164] But the neoliberal turn and the threat of jobs lost overseas put an end to that, and alienated workers take their solace in leisure activities and consumption, a cycle

161 Braverman, *Labor and Monopoly Capital*; Barbara Garson, *All the Livelong Day: The Meaning and Demeaning of Routine Work* (New York: Penguin, 1994) and *The Electronic Workshop: How Computers Are Transforming the Office of the Future into the Factory of the Past* (New York: Simon & Schuster, 1988).
162 Hochschild, *The Managed Heart*.
163 In my own field of academia I worry about the use of distance learning, lectures on tape, and the use of underpaid and insecure adjunct professors to replace professors. The intrinsic rewards of the field mitigate the alienation and allow them to be exploited.
164 Ake Sandberg, "Enriching Production: Perspectives on Volvo's Uddevalla Plant as an Alternative to Lean Production," MPRA Paper No. 10785, University Library of Munich Germany, revised 2007.

of "wanting and spending" that does not produce happiness but rather massive personal indebtedness.[165]

It was supposed to be different. Liberal sociologist Robert Blauner in his classic work *Alienation and Freedom*[166] and numerous futurologists of the last half of the twentieth century foresaw the end of alienation in the age of automation. But on the contrary: studies show that in general the more automated the job, the less control is required of the worker.[167] It could be said that we all benefit as consumers from these developments which cheapen production, and there is truth to this. However, most of us are not only consumers, but also workers for most of our adult lives. It is not impossible to have efficient production without degrading human beings in the process. It is we after all who devise and choose among technologies; technology does not dictate to us. An instructive example of the second principle of scientific management comes from the machine-tool industry, where as labor historian, David Montgomery, and David Noble, historian of technology, have shown, of two equally efficient technologies developed around the same time, the one chosen was the one that put control over the process in the hands of management.[168] Often technologies are chosen to make it easier to measure and control individual output. With electronic monitoring, as Barbara Garson points out, the worker reports on him- or herself with each keystroke.[169]

To refer to these changes in the labor process in capitalism as the "dehumanization" of work and to say they involve

---

165 Juliet Schor, *The Overspent American* (New York: Basic Books, 1998).

166 Robert Blauner, *Alienation and Freedom: The Factory Worker and His Industry* (University of Chicago Press, 1964).

167 James R. Bright, *Automation and Management* (Boston, MA: Division of Research, Graduate School of Business Administration, Harvard University, 1958), discussed in Braverman, *Labor and Monopoly Capital*, 213–23.

168 David Montgomery, "Social Choice in Machine Design: The Case of Automatically Controlled Machine Tools and a Challenge for Labor," *Politics and Society*, 3/4 (1978): 313–37. David F. Noble, *Forces of Production: A Social History of Industrial Automation* (Oxford University Press, 1986). See also: Noble, *Progress Without People: In Defense of Luddism* (Chicago: Charles H. Kerr, 1993).

169 Garson, *All the Livelong Day*, 263.

"self-estrangement" is not romantic rhetoric, but rather rests on the nature of human labor and its importance in people's lives. People want to work, a desire that has both genetic and social roots, but they want work that is worthy of them.[170] Labor in its distinctly human form is purposive, a union of thought and action. As Marx put it eloquently, "What distinguishes the worst architect from the best of bees is this, that the architect raises his structure in imagination before he erects it in reality."[171] It is precisely this union of conception and execution that is severed – intentionally – in labor under capitalism. As alienation is discussed in the mainstream literature, it is primarily a subjective phenomenon – having to do with people's feelings. What I have been describing, on the other hand, is objective: workers are subordinated to capitalists, workers have progressively less control of their labor while capitalists have more, workers' skills have become capital's, and workers are worth less while the wealth and power of capitalists has grown stupendously both in absolute and relative terms. But alienation has subjective effects. If people are treated as interchangeable commodities, with inadequate challenge and respect, this makes them unhappy. As women are at the bottom of the occupational ladder, they are therefore most subject to alienated labor. As the majority of workers on the global assembly line and in "pink-collar" service work and clerical work, sexism and capitalism combine to maximize profits and alienation. Even if it were possible to end extreme poverty in capitalism through the provision of a welfare minimum, this would not end alienation for most people, and hence even "ideal" capitalism is far from ideal for human beings.

Summary conclusion of capitalism in theory

Contrary to our popular idea of property, property is not things, nor physical possession, but rights, as most writers on property recognize. Every system of ownership, every system of property,

---

170 Howard Gardner, Mihaly Csikszentmihalyi, and William Damon, *Good Work: When Excellence and Ethics Meet* (New York: Basic Books, 2002).
171 Marx, *Capital: Vol. I*, 178.

involves certain rights or freedoms, and denies other rights and freedoms. Consider a system of common ownership versus private ownership. A system of common ownership involves the right and freedom for all to use, enjoy, and benefit from the commons. In pre-capitalist days, common people had the right to hunt, graze their animals, gather food and firewood on common land, rights that could double the income of poor families.[172] Women were and are still today around the world the principal gatherers and men the hunters. These rights/freedoms were lost with the enclosure movement, so pivotal to the development of capitalism. It is also happening at a rapid pace throughout the world due to capitalist development.[173] This *right not to be excluded* from the use of something is one kind of individual right to property. But a system of common ownership does not include the right to exclude others. Nor does it include the right to benefit from the commons by buying or selling the commons or one's portion of it. So one has a right to use or enjoy common property, but not to dispose of it. Defenders of capitalism, from Locke on, see the restrictions on rights of ownership in common property as unjustified restrictions on individual freedom. Capitalism involves a different kind of individual right to property which includes the right to buy and sell what one owns because it is a right of exclusive ownership. This means that it is a right and freedom to exclude others. So *this kind of individual right to property entails the lack of rights and freedom of all those who are excluded.* With the predominance of the market in the modern period, the second kind of ownership has almost entirely eliminated the first. C. B. Macpherson explains that as the amount of property held in common became smaller and smaller, our concept of property has also drastically narrowed.

---

172 Hill, *Liberty Against the Law*. Also Linebaugh, *The Magna Carta Manifesto*.
173 For a discussion of today's receding commons, see Anatole Anton, "Public Goods as Commonstock," in Anatole Anton, Milton Fisk and Nancy Holmstrom (eds.), *Not for Sale: in Defense of Public Goods* (Boulder, CO: Westview, 2000). David Harvey develops the concept of "accumulation by dispossession" in *The New Imperialism* (New York: Oxford University Press, 2005). The privatization of water all over the world is particularly important.

From the earliest ideas of property, say from Aristotle down to the seventeenth century, property was seen to include two kinds of individual rights: an individual right to exclude others from some use or enjoyment of some thing; and an individual right not to be excluded from the use or enjoyment of things that society has declared to be for common use – common lands, parks, roads, waters. Both were rights of individuals. Both rights were created and maintained by society or the state. Both therefore were individual property.[174] Another new kind of individual property is found in programs like social security or universal medical care; individuals have the right to draw from common resources, but not to exclude others or to sell their share. Such publicly provided goods hark back to older forms and can be considered another kind of common property, particularly important for women given their role as child-bearers and primary caregivers. Legal theorist Morris R. Cohen explains that the right to exclude, which is the essence of private property, gives it the character of political sovereignty in that it gives the property owner the power to command the service and obedience of those who are not economically independent, even if this "may be obscured for us in a commercial economy by the fiction of the so-called labor contract as a free bargain and by the frequency with which service is rendered indirectly through a money payment."[175] Interestingly, Cohen does not infer from this analysis that private property is therefore unjustified, as he leaves open the possibility that compulsion in the economic sphere might be necessary. However, he says, "we must not overlook the actual fact that dominion over things is also *imperium* over our fellow human beings."[176]

Today, at the beginning of the twenty-first century, when some individuals have more wealth than that of many countries combined, and half the world's largest economies are corporations

---

174 C. B. Macpherson, *The Rise and Fall of Economic Justice and Other Essays* (New York: Oxford University Press, 1985), 77; Linebaugh, *The Magna Carta Manifesto*.

175 According to Marx, in capitalism, relations between people are perceived as relations between things, calling this the fetishism of commodities.

176 Cohen, "Property and Sovereignty," 159.

not countries, this power over things and over others extends to the entire globe. *Indeed, it is the power to determine the future of life on earth.* If the defense of capitalism as an ideal rests on an expanded "humanized" or "compassionate" version of capitalism that would either reduce this extraordinary power or else render it benign, then everything depends on whether such a reformed version of capitalism can be realized. Otherwise the defense of capitalism amounts to an apology for a very un-ideal system.[177] What theory of politics and social change would make this plausible?

It is time to leave the realm of theory and examine capitalism as an actually existing system.

3   Capitalism in reality

Compared with pre-capitalist societies

Patriarchy: a contested concept

Let us turn directly now to the question of whether capitalism in reality is good for women. One question that immediately arises is, compared with what? And in what respects? In recent discussions of capitalism's impact on women, especially discussions in the United States and Western Europe, capitalism is contrasted to less developed, pre-capitalist, traditional societies. Unless we go way back to the earliest days of human history, these societies are almost without exception patriarchal. It would seem to follow almost automatically that from a feminist point of view, capitalism would be better. But what does patriarchal mean exactly? There is a substantial and influential body of literature that problematizes the concept of patriarchy and the assumption that it is counterposed to modernity. The definition of the concept patriarchy is male dominated or more precisely, father dominated, and the latter more restricted sense is how I will be using the concept, using "sexism" or simply "male domination" for the broader meaning. Still, even in the restricted sense, patriarchy is not a homogeneous system of male domination, by any

177 See Mills, "'Ideal Theory' as Ideology."

means, but rather has many varieties. A number of writers insist that the presumptions prevailing in many feminist discussions of patriarchy are inaccurate and stress the following points about patriarchal societies:

(1) Women are not in the same position in all patriarchal societies.
(2) Women are not totally passive victims, respondents to external forces, but almost always have some room for negotiation in these societies.
(3) Various kinds of patriarchal bargains are possible, some of which have considerable advantages for some women, particularly as they age (e.g., the infamous mothers-in-law of some societies).
(4) Patriarchal bargains also exist in modern societies, for example, the proto-typical family of 1950s middle-class capitalist America of the breadwinner father and housewife mother.[178]

In my opinion, these points have considerable validity and they help us to understand why women sometimes choose arrangements that to us today seem oppressive. Some feminists go further and argue that women are actually better off in many pre-capitalist than in capitalist societies.[179] Despite mostly being patriarchal, they maintain, subsistence economies offer more to women overall than does the globalized capitalist economy. Moreover, they say, capitalism is also patriarchal and should be described as capitalist patriarchy.

Capitalism as tendentially better for women

Notwithstanding the validity of many of the points made above, and the variety of pre-capitalist societies, I would maintain that *as a system*, capitalism has the potential to create the conditions

178 Deniz Kandiyoti, "Bargaining with Patriarchy," in Holmstrom (ed.), *The Socialist-Feminist Project*, 137–51, explains how the third point leads many older women to internalize and enforce patriarchy.
179 Veronika Bennholdt-Thomsen and Maria Mies, *The Subsistence Perspective: Beyond the Globalised Economy* (London: Zed Books, 1999); Silvia Federici, *Caliban and the Witch: Women, the Body and Primitive Accumulation* (Brooklyn, NY: Autonomedia, 2004).

for better lives for women than pre-capitalist societies – in general. However, that does not entail that *in all particular cases* and *in all respects* women will be better off in the transition from pre-capitalist to capitalist society, particularly in the short run, for there are many factors other than gender relations that contribute to overall well-being. Subsistence peasants, for example, are likely to be much worse off as they lose their homes and their livelihood and have to become wage workers in a capitalist economy. This is just as true, or more so, for women, as they lose the protections as well as the restrictions afforded by traditional societies. In the Philippines, for example, the destruction of natural resources has forced peasants out of their simple rural economies to living in Manila garbage dumps – literally.[180] This process is what Marx called "primitive accumulation," a process discussed earlier in the context of seventeenth-century England.

A crucial respect in which people's conditions of life tend to worsen in the transition to capitalism is that the amount of work they do tends to increase. This might surprise many readers since, as Juliet Schor says in *The Overworked American*, "One of capitalism's most durable myths is that it has reduced human toil."[181] While it is true, she explains, that the modern 40-hour week (the result of a long and bitter struggle) is dramatically less than the 70- to 80-hour work week that prevailed in the nineteenth century, this latter figure may have been the "most prodigious work effort in the entire history of humankind." In the Middle Ages peasants not only worked fewer hours per day, but many fewer days per year due to the domination of agricultural work by the seasons, and to the multitude of holidays, which was also the norm in ancient Greece and Rome. The very concept of time changed in the transition to capitalism from an extremely vague and loose sense to become ever more finely divided as time took on economic value and the rhythm of work was set by

180 Robin Broad with John Cavanaugh, *Plundering Paradise: The Struggle for the Environment in the Philippines* (Berkeley, CA: University of California Press, 1993).
181 Juliet B. Schor, *The Overworked American: The Unexpected Decline of Leisure* (New York: Basic Books, 1992), 43.

time-clocks rather than by nature.[182] In the United States over the past several decades hours of work have steadily increased.

With respect to strategic gender interests

Despite the above very important caveat, I say that capitalism is better than pre-capitalist societies for most women, over some time anyway, for two reasons relating both to strategic and to practical gender interests. The first reason has to do with patriarchy (i.e., father-dominated societies), the second with industrialization. Patriarchal bargains are still patriarchal whatever their variations and even if women have some maneuvering room within them. In most pre-capitalist societies, the father of a family has, by virtue of his position, a power that he has gradually lost in capitalist societies, and when he shares the power, it is with other men in the kinship group. In feudal societies, the most widespread system prior to capitalism, the peasant household was a work unit and, therefore, the head of the family was also the head of the work unit – the foreman essentially. Men also monopolized military power, which gave them considerable power throughout the society. In contrast, though the 1950s-style arrangement of breadwinner father and housewife mother could be called a patriarchal bargain, the power of the breadwinner father in such families did not translate into power in society at large. The work done in the family was for their immediate needs only, and was quite distinct from the dominant kind of production in capitalist society. What power the breadwinner fathers had outside the family was not due to their being fathers, but rather to being men, mostly white, middle-class men. And that meant that breadwinner fathers had less total power *in* the family as well, than did fathers in pre-capitalist societies. Thus, though the arrangement of breadwinner father and housewife mother could be called patriarchal, it does not have the same

---

182 Among the sources Schor cites are H. S. Bennett, *Life on the English Manor* (Cambridge University Press, 1960); Jacques Le Goff, *Time, Work and Culture in the Middle Ages* (Chicago University Press, 1980); Marshall Sahlins, *Stone Age Economics* (New York: Aldine, 1972).

overall significance for male–female social roles since it is embedded within a capitalist system. Moreover, even in the heyday of this type of family, though it was presented as the norm, it was by no means universal. Family forms varied according to class and race. I did not grow up in such a family, nor did most of my friends because our mothers had to work whether or not our fathers were in the family. And historian Temma Kaplan explains that women raising their own and others' children has, for centuries, been "the family structure of poverty under capitalism."[183] Today, families in which fathers work and mothers stay at home constitute a very small minority of American families.

The fact that no particular style of family is integral to the functioning of capitalism reflects the first reason why capitalism tends to be better for women (although for poor women, the lack of support for *any* kind of family form can be devastating, as will be discussed later). Though capitalists are predominantly male and usually fathers, they do not have power *as fathers* but rather, *as owners of the means of production* and, hence, they have no necessary relationship to women. Indeed, capitalists can be women and so can political leaders. Instead of being patriarchal, capitalism, as explained earlier, is a different kind of hierarchical system that rests on a different kind of power – ownership of the means of production – that in theory at least does not absolutely require the subordination of women. Rather, the principal "rule" or "law of motion" of capitalism is the maximization of profit. That is the goal of production in capitalism; that determines what is produced, how it is produced, and where it is produced. In principle, capitalism is "gender neutral" – it does not matter whose labor power produces the profit and who gets it.[184] This is often cited as a reason why capitalism is good for women, but it is decidedly a mixed blessing as we shall see.

---

183 Temma Kaplan, "The Disappearing Fathers Under Global Capitalism," in Holmstrom (ed.), *The Socialist-Feminist Project*, 152–57.

184 On this point *The Communist Manifesto* says, "the more modern industry becomes developed, the more is the labour of the men superseded by the labour of the women. Differences of age and sex have no longer any distinctive social validity for the working class. All are instruments of labour,

Moreover, though capitalism is gender neutral in principle, women's subordination is sometimes useful to capitalism as well as to men – women can be paid less, for example, and they do most of the socially necessary caring work for free. (Similar things can be said about race in that capitalism is also in principle race neutral, yet racism has been highly advantageous to capitalism. Despite similarities, however, the relationship of sexism and racism to capitalism are not identical, so I will not complicate my discussion any further.[185]) Marxist, socialist, and other radical feminists have debated how these competing interests within capitalism, on the one hand, toward gender neutrality for the maximization of profit, and on the other hand, the utility of women's subordination for profit maximization are related, and how these two tendencies have worked out in different historical periods and places.[186] Nevertheless, overall, over time, it is clear that there has been a gradual, though incomplete, reduction of rigid gender roles as capitalism has developed. In Molyneux's terms, women's *strategic* gender interests have generally advanced under capitalism. This is not universally the case, however; fully developed capitalist countries Chile and Ireland have laws prohibiting abortion under all conditions. Though women have these rights in the United States, it is the only developed country that has not ratified the UN Women's Rights Convention (CEDAW). So although there is a tendency in capitalism toward the advancing of women's strategic gender interests, this is not guaranteed

more or less expensive to use, according to their age and sex." Tucker (ed.), *Marx–Engels Reader*, 479.

185 Indeed, a number of scholars have suggested that racism in its most virulent modern form is *due to capitalism* because, on the one hand, conquest and slavery were instrumental to the development of capitalism, but, on the other hand, they were completely at odds with the new ideals of human equality. This contradiction between theory and reality required that the enslaved be reduced essentially to nonhumans, outside the pale of morality. Ellen Meiksins Wood makes this argument explicitly in "Capitalism and Human Emancipation: Race, Gender and Democracy," *Democracy Against Capitalism*. It is consistent with, perhaps implicit in, Mills, *The Racial Contract*.

186 There is a large literature on this topic. See among other sources, Wally Secombe, "The Housewife and Her Labor Under Capitalism," *New Left*

and is never automatic. Capitalists can live with their denial as long as capitalist economic interests are furthered. Moreover, it remains to be seen whether progress can continue to the point of complete gender equality within capitalism or whether some gender inequities are inevitable in the system.

With respect to practical gender interests

Whether women do better under capitalism with respect to *practical* gender interests is more complicated and very much depends on which women we are talking about and what we compare it with. To the extent that practical gender interests have also advanced under capitalism, this is due to the incredible productivity of capitalism. Its inherent need to develop technology increases output per hour thereby creating *the potential* to reduce labor time, though not always the actuality. But it clearly provides more consumer goods and advances scientific discovery (though with certain limits to be discussed later). In particular, the enormous advances in health in the twentieth century that dramatically decreased deaths throughout the world is enormously liberating for everyone, but especially for women given their role in childbirth and their responsibilities for childcare in addition to whatever other work they do. However, these are advantages for women of *development*, especially industrialization, not specifically of capitalism, and hence is not a conclusive argument in favor of capitalism. So in pursuing the question whether

Review 83 (January 1973): 3–24; Jean Gardiner, "Women's Domestic Labor," *New Left Review* 89 (January–February 1975): 47–57; Margaret Coulson, Branka Magas, and Hilary Wainwright, "'The Housewife and Her Labor Under Capitalism' – A Critique," *New Left Review* 89 (January–February 1975), 59–71; Ian Gough and John Harrison, "Unproductive Labor and Housework Again," *Bulletin of the Conference of Socialist Economists* IV (February 1975); Nancy Holmstrom, "'Women's Work,' the Family and Capitalism," *Science and Society* XLV (Summer 1981): 186–211. Some believe there is a parallel system of patriarchy in which men exploit women, for example, Christine Delphy, *Close to Home: A Materialist Analysis of Women's Oppression* (London: Hutchinson, 1984); Heidi Hartmann, "The Unhappy Marriage of Marxism and Feminism," in Linda Sargent (ed.), *Women and Revolution* (Boston, MA: South End, 1981).

capitalism is good for women, let us shift the point of comparison from pre-capitalist societies to other noncapitalist societies.

Compared with so-called socialist societies

Leaving aside societal forms that have not yet been realized, there have been developed societies that were not capitalist, viz. the so-called socialist societies, the Soviet Union, Eastern Europe, China, etc.[187] How does capitalism compare with them with respect to the interests of women? Immediately following the Russian Revolution in 1917, there were truly astonishing gains for women, both legally and materially. The government instituted freedom of marriage, divorce, and abortion, eliminated laws against homosexuality and the status of illegitimacy, reforms that advanced strategic gender interests beyond anything existing anywhere else in the world at that time. To appreciate just how astonishing these advances were, consider the fact that almost one hundred years later, this is still not the norm in all developed countries, much less in developing countries as Russia was at that time. Communal cafeterias, laundries, childcare all addressed women's practical gender interests in impoverished, war-torn conditions. At the end of the First World War the women's movement even forced the Bolsheviks to split factory jobs between the women who had been working there and the soldiers coming back from the war. However, the Russian Revolution degenerated very quickly; indeed, it underwent a fundamental transformation in the 1920s to a bureaucratic totalitarian system under Stalin. No independent political movements were allowed, including, of course, no independent women's movement. Similar systems were constructed after the Second World War throughout Eastern Europe under the domination of the Soviet Union, and in China after the Chinese Revolution led by Mao Zedong. Policies regarding women varied in all these

187 In my opinion these societies are most accurately named "bureaucratic collectivist," as their economies were organized collectively and property was collective, nominally owned by the whole society, but controlled totally by a bureaucracy, therefore, very different from socialism as envisioned by Marx and Engels and other classical socialists.

countries according to particular state interests, but in general, the fact is that both strategic and practical gender interests were satisfied to a fair extent. Of course, women were not liberated as was claimed, but neither were men as these were totalitarian societies, and the sexism of prior societies remained embedded to a great extent. Nevertheless, relative to what came before and in relation to men in these societies, women fared quite well. In some countries, like China, where women were practically slaves before the revolution, the improvements in women's lives were especially dramatic. The reason is that *like capitalists*, the ruling bureaucracies of these societies had no vested interest in women's subordination. Indeed, on the contrary, *unlike capitalists*, they had a clear vested interest in eliminating it. They needed to maximize the productivity of the whole society since they "owned" the whole society, not just a particular firm, so they needed to maximize everyone's input into production. Hence, they instituted freedom of marriage and divorce, abortion, equal education, childcare, health care, and other social supports enabling women to participate in production and society at large on an equal basis with men.[188] However, since the satisfaction of women's interests depended on their coincidence with state interests, this was unreliable. Romania, for example, had strong anti-abortion laws because the bureaucracy wanted to increase the birth rate.[189]

Effects of transition to capitalism

Today most of these societies are in various stages of transition to capitalism; the collective property has been privatized, which means that the property has been essentially stolen from the members of society, and social supports have been dismantled.

188 Sonia Kruks, Rayna Rapp, and Marilyn B. Young (eds.), *Promissory Notes: Women in the Transition to Socialism* (New York: Monthly Review, 1989) is a useful collection of case studies, although I disagree with their characterization of these societies as socialist.

189 The same subordination of women's interests is common in capitalism. While the United States cites the emancipation of women as a goal of its policies in Afghanistan, a look at recent history shows that the United

Again, we see a process of primitive accumulation.[190] How have women been affected by this process? A report by the United Nations Children's Fund concluded that the position of women has "spiraled downward … with increasing joblessness, abuse and deteriorating social services." Most significantly in terms of overall well-being, life expectancy has even declined in one-third of the countries studied.[191] As for strategic gender interests, there is considerable variability, but overall the trend is backward. In terms of political influence, the number of women in government has declined by about one-third. Throughout the former Soviet bloc, countless young women have migrated to work as sex workers; sometimes they are trafficked, sometimes they act in the hope it will get them a better life. In Poland, with its strong Catholic Church, women's right to abortion is threatened. In Russia and China, with no history of legally protected individual rights, and no women's movement, the switch to the market has brought sex, age, and "beauty" discrimination in employment, as employers can hire whomever they want and contract with them for whatever services they want. Market freedom for employers, but constraints for employees. As these societies are in transition, it is difficult to predict how things will evolve. It is possible that fledgling grassroots movements will succeed in regaining the strategic gender interests they enjoyed earlier, but this will be a very hard struggle in the prevailing political and economic conditions. For now it seems clear that while some women are enjoying more freedom and material goods than they ever dreamed of, primarily due to the privatization of collective property, the majority of women are worse off due to that same privatization. This deterioration in the position of most women

States was actually responsible for bringing the Taliban to power, because they supported the mujahadeen, including Osama bin Laden, against the Soviet-supported government of Afghanistan, one of whose crimes in their eyes was instituting reforms for women.

190 Nancy Holmstrom and Richard Smith, "The Necessity of Gangster Capitalism: Primitive Accumulation in Russia and China," *Monthly Review* (February 2000): 1–15.

191 Elizabeth Olson, "'Free Markets Leave Women Worse Off,' Unicef Says," *New York Times*, September 23, 1999.

with the transition to capitalism should not be surprising if we look more closely at what women have and have not achieved in capitalist countries around the globe.

Gains and losses: sweatshops and worse

As already discussed, *women's strategic gender interests* have tended to be advanced as capitalism developed, although this is not always true in all respects. How women fare with respect to their *practical gender interests* is more complicated and depends on which women we focus on. In many countries around the world, both former Soviet-style economies like China or newly industrializing countries, capitalist development has taken the form of sweatshops.[192] Unlike the early days of capitalism in Europe, it is a striking fact that the majority of workers in these factories are women. Publicity about the miserable conditions in which so much of our clothing is made helped to spark an anti-sweatshop movement on US campuses and around the world (recall the exposure of Kathie Lee Gifford and the anti-Nike campaign) and helped to ignite the global justice movement.

Nevertheless, many commentators, including some feminists, have argued that the anti-sweatshop movement is misguided. Nicholas Kristof of the *New York Times* entitled a column "In Praise of the Maligned Sweatshop."[193] Basically, four arguments are given in defense of sweatshops, and against struggles like those waged by the United Students Against Sweatshops (USAS)

---

192 The exact definition of "sweatshops" is not established. The US Department of Labor defines them as workplaces that violate two or more US labor laws. The ILO has a list of eight core labor standards which ought to be met for any worker in any country no matter what the level of development. These have to do with minimum wage, maximum hours, safety conditions, right to unionize, etc. Sometimes the laws in developing countries are quite good (for example, Bangladesh has paid maternity leave), but they are not enforced. Many countries have established special export processing zones expressly to avoid their own domestic labor laws, including freedom of association and the right to collective bargaining, and attract foreign companies.

193 June 6, 2006, "Where Sweatshops Are a Dream," January 15, 2009, among others. Mainstream economists organized the Academic Consort on International Trade (ACIT) to defend sweatshops against the critics.

for decent labor standards, purporting to show that despite poor conditions they are actually good for their employees.

The first argument is that conditions are not as bad as critics charge, especially compared with prevailing standards and cost of living in the countries where they exist. This defense is simply not credible. Numerous independent studies have documented *worsening* conditions since the 1980s due to intense competition, particularly in the apparel industry, that has resulted in what has been called a "race to the bottom."[194] The International Labor Organization (ILO) has described conditions as in many cases resembling indentured servitude. We have all heard of the Triangle Shirtwaist fire in New York City on March 25, 1911, but how many know that 2,500 women were burned in fires in China in 1992 alone?[195] The recent economic downturn can only worsen the problems as competition to hold onto a shrinking market grows more fierce.

The second defense of sweatshops is that being exploited, even super-exploited, is better than *not* being exploited because there is no work. People in these developing countries were worse off before the sweatshops came, it is claimed, and if critics fight too hard to improve conditions, the companies will close up shop and go to other countries where they will have a freer hand, leaving

194 Some, for example, ACIT above, attempt to argue that there is no race to the bottom on the grounds that multinational corporations pay higher wages than those that prevail in developing countries. That could be true, but it is a different issue. Corporations have left countries with higher wages to go to countries with lower wages: from the United States to Mexico, from Mexico to the Philippines, from the Philippines to China, and from there to Vietnam. Neither is it a powerful moral argument, since the prevailing local conditions may be truly atrocious.

195 Ellen Israel Rosen, *Making Sweatshops: The Globalization of the US Apparel Industry* (Berkeley, CA: University of California Press, 2002), 241–44. Also see extensive reports of the National Labor Committee from around the world, available at: www.nlc.org. Terrible working conditions made worse by development are not, of course, confined to factories. The conditions of miners in China are particularly horrific. Though underreported, due to government policy and corruption, it is known that nine miners die every day, forty times more than in the United States. Edward Wong, "China Charges 58 with Covering Up Deadly Mine Blast," *New York Times*, December 1, 2009.

their workers behind with no jobs. Kristof says, "For those living on a garbage mountain, labor standards can hurt." But what he does not address is how they came to be living on a garbage mountain. This brings us back to the question of whether conditions were in general worse in pre-capitalist societies. As I said earlier, it all depends: the lives of subsistence peasants in places with adequate natural resources may be limited, but materially adequate and stable. There are no garbage mountains. The introduction of capitalism deprived those peasant farmers of their means of subsistence as their farms typically were seized and consolidated into export plantations, forcing millions who can no longer survive in the countryside into cities and onto garbage mountains or migration abroad. The numbers coming into the cities makes for high rates of unemployment, poverty, and desperation. *Once this process has occurred*, people are placed between the proverbial rock and a hard place. A job in a sweatshop will in fact be better than its alternative, which could be starvation. Sometimes workers have no choice but to agree to whatever conditions employers try to impose, but not even to try to get better conditions through labor standards is to accept the logic of the race to the bottom.

Even if the best strategic choice sometimes appears to be to accept super-exploitative conditions because it is better than the alternatives, this is hardly an argument in favor of capitalism. It is, rather, *a testament to the incredible power of capitalists to impose their will*. If workers decide they have to accept sweatshop conditions, it is because it is the best of a bad lot of choices imposed by the structure of capitalism, just as a patriarchal bargain that women choose because there is no better alternative is still a patriarchal bargain, worse than a nonpatriarchal one. It is what we called earlier, a "forcing offer." That they benefit from their choice (compared with the alternatives they have) does not make it morally all right; capitalists take advantage of their desperate conditions (to which capitalism has often contributed) and benefit vastly more.[196] Rather than long-term investments

---

196 Chris Meyers, "Wrongful Beneficence: Exploitation and Third World Sweatshops," *Journal of Social Philosophy* 35(3) (2004): 319–33.

necessary to increase prosperity, capitalism's relentless pursuit of maximum profit directs investment into sweatshops. If it is really true that the only path to growth for developing countries in the global capitalist economy is indeed factories that pay sub-poverty wages in poor working conditions, this should be seen as a condemnation, rather than as a defense, of global capitalism.

There are, indeed, very difficult practical, strategic questions regarding reform struggles within developed capitalism as well. How should American workers respond to threats either to give up some of their hard-won benefits or face losing their jobs to people across the globe who prefer sweatshops to starvation? There are no easy answers, given the power of the multinational corporations they are up against. Corporations can take advantage of the crisis to force concessions from workers even when they are not economically necessary. (For this kind of behavior, some commentators have likened multinational corporations to the Mafia.) The auto industry is a case in point. As an economist for the Canadian Auto Workers Union explained, though the industry is in trouble throughout the world it is only in the United States and Canada – where "direct labor accounts for less than 7 percent of total auto costs" – where wage cuts are being demanded; "ultimately it's about politics not economics."[197] Chrysler's declaration of bankruptcy broke union contracts and forced auto workers to accept lower wages and benefits. Another example is the garment industry, one of the most globalized industries, where the rich countries allow corporations like Wal-Mart to dominate the market, which then use their market power to insist on ever-cheaper prices from their producers, who in turn squeeze their workers even tighter. The rich countries also subject poor producing countries to rules, such as no subsidies to business, which do not apply to firms in their own countries and certainly did not apply in the past when their industries were first

---

197 Jim Stanford, "The Economics, and Politics, of Auto Workers' Wages," www.theglobeandmail.com, accessed April 20, 2009. Naomi Klein's *The Shock Doctrine: The Rise of Disaster Capitalism* (New York: Henry Holt, 2007) argues that this is a dominant pattern in recent global capitalism.

developing. Then there is the role of international lending agencies which operate like predatory loan sharks imposing harsh rules and such high interest rates that the borrowing countries become indebted for life. At present, according to a World Bank estimate, developing countries pay $13 for every dollar they receive in grants, an "exchange" relationship quite similar to the height of the colonial period. Thus, the game is, essentially, fixed in favor of the biggest corporations and the richest countries of the world.[198] Fighting for regional and international labor standards, such as the "Asia Floor Wage," is one small step toward changing that balance of power and hence is in the interests of workers in both developed and developing countries. It will be a hard fight, but one that should be supported by all feminists.

The third argument in defense of sweatshops focuses specifically on women, who make up an astonishing 80 percent of the low wage workers in developing countries.[199] Some feminists support or are ambivalent about sweatshops because they believe they liberate women from patriarchal family structures and lead to personal empowerment.[200] This argument is also offered in connection with the huge increase in women's international migration which I will discuss later. It has been well established that women's freedom to work outside the home increases their freedom and well-being, but what this proves about work

198 Anannya Bhattacharjee, Sarita Gupta, and Stephanie Luce, "Raising the Floor: The Movement for a Living Wage in Asia," *New Labor Forum* 18 (Summer 2009): 72–82. For more detail see the documents launching the campaign for an Asia Floor Wage, Bhattacharjee, Gupta, and Luce. "Raising the Floor: The Movement for a Living Wage in Asia," *New Labor Forum* 18(3) (Fall 2009), at: www.asiafloorwage.org/documents/Press/Bhattacharjee%20et%5B1%5Dal.pdf. See also the film *Life and Debt*, 2001. For more information on how poverty is reproduced in the name of development, see Sarah Bracking, *Money and Power: Great Predators in the Political Economy of Development* (London: Pluto Press, 2009).

199 Rosen, *Making Sweatshops*, 245.

200 For example, see Patricia Fernandez-Kelly and Diane Wolf, "A Dialogue on Globalization," *Signs* 126 (2001): 1243–49. Naila Kabeer provides a detailed account of how specific social and economic conditions influence the lives of women garment workers in Dhaka, Bangladesh, and London: *The Power to Choose* (New York: Verso, 2002).

in sweatshops is not entirely clear. Again, it all depends on the place, the time, and the aspect of the women's lives at which we look. Women sweatshop workers should not be seen as passive victims, and sometimes it is true that their work is an escape from rural poverty, gives them greater bargaining power in their families, and improves their lives in various ways. But where patriarchal family structures are replaced by totalitarian working conditions backed up by totalitarian and corrupt governments, it is not clear how much the women are empowered overall by this transition. When their factories are in special export zones set up to evade labor laws and attract foreign companies, it is even less likely that women will be empowered by their work experience since one of the features of these zones is that there is no freedom of association or right to organize. Without that they have *little real power*, even if they are more *empowered as individuals vis-à-vis men in their families*.[201] Moreover, paid employment only increases women's autonomy if the jobs pay living wages, and seldom do women factory workers in newly industrializing countries earn enough to support a family.[202] Their jobs seldom provide a way out of poverty; indeed, conditions are sometimes so bad that their lives are cut short or they have to go back to their villages sick or almost blind, as happens to workers in electronics factories.[203] While immigrant sweatshop workers in developed countries may have reasonable hope for their children, this is not the case in poor countries. Even in the best-case scenarios, which defenders like to focus on, I would simply say that capitalism is not the only means to the end of women's empowerment and often it comes at tremendous cost.

---

201 The distinction between these two senses of power is nicely illustrated by Miriam Glucksmann aka Ruth Cavendish, *Women on the Line* (London: Routledge, 2009). Rather than being empowered in the sense of individuals having a certain psychological quality, as empowerment is usually understood, women in the factory where she worked in the 1980s had a sense of their potential *collective power* to influence the British auto industry and the economy at large.
202 Bhattacharjee, Gupta, and Luce, "Raising the Floor."
203 Rosen, *Making Sweatshops*, 241–42.

The fourth defense of sweatshops, often implicit in the previous two, could be called "the future will be brighter" position. Conceding that things are really bad for many workers today, it argues that working women were also terribly exploited in the early days of capitalism in Manchester, England or Lowell, Massachusetts and look how much better off we are today. Poor conditions are inevitable in the early stages of capitalist development, it is said, but they improve greatly over time. This argument rests on the assumption that the only direction in which capitalist development works is up, that given time, capitalist countries will all look like Sweden. While logically possible, and highly desirable, this scenario is also highly unlikely. What has been called "the Lowell model" is quite disanalogous to sweatshops today, because the conditions then, though bad, were actually not as bad as they are today,[204] but more importantly, the economic context was different. The wages of the young women in Lowell were supplementing the wages of their fathers, and sometimes husbands, who were earning higher wages in capital-intensive industries. By contrast, in today's newly industrializing countries, as already discussed, low-wage women workers are the vast majority of the workforce. The men in their lives are not working in higher paid jobs or often, in any jobs at all. The dominant industries are not capital-intensive but low-wage assembly plants. Though this division of labor may be considered less patriarchal, overall conditions for the workers are arguably worse than those that prevailed in places like Lowell. As for the future, since the early stages of capitalism in Europe and America were quite different from today's newly capitalist countries, there is no reason to think that history will repeat itself in the later stages in these countries. In particular, the newly developing countries have been forced to accept trade agreements and WTO rules which forbid them from giving the kind of supports to domestic firms that the rich countries gave when their industries

---

204 Rosen, *Making Sweatshops*, 244; as increased competition brought worse conditions to Lowell, the native-born workers protested and were replaced by immigrant workers.

were first developing.[205] We can see the results of the global garment industry's extremely inequitable power relationships in the fact that:

> although Bangladesh has succeeded in developing its garment industry over the course of the past thirty years, it has not been able to significantly raise its standard of living, and their garment worker wages are still the lowest in the world. In real terms, garment wages in Bangladesh fell from 1994 to 2006, despite an enormous growth of the industry … The structure of the supply chain … keeps Bangladesh-based firms and workers down.

The authors of the study conclude that just as Walter Rodney showed that Europe underdeveloped Africa, the current system "underdevelop[s] garment-producing countries with grave consequences for garment workers."[206]

Moreover, the trajectory as capitalism develops is not necessarily up. It can remain the same, go down, or go up and then down again. In the United States, garment workers fought long and hard to get labor unions that succeeded in ending sweatshop conditions. In 1933 Frances Perkins, US Secretary of Labor, said, "The red silk bargain dress in the shop window is a danger signal. It is a warning of the return of the sweatshop, a challenge to us all to reinforce the gains we have made in our long and difficult progress towards a civilized industrial order."[207] But now more than seventy-five years later, her warning is still apt. Sweatshops are back; in fact, it is estimated that 75 percent of New York City garment firms are sweatshops.[208] So when apologists for sweatshops say wages are not bad compared with the wage standards and the cost of living prevailing in the region, they should include New York City in their calculations! The retail industry is another

---

205 Early capitalist development in Europe also relied on deceit and brute force, for example, the Opium Wars. See Ha-Joon Chang, *The Bad Samaritan: The Myth of Free Trade and the Secret History of Capitalism* (London: Bloomsbury Press, 2008).
206 Bhattacharjee, Gupta, and Luce, "Raising the Floor," 76.
207 Quoted in Rosen, *Making Sweatshops*, 1.
208 Rosen, *Making Sweatshops*, 227.

industry employing many women where wages and conditions have deteriorated. Unionized department stores like Macy's are in decline, replaced by nonunion Wal-Mart, which is currently the largest employer in the country. GM used to be the largest employer in the United States, in the days when one in six US jobs was connected to the auto industry. But the US auto industry was in serious trouble when I began this project and is now "on life support" as some dark humorist put it. Millions of working women (and men) who had comfortable standards of living have lost them due to capitalist development and may lose their pensions as well.[209] This is in the richest country in the history of the world. We will look at the global picture later. Briefly, however, though conditions in developing countries are generally worse for working people, it should not be assumed that this is universally the case, that even relatively poor people in the United States are better off than those in poor countries. In fact, African Americans, both women and men, have a shorter life expectancy than Indians in Kerala and several other poor countries.[210]

Competitive market constraints

Could these tendencies within capitalism be reversed? Could capitalists somehow be prevailed upon to make different choices that would be better for their employees? In the earlier discussion of freedom in capitalism, my focus was on freedom for the majority of people in capitalism, but it is worth asking: how free are capitalists? Certainly, they are freer than the majority of people in capitalist societies. We have seen how much more freedom wealthy people have in their individual lives, and capitalists certainly tend to be wealthy, and we have seen how much more freedom owners of the means of production have to determine economic and political decisions than nonowners. However, this latter freedom is strictly constrained by the nature of the market system. Individuals

---

209 Another example of the imbalance of political and legal power between corporations and working people is that in bankruptcies courts give priority to repayment of debts to banks and other secured creditors over repayment of workers' wages.

210 Sen, *Development as Freedom*, 22f.

acting in their role as capitalists *must* make decisions that they think will maximize profits. A recent report on the declining US auto industry states that "Shrinking market shares have *forced* GM, Chrysler and the Ford Motor Company to close more than a dozen assembly plants and shed tens of thousands of workers in recent years" (my emphasis).[211] Of course, they had choices, they made decisions, but if an individual capitalist made profit maximization secondary to some other goal, such as maximizing the well-being of his employees, or the health of the planet, or some purely personal caprice, his shareholders would protest and sell their stock in his company. Indeed, such conduct would violate the fiduciary responsibility owners have to their shareholders which is to pursue profit over all else; hence, it would be illegal. Corporations that do not have shareholders can legally do what they want but they are caught in the same system; they are all in competition together with other corporations that believe they *must* pay the cheapest price they can in order to compete – and often they are right. Laws are necessary to constrain them *all* so that individual corporations are not under competitive pressure to search for the lowest wage workers, perhaps even slave laborers. And these laws must be international laws, given that corporations are multinational. It is worth struggling, therefore, for international labor standards that require living wages in all countries. Though necessary, laws are not enough, however; there are laws against slave labor but it has not been eliminated, as will be discussed later. The laws must be enforced, and competitive pressures lead to corruption. In sum, the structure of capitalism simply makes it hard for capitalists to "do the right thing."[212]

Changed gender roles in context

Turning back to how women are affected by capitalism, are the losses for women workers described above balanced by gains for

---

211 Nick Bunkley and Bill Vlasic, "With Plants Shutting, the SUV Lumbers Near the End of the Line," *New York Times*, December 24, 2008, B4.

212 The film *The Corporation*, 2009 is a powerful exposé of the pathological legal "person" that it calls the dominant institution of our era.

other women workers – either here or abroad? Is this dismal picture just a piece of changing social and economic conditions in which women on the whole are doing as well or better than ever before? To some extent, yes, of course. Women in developed countries are in positions they were never in before, from doctors and lawyers to professors, corporate executives, and politicians. The question, then, is how do we understand and evaluate the changed gender roles of the past fifty years? Have women gained *overall*, even though some have lost? If so, what have they gained?

In the United States, which I will concentrate on, the women's movement was certainly crucial in making gains for women. The gains did not come automatically with the development of capitalism, but had to be fought for and won. That is the positive side of the story which feminists all celebrate. Earlier I discussed the decline of the patriarchal family – breadwinner father and housewife mother – as an indicator of the changing gender order which constituted progress for women. But not everyone was happy with this change – and those who were unhappy were not all patriarchs or conservative women – because this change has a downside. *Not many men today earn enough to support a whole family, the so-called family wage.* Though women now earn 77 percent of what men earn, up from 59 percent, this is not because women have done so well, but because men's wages have declined faster than women's.[213] Historian Nancy Maclean argues that even more important than the women's movement in explaining the changing gender relations in the postwar period was the end of the family wage.[214] More families needed more people in the workforce; to sustain the family wage, it now takes 80 hours

213 Stephanie Luce and Mark Brenner, "Women and Class: What Has Happened in Forty Years?," *Monthly Review* July–August (2006): 83. They also point out a recent study that shows that over their lifetime, the wage gap between women and men is actually 38 percent. In full-time work, women earn 80 percent of what men earn. Catherine Rampell, "As Layoffs Surge, Women May Pass Men in Job Force," *New York Times*, February 6, 2009.

214 Nancy Maclean, "Post-War Women's History: The 'Second Wave' or the End of the Family Wage?," in Jean-Christophe Agnew and Roy Rosensweig (eds.), *A Companion to Post-1945 America* (Malden, MA: Blackwell, 2002).

of paid labor, instead of the 40 hours of the 1950s. After winning the 40-hour week, the number of hours worked started to rise in the United States after 1969 resulting in an extra month of work.[215] While women's paid employment has been beneficial for women *in relationship to men of their class*, it is an expression of declining conditions for most families and, in particular, for women workers with young children whose work week is conservatively estimated at an average of 65 hours per week.[216] There has also been a massive increase in personal indebtedness as families struggle to survive. Today's economic crisis is bringing the possibility of further changes in gender roles, but the news is not therefore good from a feminist point of view. In February 2009, it was reported that for the first time in American history, women may surpass men in the workforce – but the cause is that 82 percent of the jobs lost had been held by men. Since the jobs women hold are more often part-time without benefits, and lower paid, this is very bad news for most families.

If we look at the gains for women in the United States since the women's movement, we can see both the enormous achievements women have won under capitalism, but also the limits posed by capitalism. Essentially, what women achieved is their democratic rights. The law no longer prohibits women from doing whatever men can do; in fact, the law prohibits private institutions from discriminating against women. So women are legally free to contract and compete on the same basis as men. Legal restrictions on the exercise of reproductive freedom – which is fundamental to the exercise of all rights – have mostly been eliminated, though this is an ongoing struggle. Some gains have been made in protecting women from violence. These objective advances of strategic gender interests and the concomitant sea change of consciousness have allowed unprecedented freedom of opportunity for women. That is the good news.

Yet for all this, the wage gap between the sexes, though reduced, is still one of the largest in the world. For college graduates, the

---

215 Schor, *The Overworked American*, 29.
216 Schor, *The Overworked American*, 21.

gap has actually increased.[217] Labor economists have shown that this is not explained primarily by discrimination, but rather by our country's "unmatched and ever-widening levels of overall economic inequality." One commentator described the trends of the last thirty years in the United States as "the largest transfer of wealth and income in the history of the world – far larger than what occurred during either the Russian or the Chinese revolutions." From 1970 to 2000, the share of the total income of the richest 0.01 percent of Americans had gone from being 53 times the national average to 306 times the national average. Wealth is even more unequal; for example, the top 1% has 45% of the wealth, a ratio not seen since 1929.[218] A correlate (perhaps a consequence) of this inequality is a stark decline in overall measures of human development for Americans, in the boom years as well as today. The American Human Development Index (HDI) showed a decline from second in the world in the 1980s, down to sixth by the mid-1990s to fifteenth in 2006.[219] Thus, "American women … were essentially swimming upstream in a labor market increasingly unfavorable to low wage workers."[220] A similar story can be told for black Americans of both sexes.

Another piece of the explanation for the wage gap, as sociologist Johanna Brenner explains,[221] is that the women's movement did not succeed in changing the most important aspect of the gender division of labor, viz. that women are still predominantly responsible for all kinds of caregiving: of the household,

217 David Leonhardt, "Scant Progress on Closing Gap in Women's Pay," *New York Times*, December 26, 2006.

218 Felix Rohatyn, "Saving American Capitalism," *International Herald Tribune*, June 29, 2009. See also Michael Perelman, "Some Economics of Class," *Monthly Review* July–August (2006): 18–28. Excellent sources for figures on inequality in the United States are the home page for Emmanuel Saez at: http://elsa.berkeley.edu/~saez and the website for United for a Fair Economy (UFE) at: www.faireconomy.org.

219 Dalton Conley, "America is … # 15?," *The Nation*, March 23, 2009, 29.

220 Francine D. Blau, "Gender and Economic Outcomes: The Role of Wage Structure," *Labor* 7 (1993): 73–92, 85 quoted in Maclean, "Post-War Women's History," 237.

221 Johanna Brenner, *Women and the Politics of Class* (New York: Monthly Review Press, 2000).

children, the elderly, and disabled. And neither did it succeed in winning social supports for these roles, which would have cost a lot more than the legal and policy changes they did win. As the United States has the least developed welfare state of all the developed capitalist countries, this means that the burden falls on individual women. This is still true today when women are becoming the majority of the workforce. Heidi Hartmann, president and chief economist at the Institute for Women's Policy Research, says, "Over a long 20-year period, married men have stepped up to the plate a little bit, but not as much as married women have dropped off in the time they spend on household chores."[222] Clearly, men benefit to varying degrees from standard gender roles, and so do capitalists since they can pay less. Many families rely on take-out food, whether it is from McDonald's or gourmet restaurants. Some women can afford to buy their way out of more time-consuming household work – by employing other women as nannies, housecleaners, home health aides – but most cannot.[223] Thus, the class divide among women in our society has widened, as has the gap between rich and poor as a whole. *While attention has focused on the glass ceiling, the reality is that most women cannot climb out of the basement; thus, one-third of female-headed households of all races are living in poverty.*[224] Today, one out of eight people (and one out of four children) rely on food stamps.[225] The economic crisis has taken a particularly heavy toll on African American women, who were disproportionately hurt by the subprime and housing crisis. Given that most wealth in the African American community is in the form of home

222 Rampell, "As Layoffs Surge, Women May Pass Men in Job Force."
223 This is true in Western Europe and developed countries of Asia as well. One writer describes this phenomenon in Taiwan as "subcontracting filial duty." Pei-Chia Lan, "Among Women: Migrant Domestics and their Taiwanese Employers Across Generations," in Barbara Ehrenreich and Arlie Russell Hochschild (eds.), *Global Woman: Nannies, Maids, and Sex Workers in the New Economy* (New York: Henry Holt, 2002).
224 See Luce and Brenner, "Women and Class," for other important figures and analyses.
225 Jason Deparle and Robert Gebeloff, "Food Stamp Use Soars Across US, and Stigma Fades," *New York Times*, November 29, 2009.

equity, this loss "represents the largest loss of black wealth since the Reconstruction."[226] People at all economic levels are working longer hours than ever before.[227] What women would need for genuine – not just legal – equality with men in our society has proved to be very difficult to achieve: at a minimum, free childcare, health care, shorter hours of work at higher wages, all of which would require a significant redistribution of wealth. Instead, we are going backwards. So-called welfare reform, supported by Hillary Clinton, has meant that for the first time in fifty years, women and children cannot count on support if they need it. And now, in the richest country in the history of the world, many more are in need. As Johanna Brenner explains, it will take a revival of broad social movements to reverse these trends.

The global picture

On a global level the gap between rich and poor has also widened – to such obscene levels that the figures are almost incomprehensible. Both in absolute and relative terms, poor countries are poorer today, even though the 1990s were a boom period. The most recent figures from the World Bank show that one out of four people in the developing world live on less than US$1.25 per day and almost half live on less than US$2.[228] One-third of

226 Avis Jones-DeWeever, research director of the United Council of Negro Women, quoted in Dominique Haoson, "Few Safety Nets for Women of Color," Interpress News Service, March 4, 2009.

227 ILO report cited in Ehrenreich and Hochschild (eds.), *Global Woman*, 8.

228 These figures were released in September 2008 but date from 2005 – *before* rising food and fuel prices and *before* the unfolding global economic crisis which almost certainly have worsened these figures. World Bank, "World Development Indicators Poverty Data," 2009, available at http://siteresources.worldbank.org/DATASTATISTICS/Resources/ WDI08supplem, accessed October 5, 2009. See UN Development Reports www.hdr.undp.org/publications/papers.cfm. According to one study by the UN Development Programme, sixty countries were worse off in 1999 than 1980. For the 1990s, see Robert Wade, "Global Inequality," *The Economist*, April 28, 2001, 72–74; Judith Miller, "Globalization Widens Rich–Poor Gap, UN Says," *New York Times*, June 29, 1999.

all annual deaths in the world can be traced to poverty. As Mary Robinson, former United Nations Commissioner on Human Rights,[229] noted in an interview on International Women's Day 2009, poverty affects women in particular. As a result of this global polarization, the middle class of the Third World now earns less than the poor of the First World, so a woman migrating to wealthier countries to be a maid or nanny may come from a family of schoolteachers in Mexico or the Philippines. Contrary to the standard optimistic picture of globalization, Saskia Sassen has shown that growth sectors of the new global economy create not only decent paying professional jobs, but also a large number of low-wage dead end jobs to support the professionals at work, at home, and at play.[230] In the capitalist democracy of India, studies show that sweatshop and other low-wage work is perpetuated generation to generation, and is even growing. Despite the growth of the Indian economy, 2.5 million children die annually, the number of underweight children has hardly declined, and the number who are fully immunized has actually declined.[231] *There are now more child laborers throughout the world than ever in history.* Though capitalist development has improved the lives of many in the developing world, it has also brought growing immiseration to many poor countries, through a combination of development, massive indebtedness, followed by the austerity policies imposed by international institutions like the IMF and the World Bank such as wage freezes, cuts in social services, and devaluation of local currencies. Rather than improving their economies as promised, the terms of the loans are such

---

229 Interview with Mary Robinson on *Democracy Now*, radio March 9, 2009. Robinson was the first woman President of Ireland, UN High Commissioner for Human Rights, President of Oxfam and of the International Commission of Jurists.

230 Saskia Sassen, "Global Cities and Survival Circuits," in Ehrenreich and Hochschild (eds.), 254–72.

231 Pankaj Mishra, "The Myth of the New India," *New York Times*, July 6, 2006; Somini Sengupta, "Indian Prosperity Creates Paradox; Many Children are Fat, Even More are Famished," *New York Times*, December 31, 2006 and "As Indian Growth Soars, Child Hunger Persists," *New York Times*, March 13, 2009.

that even though the countries have paid off their original loans many times over, many have ended up even more indebted.[232] As a result, billions of people have been left destitute (a disproportionate number of whom are women), and there has been a mass migration of women and men, mostly people of color, from poor countries to rich countries. With men gone or unable to support them, women have had to leave their own countries and families to work in developed countries as nannies, janitors, health aides, and sex workers.

Throughout history, women have migrated to do the very same jobs, but never on this scale; women now constitute about half of the world's 120 million legal and illegal migrants, and they are the majority from some regions.[233] Some have called this the feminization of migration. In the best cases with the least abusive conditions, particularly in the care sector, migrants are able to provide for their families and achieve more personal independence than they could have achieved at home. But feminists cannot be happy about even the best-case scenario because it comes at untold emotional cost to the women who migrate and to the children they have left behind. Arlie Hochschild calls it a new kind of imperialism. Instead of the male-centered extraction of gold, ivory, and rubber by direct forms of coercion in the nineteenth century, today's imperialism involves the extraction of emotional resources and does not operate through the barrel of a gun: "The yawning gap between rich and poor countries is itself a form of coercion, pushing Third World mothers to seek work in the First for lack of options closer to home. But given the prevailing free market ideology, migration is viewed as a 'personal choice' ... and the consequences 'personal problems.'"[234] Feminists know better than that.

In the worst cases, these immigrant workers were trafficked; even when they chose to migrate they may end up as virtual

---

232 See Richard C. Longworth, *Global Squeeze: The Coming Crisis for First World Nations* (Chicago: Contemporary Books, 1998).

233 Ehrenreich and Hochschild (eds.), *Global Woman*, 5.

234 Arlie Hochschild, "Love and Gold," in Ehrenreich and Hochschild (eds.), *Global Woman*.

slaves. The extreme, even slave, conditions of many migrant workers are not directly due to capitalism and the reforms advocated to correct them are, theoretically, compatible with capitalism. However, *capitalism is indirectly responsible in that it creates the conditions that render workers, particularly women, vulnerable to such abuses.* As scholar and activist Joy M. Zarembka explains, "The global economic changes that push women from developing nations to migrate for domestic work have also contributed to the recent rise of domestic worker abuse."[235] Immigrant workers outside the domestic sphere are also vulnerable to abuse as they have no legal rights. A horrific recent example comes from Greece where a Bulgarian woman unionist was blinded and almost killed to punish her for her activism against the prevailing conditions of "medieval servitude." Her case was ignored by the police and the press until her coworkers' protests brought it to public attention and an international petition to open an inquiry. The petition circulated about the case describes how *"gangster practices are becoming a regular part of the world of work."*[236]

Probably the worst abuses are found in the sex industry. Thailand provides a rich case study of the good and bad consequences of capitalist development in a sexist and hierarchal society long accepting of nonmarital sex for men.[237] Given its natural resources, few people starve in Thailand, except in the north where poor conditions sometimes led families to sell a girl child as a servant or slave. But today "The small number of children sold into slavery in the past has become a flood." The customary ill-treatment of women combined with the relentless pursuit of

---

235 Joy M. Zarembka, "America's Dirty Work: Migrant Maids and Modern-Day Slavery," in Ehrenreich and Hochschild (eds.), *Global Woman*, 144. There are also noneconomic causes of migration such as unhappy, abusive family situations, and positive reasons like a desire for adventure and self-improvement. Research does not show the percentages in each of these categories, but what research exists shows that the overwhelming majority are driven by poverty.

236 Justicepourconstantinakouneva@gmail.com.

237 The following statistics and quotes are all taken from Kevin Bales, "Thailand: Because She Looks Like a Child," *Disposable People: New Slavery in the Global Economy* (Berkeley, CA: University of California, 1999).

profit in the new economy has brought horrendous results for women. In a country with (a conservative estimate of) over 1 million prostitutes, about one in twenty are enslaved, again a conservative estimate. Economic development has brought both greater supply and greater demand. Prices have risen overall, but returns for agricultural products have not. Yet peasants are everywhere exposed to new and tempting consumer products. So girls are now sold not to feed a family, but "to buy color televisions and video equipment." The demand can also be traced to development as more men can now afford to pay for sex. "Who are the modern slaveholders? The answer is anyone ... with a little capital to invest." At the bottom are the pimps and brothel keepers who appear to own the girls, then there are the brokers and agents, but "the real slaveowners tend to be middle-aged businessmen ... the slaveholder may in fact be a partnership, company or corporation" for which brothels are just one of many capital investments, often masked as part of the entertainment or tourism industries central to many countries' development plans. It is a particularly lucrative part of an investment portfolio, with low capital investment, low risk, and high turnover, as the girls are destroyed and replaced by others. The positive results of development have somewhat curtailed the supply of prostitutes from the north of Thailand, but brokers (i.e., slavers) have simply moved across the border to Burma and Laos.

Nor is slavery confined to the sex industry. Though it is illegal everywhere, the world's leading expert on modern-day slavery, Kevin Bales, estimates that the total number of slaves today is *27 million, more than all the people stolen from Africa during the time of the transatlantic slave trade*.[238] The population explosion and the impoverishment of millions has created a glut of potential slaves in the poorest societies. With government collaboration, slavery takes different forms and is found throughout the world, touching the lives of all of us:

238 Bales, "The New Slavery," *Disposable People*, 1–33. This estimate is larger than government estimates but smaller than that offered by activist organizations. All the quotes and figures in this paragraph are from this chapter.

Slaves in Pakistan may have made the shoes you are wearing and the carpet you stand on. Slaves in the Caribbean may have put sugar in your kitchen and toys in the hands of your children. In India they may have sewn the shirt on your back and polished the ring on your finger ... They made the bricks for the factory that made the TV you watch. In Brazil slaves made the charcoal that tempered the steel that made the springs in your car and the blade on your lawnmower. Slaves grew the rice that fed the woman that wove the lovely cloth you've put up as curtains. Your investment portfolio and your mutual fund pension own stock in companies using slave labor in the developing world. Slaves keep your costs low and return on your investments high.

How should we understand the relationship of these horrors to capitalism?[239] Defenders of capitalism would say it is totally anomalous, a remnant of earlier systems and not to be blamed on capitalism. Slavery would seem antithetical to capitalism (certainly it is in theory) because capitalism rests on "free" labor. However, as we know, slavery in the Americas played a critical role in the early days of capitalism. Through what was known as the "triangle trade" between Africa, the Americas, and Europe, slavery was an integral part of the burgeoning world capitalist economy. And, indeed, the very division of the world into developed and undeveloped, rich and poor, the "First World" and the "Third World," which most people in the former countries take as "natural," came about through the use of horrific violence by the powerful at crucial historical junctures.[240] Today's slavery differs in several respects from that found in early capitalism,[241] but its prevalence and its character also have to be understood in terms of the global capitalist economy. The race to the bottom, which at the high end moves jobs out of developed countries, has much worse consequences at the low end of the global economy as poor

239 Miles, *Capitalism and Unfree Labor.*
240 See Mike Davis, *Late Victorian Holocausts: El Niño, Famines and the Making of the Third World* (New York: Verso, 2001); Thomas Pogge, *World Poverty and Human Rights,* offers arguments to show that individuals in rich countries today are responsible for *sustaining* the harm suffered by the poor.
241 Most important are the absence of legal ownership and attempts to justify it in any terms other than economic.

farmers have to compete with slave labor and are pushed into debt bondage themselves. The new slavery is actually more profitable than the earlier form because it is less capital intensive (the supply is closer to hand) and slaveholders are not responsible for the unproductive – the young, the old, the injured, and the sick. If a slave is not productive, she or he is simply disposed of. "In the new slavery, the slave is a consumable item, added to the production process when needed, but no longer carrying a high capital cost." *Thus, capitalist development brings both freedom and slavery in its wake, depending on where and at whom we look.* As Bales says, if the powerful capitalist countries and international organizations like the IMF and the WTO gave as much attention to the stealing of lives as they do to the stealing of copyright, slavery could be eliminated. Capitalism is antithetical to slavery in theory, as it is to sexism and racism, but is quite compatible with it in reality. When the values supposedly inherent in capitalism of individual freedom and equality of opportunity come into conflict with its drive to maximize profit, the latter overrides the former.

In theory women's practical gender interests could all be satisfied under capitalism; the Scandinavian countries come close, and the New Deal was a step in this direction. However, economic and political conditions have changed. As already discussed, the model of capitalism dominant in the United States since the 1980s, known as neoliberalism, was a throwback to pre-New Deal style capitalism. As corporations searched the globe for the lowest costs, the New Deal was being dismantled, by the Democrats as well as the Republicans in the United States, and the welfare states of Europe and Japan came under increasing pressure to adapt to US-style capitalism.[242] The current economic crisis has led to a loss of credibility of that ideology, but conditions are not favorable for advancing the interests of working people and creating a less brutal form of capitalism. The mobility of transnational corporations is crucial in allowing

242 For example, Martin Fackler, "In Japan, New Jobless May Lack Safety Net." "As never before, the global downturn has driven home how a decade of economic transformation has eroded Japan's gentler version of capitalism, in which companies once laid off employees only as a last resort." *New York Times*, February 8, 2009, 6.

them to influence politics in a direction favorable to them. The labor movement and other social movements are on the decline, fighting defensive battles to keep some of the gains they won under more favorable conditions; there is always someone more desperate who will take their position if they say "no."

Could the economic crisis change this gloomy prognosis? Early in 2009 the Director of National Intelligence, Dennis C. Blair, described the financial crisis as the top near-term security threat facing the United States;[243] the rising unemployment rates and resulting protests all over the world are seen as a threat to stability;[244] commentators have likened our current conditions to those preceding the rise of fascism and the Second World War, and there are debates on the Internet as to whether the current crisis could spawn new extremist movements as they did then. It is possible that a combination of militancy, moral arguments, and pragmatic fears that "the poor will help themselves" may prevent the conditions of the majority from being worsened. However, this scenario is still a far cry from transforming all capitalist countries into Sweden. While it is logically possible, and would certainly be preferable to what we have now, a more ideal, more compassionate version of capitalism, a global social democracy, such as advocated by liberal economists like Joseph Stiglitz and Paul Krugman (and which may be close to my debate partner's ideal capitalism), does not seem to be anywhere on the horizon. Indeed, the reverse seems more likely as the brutal logic of competitive global capitalism pushes down the majority of the people of the world.

4   Human interests are women's interests

Thus far my discussion of capitalism's impact on women has focused on gender- and class-related interests. But women have interests that are not uniquely gendered or tied directly to class.

---

243 Walter Pincus and Joby Warrick, "Financial Crisis Called Top Security Threat to US," *Washington Post*, February 13, 2009.
244 Nelson Schwartz, "Job Losses Pose a Threat to Stability Worldwide," *New York Times*, February 14, 2009.

As many feminists have come to recognize, women's gender interests cannot be analyzed separately from their race, class, and other aspects of their identity, an approach often referred to as "intersectionality." I suggest that we need to go further and give full recognition in feminist discussions not only that we are all different but interrelated in all kinds of respects, but that we are also *alike simply by virtue of being human*. This point is already expressed in the strong feminist claim that women's interests are human interests, women's rights are human rights. It is equally true and important that human interests are women's interests – whether or not they are differentiated by gender. Feminists should not limit their concerns to those uniquely or primarily affecting women. I will turn now to three reasons why capitalism is bad for women – and for all living creatures.

First, is capitalism's propensity toward war. Most wars in the nineteenth, twentieth, and twenty-first centuries have been between capitalist countries over resources and markets. This was obscured in the second half of the twentieth century by the Cold War between capitalist and communist countries, which was used to justify massive expenditures on weaponry, particularly by the United States. However, the collapse of communism did not bring a "peace dividend" as many had hoped because "rogue states" and "terrorists" were used to justify the same old policies. The United States has over seven hundred military bases in foreign countries[245] and spends an average annual 51 percent of its budget on the military, with the war in Iraq likely to cost a trillion dollars.[246] Capitalism's inherently competitive nature makes wars inevitable as long as there are nation-states as each country competes for the resources it needs for development. From colonial times, to contemporary struggles over oil and water, resource plunder is key to capitalist development, which

---

245 Chalmers Johnson, *The Sorrows of Empire: Militarism, Secrecy and the End of the Republic* (New York: Metropolitan, 2004).

246 For documentation of these numbers and what else the money could have been spent on, see "Where Your Income Tax Money Really Goes," published by the War Resisters League, February 2010, available at: www. warresisters.org.

will only intensify with the expansion of capitalism throughout the globe. Wars affect all living creatures, but in modern wars the bulk of the casualties are noncombatants, which means *mostly women and children.* Women are also subject to horrific sexual violence and make up the bulk of refugees displaced by wars, whose deaths from malnutrition are not counted as war casualties. Humans have always fought wars, but capitalism's inherent propensity toward war, combined with its inherent tendency toward technological development, has resulted in weaponry that could destroy all living creatures on the globe several times over. And competition leads to self-destructive contradictions. For example, Cold War interests in Afghanistan led the United States to ignore, even to aid and abet, Pakistan's development of nuclear technology,[247] which has now been exported to other countries around the world and is widely cited as one of the greatest dangers faced by the United States. We need to develop a system that does not encourage the worst of human capacities and tendencies, but instead fosters capacities like compassion and cooperation.

How we think about "security" has to be broadened, both how to get it and what it means. As Nobel Peace prize winner Bishop Desmond Tutu said recently, "you don't get true security from the barrel of a gun."[248] We have to think about its meaning differently too. Especially in the United States after 9/11 security is conceived exclusively in terms of protection against intentional threats to our safety and well-being, which, of course, means they are threats by individuals, groups, or nations. But the concept has a broader sense, of protection against threats of all kinds, whether intentional or not. These two conceptions of security are highly gendered. When we think of security in the narrow sense (as in "Department of Homeland Security") we know that it is overwhelmingly men who will be defending us against other men who are attacking us. One invariant of the sexual division of

247 David Armstrong and Joseph J. Trento, *America and the Islamic Bomb: The Deadly Compromise* (New York: Random House, 2007).
248 Reported on *Democracy Now*, August 28, 2009, speaking in Israel.

labor is that men have had the responsibility for violence. This is true today even with women in the US military, especially as we go up the military hierarchy and into the realm of military technology. On the other hand, if we think of security in the broader sense of social security and security blankets then women enter the picture, as the other invariable piece of the sexual division of labor is that women do the bulk of the caregiving. To truly protect our well-being, we need to conceive of security in the broadest sense and devote our resources to this end, as in fact the biggest threats facing humanity today are not from intentional acts. Just one example is that "unsafe water and lack of basic sanitation cause 80% of all sickness and disease and kill more people *than all forms of violence, including war.*"[249] It is important to note, however, that although these deaths are not the result of direct intentional acts, many intentional acts contribute to the lack of access to safe drinking water, from polluting streams and rivers to privatizing water.

A second life-threatening implication of capitalist development in the age of globalization can be summed up in the titles of two recent books: Mike Davis' *Planet of Slums* and Laurie Garrett's *The Coming Plague.*[250] Capitalist development around the globe has meant that for the first time in human history, more people live in cities than not, and the biggest cities are in the developing world: Bangkok, Mexico City, Cairo, and Nairobi. Combined with another trend of global capitalism – the growing extremes of wealth and poverty – these cities have vast slums that are potent breeding grounds for infectious disease. Centuries of capitalist development has brought us a planet of slums. The spread of industrial-style agriculture throughout the world means that animals are living in vast slums too, known as confined animal feeding operations (CAFOs), with horrendous consequences for our health. When we add to this equation the privatization of

---

249 www.Charitywater.org, accessed July 19, 2010.
250 Mike Davis, *Planet of Slums* (London: Verso, 2006); Laurie Garrett, *The Coming Plague: Newly Emerging Diseases in a World Out of Balance* (New York: Penguin, 1995); Mike Davis, *The Monster at Our Door: The Global Threat of Avian Flu* (New York: New Press, 2005).

everything from water to education to health care that world capitalist institutions like the IMF and the World Bank mandate, and we consider the fact that more people died in the flu pandemic of 1918–19 than in the First World War, we can see the catastrophic possibilities today when millions of people and things traverse the globe every minute. That most of the ingredients for the drugs used to treat disease come from China does not inspire confidence regarding either the availability or safety of the drugs we would need in an emergency.

Finally, if all countries develop along capitalist lines, life will be unsustainable on this planet. Al Gore's powerful film about global warming, *An Inconvenient Truth*, starts out with charts showing the historic rise in atmospheric temperature. It began to take off in the mid-nineteenth century and is now "off the charts," very rapidly approaching the point where human life will simply not be sustainable. The United Nations Population Fund has warned that women in developing countries will bear a disproportionate burden of global warming. And this is not the only threat to global survival. As the United Nations Millennium Ecosystem Assessment concluded, *almost two-thirds of the natural resources necessary to sustain life* on this planet are being degraded and destroyed by human action: the oceans are being depleted of fish; deforestation is proceeding at record rates; rivers, lakes, and wetlands have become toxic; 50,000 species become extinct every year, etc., etc. "In effect, one species is now a hazard to the other 10 million or so on the planet and to itself."[251] Why human behavior now threatens human survival, and how we can stop it, is not addressed. And *there is no guarantee that we can stop it*. As demonstrated by Pulitzer Prize winning author Jared Diamond's book *Collapse*,[252] a number of societies in the past essentially committed ecological suicide because they exhausted their natural resources and refused to make the changes in their values and

---

251 March 30, 2005, www.millenniumassessment.org. The report was prepared by 1,360 scientists from ninety-five countries.

252 Jared Diamond, *Collapse: How Societies Choose to Fail or Succeed* (New York: Viking, 2005).

ways of life necessary for survival. Diamond worries that we are on the same path, but this time it is not just individual societies but the whole planet. Like Al Gore, he concludes with the usual good ideas about what we should do, from using more energy-efficient light bulbs, to lobbying, consumer boycotts, pressing corporations to adopt eco-friendly policies, and so on. But these have all been tried (with some modest successes) – and yet the problem is getting *much worse very rapidly*. The problem is that an even more inconvenient truth than global warming is that the standard measures proposed will do very little to stop it (or any of the other threats to the planet's ecosystems) as long as capitalism continues. Because capitalism is – for better and for worse – an economic growth machine. *The world economy now produces in less than two weeks the equivalent of the entire physical output of the year 1900, and global economic output now doubles every twenty-five to thirty years.*[253] The transition to capitalism of the Soviet bloc countries will likely increase this rate. Although communist and pre-capitalist societies were often terrible for the environment, ironically, it is the chief virtue of capitalism – its incessant need to innovate and develop – that is now the single greatest threat to our future. China, for example, plans to put as many cars on the road by 2020 as the United States has now. While the economic downturn has slowed this process, it will continue if capitalism revives. Clearly this cannot go on.

Defenders of capitalism would disagree with this pessimistic prognosis. Leaving aside a rejection of the facts – which I take to be irrefutable – and the psychological need to deny such a terrifying prospect, they would likely offer two reasons for their optimism: the basic rationality of capitalists who will also be destroyed if trends continue; and the prospects for addressing the problems within capitalism, by the growth of green industry, for example. To support their position, they could point to the report issued in 2006 by former UK Treasury Secretary and World Bank chief economist, Sir Nicholas Stern, which pointed out the

253 Jonathon Porrit, *Capitalism As If the World Matters* (London: Earthscan, 2005), 77.

devastating economic – as well as ecological – effects of allowing current trends to continue, concluding that it was both necessary and economically rational to intervene to reverse them. Then Prime Minister Tony Blair agreed, urging "radical measures." And yet, these radical measures have not been taken. The problem, as Diamond's book shows, is that people do not always act in rational ways even when the alternative is catastrophe.

Capitalism's constraints on rationality

The gap between, on the one hand, the now accepted fact that either we fundamentally change our economic practices or we die, and, on the other hand, the meager steps actually taken to address this, suggests how fundamental and systemic the problem is. It is not simply that people do not want to face the difficult choices, but that *capitalism poses structural constraints on our ability to act rationally*. The subtitle of Diamond's book is *How Societies Choose to Fail or Succeed*. But is it really a matter of "choice"? Who is it that gets to choose whether our societies continue to pursue eco-suicidal practices? Or is it rather the fundamental requirements of capitalist reproduction on a day to day basis?[254] Certainly, all of us should do what we can to reduce our individual destructive impact on the earth. But it does not matter much whether I choose public transportation or a bicycle instead of a car if auto manufacturers are producing exponentially more cars every year. Nor, as discussed earlier, can individual corporations simply choose to promote environmental security rather than profit. The occasional CEO who seems to understand the problem is caught in a bind. For example, in the 1990s BP's CEO warned that fossil fuels accelerate global warming, adopted the slogan "Beyond Petroleum," and invested in solar power.

254 Much of my discussion here relies on the following articles: Richard Smith, "Capitalism and *Collapse*: Contradictions of Jared Diamond's Market Meliorist Strategy to Save the Humans," *Ecological Economics* 55(2) (November 2005): 294–306; "The Eco-suicidal Economics of Adam Smith," *Capitalism Nature Socialism* 19(2) (June 2007): 22–43; Nancy Holmstrom and Richard Smith, "Their Rationality and Ours," in Anatole Anton and Richard Schmitt (eds.), *Toward a New Socialism* (Lanham MD: Lexington Books, 2006).

However, 99 percent of their investments remain in fossil fuels *and they are increasing*. If he did not follow this tried and true avenue to higher profits, he would be out of a job. Possibilities would seem to exist for change within capitalist terms, but they too are subject to the constraints of the market system. Wind and solar power were growing, and were expected to grow more with President Obama's commitment to greener energy, but now "because of the credit crisis and the broader economic downturn, the opposite is happening: installation of wind and solar power is plummeting."[255] Even if we switched to less destructive technologies, this does nothing to reduce and could even increase the overall levels of resource consumption. The basic problem is that our finite planet cannot bear the consumption of resources entailed by endless growth. Even, for example, if we were to switch to cleaner, greener cars, if we continue to produce ever more cars, the resources and materials for building, maintaining, and transporting the cars would cause more pollution than we have at present.[256]

The basic problem lies in the conflict between the individual rationality enforced by the competitive market system and what is rational from a social point of view. Each firm is compelled to act to maximize its own interests, and this goes on and on – until it is too late. As economist Lester Thurow of WorldWatch Institute put it, "Each generation makes good capitalist decisions, yet the net effect is collective social suicide."[257] As I write, the US Congress is considering legislation to deal with global warming. Producers of coal, oil, natural gas, wind and solar energy are all lobbying intensely and "battling one another over policy decisions worth billions of dollars in coming decades."[258] Some

---

255 Kate Galbraith, "Dark Days for Green Energy," *New York Times*, February 4, 2009, B1.
256 John Whitelegg, "Dirty from Cradle to Grave," available at: www.worldcarfree.net/resources/freesources/DirtyfromCradletoGrave.rtf.
257 Lester Thurow, *The Future of Capitalism: How Today's Economic Forces Shape Tomorrow's World* (New York: Penguin Books, 1996), 302f.
258 John Broder and Jad Mouawad, "Energy Firms Find No Unity on Climate Bill," *New York Times*, October 19, 2009, 1.

supporters are hoping that the divisions will improve the chances of some legislation passing. Perhaps, but is this really a rational way to deal with the global ecological crisis we face – to have it determined by which lobbyists have the greatest clout? Adam Smith famously maintained that the best way to promote collective well-being was by pursuit of self-interest. In the eighteenth century this philosophy could not do too much harm to the natural world. But today, when "a global engine of development of staggering power has the capacity to melt the icecaps, transform the climate, strip mine the oceans to extinction, denude entire continents of forests, wipe out tens of thousands, if not millions, of species in a few decades, and poison the global atmosphere, all our fresh water sources, and even entire oceans,"[259] it is time to reject the theory. The environmental crisis is only the most dramatic example of the inherent conflict between the satisfaction of human needs in all their complex dimensions and an economic system that has profit maximization as its be all and end all. Women are disproportionately among those harmed by this system due to their childbearing and caregiving roles. It is time to reject a system where everything has a price and nothing has a value.

5   Conclusion: what is the alternative? and what should feminists do now?

The burden of my argument has been that capitalism creates the conditions for genuine human liberation, but at the same time it puts up systematic barriers to its realization. The technology exists today both to make work more fulfilling and to reduce necessary work allowing people time to use just as they wish – to spend with family, to develop their interests and talents, or to sleep. But as we have seen, this has not happened; capitalism has brought neither greater freedom *from work*, nor *in work*. The so-called socialist countries were no better. In both systems the advances women made are those compatible with the interests

259 Smith, "The Eco-suicidal Economics of Adam Smith," 36.

of the dominant class; those not so compatible were not realized. Throughout this chapter I have argued negatively because the question was whether capitalism was good for women, not what should replace capitalism. But the critique gives us the basic guidelines for an alternative. What women need to advance their strategic and their practical interests and to lead fulfilling lives is a genuinely democratic society at all levels, economic as well as political, where they are free to organize and press for their interests as they see them, and where no structural barriers stand in their way. Given the conflicts between profitability and the satisfaction of human needs in all their dimensions, we need to move to a society that aims *directly* at the satisfaction of social need. And not just individual societies, but on a global scale, because increasingly the world's people are all interconnected and ultimately one. I mean this not only in a moral sense – that every individual has equal value no matter where they happen to live – but as an urgent practical claim. Whether threats come from environmental disasters, or wars, or terrorism, no one can be truly secure in the world as it is organized at present. The resources of the world must be seen as a common treasury belonging to all humankind, not owned by a tiny minority.

The potential conflicts between what is rational from an individual point of view and from a collective point of view require that collective rationality prevail in cases of conflict. This entails that while there should be some role for a market, the most fundamental decisions facing society must be made by democratic planning. This is not a restriction on freedom or autonomy as some might fear. On the contrary, it is the only way that people can realize their freedom and autonomy on a collective scale. To limit our ability to plan for our social needs is to limit our freedom as well as to limit democracy. Thus, rather than an inherent conflict between planning and freedom, the two coincide if planning is democratic. Social planning is the only way we can expand our freedom beyond the scope of individual control in ways that matter most to us. It is the only way we can "control our destiny." Constraints can and should, however, be put on the power of the collectivity, which is another way of saying that there must be a recognition of certain individual rights. Women need rights both as individuals and as part of collectivities.

As Noam Chomsky has said: "The task for a modern industrial society is to achieve what is now technically realizable, namely, a society which is really based on free voluntary participation of people who produce and create, live their lives freely within institutions they control, and with limited hierarchical structures, possibly none at all."[260] Is this alternative socialism? The word "socialism" has been applied to so many different, indeed, incompatible models – from early utopian projects to social welfare capitalist societies to different totalitarian models of the twentieth century – that I am somewhat hesitant to use it for fear of misunderstanding. Hal Draper, the Marxist scholar and activist, has argued that the most fundamental division among the different models that have been called socialist is between what he called the "two souls of socialism": socialism-from-above and socialism-from-below.[261] The totalitarian "state socialist" and the welfare capitalist models, as well as most of the utopian socialist schemes, would belong in the "socialism-from-above" camp. But there was always another socialist tradition of socialism-from-below, of *self-emancipation as both the means to, and constitutive of, socialism*. This vision was exemplified by Marx's slogan for the First International Workingmen's Association: "the emancipation of the working class must be the act of the working class itself." So the vision I am projecting would be socialist in this sense.

But the word does not matter. Call it socialism, or call it eco-feminist, or libertarian socialism, or economic democracy – or some totally new name. As William Morris said, "Men fight and lose the battle, and the thing they fought for comes about in spite of their defeat, and when it comes turns out to be not what they meant, and other men have to fight for what they meant under another name." Women have always fought too; indeed, early

---

260 Quoted in Michael Albert and Robin Hahnel, *Looking Forward: Participatory Economics for the Twenty-First Century* (Boston, MA: South End, 1991), 13.

261 Hal Draper, Marxists Internet Archives, "The Two Souls of Socialism," available at: www.marxists.org, accessed July 22, 2010. See his five-volume *Karl Marx's Theory of Revolution* (New York: Monthly Review Press, 1977–90).

women radicals like Flora Tristan, or Eleanor Marx, or Emma Goldman, Louise Michel, or Alexandra Kollontai (some of whom were "utopian" socialists, others anarchists, and still others were Marxists) fought against capitalism, against colonialism and slavery and for women's liberation in all its dimensions. Expanding her father's famous slogan Eleanor Marx wrote, "Both the oppressed classes, women and the immediate producers, must understand that their emancipation must come from themselves." Many anticipated the insight usually attributed to second-wave feminism, incorporating the personal, intimate, aspects of our lives as part of their liberatory vision because they understood that the economic and political and "personal" were interrelated relations of power.[262] As discussed earlier, the Russian Revolution not only instituted such measures as communal childcare and laundries, but it also eliminated laws against homosexuality and the status of "illegitimacy." There is a logic and a momentum to struggles against oppression, as attested by the many American women who participated in the civil rights and anti-war movements of the 1960s and then went on to the women's liberation movement. Today, that deeper vision of liberation from *all* sources of oppression, be they economic, sexist, racist, or homophobic, is widely understood on the left and in popular movements around the globe, even if there is debate about their interrelations and relative importance and some slow feet.

In defense of her neoliberal policies Margaret Thatcher liked to say, "There Is No Alternative," repeating that phrase so often that it was abbreviated as TINA. An interesting thing about this claim is that if people believe it, then it becomes true; there is indeed no alternative. And then, if what I have argued above is true, humankind is doomed. I prefer to believe the slogan of the global justice movement: "A Better World is Possible." That claim carries no guarantee of truth, even if we all believe it. But if enough people believe it and act on it, we have a chance of

262 See Barbara Taylor, *Eve and the New Jerusalem: Socialism and Feminism in the Nineteenth Century* (London: Virago Press 1983). Excerpts of socialist-feminist "foremothers and fathers" are found in Holmstrom (ed.), *The Socialist-Feminist Project*.

building a better world. The good news is that many people the world over are fighting for control over economic policies that dominate their lives, animated by the idea that everyone in the world who is affected by economic and environmental decisions should have some say in them. There is no grand master plan for all times and places, nor do all activists in the movement support a model of economic democracy as opposed to capitalism free of the ravages of neoliberalism. (Nor do all proponents of economic democracy have the same conception; some in the anarchist direction want to stick with local nongovernmental models, while others are committed to using and transforming local and even nation-states and building global institutions.[263]) Nevertheless, economic democracy is the logic of the movement that offers hopeful examples of sustainable democratic ways of living together, such as the participatory budgeting developed in Brazil, which has involved hundreds of thousands of people. Via Campesina is an international organization of peasants, agricultural workers, rural women, and indigenous communities that fights for food sovereignty, also called food democracy, and cites gender parity as one of their main objectives. As the agricultural practices they favor grow out of centuries of their own experience, they are more sustainable ecologically than the top-down technocratic solutions like genetically modified organisms (GM food) that are favored by multinational institutions and corporations. In India 5 million peasants have shared seeds in violation of Indian seed patent laws.[264] Most examples of economic democracy are local, but there are models being developed for broader

---

263 For examples of the latter approach see Hilary Wainwright, *Reclaim the State: Experiments in Popular Democracy* (London: Verso 2003).

264 This fits my point made earlier about choices among technologies reflecting power relations. See AAAGRrrr! (accessed July 22, 2010), "an e-newsletter for information on African agro-ecological alternatives for food sovereignty: the right of all people to healthy and culturally appropriate food produced through ecologically sound and sustainable methods, and their right to define their own food and agriculture systems. This newsletter provides updated information on the Alliance for a New Green Revolution in Africa (AGRA), a $500 million project to re-introduce the decades-old Green Revolution into African food systems. This new Green Revolution is

global institutions and policies that are necessary to deal with our increasingly global problems and to create solidarity across local, national boundaries.[265] The goal should be to combine as much local, regional, and national autonomy as possible, drawing on local knowledge and passion, with broad, even global, regulation as necessary, in particular, to deal with environmental problems. An intriguing example comes from the world of cyberspace where the open source movement is creating what one observer calls a "global collectivist society ... a new socialism."[266] We need to bring this model from cyberspace into real space, fusing individual creativity and autonomy with collective democratic controls that are necessary to protect and enhance the well-being of all humankind. In the famous phrase of Italian Marxist, Antonio Gramsci, we need to cultivate pessimism of the intellect, but optimism of the will.

being led by seed and fertilizer companies, is targeting traditional African food crops, and plans to prepare African agriculture for the widespread introduction of genetically modified seeds." See: http://pambazuka.org/en/category/enewsl/53590. See also Beverley Bell and the Other Worlds Collaborative, "Who Says You Can't Change the World: Just Economies on an Unjust Planet," vol. 1, June 2009, at: www.otherworldsarepossible.org.

265 British economist Pat Devine has developed a model of democratic, participatory planning in *Democracy and Economic Planning: The Political Economy of a Self-Governing Society* (Cambridge: Polity, 1988). For another model see Albert and Hahnel, *Looking Forward*. For more discussions, see Raymond L. Goldsteen and John K. Schorr, *Demanding Democracy After Three-Mile Island* (Gainesville, FL: University of Florida Press, 1991); Adolf Gundersen, *The Environmental Promise of Democratic Deliberation* (Madison, WI: University of Wisconsin Press, 1995); Greg Palast *et al.*, *Democracy and Regulation: How the Public Can Govern Essential Services* (London: Pluto, 2003); William Fisher and Thomas Ponniah, *Another World is Possible* (London: Pluto Books, 2003); George Monbiot, *The Age of Consent: A Manifesto for a New World Order* (London: Flamingo, 2003); Michael Fox, *Beyond Elections: Redefining Democracy in the Americas*, 2008 a documentary film. Also see Marx's discussion of the first workers' government – the Paris Commune.

266 "When masses of people who own the means of production work toward a common goal and share their products in common, when they contribute labor without wages and enjoy the fruits free of charge, it's not unreasonable to call that socialism." Kevin Kelly, "The New Socialism: Global Collectivist Society is Coming Online," available at: www.wired.com, May 22, 2009.

In the meanwhile, feminists should push to get the most from capitalism for the most women, not simply the freedom to exploit and be exploited on the same basis as men. This means they have to focus on practical, as well as strategic gender interests. For example, rather than fighting simply for the right to abortion, all feminists should embrace the concept of reproductive freedom for all women, which includes adequate medical care, childcare, decent paying jobs for women. These cannot be separated from economic and political rights.[267] Using the terminology developed earlier, women's strategic gender interests must be united with practical gender interests. Though one cannot take on all issues at once, this is an example of how feminists must integrate the issues that affect women in all their multidimensionality, even ones that are not explicitly gendered. In the United States, a struggle for public goods like universal medical care, childcare, and elder care would enhance the interests of all women who are not rich and would increase the areas of society that are subject to democratic control.[268] They also point beyond a society based on private property. But it is not only women in the developed world who are worthy of feminists' moral regard. For women in the developing world, securing these rights, and even the right to food, shelter, and clean water, require a struggle against global capitalist institutions like the World Bank which have imposed structural adjustment programs that cut back already meager government services in order to pay back criminally onerous debts to the richest countries and institutions in the world. Complete cancellation of Third World debt is a necessary and just first step that all feminists must support. The call raised by developing countries for reparations from wealthy

267 See Rosalind P. Petchesky, "Human Rights, Reproductive Health and Economic Justice: Why They are Indivisible", in Holmstrom (ed.), *The Socialist-Feminist Project*. The broad notion of reproductive rights was developed in the 1970s by black feminists and socialist feminists in opposition to the narrow focus on the right to abortion in the mainstream (white) women's movement. See Jael Silliman, Marlene Gerber Fried, Loretta Ross, and Elena R. Gutierrez (eds.), *Undivided Rights: Women of Color Organize for Reproductive Justice* (Cambridge: South End, 2004).

268 Anton, "Public Goods as Commonstock."

countries to their countries for the devastating effects of climate change (wealthy countries create 75 percent of the pollution) is a just demand and a specifically feminist one since women suffer disproportionately. Another injustice that must be fought is the fact that while capital moves freely around the globe displacing people in its wake, the movement of people is increasingly controlled and criminalized. The fight to declare "no one is illegal" is a just one that speaks to the interests of all working people, as "illegal" immigrants are a pool of low paid labor. Aside from moral reasons, there are also selfish reasons why feminists cannot limit their concerns to their own societies. Our problems are increasingly global. As already discussed, the most important public good must be the environment which knows no national boundaries. Women are disproportionately among the world's poor who are bearing the brunt of ecological destruction, and it is striking that women have been at the forefront of environmental struggles around the world.

Finally, it is also important that feminists stress the very different values and understandings that motivate us from those that dominate capitalist culture. Individual autonomy is a crucial goal for women. But as women know better than anyone else humans are interdependent beings, so we should stress that autonomy is not counterposed, but rather complementary to the values of caring, compassion, solidarity, and security in the fullest sense of the term. And we should resist the capitalist logic which turns all areas of our lives into commodities, where everything has a price and nothing has a value.

To close with the optimistic words of writer and activist Arundhati Roy: "Not only is another world possible, she is on her way. On a quiet day, I can hear her breathing."[269]

269 Bell, "Who Says You Can't Change the World."

Part III

3   Ann Cudd's reply to
Nancy Holmstrom

P ROFESSOR HOLMSTROM AND I AGREE ON many things. We agree
that poverty is a serious problem, and that the wealthier persons of the world should do more to alleviate it. We agree that
women are overrepresented among the poorest of the world,
and that in many places women suffer from severe oppression.
We also agree that philosophers and economists have in the past
largely failed to attend sufficiently to the concerns of the poor,
the sick, and the vulnerable, and, until recently, have virtually
ignored women. What we disagree on, for the most part, is the
best means of ending poverty and oppression. Where I see capitalism as an essential means to that end, she sees it as an inevitable obstacle to progress. Part of our disagreement hinges on the
conception of freedom and human well-being. But we both also
agree that neither material goods nor freedom are incommen-
surable; they permit tradeoffs, though we might disagree on how
those tradeoffs are to be made.

Our main disagreement, however, is over the economics of
poverty and well-being. By "economics" I mean two things. First,
is the economic theory that should be applied in the debate.
Professor Holmstrom accepts a Marxist theory of production and
wages, which I maintain is outdated and false. I accept a neoclassical account of wage and price determination, which she
rejects as ideological and naive. I have attempted to spell out
the assumptions and principles of the theory that I support, in
order for readers to decide for themselves. Second, by "economics" I also mean that the economic facts are in dispute, and by

"facts" I mean claims about data, such as how many people are there?, how long do they live?, how much income do they earn? While these facts are laden with theory, there are some facts that I believe are relatively uncontroversial and crucial for the argument over whether capitalism can hope to bring about a feminist political transformation. Some of these I have reported in my main contribution. But now that both sides of the debate have been clearly stated, the point of disagreement can be sharpened. I begin my reply with this question of economic fact.

The world's poor: who they are, where they live, what they do

Much of the empirical disagreement in our two positions hinges on two questions: (1) how bad is the capitalist world for the worst off; and (2) is it getting better or worse for them with capitalist development? So I will begin with an empirical assessment of the first question by asking who are the poor: where do they live, how poor are they, and what do they do for a living?

First, what counts as living in poverty can be debated, but a reasonable place to start would be the level of consumption set by the UN Millennium Goals, the first of which is to cut in half by 2015 the number of persons living on less than US$1 per day, assessed by the constant purchasing power parity (PPP).[1] This is extreme poverty, to be sure, but it is the level that social scientists and activists have used to estimate the number of persons in extreme poverty around the world. So this level allows us to make the most accurate estimates of the numbers of impoverished persons. According to this standard, the number of people

---

1 "Tracking the Millennium Development Goals," 2007, available at: www. mdgmonitor.org/goal1.cfm; "purchasing power parity" (PPP) refers to an estimate of the monetary value of an equivalent basket of goods in different places. This estimate allows one to factor out the differences in nominal prices of goods to get to the question of what resources individuals have available to them. Although it is controversial in the literature exactly how best to gather the data for and compute PPP, there is no real controversy about the need to use constant PPP in order to estimate the changes in global poverty rates.

in dire poverty in the world in 1981 was 1.47028 billion, while the number in 2004 was 0.96948 billion.[2] Considering that the population of the earth rose in that period of time from 4.5 billion to 6.4 billion, the massive reduction in the absolute numbers of people living in dire poverty is truly remarkable.[3] In percentage terms, while in 1981 40.14% of the world's population lived on less than a dollar a day, in 2004 that was down to 18.09%. Much of this dramatic improvement is due to changing conditions in China over this period of time, where in 1981 0.63366 billion people or 63.76% of its population lived in dire poverty, while in 2004 those numbers had fallen to 0.12836 or 9.9%. If we double the standard for poverty to US$2 per day (again, in constant PPP terms), then we see that the total number living at this level has slightly increased, from 2.45247 billion to 2.54794 billion, which is still an impressive decrease in percentage terms of 66.96% to 47.55%. Here China's numbers are even more impressive considering the higher bar: the absolute numbers have fallen from 0.87577 billion to 0.45225 billion, and in percentage terms from 88.12% to 34.89%.[4] It is important to note here, of course, that China has changed from a centrally-planned communist state to a market-driven economy in that time, and there is no doubt that this drastic decrease in poverty is due to that change.

Second, where do the world's poor live? Professor Holmstrom's contribution would have one believe that they live in urban areas, having been forcibly evicted from their traditional, rural homelands in capitalist countries. But this is, in fact, not true. In 2002 the urban share of the population in the world was 42.34%, while the urban share of the world's poor at the US$1 dollar standard was 24.55%, and 26.37% at the $2 standard.[5] We can

2 Shaohua Chen and Martin Ravallion, "How Have the World's Poorest Fared Since the Early 1980s?," World Bank Policy Research Working Paper No. 3341, June 2004, table 1.
3 US Census Bureau International Data Base, available at: www.census.gov/ipc/www/idb/worldpop.php, accessed August 24, 2009.
4 Chen and Ravallion, "How Have the World's Poorest Fared Since the Early 1980s?," table 2.
5 Chen and Ravallion, "How Have the World's Poorest Fared Since the Early 1980s?," table 4.

also look at how wealth is distributed between rural and urban households. Worldwide, only 8% of the poorest quintile (20%) of households as measured by wealth (rather than income, as with the US$1 standard) live in urban areas, although in the Near East and North Africa that number rises to a high of 23%. Still, overwhelmingly – almost 75% – the poorest people in the world live in rural areas.[6] One might ask whether the relatively few poor who do leave rural areas leave because of their poverty and a desire to seek better conditions in urban areas, or because they are pushed out of their impoverished rural homes only to land in equally impoverished conditions in the urban areas. The data that I have found does not answer this question, and it certainly bears further investigation. In either case, it is not reasonable to conclude that capitalism has impoverished more people, let alone that it has done so by pushing them off the land in order to create a reserve army of labor for urban sweatshops.

So, third, what do the poor do for a living? This is a particularly difficult question to answer, since most of them live, as we have just seen, in rural areas of the least developed countries. But most of them therefore cannot work in export-related industries or factories. In rural areas, what businesses do exist are small and often family operated. Most of the rural poor are agricultural laborers and small farmers; most of such employment is informal.[7] Informal work is less well paid and less stable than formal work, and comes with fewer social and legal protections. There are no global statistics yet on the numbers and pay of workers in all sectors, but according to a study of six developing countries done by the United Nations Development Fund for Women (UNIFEM), only 14 percent of women in India are informally employed in nonagricultural paid work. The majority of persons, male or female, who work in the informal economies studied are self-employed.[8]

6 International Labor Organization, *World Employment Report*, 2004–5, 121.
7 Martha Chen *et al.*, "Progress of the World's Women 2005: Women, Work and Poverty," United Nations Development Fund for Women, 2005, 46.
8 Chen *et al.*, "Progress of the World's Women 2005," tables 3.1 and 3.2.

So what does this mean? To the degree that we can generalize, the poorest people of the world are self-employed workers in rural areas, most of them engaged in small-scale agricultural production. They are not working in sweatshops or export industries; global capitalism has not changed their lives very much; they live much as their ancestors did. Where capitalism has a significant foothold, employment tends more often to be formal and urban, and where it is formal, wages are generally higher and social and legal protections are greater.

Thus, my first response to Professor Holmstrom is to say that world poverty is falling, and dramatically so as capitalism expands globally, though, to be sure, poverty is still horrific and much more remains to be done. Furthermore, the poverty that continues to exist in the world is largely in rural areas that are as yet virtually untouched by capitalist development. The problem, I contend, is not too much capitalist development, but too little.

A false or confused picture of capitalism

The second response is that Professor Holmstrom's argument is based on an incomplete and misleading set of statistics at several key points. First, she cites statistics about poverty in the world without citing the statistics of previous years or eras, then claims that things are getting worse. If we want to know whether capitalism is a progressive force fighting poverty, however, then we must compare earlier times with current times. When we do so, we find that, in fact, things are getting better, as I have documented above with respect to the number and percent living in dire poverty, or the percentage of persons living under the lesser, US$2 per day (PPP), standard of poverty. Although she and I agree that there is great and horrendous poverty in the world, and that much could be done to relieve it with good will from rich countries and individuals, and greater genuine efforts to solve problems by governments of poor ones, it is still the case that fewer and fewer people in the world are desperately poor even despite the ever growing population of the earth. Since we also agree that capitalism is a global hegemonic force, it is likely that capitalism is a large part of the *progress* that the world has made in reducing poverty.

Second, Professor Holmstrom makes a rhetorical appeal in her discussion of "sweatshops" and the alleged "race to the bottom" in capitalism. But this appeal is not grounded in fact or reasoned argument. Let me quote the most egregious example, which comes as she is discussing defenses of so-called "sweatshops":[9]

> The first argument is that conditions are not as bad as critics charge, especially compared with prevailing standards and cost of living in the countries where they exist. *This defense is simply not credible*. Numerous independent studies have documented worsening conditions since the 1980s due to intense competition, particularly in the apparel industry, that has resulted in what's been called a "race to the bottom." (p. 224, emphasis mine)

But the defense is credible and documentable with reliable statistics; the "race to the bottom" does not exist on a statistically significant scale. This can be seen by examining how wage rates and total work compensation has changed over time in capitalism. Global statistics are not well kept and difficult to generate, but studies have improved recently as more economists have focused their lenses on the state of the world's poor. Estimates of recent trends show that from 1995 to 2007 global real wages grew by 0.75 percent annually. While the rate of growth varies greatly around the world, most countries for which the ILO has reliable statistics experienced rising real wages.[10] There is also evidence about what happens to wages in developing countries when multinational firms enter. Studies suggest that such firms

---

9 I say "so-called 'sweatshops'" because the term is unclear and would not be used by the defenders of capitalist factories or transnational enterprises that this term is loosely used to refer to. If "sweatshops" refers to whatever factories are violating labor laws, then no one would defend *those* factories. But if they are referring to any factories that simply pay lower wages than factories in other countries, then it begs the question to imply that this violates morality.

10 International Labor Organization, *Global Wage Report*, 2008–9, 13.

pay much higher wages than local firms, and that as they enter local markets, local employer wages rise as well.[11]

Of course, these higher wages are probably not due to those that Professor Holmstrom would call sweatshops, but rather to firms that, she would agree, are doing good in the world. There are no doubt firms that violate local labor laws or well accepted international standards and also pay good wages by local standards, and here we might or might not disagree about their overall value. Are such firms doing good things? I think this depends on what law is being violated (is it a protectionist law or does it really matter for health and safety?) and how the treatment of workers compares with how they would live with their other options. If their other options are much worse than working in the multinational firms, then perhaps that is an improvement that the activist world should be willing to live with until better options can be produced. I am not sure that Professor Holmstrom would allow for this sort of partially favorable judgment.

The data on wages and conditions for the United States are much better because of data collection efforts by the Bureau of Labor Statistics (BLS). The United States is the largest capitalist economy in the world, and so if the race to the bottom were a real phenomenon, one might expect it to be most apparent here. Yet the opposite has occurred; wages and overall compensation have soared. According to a report on employment, wages, and income in the twentieth century, compiled by the BLS:

> In 1900, per capita income (in 1999 dollars) was $4,200; it was about $33,700 in 1999. The average hourly pay of manufacturing production workers in 1999 was $13.90; in 1909, the first measured year, it was about $3.80 (in 1999 dollars). In addition to wages and salaries, benefits comprised a major part of employee compensation at the end of the 20th century.

11 Drusilla K. Brown, Alan Deardorff, and Robert Stern, "The Effects of Multinational Production on Wages and Working Conditions in Developing Countries," in Robert E. Baldwin and L. Alan Winters (eds.), *Challenges to Globalization: Analyzing the Economics* (University of Chicago Press, 2004).

Statistics show that benefits averaged $5.58 per hour – or 27.5 percent of total compensation – in 1999.[12]

The race to the bottom theory also predicts that more and more children will enter (or be forced into) the workforce, since they are cheaper to reproduce than adult workers. Yet the number of child laborers (aged 10 to 15 years) in the United States over this time has fallen from 1.75 million or 6 percent of the legal, full-time workforce in 1900 to no legal full-time workers in 1999.[13] The theory also suggests that capital has so much market power that it can dispense with safety regulations. Of course, in the United States, workplace safety is dramatically better today than a century ago.

Work also became steadier over the twentieth century. Again citing the same source:

> Unemployment is estimated at 5 percent in 1900; in 1999 it averaged 4.2 percent. While these two figures are not much different, they reflect very different dynamics. Data from four States – California, Kansas, Maine, and Michigan – and the 1910 census suggest that workers around the turn of the century faced a high probability of being laid off or unemployed sometime during the year.[14]

Thus, capitalist development on the whole does not tend to lower wages, increase child labor, put workers in more dangerous situations, or expose them to greater uncertainties over time. In fact, it is quite the opposite, as far as we can tell. There are no doubt exceptions to these statistical trends. There are also egregious violations of law, where children and adults are enslaved. And unemployment periods for some are permanently devastating. But on the whole the system does not impoverish; it lifts the masses out of poverty. To deny this sort of development to masses of people because of the experience of some would seem unwise

12 Donald M. Fisk, "American Labor in the Twentieth Century," US Bureau of Labor Statistics, available at: www.bls.gov/opub/cwc/cm20030124ar02p1.htm#13, accessed August 29, 2009.
13 Fisk, "American Labor in the Twentieth Century."
14 Fisk, "American Labor in the Twentieth Century."

and unfair. Thus, the exceptions call out for incremental, not systemwide, change, and to heed the normal moral imperative to show charity and good will toward all those who are worse off than oneself.

The "race to the bottom" is a myth generated by a flawed and largely discredited Marxist economic theory. According to Marxist economics, capitalist firms are compelled by the force of competition with other firms to cut wages until the wages fall to subsistence level for the worker (or even lower, provided that there are enough reserve laborers willing to work for less than subsistence rather than starve immediately). This theory is mistaken in multiple ways. First, it relies on a mistaken price theory that holds that prices are determined by the cost of production in terms of cumulative (socially necessary) labor power required to produce the item. But this fails to take account of the consumption or demand side of the equation. To put it in simple terms, wages are the price of labor. According to contemporary price theory, the price of a good (or an input to production, such as labor) is determined by the demand and the supply of that good or service. In turn, the demand for the good depends in part on the other options that a consumer (producer) has for substituting other items for that good. Applying this insight to the determination of wages, if there is any competition for labor, the demand for labor should have as much effect on the wage rate as the cost to produce the labor. Second, Marxist economic theory relies on the assumption that there is no competition among firms for laborers, not even their opting for home production, entrepreneurial activities, or the informal economy, which is another way of saying that it assumes that laborers have no outside option besides starvation. But this is clearly not true in reality. People in the poorest parts of the world do live largely on informal work or self-employment. The existence of (illegal) slavery suggests that merely providing subsistence for workers would be a good deal, since that would save the costs of finding, coercing, and keeping hidden the slaves (or bribing the police). Furthermore, the data shows that the race to the bottom does not happen in reality. The data on rising wages stands as a strong argument in favor of firms that push forward capitalist development, providing greater than average wages locally, even if those wages are lower than those paid in other countries.

Professor Holmstrom conflates inequality and poverty. Inequality is, of course, a relative measure, while poverty is an absolute standard. One can be much poorer than, say, Bill Gates, without being the least bit poor or lacking in any way the material wherewithal to develop one's capacities fully. Surely all of the professors and artists on earth are much poorer than Bill Gates, yet they have all had the freedom to develop their capacities to such an extent that no one would worry about whether they are impoverished by the system. Material inequalities matter only when they imply some sort of impoverishment in terms of the ability to do something essential to human life. Professor Holmstrom does not seem to recognize this, however, when she writes:

> Material inequalities, moreover, are also inequalities of power and freedom and general well-being. The connection between general well-being and material goods seems so obvious that it is not necessary to elaborate except to point out, first, that it can literally be a matter of life and death, and, second, that material inequalities are correlated with other problems usually perceived as unrelated, such as domestic violence for example. (p. 194)

In this quote, she slides from material inequality in the first sentence, to impoverishment in the first two clauses of the second sentence, and back to inequality in the final clause of the second sentence. It is important to note, though, that material inequalities do not necessitate inequalities of power or freedom or general well-being. Think again about the comparison of Bill Gates with the professor. Even less do inequalities in material goods necessitate a lack of freedom or general well-being. But severe poverty, of course, does. Bringing in the point about domestic violence makes her point even less clear. Material inequality between domestic partners is not nearly as great within as across societies, yet I would agree that inequalities of various kinds between partners is cause of domestic violence. But surely that inequality – the inequality between domestic partners – is not due to capitalism.

Professor Holmstrom argues that relative equality is necessary for freedom and self-expression because only with relative (material) equality will there be political equality:

> Only a society that was fairly egalitarian would eliminate these internal barriers to freedom and self-expression, as all groups in society would be involved on an equal basis in the institutions that shape them. Only in such a society that allowed for both personal and political autonomy would freedom as self-realization be possible. (pp. 197–98)

But we can imagine a society in which there is great wealth for some and inequality in the distribution of goods, but in which no one is denied the material support for developing their capacities. Personal autonomy does not seem to require material equality, though it surely requires some base level of income of material goods. Furthermore, in such a society we can imagine individuals who begin at the low end of the scale of wealth and income who could rise to the top politically, at least in a democracy. President Barack Obama is a good example: he comes from neither privilege nor deprivation, he is identified with a less privileged group politically, and the United States is not even a society where everyone can develop their capacities. It would not be plausible to suppose that if those living in deprivation in the United States were brought to a young Obama-like level of material well-being, then none of them could come to have political autonomy. It is not plausible to require everyone in every group to have the ability to "be involved on an equal basis in the institutions that shape them," since some of us lack the personal charisma that such influence requires. So equality seems not to be necessary for political autonomy, either. Equality is clearly not a sufficient condition for autonomy or freedom as self-realization – one needs to have sufficient material resources, among other things. Finally, bringing about economic equality would not necessarily bring political equality. Indeed, if the communist experiments of the twentieth and twenty-first centuries are any guide, what has to be done to achieve absolute equality seems to be itself an impediment to political equality. So, equality is neither a necessary nor a sufficient condition for personal or political autonomy, and inequality is not necessarily a hindrance to either personal or political autonomy. Inequality seems to be problematic only when the inequalities are so great as to amount, at the lower end, to material deprivation. But in that case it is really poverty that we should be discussing, not inequality.

Professor Holmstrom argues that inequality is rising in the United States, and that this is problematic. Let us examine this claim. If inequality is to count as a critique of capitalism, given the argument I have just made, then it must be because inequality is due to declining wages and compensation among the poorest. Rising inequality can be due to a falling bottom, a flying top, or a polarization situation. If it is a flying top, then, granting my previous argument, that should be acceptable, particularly if the bottom is also rising to some degree. According to the *Global Wage Report* cited above, rising wage inequality in the United States is mostly due to a flying top when comparing wage differentials over time.[15] There are some senses in which wages are becoming less polarized, namely, the wage gap for men and women is falling (although that there is any wage gap at all is, of course, a bad thing for women). Professor Holmstrom laments that in the United States the wage gap has fallen mainly because men's wages have declined. But how problematic is this really? This, after all, is a falling top, not a falling bottom, at least with respect to the comparison of men with women. If men's wages are falling mainly because they have lost an automatic privilege over women, and women's wages have risen, then it may not be so problematic, particularly from a feminist point of view. The loss of undeserved privilege is not, in itself, morally bad. A relevant question is whether all wages have increased, and whether it now takes less working time to buy subsistence for the worse off. As I reported earlier in this reply, the trend in the United States is toward better wages and working conditions.

15 *Global Wage Report*, 28.

Considering changes over time in the United States leads us to the claim Professor Holmstrom makes that by one measure of well-being, the Human Development Index (HDI), the United States is declining. But she mistakenly compares the US rankings at different times rather than the raw scores the US receives at those times. Comparing the ranking of the United States at different points in time on HDI is irrelevant to the question of whether the quality of life is improving over that time period. The rank may go down, while the quality of life as measured by the index goes up if other countries are making even greater progress. Furthermore, the way the index is calculated has changed over time, so the difference in ranking may be an effect of a change in emphasis of the index. It is important, then, not only to look at the raw indices, but also the methodologies for computing the indices in order to make this sort of comparison. Although she cites the rankings using only a secondary source,[16] the original source from which that comes, the United Nations Development Programme, 2008 Human Development Report Statistical Update, used the 2006 methodology uniformly to compute the indices going back to 1980. This source shows that in 1980 the United States had an HDI of 0.892, by 1995 it was 0.933, and as of 2006 it was 0.950. So in the United States the HDI has improved substantially over those twenty-six years. That the ranking of the United States has declined says more about the improvements of other countries. The fact that other capitalist countries have improved their HDI by more than the United States over that time is scarcely a condemnation of capitalism.

Capitalism: partial failures, partial successes, and progress

Professor Holmstrom focuses on the partial failures of capitalism, without acknowledging partial successes or progress. Capitalist development has enabled enormous progress in life span, health,

16 The reference is Dalton Conley, "America is … #15?," *The Nation*, March 23, 2009.

and material standards of living for a vast number of people, as I have documented. While it is true that there remains much to be done to bring the poorest out of poverty, it is not clear that this is so much caused by capitalism as is due to a lack of capitalist development. Still, there are partial failures, such as where capitalist firms have violated laws or pressured governments into overlooking them. However, many of the partial failures are due not to capitalism, but rather to the adherence to traditionalism in some sectors of society, even where that conflicts with the general logic of capitalism.

Modern slavery combines both of these categories of partial failures. In almost every place where people are forced to work for no pay, this is illegal. Because of either corruption or incompetence of local police, the slavers are able to get away with their evil deeds. Still, we have to see this overall situation as, first, an advance over the times when slavery was legal, and, second, a contradiction of the logic of capitalism. Capitalism requires labor (as well as capital) to be free to be put to work wherever it will be most in demand. As long as some are able to skirt the law and take rather than compete for inputs to their products, there will be in effect a market failure. The problem is the failure to enforce rights, property rights in the self. In each country that Kevin Bales examines in his groundbreaking exposé of modern slavery, the causes are different and complex.[17] While in some it is a type of highly organized international crime, in most places it is the continuation of traditional practices, such as in Pakistan, where children have traditionally been bonded to carpet makers and essentially made into slaves. The real question with both types of modern slavery, though, is whether it would disappear if we were to move to the democratic socialism Professor Holmstrom recommends, and that is just not clear. It is, after all, in the most developed capitalist countries that we see the least slavery.

Does capitalism cause more wars? This has long been an argument of socialists against capitalism, but it seems a flimsy one.

17 Kevin Bales, *Disposable People: New Slavery in the Global Economy* (Berkeley, CA: University of California Press, 1999).

First, it is clear that the communist experiments of the twentieth century were every bit as militaristic and capable of aggressive wars as the capitalist ones. Second, it is commonly asserted, and I think Professor Holmstrom would agree, that democratic nations do not wage war against each other. But democratic countries tend toward capitalism, since that seems to be what people choose when given the chance. As with slavery, the logic of capitalism tells against war, in general, as that wipes out potential trading partners. Capitalist competition is a positive-sum game, not a zero or negative sum. I agree wholeheartedly with Professor Holmstrom's assertion that security is broader than military security; the security of persons and property generally is the necessary condition for capitalist development.

Professor Holmstrom cites only the downsides of growth: in the early sections of her contribution, she criticizes capitalism as not productive enough to prevent poverty, yet in the final section she criticizes it for being too productive in that it causes overpopulation and overpollution. Does capitalism cause overpopulation and overpollution? Admittedly, development can be a two-edged sword of capitalism: it enables great material productivity, but this productivity uses natural resources and creates waste; it enables greater life spans for more persons, but then we have more people. However, capitalism cannot really be faulted for overpopulation. As I demonstrated in my main contribution (see section "Lower infant mortality and lower fertility" and Table 1.1), fertility falls with greater development. The real population growth in the world is due to population growth of the least developed nations, not capitalist ones.

I agree with Professor Holmstrom that we should be very concerned with pollution, and particularly with climate change, but in my view, this points us toward private ownership of property and not collective ownership of scarce resources. As has been proven repeatedly by experience, and as is clear from theory as well, when goods are collectively owned they are subject to the problem known as the "tragedy of the commons." The tragedy of the commons is the overuse of a scarce resource that happens because no one has the incentive to preserve and protect the resource for the long term. Common ownership sets up a race to use the resource before it is used up by someone else, or exhausted. Even with the best of intentions on one's own part, if one cannot be sure that others will preserve and protect the resource, then it is only rational to make full use of it while it lasts. In game theoretic terms it is like a "prisoner's dilemma" in which there is no equilibrium strategy that would counsel preservation of the resource; anyone who refrains from using the resource in order to preserve it for later generations would be played for a sucker. Real world examples abound of the tragedy of the commons: the depletion of the world's ocean fisheries; overpollution of the atmosphere; overgrazing of common pasturelands; over-gathering of firewood. This last is a particular tragedy in many places in Africa today for women, where they must search farther and farther from home to find enough fuel.

Private ownership of property provides owners with an incentive to preserve their property for the long term. It is precisely the ability to exclude others from using it that allows one the security to be able to invest in it, by improving the pasture, protecting the trees, refraining from fishing at times, or taking only the mature animals. No one worries that cattle, which are owned privately and therefore cultivated, will disappear after all. But we are very worried about the disappearance of cod in the North Atlantic. Private ownership allows one to sell the good in the market if, and only if, those who would consume the good are willing to pay the price that reflects the relative scarcity of the good and the expense of preserving it. The ability to own a competing resource privately and sell it means that alternatives can be cultivated as well, which removes some of the pressure from the more scarce, and therefore more expensive, privately owned good.

The tragedy of the commons can also be relieved through collective means, as Professor Holmstrom claims. The common owners can conceivably come together to agree on a limitation mechanism and an enforcement mechanism, but this requires intrusive monitoring and coercive enforcement if it is to work. Furthermore, the collective must agree on the correct degree to which the resource should be exploited. Finally, they must also exclude all others outside the collective from using the resource, which may also require applying coercive means. There are some renowned examples where this has worked,[18] but there are many more where it has tragically failed.

Misunderstanding the economics of capitalism

Professor Holmstrom, and anti-capitalists generally, present a mistaken picture of the economics of capitalism. They tend to focus on production without taking account of the consumption side, as I noted earlier. The point of production is viewed as job creation for workers, and not creation of goods that are demanded by consumers in the market. When the demand side of the market is overlooked, so is the efficiency with which capitalism conveys information through that demand. But this information efficiency is one of the primary advantages of the market over central planning economies. Anti-capitalists also assume a static world in which there is no innovation or change. While capitalism is not very good at providing full employment in a static world, that is not where its internal logic drives it. As Schumpeter observed, capitalism is all about creative destruction, and it is driven by the desires of consumers or potential consumers of good.

An example of how Professor Holmstrom misconstrues the logic of capitalism comes when she writes: "Rather, the principal 'rule' or 'law of motion' of capitalism is the maximization of profit. That is the goal of production in capitalism; that determines what is produced, how it is produced, and where it is produced" (p. 217). On the contrary, however, it is the choices of consumers, or firms' best guesses of those choices, that determine what is produced. Firms need to cover their costs, which include inputs to production and distribution, as well as interest

---

18 J. E. M. Arnold and J. G. Campbell, "Collective Management of Hill Forests in Nepal: The Community Forestry Development Project," *Common Property Resource Management* (Washington, DC: National Academy Press, 1984), 415–54.

payments on whatever loans they have made, and the opportunity costs for the owner, who could choose to invest her or his capital in other ways. Once those are covered, any additional profits are "rents" – unnecessary to bring the goods to the market. When firms manage to produce what consumers will buy, then they may make enough profit to continue to compete for employees and the other inputs, each of which faces other opportunities for employment either in or out of the formal market, in order to continue production. Firms may or may not also receive rents, and they may or may not maximize their profits in the real world, where information is not perfect; everyone is simply making their best estimates about their opportunity costs of utilizing their resources.

A similar point can also be made regarding the differences in the definitions of capitalism that she and I give. There are two important differences. Whereas I stress free markets and nondiscrimination, she stresses production for profit. With free markets, under ideal conditions, production for profit is likely to occur, but only if the producers are rational and profits are necessary to remain in the market. This is true only under very competitive conditions. With less competitive conditions, maximization may neither be reached nor necessary for survival of the firms in the market. As with evolution in the natural sphere, competition guarantees that only the "good enough" survive, but does not necessarily lead to the maximum profit.

The second difference between her definition of capitalism and mine is that Professor Holmstrom refers to the "brutally competitive system" of capitalism in a way that misunderstands the nature of competition. When the tooth and claw fight to the finish of prey and predator interaction in nature is taken as the paradigm of competition, many positive and cooperative aspects of market competition are overlooked. If sport is taken as the paradigm of human competition, however, we can view competition in a more nuanced light that is more appropriate as an analogy to the competitive nature of capitalism. Competitive sport is characterized by a set of rules for the game (similar to the laws that structure property rights and trade), and players who intend to play by the rules or at least must try to do so for the most part in order for the game to continue (and so for them to gain from its existence in the long run). The outcomes of competitive sport typically involve a winner, and perhaps also a loser or at least runners-up, but the losers almost invariably see themselves as having gained through the participation in the competition; they are not the vanquished of war or the prey of nature. And perhaps most importantly, sport and its competition tends to bring out the best in the competitors. At its best, competitive sport brings about what Rawls (following Humboldt) calls a "social union," where each member of the group takes pleasure in the achievements of the other as well as their own. Capitalist markets can also create this kind of synergistic, communal system by bringing out the best in competitive firms to create more and better products, and giving each other the incentives to create, innovate, and invest. And with both capitalism and sports, a social union can arise among persons who previously were strangers, and who have come together only for the sake of the market opportunities or the desire to play in the game.[19] Of course, games can devolve into shouting matches or fights, and capitalists can use dirty tactics to win at any cost. This counsels us to design good rules, which evolve when tactics become unfair and upset the balance, as well as good referees to monitor the players and punish violators. It does not suggest that we give up playing sports altogether.

Capitalism gives everyone in the system an incentive to ensure that all the participants continue to function well, even while each wants to perform better than the next one. Professor Holmstrom sometimes writes as if the last capitalist standing is the one and only winner. In comparing capitalism with so-called socialism as it has worked out for women, she writes that:

> In some countries, like China, where women were practically slaves before the revolution, the improvements in women's

19 I elaborate this sport metaphor of capitalist competition in "Sporting Metaphors: Competition and the Ethos of Capitalism," *Journal of the Philosophy of Sport* 34 (May 2007): 52–67.

lives were especially dramatic. The reason is that *like capitalists*, the ruling bureaucracies of these societies had no vested
interest in women's subordination. Indeed, on the contrary,
unlike capitalists, they had a clear vested interest in eliminating it. They needed to maximize the productivity of the whole
society since they "owned" the whole society, not just a particular firm, so they needed to maximize everyone's input into
production. (p. 221, emphasis in text)

One could just as easily say that capitalists also have a vested
interest in making sure that everyone is available as a laborer
and a consumer, since that would increase the supply of labor
and the demand for their goods.

A common Marxist exaggeration that Professor Holmstrom
indulges is that capitalism is a system of forced labor. The reason for this is that for many workers lack the means to produce
a marketable good or service on their own, and so they must
contract their labor for wages. Even granting that workers have
no outside option whatsoever (which I have already suggested
is dubious), it is a huge difference to say that one must sell one's
labor to some capitalist, as opposed to being bonded to a particular capitalist. The latter situation is almost slavery (with a wage),
but the former is clearly not slavery. After all, one has to make
some efforts just to live, even if the effort is just swallowing. But
it does not follow from that that one is forced to swallow, at least
not in any morally relevant sense of force! One might object that
having very bad outside options (no education, no tillable land,
no marketable skills, no family support, dependants) means that
one is rational to choose to work even for very low wages. The
whole question is one of degrees and choices. It is not true to
say, as Professor Holmstrom does, that there is forced labor only
when one does not own the means of production and appropriation. Even then one has to produce something and appropriate something, and one has to labor to do these things, even to
choose which things to make or appropriate. So when she says
that the only difference between indentured servitude and the
free labor of capitalism is a matter of degree of force, that too can
be said of any system one can imagine. Only the state of nature

would contain no force that is supplied by persons or systems created and enforced by persons, but the state of nature is not what we would call free either, since most of us would not be able to realize our capacities in such a state.

Perhaps most crucial for evaluating the alternative she offers, Professor Holmstrom fails to appreciate the efficiency of information transfer of capitalism and how difficult that would be to replace in a nonmarket system. As I argued on pp. 75–78, in a nonmarket system, bureaucrats are needed to make the kinds of decisions about what to produce, where, by whom, and how and to whom and how much to distribute that markets make automatically through the price system. Since the bureaucrats would have access to information that others do not have, there will be even more asymmetries of information and the accompanying problems that creates than in a market system. Finally, if the bureaucrats want to make distribution and production decisions based on some information, they will have to ask for it from the citizens, and this creates information asymmetries now favoring the citizens. All of these problems, at least, are avoided by a market system that sends inputs to production to the firms most readily willing and able to pay for them, given the available alternatives, and goods and services to the consumers most willing and able to pay for them, also given the available alternatives. No one has to count or even decide what has to count, let alone depend on the producer or consumer to accurately reveal their preferences or needs.

Finally, in today's world it is anachronistic to suggest that one has to control some large amount of capital in order to be able not to work for a capitalist. Most of the world's poor do not, in fact, work for capitalists. But this does not prevent them from being poor. Whether individuals control the means of production is a red herring in the argument about whether capitalism is a coercive system. The real question is whether people have enough good options so that they can buy or create a decent standard of living. What the working poor need is relief from poverty so that they have a better bargaining position from which to choose what labor to perform and what to refuse to perform.

The critique of liberal feminism

Professor Holmstrom's feminist critique of capitalism is also a feminist critique of liberalism that centers on a critique of liberal marriage and property rights. Although I take it that it is not my task here to defend liberal feminism, I will comment on one point in her critique that is closely tied to the critique of capitalism. Here she offers a reading of Locke on the foundation of property and conjugal rights, which ties the two together. The key uniting feature of the arguments on her view is that it is supposed to demonstrate that "free, equal and rational people would freely consent to loss of freedom and equality" (p. 159). In the case of men, they give up freedom when they tacitly consent to the rule of law, because this is the best way to protect their private property rights. But since the right to private property is to unlimited appropriation of private property, this means that many men will actually be unable to own private property, once all the good land is appropriated. In the case of women, they give up their freedom to their husbands when they consent to marry because the man is "abler and stronger." "Thus … classical liberal theory defended a property form and marriage based on that form that *necessarily* put limits on women's rights and freedom" (p. 166), emphasis mine). But does Lockean private property necessarily put limits on women's rights and freedoms? Of course, there always must be some limits to rights and freedoms under any moral system, so those that Professor Holmstrom has in mind here must be sexist or discriminatory limits: limits that do not apply to men. Absent the sexist assumption that men are "abler and stronger," there is no reason to assume that the Lockean theory of property rights entails such discriminatory rights. Furthermore, what does Professor Holmstrom mean by her use of the present tense – does she suggest that capitalist private property rights always put the same limits on women's rights and freedoms as those that existed in the eighteenth century? Or just some limits on women's rights and freedoms, which of course is true, and true for men as well. For instance, we do not have the right or freedom to treat as ours the private property of someone else. But this lack of freedom can be defended if the whole system of capitalist private property can be, as I am arguing. She goes on to say that liberal feminism cannot get away from this conclusion, however. "Would it be possible to rewrite his story to allow for equality between men and women as today's liberal feminists would like to do? No, for as Lorenne Clark explains, 'One of Locke's major objectives was to provide the theoretical basis for the absolute right of the male to pass his property to his rightful heirs'" (p. 166). But this is not to say that he succeeded! After all, someone might say that his aim was to defend slavery or the genocide of Native Americans, but that's not the liberal feminist aim.

The alternative to capitalism

Professor Holmstrom does not propose anything like a workable system as an alternative to capitalism. Yet even as she acknowledges, we cannot answer whether capitalism is good for women unless we ask "compared with what?" Professor Holmstrom proposes democratic socialism, which involves a centrally-planned economy in which decisions are made democratically. Her proposal for democratic socialism is only lightly sketched, but she offers a few guiding principles. First, the democracy should be a direct democracy, or at least the representatives should earn the average income of those they represent and be subject to immediate recall. Because of the immediate recall provision, this is essentially a direct democracy. But this fails to take into account the tyranny of the majority problem. A direct democracy is likely to force on an unwilling or oppressed minority its own interests. Professor Holmstrom makes clear that she does not recognize the importance of this point when she criticizes James Madison's *Federalist Paper No. 10* for his recommendation of a representative democracy, which he offers to solve the problem of "factions," or the tyranny of the majority. But this is only the political problem with direct democracy.

To determine whether in her imagined society there would be freedom we need to see how production and distribution are in fact organized. Is it economic anarchy? Then there will be no collective production, except on a very small local basis, because when there are more than a small number of persons working together, the allocation of effort and product will have to be decided by someone or some majority. If it is central planning, then there must be some force that determines what will be produced and consumed. Does she assume that people will come to an immediate consensus for all such decisions? That is surely an implausible assumption about human emotional make-up, material need, and epistemic and empathetic capacity. But without consensus the possibility of a tyranny of the majority will arise and decisions will come about too slowly to direct production. Even without these problems, it is hard to imagine how an entire society's production and distribution decisions could be made by a democratically controlled central planner. Many decisions would require expertise in engineering and manufacturing, others would require knowledge of medicine, still others would concern food production. Would the citizens need vast knowledge of all of these things in order to vote reasonably? Or would they cede their vote on those matters where they lack expertise? This would incline the system toward a two-tier system of elite managers and uninformed users, which raises serious informational asymmetry problems and is not a direct democracy.

The tyranny of the majority and the tragedy of the commons arise when and because people do not feel the need to seek the social good over their own selfish interests. Professor Holmstrom seems to assume that this impulse to seek one's selfish interest arises in capitalism but would not arise in socialism, and that people would be much more willing to work for the good of all in a noncapitalist society. They would not feel forced or compelled, and they would be willing to volunteer for the dangerous or dirty jobs that would still be needed. This seems to me to be implausible, even granting that to some extent our characters and desires are endogenous to our economic and social systems. Each of us wants some realm of choice and autonomy, yet this is a selfish desire. Evidence for my view is that when groups of people are oppressed, they generally come to resent and resist it, even if the ideology of the society tells them that this is their natural place or what they deserve. Societies have relied on women to clean up after their families, for example, and virtually everything about society has been geared to making them think that this is their natural role, but women have still resented and resisted this. Although we are capable of fellow feeling and altruism some of the time, we are also prone to selfishness much of the time. Capitalism takes the selfish impulse and turns it toward the collective good by coaxing people to consider the interests of strangers, namely their needs and desires, in order to maximize one's own welfare. Socialism does not offer a similar set of incentives, and therefore must endure the selfish impulse when it arises.

In sum, I agree with Professor Holmstrom that we ought not to focus on an ideal of capitalism, but on its reality. But by the same token we need to compare it with a feasible alternative to capitalism, and she has not offered us one. Rather, she has offered us a pie in the sky of what democratic socialism might be, without a realistic assessment of either democracy or the past experiments with socialism. In my part of this book I have attempted to assess capitalism as it is and as it could be. This necessitated offering a conception of what might have been and what might yet be without capitalism. I have argued that we can see the feasible alternatives to capitalism by looking at those that exist and have existed in the world: in rural areas, for instance, where capitalism has barely touched people's lives, in historical accounts of how people lived before capitalism developed, and in the great communist experiments of the twentieth century. In each of these, life is or has been nasty, brutish, and short. Traditional societies, as I have argued, have traditionally oppressed women most of all, offering little chance for autonomy, or even for the basic material goods needed to be able to expect to have a long, healthy life with one's children and grandchildren. While women achieved some level of social equality in the communist societies, it was largely due to the leveling of all the people, and did not go as far as what women have achieved in the capitalist West in political or material terms. Capitalism no doubt can be refined and reformed to do even better by women and the world's poor, but it provides people with the kinds of incentives that bring forth great efforts that result in innovation, and the information that allows for more efficient production and distribution than any other economic system on offer. Capitalism requires restraint and intervention if it is to be justifiable, that is, if it is to achieve efficiency and avoid imposing negative externalities. It is false to say that "there is no alternative," but it is not false to say that capitalism poses a range of alternatives, some of which are good for the vast majority of human beings. What we need, then, is to work toward those reforms of capitalism rather than seeking to destroy it altogether.

4   Nancy Holmstrom's reply to Ann Cudd

Introduction: ideal versus nonideal theorizing

THERE IS MUCH THAT PROFESSOR CUDD and I agree on in this debate regarding feminism and capitalism. Most basically, of course, since we are both feminists, we believe that women are oppressed and that this is morally wrong. *In words at least*, we share the same goal of social freedom (though both her goal and its relationship to capitalism are ambiguous). We also agree that capitalism creates conditions that make the liberation of women possible and we would support many of the same reforms to capitalism. Furthermore, we agree that the bureaucratic model of the former Soviet Union is not a desirable alternative to capitalism. Beyond that, however, we part company. The burden of my argument has been that while, on the one hand, capitalism creates the potential for genuine human liberation, at the same time it puts systematic barriers to its realization. This is especially true for women as they tend to be among the least powerful in all societies. The source of improvements under capitalism is development, which is not unique to capitalism; hence, advances achieved since capitalism began are not a definitive argument in favor of it today. Moreover, as I have tried to show, while capitalism *was* a progressive force in human history, it is so no longer. Indeed, it threatens the future of humankind. Women need a society organized on a very different basis – one oriented to the satisfaction of human needs as democratically determined, rather than to the maximization of profit.

Fundamental to our disagreements is a difference in methodology. In her defense of capitalism from a feminist point of view, Professor Cudd relies on an abstract idealized model of capitalism. Not simply when she considers the model perfectly competitive market (PCM), nor when she describes her ideal enlightened version of capitalism, where abstract ideal models are appropriate, but, I contend, her entire discussion of capitalism (except for some statistics), both how it works and of how it might work, rests on an abstract idealized Adam Smithian model of capitalism rather than on capitalism as an actual historically varied economic system in the real world. Nor is it always clear exactly what she is defending: simply her ideal version of capitalism or real world capitalism; sometimes she says "the ideal capitalism I am defending" while at other times she defends capitalism without qualifiers. But since her title is "For capitalism as a feminist ideal and reality," I will take her to be defending both. Her abstract idealized approach is typical of mainstream economists, especially in the United States, so it is not surprising, but it is nevertheless a serious weakness. (Could this be because reality does not support her theory?) If my criticism is correct, as I will try to show throughout this response, this makes her contribution to the debate as to whether capitalism is good for women a paradigm case of what has been called ideal theory. As explained by Onora O'Neill and Charles Mills,[1] ideal theory is theory that abstracts from, that is, ignores or marginalizes the actual oppressive social world, conceptualizing that reality in ways that reflect the status quo, and therefore idealizing it. Whether intended or not, ideal theories function to justify the structures of domination that are in place. Feminists have been among the clear-sighted in discerning the idealization of mainstream theory (sometimes called "malestream" to make the point), so it is disappointing

---

1 Onora O'Neill, "Justice, Gender, and International Boundaries," in Martha C. Nussbaum and Amartya Sen (eds.), *The Quality of Life* (New York: Oxford University Press 1993); Charles Mills, *The Racial Contract* (Ithaca, NY: Cornell University Press, 1997) and "'Ideal Theory' as Ideology," in Peggy DesAutels and Margaret Urban Walker (eds.), *Moral Psychology* (Lanham, MD: Rowman & Littlefield, 2004).

that a feminist like Professor Cudd makes the same error (or so I claim) when approaching economic theory and reality. Since I am committed to doing nonideal theory, my contribution to this debate is full of messy, unsavory, and decidedly nonphilosophical facts about our current world that would be quite inappropriate in mainstream political philosophy.[2]

"Capitalism" and "patriarchy": definitions and intersections

What is capitalism?

For obvious reasons, Professor Cudd and I both start our presentations with definitions of capitalism: to judge whether capitalism is or is not a good system for women, we have to decide which societies count as capitalist. We agree that private ownership of the means of production is essential to the definition; that there are different versions of capitalism, with more or less government regulation (pure laissez faire capitalism is a fantasy); and therefore we agree that Sweden is capitalist, rather than socialist as it is usually described by defenders of a more free market version of capitalism.[3] As Sweden is a pretty attractive society, especially from a feminist point of view, this is good for her side of the debate. Beyond this, however, our definitions diverge because, I think, our approaches to determining a proper definition differ.

2 I have long found it strange that while fields of philosophy like philosophy of science and philosophy of mind are done in close connection with the relevant empirical science and Quine pushed epistemology in a naturalistic direction, ethics and political philosophy have persisted in their abstract ideal mode.

3 She seems to be inconsistent, however, since later on she describes India as "until the 1990s a socialist country." But the changes in India in this period were not from socialist to capitalist, but from a more state-involved capitalism to a more free market version. India had less of a public sector than Sweden. See Vivek Chibber, *Locked in Place: State Building and Late Industrialization in India* (Princeton University Press, 2003). That the Indian government in this period called itself socialist is no more reason to say that it was socialist than the name of East Germany under communism – the "German Democratic Republic" – is a reason to say it was democratic.

She talks of a "descriptive ideal" of capitalism as distinct from her ideal version of capitalism, but which she says is based in part on normative background assumptions regarding property, the market, and free wage labor. Although I confess I am confused about her approach (what is the difference between defining conditions and background conditions, for example?), it seems to me that her definition of capitalism is a "persuasive definition," that is, a definition that includes elements intended to persuade someone in favor of the thing defined: "stacking the deck," in other words. I say this because she includes in her definition of capitalism the assumption that "ownership and participation in markets is to be nondiscriminatory." She uses this criterion to exclude Saudi Arabia from the list of capitalist countries in the world, which is favorable to her case as Saudi Arabia is such an unappealing society, especially from a feminist point of view. She justifies this limitation on what will count as a capitalist society on two grounds: that nondiscrimination is more efficient and that it is more free. But my response is: if so, so what? These rationales are part of *the theory* of capitalism, whereas *in the real world*, as she knows, many capitalist societies have allowed or even mandated discrimination in the market; a particularly important example for American history being the market in human beings when the status of slave was restricted to members of the black race, that is, people of (some degree of) African ancestry. Other examples throughout American history abound. Did the United States become capitalist only in 1965 with the passage of the Civil Rights Act? Of course not. Hence, the list of countries with capitalist economies in the real world should include Saudi Arabia as well as Sweden.[4] This entails that capitalism runs the gamut with respect to gender equality: a report by the World Economic Forum on gender equality in 2009 ranks Iceland and three other Nordic countries highest, the United States was thirty-first, and

---

4 She also argues that Saudi Arabia is not a clear case of private ownership because the same family rules both the government and the economic sphere. But this makes it an example of oligarchic capitalism, like others she cites.

the *New York Times* article does not even mention Saudi Arabia, but we can assume that it is close to or at the bottom.[5]

The fact that capitalism and dictatorship can co-exist brings out a familiar ambiguity in a definition of capitalism that Professor Cudd cites as similar to hers, an ambiguity that creates another persuasive definition. Philippe Van Parijs, in her footnote 6, includes, after private ownership of the bulk of society's means of production, the condition that "people in some important sense own themselves." This sounds good, but as I discussed at length in my main contribution, what does it mean? If it means that individuals in capitalist societies necessarily have moral rights or political freedom, then it is false. There are capitalist societies where no one has moral rights and capitalist "democracies" have existed where many or most people lacked these rights. On the other hand, if it just means that individuals can sell their labor power, that is, that wage labor is a necessary feature of capitalism, then we agree – but this should be made explicit, as in my definition of capitalism. In fact, I suggest, an important function of the claim that individuals "own themselves" is to imply that everyone in capitalism owns something and they all just meet in the marketplace to voluntarily exchange their various wares, thereby suggesting an equal and fair exchange. But this children's book picture serves to obfuscate the *vast* difference in power between those who own the means of production and those who, in Marx's words, own "nothing but their own skins." The relationship between these two groups is the core relationship on which capitalist societies rest.

The same obfuscation occurs in Professor Cudd's criticism of Marx's analysis of capitalism on the grounds that there is no longer a sharp distinction between classes as there was in his day because so many middle-class people today are partial owners through their pension funds, and yet "they are hardly the capitalists of Marx's imagination." Indeed. Even to call it "ownership" is somewhat misleading since ownership of a thing tends to

5 Reuters: World Briefing Europe, "Iceland: Nordic Countries Lead in Gender Equality, Report Says," *New York Times*, October 28, 2009.

imply some power over it, which such "owners" lack.[6] Of course, neither Marx nor any contemporary Marxist would imagine that because a worker in a private hospital in New York City (predominantly women of color) has a pension from her union that invests in the stock market, this does *anything at all* to lessen the crucial difference in social power between the class of people who live through ownership of the means of production and those who live through their labor, whether it is more or less remunerative. The former have only become vastly richer and more powerful than in Marx's day. Yes, there are today – and were historically – other classes in capitalist society, but these are the two most fundamental – wherever the latter's pensions are invested (if they are lucky enough to have a pension).[7] The issue is the differences in power between the two groups and the relationships of domination and subordination between them that this entails.

Other features of contemporary capitalism that Professor Cudd contends show that Marx's account is outdated also miss their mark. Neither some (limited) government restrictions on private ownership nor the greater investment today in financial capital as opposed to industrial production change the fact that the bulk of the means of production (whether they are land or factories or banks) are in private hands and that the owners make the crucial investment decisions. Furthermore, she exaggerates the extent to which production of material goods has been replaced by production of financial goods and by services. So although there is some reorganization of the global economy such that investment in New York or London is heavily concentrated in financial services, on a global scale there is ever more production of material goods, and indeed, that is where Citibank, Goldman Sachs, etc. invest their funds. Consider the fact that in 2008 manufacturers

---

6 See Edward Wolff, *Top Heavy: The Increasing Inequality of Wealth in America and What Can Be Done About it*, 2nd edn. (New York: New Press, 1996).

7 A good source for Marx's view of class is Hal Draper on classes. The best contemporary analysis of class influenced by Marx is found in the work of Erik Olin Wright, particularly *Classes* (London: Verso, 1985).

in China produced more vehicles than they did in the United States and their plan is to increase auto production.

I contend that the definition of capitalism that I offered is the most perspicuous: private ownership of the bulk of the means of production, production for profit, and wage labor as the most important form of labor. This definition captures the features of an economic system that developed in the seventeenth century in Europe and is today dominant throughout the world. Although markets had existed before this, never before in history was a whole society organized around and dependent upon the market. Never before was labor a commodity and, moreover, the dominant form of labor on which the society depended. While Marx coined the word capitalism for this new system, it is not only Marxists who understand capitalism in this way. In his classic work, *The Great Transformation*, economic historian Karl Polanyi theorized the momentous significance of the expansion and dominance of the market which involved the state establishing land, labor, and money as commodities;[8] it was not simply a "natural," evolutionary process. It is the dependence of everyone in society on the market and the competition that drives the market that is so radically distinctive of the economic system that now dominates the world. This definition of capitalism I am using allows us to understand the apparently inexplicable – why the system is driven to ceaselessly expand even to the point of environmental catastrophe. (It has been analogized to a perpetual motion machine by a critic or like rats in a cage by a defender.[9]) It also helps us to understand the process of transition to capitalism that the countries in the former Soviet bloc have made in the past few decades. In most of Eastern Europe and Russia, and to some degree in China, it is now individuals, rather than the state, who control the means of production; production is for the market; and individuals are "free" to sell their labor, that is, *they*

8 Karl Polanyi, *The Great Transformation* (Boston, MA: Beacon Press, 1957).
9 The critic is Alex Callinicos, *An Anti-Capitalist Manifesto* (Cambridge: Polity, 2003); the defender is Paul Krugman who goes on to say why it is essential that the rats continue running around the cage. "Money Can't Buy Happiness. Er, Can It?," *New York Times*, June 1, 1999.

have no choice but to sell their labor since the social supports they had previously, from guaranteed jobs to housing to medical care and education, have been taken away.[10]

What is patriarchy?

Professor Cudd and I agree that in the real world capitalism has been marked by the subordination of women. (This is why we became feminists!) In her words this is patriarchy; I call it sexism, reserving the word "patriarchy" for its original more specific meaning of father-dominated societies. The difference of a word is not important except insofar as the use of "patriarchy" encourages her to conceive of it as a transhistorical system distinct from capitalism. She acknowledges some relationship between the two as she allows that capitalism capitalizes on patriarchy, for example, by paying women less, but she says capitalism does not cause patriarchy, seeing it as in some sense a parallel system that can exist with more than one economic system. Hence, she argues that feminists should blame patriarchy rather than capitalism for wage differentials and other disadvantages women endure in capitalist societies. "Patriarchy creates coercive background conditions for women, and thus patriarchy, not capitalism, is to blame for women's exploitation under capitalism." Everything is fine and fair in capitalism it seems except if women are disadvantaged relative to men (or blacks relative to whites). Her attempt to differentiate between the economic system of capitalism and its background conditions does not work in this case. Again I believe she is relying on an abstract idealized model of capitalism that does not include sexism (or racism). But as I have discussed, even though sexism is not unique to capitalism, existing both before capitalism and after in the so-called socialist countries, nevertheless, sexism has been part of capitalism, to varying degrees, in all its manifestations in the real

10 How this primitive accumulation is carried out is suggested by the fact that "91% of 3,220 Chinese citizens worth 100 million yuan ($14.6 million) or more are the children of high-level Communist Party officials." *Newsweek*, July 20, 2009, 10. Thus, members of one ruling class have moved themselves into another ruling class.

world. Since sexism is not part of its very definition, it is true that one could *imagine* a version of capitalism that was not sexist (or racist) – and this seems to be what Professor Cudd identifies as capitalism. However, to suppose that the logical possibility of a nonsexist capitalism implies that real world capitalism is not sexist is an instance of ideal theory. The logical differentiation of the two is not enough to exculpate real world versions of capitalism since, contrary to the pure theory of capitalism, *there are causal relationships between sexism and capitalism even though capitalism did not cause sexism.* It is in the interests of capitalists to take advantage of (even sometimes to create or augment) any divisions, prejudices, and vulnerabilities within the working class in order to maximize profit. Equal pay for comparable work and free childcare would benefit working-class women primarily, but as they are not opposed to the interests of working-class men, it cannot be "patriarchy" that explains their absence in the United States. Rather, since both reforms would cost money, they have been difficult to achieve except where working-class movements were very strong, as in Western Europe after the Second World War. Thus, sexism is not simply a useless remnant of earlier economic systems.

How should we understand the relationship between sexism and capitalism? My examples in the previous paragraph certainly do not imply that all instances of sexism in capitalist societies are to be explained by the interests of capitalists. Sexist oppression cannot be reduced to class oppression. Often it is clear that men gain from women's oppression, both in capitalist and noncapitalist societies (most obviously in the fact that women do the bulk of household labor even when they work outside the home); sometimes both men and capitalists benefit; and sometimes men and/or capitalists can have interests that pull in both directions. Professor Cudd suggests that capitalism is less hospitable to patriarchy/sexism than is socialism because they are both collectivist, whereas capitalism is individualistic. However, this feature of capitalism can combine with patriarchy to work against women, in particular, when the crucial work of care is left to individuals. (Women would do best in a society with the right mix of individualism and collectivism.) To understand how all these relationships work, including the changes that have occurred, does it help to posit a more or less parallel system of patriarchy to account for women's oppression within capitalism as Professor Cudd and many other feminists think? If so, then one would surely also need a "system" of racism (and perhaps other systems to account for other hierarchies like sexual orientation). But what exactly constitutes a system?; how many are enough? This gets complicated. While most societies have been male dominated, this is not enough, in my opinion, to constitute a transhistorical "system," as the sexism of capitalism is very different from that of pre-capitalist societies. I believe it is clearer to describe the system in which we live as one integrated system of capitalism which is sexist and racist (to greater and lesser degrees at different times and places). In any case, whether one prefers to speak of one system with different facets, or several systems, one has to recognize how totally integrated these "systems" are. An early articulation of what has become known as an intersectional analysis is the Combahee River Collective's Black Feminist Statement that "the synthesis of these oppressions [racial, sexual, heterosexual, and class] creates the conditions of our lives."[11] All

11 Combahee River Collective 1977, reprinted in Gloria T. Hull, Patricia Bell Scott, and Barbara Smith (eds.), *But Some of Us Were Brave* (Old Westbury, NY: The Feminist Press, 1982), 13. For influential dual systems analyses see Christine Delphy, *Close to Home: A Materialist Analysis of Women's Oppression* (London: Hutchinson, 1984) and Heidi Hartmann, "The Unhappy Marriage of Marxism and Feminism: Toward a More Progressive Union," in Lydia Sargent (ed.), *Women and Revolution* (Cambridge: South End Press, 1981) and discussions/critiques of Hartmann in *Women and Revolution*. Though Carole Pateman uses the word patriarchy for capitalist and pre-capitalist societies, she makes clear that in her analysis, "there are no feudal relics in civil society," Carole Pateman and Charles Mills, *Contract and Domination* (Cambridge: Polity, 2007), 209; see also ch. 5 for her intersectional analysis. Discussions of intersectionality often leave out class; people of color, especially black women, become stand-ins for poor and working-class people. While this was never analytically accurate, its inadequacy should be more obvious today given the widening class divide among both women and black Americans, exemplified dramatically by individuals like Condoleeza Rice. For a corrective, see Johanna Brenner, "Intersections, Locations and

this means that we cannot simply blame patriarchy rather than capitalism for women's lower pay relative to men, for inadequate childcare, etc.

Sex, race, class, and justice

If sexism and racism could be eliminated from capitalism, that is to say, if we could continue to progress to the point of complete gender and racial equality within capitalism, this would be a great moral victory. I do not need to stress how truly wonderful it would be if all children had an equal chance at a fulfilling life regardless of whether they were born male or female and if race were an outmoded concept. If this were ever to happen, it could only be the result of a great deal of struggle, so all feminists strive for it, including those who are skeptical that such equality is compatible with capitalism. However, were it to be achievable, so that women and men and people of all races[12] were distributed equally throughout the economic pyramid, feminists ought not to be satisfied. For this would still leave the majority of women in the base of the pyramid. The only difference is that the base would no longer be *disproportionately* female (and dark-skinned); men would be there in equal proportions to their numbers in the population. The point is that while it is theoretically, that is, logically, possible to eliminate sexism and racism from capitalism, it is not even logically possible to eliminate class differences from capitalism. Indeed, they are constitutive of the system. (If we applied this point beyond our society to the globe, it would be even more difficult to distinguish inequalities due to gender and race and those due to global capitalism.) And inequalities due to gender are, in fact, a lot less than inequalities due to class.

Capitalist Class Relations: Intersectionality from a Marxist Perspective," in *Women and the Politics of Class* (New York: Monthly Review Press, 2000).

12 This is an easy but incorrect way of expressing what the end of racism would mean. If race is actually a social construct, as I believe has been demonstrated, then with racism gone, we would no longer categorize people by race. All we could say is that people of all different physical descriptions are found throughout the economic pyramid.

Though men have advantages over women *within the same class*, a woman in developed capitalist countries is far closer in her material conditions and opportunities to men in her class (and race) than to women of other classes. For example, the average hourly pay for Wal-Mart employees is US$10 an hour; a sex discrimination suit revealed that the annual difference between men's and women's wages at Wal-Mart comes to about US$1,100. Though the women employees are worse off, both women *and men* who work for Wal-Mart (the largest employer in the United States) are pretty poor! And their lives are shaped by this fact. In another sex discrimination case – this one against Morgan Stanley – the bond saleswoman complainant made over US$1 million annually, while her male counterparts earned even more, and hence the suit.[13] Though there is no moral justification for her earning less than her male colleagues, both the male *and the female* bond salespeople are fabulously wealthy – and their lives are shaped by this fact. At the outer ends of US society (leaving aside the global gap), while those in the very top of the pyramid have wealth exceeding that of many countries, there are now 39.8 million people in the United States who are below the poverty line, defined as US$22,025 for a family of four, and next year's figures will be worse.[14]

Moreover, there is not a great deal of mobility between classes. The class into which one is born is the single most important determinant of where one ends up in adulthood. And yet it is ultimately an accident. If it is unjust that girls should have fewer opportunities than boys, or blacks than whites, why should it be OK from a moral point of view that someone born to a poor or working-class family should have fewer opportunities than a child from a higher class family? Individual variations in personality and intelligence exist, but they do not account for the statistical differences in outcome. Consider the fact that the best predictor of SAT scores is the

13 See Walter Benn Michaels, *The Trouble with Diversity: How We Learned to Love Identity and Ignore Inequality* (New York: Henry Holt, 2007), 114–17.
14 Erik Eckholm, "Last Year's Poverty Rate was Highest in 12 Years: Median Family Income Fell," *New York Times*, September 11, 2009, A12.

net worth of the parents – not surprising since wealthy parents can afford to pay for schools with small classes and tutors on top of their teachers.[15] Since Americans tend to think schools are meritocratic, it confirms their conviction that the rich deserve their riches and, therefore, the vast majority who are not rich are not deserving. This personalized responsibility for failure in competitive capitalist societies creates internal barriers to equal opportunity as well.[16] While there is greater class mobility in capitalism than in pre-capitalist societies where laws and rigid traditions restrict mobility, and greater mobility in Western Europe today than in the United States, it remains a fact that most people will end up in the class into which they were born. Indeed, how could it be otherwise?; who would be the workers if we were all capitalists? A model of capitalism that would better fit Professor Cudd's claims that capitalism stimulates innovation and rewards achievement, and would therefore be more fair, would eliminate inheritance. Do the children of the rich really show more initiative and contribute more to society than do the children of the majority? Not, of course, that capitalism without inheritance is a realizable model. While currently estates as great as US$7 million are exempt from inheritance tax, there is a powerful movement of the super-rich in the United States today to eliminate the estate tax entirely (which would give the Waltons who own Wal-Mart, US$30 billion).[17] A feminist concerned with the oppression and lack of freedom for

15 Dalton Conley, *Being Black, Living in the Red* (Berkeley, CA: University of California Press, 1999), 7. An acquaintance of mine in New York City has a lucrative business as a math tutor to private school students, spending the summer in the Hamptons so she can tutor them at their vacation homes as well as during the school year. She reports that often other tutors are meeting before or after her, helping the students write essays and anything else they might need. The tutoring advantage is, of course, just added on to the many advantages of private schools (or public schools in rich areas), like small class sizes. A new company prepares 4- and 5-year-olds for the test important for admission to private pre-schools. Susan Dominus, "Connecting Anxious Parents and Educators, at $450 an Hour," *New York Times*, August 18, 2009.

16 See Everett Carl Ladd and Karlyn H. Bowman, *Attitudes Toward Economic Opportunity* (Washington, DC: AEI Press, 1998).

17 This is roughly the gross domestic product of Jordan, points out Michael Crowley in "The 'Death Tax' Scam," *Rolling Stone*, June 11, 2009. Crowley

women should be no less concerned if the cause is the class system than if it is sexism. Defenders of capitalism like Professor Cudd believe in individual initiative and competition, but they ignore the evidence showing that the competition is – essentially – fixed. Thus, I contend that if one shares the liberal value of individual freedom and opportunity one needs to go beyond capitalism with its inherent – and widening – class differences.

Are class differences just? Class and freedom

Professor Cudd disagrees. While granting that most capitalist societies do contain gross inequalities, she argues that this is not essential to capitalism and would not exist in her enlightened version because it would have a welfare minimum. She contends that everyone is better off in capitalist society due to its productivity as long as the floor of the economic pyramid is raised, in which case as she sees it, the society would contain no gross inequalities. In the absence of discrimination or "absolute poverty," she contends, individuals simply agree without coercion to work for the owners of capital for a particular return and a worker "is just as able to demand her share of the surplus as the owner of the capital inputs to production." In such a case there may be exploitation, she says, but it is not morally problematic. I have two responses.

First, though a welfare minimum is certainly a good thing worthy of support by all feminists, it would not eliminate the vast differences in power, freedom, material well-being, and opportunity that are inherent in any capitalist system. How high could such a floor be? In any case, a "floor" is not a ceiling and thus does not eliminate the inequalities described above, which I contend should count as "gross inequalities"; they affect the freedom of the wage–labor relationship, they entail that some can give orders to the

also explains why the liberal senators from Arkansas and Washington support the proposal to raise the exemption to US$10 million, viz. that two of the key organizers of the estate tax repeal effort are from their states and essential to their re-election.

rest, and they should be seen as morally problematic. As Andrew Sayer puts it, "Class matters because it creates unequal possibilities for flourishing and suffering."[18] It is not clear why Professor Cudd thinks that a worker will be able to get "her or his share" as long as she or he is able to unite with others (i.e., via labor unions?), nor just what Professor Cudd thinks should be "her or his share." In Professor Cudd's view it is morally fine if two agents agree to share the surplus produced by their interaction or if one voluntarily agrees that the other should get the entire surplus. Yes, one can imagine hypothetical cases like these. But the question is how does she think this applies to real world relations between capital and labor? *How* exactly do they share, that is, who gets how much of what "they produce"?[19] Is this a case where they "voluntarily agree" that one side should get all the surplus? Why would they do that? Or is it not truly voluntary? In fact, whatever capital and labor agree on in any particular case, it is a result of a hard fought struggle between two groups of very unequal power.[20]

Although labor unions give workers a bit more power vis-à-vis capital, they hardly equalize the power of the two sides in the labor market – as seems to be implied by Professor Cudd's claim that a worker not limited by inequality or poverty is "just as able to demand her share" and that "there is nothing in the theory of capitalism to require that workers go it alone." How many employees, even those in unions, and even in countries with

---

18 Andrew Sayer, *The Moral Significance of Class* (Cambridge University Press, 2005), 218.

19 I put "they produce" in scare quotes because I do not want to get into the complicated and contested question of just where profit comes from in capitalism. For an incisive critique of the assumption that capitalists, by virtue of their ownership, make a productive contribution and therefore deserve most of the profit, see David Schweickart, *Against Capitalism* (New York: Cambridge University Press 1993), ch. 1. For more of my views of exploitation, see "Exploitation," in Will Kymlicka (ed.), *Justice in Political Philosophy* (Cheltenham: Edward Elgar, 1992); "Coercion, Exploitation and Labor," *APA Newsletter on Philosophy and Law* 94(1) (Fall 1994), 84–88; "Exploitation" in *International Encyclopedia of Ethics,* forthcoming.

20 There are occasional exceptions when labor of a certain kind is in scarce supply but high demand, but these situations of more equal bargaining positions are temporary.

more social welfare than we have, have ever felt that they were *"equally able* to get their share" as were their employers? *From whose point of view* is Professor Cudd speaking? Moreover, even the very limited power that unions have in the United States is on the decline as union membership has declined due to what commentators have called "an employer's offensive." Although US law protects the right to organize unions, there is little enforcement, so workers are intimidated and fired and employers do not hesitate to use threats to relocate to kill union organizing drives. In 2004 only 8 percent of private sector jobs in the United States were unionized but "fully 39% of jobs being shifted outside the US were from unionized facilities."[21] Today, only 12.4 percent of American workers are in unions.[22] Though these facts may not be part of the "theory" of capitalism, as Professor Cudd says, extreme inequalities and attendant lack of power and freedom for the majority are definitely part of its reality.[23] They are also part of people's *experience*, except for the most privileged among us.

As for the capital side of the capital–labor relationship, Professor Cudd assures us that capitalism certainly does not condone collusion among capitalists. But what counts as "collusion"? And how precisely is collusion distinguished from cooperation, which certainly cannot be forbidden? Though individual capitalists are in competition with one another, they share many common interests and act on them via organizations like the National Association of Manufacturers and innumerable industrywide organizations. Pfizer and Merck are competitors, for example, but they share an interest in limiting generic and alternative medications. What

---

21 Kim Moody, *Workers in a Lean World* (New York: Verso, 1997). In a 2000 report Human Rights Watch found "a pattern of threats, intimidation, and firings of nursing home workers trying to form and join unions and of employers' refusal to bargain when workers succeeded." Cited in Gertrude Ezorsky, *Freedom in the Workplace?* (Ithaca, NY: Cornell University Press, 2007). See *Labor Notes* www.labornotes.org for ongoing coverage of these issues, accessed July 21, 2010.

22 www.bls.gov/CPS, accessed July 23, 2010.

23 I believe she would say that these are part of the background conditions, but not part of capitalism, but again, I do not see how this distinction can be sustained except by another retreat into ideal theory.

laws prevent them from organizing together to restrict them via laws about intellectual property, etc.; indeed. since corporations have the status of persons under US law, any attempts to limit their political activity has been interpreted by the courts as a violation of their right to free speech. Given their commonality of interests, newspapers report simply on how much a given politician has received from, for example, "the health care industry" without bothering to differentiate the different firms. And then there is agro business that has organized for decades to secure massive subsidies, with the result that fast food is cheaper than healthy food. Business interests bragged about how they had used the threat to relocate in order to get NAFTA (the North American Free Trade Agreement) passed. I could go on and on, but even on the (false) assumption that capitalists never violate the laws of capitalist societies, capitalists can combine to increase their strength, just as workers can. In any case, even without cooperation/collusion, a single large corporation has vastly more wealth and power than its employees even if they are organized. It is difficult for me to believe that anyone can seriously claim that in general labor organizations (where they exist) have equal power in capitalism with employers and their organizations.

According to Professor Cudd, the inequalities of capitalism are mostly due to intelligence and hard work (and, she grants, some advantages and disadvantages of birth), and are therefore acceptable, unlike inequalities in dictatorial societies. But the latter inequalities are unacceptable morally, I presume, because they are not under individuals' control; my argument has been that most of the inequality in capitalism is not under individuals' control either. A handful of individuals in global financial institutions make the decisions that impact billions of people. A truly democratic system would not have to be perfectly equal in material terms but a lot closer, and people could decide how to balance material equality and other goods.[24] For example, it might

---

24 It is plausible, however, to say that inequalities would never be so great as to interfere with democracy, for why would people democratically decide to allow this?

prove necessary to provide more material incentives to get people to do certain types of work (more likely undesirable work that could not be mechanized, rather than work that carries intrinsic rewards). But other people would prefer to do the unpleasant work for more leisure time rather than more material goods.

Professor Cudd's claim that any coercion in the worker–capitalist relationship could be eliminated rests on the provision of a welfare minimum. Interestingly, the idea of a guaranteed basic income was quite popular in the 1960s and 1970s in the United States (and enjoys some popularity around the globe today). Even Richard Nixon endorsed it. A diluted version passed the House of Representatives in 1972, but was defeated in the Senate and has since dropped out of mainstream discussion.[25] I would certainly endorse such a minimum because it would help those in need and because it would establish a precedent for public provision of need. However, I do not believe it would eliminate all coercion, which I have argued is inherent in capitalism because private ownership of the means of production/subsistence leaves the majority with no choice but to work for those owners in order to secure their means of survival. A welfare minimum would have to be awfully generous to remove that necessity, and certainly could not *equalize* their bargaining positions.

But let us suppose we grant the premise that a welfare minimum would eliminate all coercion in the capital–labor relationship. Then, the crucial next step in Professor Cudd's defense of capitalism as ideal and reality would be to show that this enlightened version of capitalism is realizable in the real world of global capitalism. But she has not done this. What is her theory of the state and its relationship to the economy? Even if it were

---

25 "A BIG Idea: A Minimum Income Guarantee," an interview with Karl Widerquist, member of the coordinating committee of the US Basic Income Guarantee Network (USBIG), *Multinational Monitor*, May/June 2009, 30–34. He explains that it was defeated by a coalition of conservatives and those who thought it did not go far enough, many of whom were also worried that it would threaten other welfare programs. Some BIG proposals are restricted to the poor who need it most while others are universal, thereby promising broader support.

realizable in a particular society, how could it be sustained in the face of global competition? In other words, why would it not just be more incentive for corporations to go to less generous countries? She does not tell us. A recent study shows that low-wage workers in many US industries, especially women, are not even paid the minimum wage they are due. Many small businesses "say they are *forced* to violate wage laws to remain competitive" (my emphasis).[26] Professor Cudd acknowledges that material inequalities can be so great as to influence the political process. So one must ask, isn't this clearly the case in our present system? And doesn't it follow that her enlightened capitalism is not realizable? If an ideal version of capitalism is not realizable, then a defense of capitalism amounts to a defense of a system that is far from ideal and enlightened, especially for women. (I have discussed these issues at greater length in my main contribution in the sections on freedom and ideal capitalism, so readers can decide which account they find most convincing.)

Though Professor Cudd grants the present system is bad, she defends it nevertheless, for three reasons, two of which are among the defenses of sweatshops that I discussed in my contribution: first, that it is better than what went before, and, second, that things will improve. Her story of the Danone yogurt ladies is like the many moving stories of individual women in the Third World who become micro-entrepreneurs through the aid of micro-loans. Though individual women may improve their lives in this way, it is fanciful (and comforting to the powerful) to think that this could be a successful general development model. For one thing, it is confined to the informal sector; micro-entrepreneurship is not a model generalizable to a whole

---

26 Steven Greenhouse, "Low-Wage Workers Are Often Cheated, Study Says," *New York Times*, September 2, 2009. The percentage of workers saying they were paid less than the minimum varied from 12 percent in home health care to over 42 and 43 percent in private households, repair services, and the apparel and textile industries, amounting to a 15 percent loss of pay. The researchers were surprised by "how successful low-wage employers were in pressuring employees not to file for workers' compensation." Only 8 percent of those seriously injured filed claims.

society (a whole society composed of individuals trading with and working for one another?). There is also evidence that the economic and anti-patriarchal success stories have been over-blown.[27] Returning to the formal sector of the economy, I will not repeat my critique of the current sweatshop model of development, except to say that it is *not* always better than what went before (are the people of the Ecuadorian Amazon better off since Texaco/Chevron destroyed their land and their health?);[28] second, that if it is better this still does not justify it because there are other better alternatives; and, finally, that it is far from clear that things will improve for the majority of people in the world if capitalism continues. The Scandinavian countries (which are as close to Professor Cudd's ideal as exist) are all small countries with abundant natural resources and they developed their social welfare systems in very specific historic circumstances. When the United Nations estimated that for the first time in human history 1 billion people (one in seven on the globe) would go hungry in 2009 due to the financial crisis,[29] and the natural resources of the planet are nearing depletion, one should not accept the progressivist model as an article of faith. The third reason Professor Cudd defends the current system (only implicit in her contribution, but probably more developed in her response to my contribution) is that she sees no alternative to capitalism except the discredited bureaucratic model of the Soviets. I attempted to address this understandable concern in the conclusion to my contribution and will do so again at the end of this response.

Health, well-being, and capitalism: the Smithian model

Professor Cudd opens her presentation of the theoretical explanation for capitalism's alleged success at promoting material

27 See Uma Narayan, "Informal Sector Work, Microcredit and Women's Empowerment: A Critical Overview," unpublished, October 18, 2006.
28 See *Crude*, 2009 the film, or check information from Amazon Watch, www.amazonwatch.org, accessed July 23, 2010.
29 Geoffrey Lean, "Year of the Hungry: 1,000,000,000 Afflicted," *The Independent*, December 28, 2008.

prosperity and freedom with a long discussion of economists' use of an idealized model of the perfectly competitive market (PCM). Central to this model is the criterion of Pareto optimality (a situation where no one can be made better off without making someone else worse off), which she argues is better than utilitarianism for morally evaluating societies. While she agrees that not all Pareto outcomes are just, in particular, if the starting points are unfair or coercive, she thinks "there is a connection to justice for anyone who thinks that liberty is one component of it." Perhaps I simply fail to understand the economics involved here, but I find this whole discussion extremely unpersuasive for reasons she herself acknowledges:

- What is the connection of this model to the ideal capitalism she defends, much less to real world capitalism? It seems to be just another example of ideal theorizing, the flaws of which have already been discussed.
- What is optimal about Pareto optimality from a moral point of view? And why should it be persuasive to a feminist? Any oppressive relationship can be ended only by making the oppressor worse off – hence, not a Pareto optimal outcome – and this is the right thing to do. Limiting the freedom of the oppressor can be justified on many moral grounds, including that of expanding the freedom of the oppressed.

Since I do not see the relevance of this whole discussion, I will turn instead to other aspects of her theoretical defense of capitalism.

Professor Cudd spends a fair bit of time arguing, against alternative explanations, that the development of capitalism was responsible for the dramatic improvements in life expectancy and infant mortality and fertility rates over the last couple of centuries. I agree with her – indeed, it seems fairly obvious – but I do not think she proves as much as she would like. First, what she shows is that the development of capitalism was *necessary*, whereas others argue that it was *not sufficient*, because scientific discoveries and governmental commitment to public health measures were necessary. These are compatible explanations. And most such improvements, both in the past and in the contemporary context, also required struggle, often against capitalist opposition, for example, by AIDS activists. Second, while capitalism played this essential role in many parts of the world in the period she discusses, it was not necessary everywhere. Life expectancy, infant mortality, and fertility rates also improved in Russia and China in the twentieth century under the bureaucratic system (despite China's disastrous Great Leap Forward), and the health statistics of Cuba, despite the US embargo, are known to be excellent. The point is that one cannot simply compare pre-modern and modern societies and equate capitalism with the modern, as Professor Cudd does. It is *development, not capitalism per se*, that was responsible for these dramatic improvements in health.[30] Yes, capitalism was historically the first engine of development and made possible the scientific revolution, but *it does not follow* that it is crucial today. Indeed, in today's world capitalism plays a mixed role at best with respect to health and well-being. As discussed earlier, *with the transition to capitalism in Russia, life expectancy has actually gone down* from what it was in Soviet days. Millions of people around the world die of preventable diseases because they are hungry and because they cannot afford basic medicines, women a higher percentage than men. *What is necessary to save them is not the medical innovations capitalism is allegedly so good at, but the freeing of global capital from private hands!*

In fact, the medical advances developed by pharmaceutical companies today are not, for the most part, explicable as capitalists' response to consumer demand. As Noam Chomsky said in a recent interview:

> Just about everything comes out of state initiative I mean, what is MIT? MIT is overwhelmingly a taxpayer-funded institution, in which research and development is carried out at public cost and risk, and if anything comes out of it, some private corporation ... will get the profit from it ... [Y]ou run through the

---

30 Her graphs from 2008 correlating female life expectancy and fertility with per capita income are odd. In 2008 where are the developed noncapitalist countries? There are none. To correlate these with income is hardly surprising. In fact, the same correlation exists within capitalist countries; rich women live longer and have fewer children than poor women.

dynamic parts of the economy, that's where they come from ...
with things like, say, computers and the Internet, for example,
consumer choice had no role at all![31]

Furthermore, those advances developed by capitalism are
mostly those expected to produce profit. Thus, we have Viagra,
Prozac, many minor variations of the same medicines developed
simply in order to extend patents, but no cure for malaria. A
society based on the satisfaction of need would not be limited in
its medical developments by the need to make a profit.[32] Finally,
in the case of many of today's health problems, capitalist development is arguably the problem rather than the solution – problems due to toxic pesticides and air pollution, in particular. Thus,
one cannot talk of the impact on material well-being and political rights of capitalism *per se*, because this depends on many historical factors, which are not captured in an ahistorical model of
capitalism or one based on particular periods and places.

Professor Cudd's discussion of capitalism and environmental
problems is particularly weak and exemplifies the problems of her
individualistic market approach. Though she is not a neoliberal like
Milton Friedman since she endorses some government support for
social need, her discussion comes close to Friedman's blasé free
market approach to environmental problems. Friedman opined,
"without modern technology, pollution would be much worse.
The pollution from horses was much worse than what you get
from automobiles. If you read descriptions of the streets of New
York in the nineteenth century."[33] Professor Cudd devotes barely
one page of her contribution to the criticism that massive environmental problems are engendered by capitalism's productivity
(which she misleadingly calls "efficiency"), dubbing the criticism
"the junkyard objection." Rightly dismissing the aesthetic interpretation of the objection, she says, "the environmental worry

31 Interview, reprinted in Wallace Shawn, *Essays* (Chicago: Haymarket Books,
    2009), 66f.
32 Jim Dwyer, "A Lifesaver Out of Reach, For Want of a Profit," *New York Times*,
    October 18, 2009.
33 Carla Ravaioli, *Economists and the Environment* (London: Zed Books, 1995),
    11.

arises because many goods create negative externalities upon obso-lescence" and claims that in her ideal capitalism, this will be solved by taxes for recycling and clean-up and incentives for firms to be more environmentally sensitive. But the environmental problems engendered by capitalism go way beyond disposing of all the junk individuals buy. The problem – in one sentence – is that *almost two-thirds of the natural resources necessary to sustain life on this planet are being degraded and destroyed through global warming, deforestation, desertification, depletion of the oceans, extinction of species*, etc., etc. Note that these environmental problems are not primarily problems of *disposal* of all the junk produced under capitalism, but arise from *their production* in the first place, which is increasing exponentially as capitalism spreads throughout the globe. It is not that the Soviet system was enlightened in respect to the environment, but that it was not *driven by market competition to produce ever more stuff*. Yes, individuals ought to be more environmentally conscious in their consumer choices and we all ought to recycle even more than we do, but this is trivial compared with the larger systemic problem. Professor Cudd's trust in the market and legislation to solve the problem is very naive; it has after all been tried, but the problem keeps getting dramatically worse. Just since 2004, chemical fac-tories and other polluters in the United States have violated the US Clean Water Act more than half a million times with virtual impunity.[34] At this stage in human history, we have to face the fact that what was a virtue of capitalism could be our death knell.[35]

Capitalist markets, information, and rationality: the Smithian model again

On the contrary, Professor Cudd argues. It is because of the mar-ket system's superiority as an aggregator of information that cap-italism is able to meet people's needs better than any planned

---

34 Charles Duhigg, "Clean Water Laws Neglected, at a Cost in Human Suffering," *New York Times*, September 13, 2009, 1.

35 Richard Smith, "The Eco-suicidal Economics of Adam Smith," *Capitalism Nature Socialism* 19(2) (June 2007): 22–43.

system could do. How is this supposed to happen? Not by planning, but by the market, which just collects information via consumer choices; "markets cause the resources to flow to fill consumer demands." In short, demand determines supply, as Adam Smith argued long ago. There are, however, many things wrong with this traditional Smithian model: first, it is obvious that people have needs for many things unavailable on the market, for example, affordable housing, so it is not demand, but "effective" demand, that is, demand that is backed up by enough money to pay for what is needed, that is registered in consumer choices. (Obviously Professor Cudd knows this, but it is important to point out that according to the model it is not sufficiently important to qualify the claim.) There are also many needs, like public transportation, that individuals cannot purchase even if they do have money, that capitalists will not supply because they are not sufficiently profitable, but which in fact require social planning. This brings out the point that *supply determines demand, as much as the reverse.* I would prefer good public transportation, but as it is not available I buy a car. The (lack of) supply forces me to change my "demand." Similarly, I wish that we had the solar power systems that would be sufficient to supply the world's energy needs, but as this potential has not been realized,[36] I install the more expensive and less efficient solar panels on my roof if I can, or, far more likely, buy energy supplied by fossil fuels. Once again, supply determined demand, but this is not registered on the market. In fact, *in the real world*, rather than being the best system for maximizing necessary information, it can be the reverse, as *capitalists often have an interest in suppressing information*. For example, for decades they suppressed scientific research showing the dangers of nicotine which has caused untold suffering and death, and they have fought to prevent labels on food that say "non-GMO," or "no Bovine Growth Hormone." This is

36 Dr. David Mills, "Solar Thermal Electricity as the Primary Replacement for Coal and Oil in the US Generation and Transportation," www.ausra.com, accessed July 23, 2010. This potential has not been realized because of the enormous political influence of the fossil fuel industrial complex.

information vitally important to consumers, but do not expect capitalists to collect it or to make it available if they have it. The information that capitalists are good at collecting is information about what they can best sell (the whole discipline of marketing is organized to do this), but what they can best sell is – to put it mildly – not necessarily what the world most needs. (For example, despite the recession, the United States has expanded its role as the world's largest weapons supplier, supplying 70 percent of all deals with developing countries.[37])

Another problem with the Smithian model is that it implies that capitalists simply collect and respond to information. But, in fact, capitalists are not passive receivers and responders. With respect to the choice between private versus public goods/services, it is not the case that they simply supply goods on the market and leave it to the political process to determine whether or not public goods are provided. Rather, they often act systematically to limit our choices; for example, research has shown that they organized to kill public transportation in Los Angeles and Detroit.[38] Nor are they neutral with respect to which possible consumer goods they supply. The more energy-efficient electric car was a threat to their gas-fueled cars, so they made sure consumers could not choose it.[39] Today, a similar struggle is being played out with respect to health care. Capitalists in the health care industry in the United States are doing everything they possibly can to prevent Americans from getting health care provided as a public good or even having the choice of public versus private health care options. The point is that the system's overriding goal of *profit maximization determines what information is acquired, what information is responded to, and what information is made public.* Again, Professor Cudd is relying on the abstract idealized model of capitalism dominant in economics courses in the United States.

37 Thom Shanker, "Despite Slump, US Role as Top Arms Supplier Grows," *New York Times,* September 7, 2009.
38 Stanley I. Fischler, *Moving Millions: An Inside Look at Mass Transit* (New York: Harper & Row, 1979).
39 See the film *Who Killed the Electric Car?,* 2006.

Tradition/religion, fetishes, and desires

I am in general agreement with Professor Cudd's criticisms of religion and tradition, but capitalism's relationship to tradition and religion is not quite as straightforward as she suggests. In general, capitalism has played a progressive historic role by destroying oppressive and backward traditions, but so did the Soviet system. In Afghanistan, for example, the Soviet-backed government of the 1980s advanced women's strategic gender interests, thereby arousing fierce opposition – but for Cold War reasons, the United States supported the opposition mujahadeen (including Osama bin Laden) against the government. Then it used feminist rhetoric to justify the war, even drawing on the great feminist authority Laura Bush to spread the message.[40] In Iraq, US occupation forces privatized the oil industry. Will this be in Iraqi women's practical gender interests? They have also supported, against feminist opposition, changes in Iraqi law giving religious groups more power over "private" issues. Furthermore, it is sometimes the material and cultural depredations of capitalism that incline people to seek solace in religion. If people's lives are not improved, they may look backward nostalgically. In today's world, where even the bad Soviet model no longer exists, where can people turn? Religion often seems the only answer. Rather than simply criticizing the oppressive role of religion, as Professor Cudd does, feminists should examine the context in which it is (often surprisingly) thriving. For example, while she justly critiques Thai Buddhism for encouraging sex slaves to passively accept their fate, she omits the facts that sex slavery is big business and the number of sex slaves has vastly increased due to capitalist development. As Marx expressed it so well, religion is "the sigh of the oppressed creature, the sentiment of a heartless

---

40 The overlap of a limited feminist vision with capitalism and the cynicism with which the US Government has deployed feminist rhetoric has led some socialist feminists to warn that feminism is being hijacked by capitalist interests. Hester Eisenstein, *Feminism Seduced: How Global Elites Use Women's Labor and Ideas to Exploit the World* (Boulder, CO: Paradigm Publishers, 2009); Nancy Fraser, "Feminism, Capitalism and the Cunning of History," *New Left Review* 56 (March/April 2009).

world, and the soul of soulless conditions ... The call to abandon their illusions about their condition is a call to abandon a condition that requires illusions."[41]

Professor Cudd's discussion of fetishism and adaptive desires is a useful contribution to an understanding of the internal dimensions of freedom and how internal barriers can both reflect and reinforce oppression. Although the concept of false consciousness had fallen out of favor due to the suggestion of elitism and a self untouched by social influences, and due to the influence of post-modernism that rejects all notion of authenticity, it is too important to radical critique to abandon. Properly understood, the concept does not imply a true self separate from social influences, but rather the possibility of a more authentic self if freed from *oppressive* social influences. My only criticism is that Professor Cudd does not carry the concept far enough to capitalism as such, an inherently hierarchical system. Ordinary people certainly do not control the processes by which consciousness is acquired and they never will in capitalism.[42]

Another world is possible: opening our imaginations

Capitalism is compatible with a limited kind of feminism, but not with the radical emancipatory vision that is at the heart of feminism. Professor Cudd seems drawn to that radical vision, but her commitment to capitalism in theory and reality makes that impossible. As I have argued throughout this reply, her picture of capitalism as a rational system that on the whole has enhanced material well-being and freedom and that can be reformed to make it ideal from a feminist perspective, rests on an idealized picture of capitalism. I expect that Professor Cudd and critical

41 Karl Marx, "Contribution to the Critique of Hegel's *Philosophy of Right*: Introduction," in Robert C. Tucker (ed.), *Marx–Engels Reader*, 2nd edn. (New York: W. W. Norton, 1978), 53.

42 See Nancy Holmstrom, "Free Will and a Marxist Concept of Natural Wants," *Philosophical Forum* 6 (1975): 423–45 and "Firming Up Soft Determinism," *The Personalist* 58 (1977): 39–51.

readers are likely to raise a similar objection to me, viz. that I am guilty of ideal theorizing, naivete, and utopianism. In this conclusion I will try to show that we are not equally vulnerable to this objection and to say more about why her critiques of Soviet-style planning do not apply to all noncapitalist models.

First, my sketch of an alternative to capitalism is, of course, ideal, if all this means is that it expresses a normative ideal, motivated by moral principles – as does feminism or liberal theory. So this sense of ideal theory should be uncontroversial. In fact, opponents of capitalism like me are motivated by the same ideals of liberty, equality, and solidarity professed throughout the Western world, but we argue that our alternative would not have the same barriers to realizing them that capitalism does.[43] Our criticism of capitalism is reminiscent of Gandhi's response to the question of what he thought of Western civilization: it would be a good idea, he said. But capitalism is more than ideals; it is an actually existing economic system. To argue for a reformed capitalism on the basis of moral ideals, as Professor Cudd does, is fine, but my charge was that her theory *of this actual system* was *idealized* in the sense that it was not an accurate picture of how it works and how it might be changed. Her account of what she believes capitalism *should* and *could* be was mixed up with her account of what capitalism *is*.

I am not in the same position. Since there is no actual system existing in reality that I am defending, I cannot be accused of idealizing it. Certainly, many people over the years have been guilty of defending idealized versions of Soviet-style systems, but I have made abundantly clear that I am not defending this non-capitalist alternative, even though I pointed out that they made many of the same advances as capitalism. In my case, there is no gap between theory and reality because there is no actually existing system to measure it against. Ah ha! I can hear critics say: you see, your theory is utopian. But the charge does not follow, any more than favoring the end of slavery or equality for women, or "free" wage labor was utopian at earlier stages of history. These ideals and social relations were unimaginable to

---

43 Thanks to Callinicos, *An Anti-Capitalist Manifesto*, for this formulation.

most people before they came into being; they seemed to violate not only the law (and sometimes God's law), but human nature, and "women's nature." But that has turned out to be untrue; the small minority thought to be crazy was right. Advocacy of these changes was utopian in a bad sense only if historical conditions absolutely precluded them at that time – which is what defenders of the status quo always claim until history finally proves them wrong. The precarious, fragile, human-made nature of societies is hard to perceive until they are close to the end. The alternative that I and many in the global justice movement favor (whether we call it libertarian socialism, eco-feminist socialism, economic democracy, or whatever) was not possible earlier in history, but is more than possible today. Thanks in part to the tremendous wealth created by capitalism, all of humankind could live decent lives if the world's resources were directed to this end rather than to the endless accumulation of profit. This is *not only possible but necessary*, as I have argued that present social and ecological conditions in fact make the continuation of capitalism unsustainable and therefore utopian. "Socialism or Barbarism" was the great Polish/German socialist activist and theoretician Rosa Luxemburg's assessment of the choice facing the world on the eve of the First World War shortly before she was assassinated. It is more apt than ever. Therefore, the challenge to come up with an alternative is not just mine. We all need to unleash our imaginations and collectively work out what such an alternative would look like. I agree it is a long shot, but as the lively socialist writer Barbara Garson put it, "I don't think it's so foolish to play a long shot when it's the only possible win."[44]

Alternative models: markets versus planning; bureaucratic versus democratic

Professor Cudd is not alone in assuming that there is no alternative to capitalism other than Soviet-style central planning (or

44 *All the Livelong Day: The Meaning and Demeaning of Routine Work* (New York: Penguin 1994), 271.

pre-capitalist modes of production, which I will ignore, as they are neither desirable nor practicable in the modern world). It is particularly difficult to imagine an alternative to capitalism if you do not understand the specificity of capitalism, if you think of capitalism as just a big complicated market society, and if, moreover, you think markets are just a natural form of interaction between people. Then it seems inevitable. But there are markets and markets. Markets existed before capitalism and could well exist after capitalism. The question is the markets' relationship to other institutions in society: do they dominate the society, as in capitalism?; is the allocation of society's resources the unintended consequence of competition among capitalists?; or are markets subordinate, embedded in other social institutions, and subject to control? as Polanyi described in earlier periods of history.

Some proposed versions of socialism envisage a central role for markets. Proponents of this kind of anti-capitalist model believe it is possible to get the good things that capitalism gets from markets but to control them democratically, for example, through workers' cooperatives which would eliminate the exploitation of the capital–labor relationship. This approach is called by its proponents "market socialism" and is probably the most popular of anti-capitalist visions, at least among academics. Some models are highly elaborated.[45] But other critics of capitalism question the viability of such a market socialist "middle ground," arguing that either we would still have the waste, inequalities, and instabilities of a market system, or if these were brought under democratic control, that it would be more or less the same as

45 Oscar Lange, "On the Economic Theory of Socialism," in Benjamin Evans Lippincott (ed.), *On the Economic Theory of Socialism* (Minneapolis, MN: University of Minnesota Press, 1938) was an early classic; Alec Nove, *The Economics of Feasible Socialism* (London: Routledge, 1983); J. Le Grand and S. Estrin (eds.), *Market Socialism* (Oxford: Clarendon Press, 1989); P. Bardan and J. Roemer (eds.), *Market Socialism* (New York: Oxford University Press, 1993); David Schweickart, *After Capitalism* (Lanham, MD: Rowman & Littlefield 2002); Diane Elson, "Market Socialism or the Socialization of the Market?," *New Left Review* 172 (November/December 1988), are among the most important proponents of market socialism.

democratic planning (also called participatory economics or participatory planning).[46]

I am most sympathetic to the latter position. The technical feasibility of planning in the age of computers has been proven I believe, and there are plausible, though hardly final, models of economic planning. Details differ, but they aim to combine decentralized cooperation and negotiation among producers, consumers, and others affected, thereby drawing on tacit knowledge. Their negotiations would occur within broad economic parameters set nationally by democratic bodies voting on alternative plans drafted by experts – a combination therefore of horizontal and (democratically controlled) vertical relations. "Prices" could be used as accounting devices for convenience in planning, but they would be set to include social costs. Though the models are worked out for the national level, they could be extended to the international level. In addition to eliminating the problems I believe are inherent in market-dominated systems, these models of decentralized economic planning can provide the coordination and innovation allegedly found only in capitalism, but for a different purpose.

They are also attractive morally in that they express a belief in the right and the ability of ordinary people to consciously and collectively control their destiny. This is not naive, though we have all been conditioned to believe it is impossible. In addition to revolutionary examples throughout history like the Paris Commune, there are exciting examples of local struggles and experiments showing these possibilities. While experts are necessary to explain the consequences of one choice or another, individuals can then decide which choice is best in the light of their

---

46 David McNally, *Against the Market: Political Economy, Market Socialism and the Marxist Critique* (New York: Verso, 1993); Fikret Adaman and Pat Devine, "On the Economic Theory of Socialism," *New Left Review* 221 (January/February 1997): 54–80; M. Albert and R. Hahnel, *The Political Economy of Participatory Economics* (Princeton University Press, 1991); Pat Devine, *Democracy and Economic Planning: The Political Economy of a Self-Governing Society* (Cambridge: Polity, 1988) offer the most important models of democratic planning.

own needs and values. In a powerful book, *Demanding Democracy After Three Mile Island* (the near-meltdown of a nuclear energy plant), a grandmother explains that if they had only told her that the nuclear plant could be dangerous she would have preferred to do without cheap energy and hang out her laundry to dry.[47] Such a decision requires no expertise. The examples from Argentina of worker takeovers of factories abandoned by their owners, or of land by the MST in Brazil (the landless peasants' movement), or the participatory budgeting process in which 100,000 people have participated, point in this direction. Whether such models of democratic planning are viable, and how much of a role markets would have to play in a democratic noncapitalist society is beyond the scope of this book. It is a question, moreover, that needs to be explored theoretically, but ultimately must be decided collectively by those attempting to build one.

Some, however, would object that the failures of the Soviet Union's model of central planning show the impossibility of any economic system based on planning. (It should be noted that their record was not one of total failure; in addition to admirable records in education and health, they did manage to be first in the space race.) The massive inefficiencies for which they were known can be explained by their political/economic structure. They were dictatorships run by and for the bureaucracy, which was not concerned to satisfy social needs any more than was in their own interest to do so.[48] The alienation from the government that this conflict of interest inevitably engendered led to those massive inefficiencies. As the adage went, "we pretend to work and they pretend to pay us." Thus, just as I have argued is true of capitalism, the Soviet model had built-in barriers to

---

47 Raymond L. Goldsteen and John K. Schorr, *Demanding Democracy After Three-Mile Island* (Gainesville, FL: University of Florida Press, 1991).

48 Professor Cudd defends the economic systems both of "socialism" (by which she means the bureaucratic Soviet model) and capitalism against criticisms that governments may intervene to outlaw unions or break strikes. But on my view, neither defense is valid. In capitalist societies, the government and the economy are distinct, but the government reflects the interests of the capitalists. In the bureaucratic model, economic and political power are fused in an undemocratic form.

collecting and using information to satisfy social needs. In an economic system oriented to the satisfaction of people's needs as democratically determined, while there would be mistakes, there would not be the same built-in barriers to collecting and disseminating important information found in the class systems of capitalism and bureaucratic collectivism. On the contrary; if people participate in making the decisions that affect them, they are not passive alienated products, but are likely to be committed to making the process most effective. Moreover, collective rule-from-below is not only how such a society would be constituted, but it could have come into being only through a process of self-emancipation, in which ordinary people's creative capabilities and self-confidence had been developed.

A final word: suppose I am wrong and there really is no alternative to capitalism? What would follow if this were true? Let us be clear: it would not follow that feminists ought to endorse capitalism as theory or reality – because my negative argument could be correct even if my positive alternative is impossible. This would mean – if my most pessimistic prognosis is correct – that humankind is doomed. Short of that, that we continue in our current obscenely unequal, crisis-ridden way, with the world's majority, particularly women, living harsh and short lives. If this is truly all that is possible, it does not make it good.

Bibliography

Adaman, Fikret and Pat Devine. "On the Economic Theory of Socialism," *New Left Review* 221 (January/February 1997): 54–80.

Agarwal, Bina. "Bargaining and Gender Relations: Within and Beyond the Household," *Feminist Economics* 3 (1997): 1–51.

Aguilar, Delia D. and Anne E. Lacsamana (eds.). *Women and Globalization.* Amherst, NY: Humanities Books, 2004.

Albert, Michael and Robin Hahnel. *Looking Forward: Participatory Economics for the Twenty-First Century.* Boston, MA: South End Press, 1991.

The Political Economy of Participatory Economics. Princeton University Press, 1991.

Allison, Dorothy. "A Question of Class," *Trash: Short Stories.* Ithaca, NY: Firebrand Books, 1988. Reprinted in Holmstrom (ed.), *The Socialist-Feminist Project.*

Alter, George. "Theories of Fertility Decline: A Nonspecialist's Guide to the Debate," in John R. Gillis, Louise A. Tilly, and David Levine (eds.), *The European Experience of Declining Fertility, 1850–1970.* Cambridge, MA: Blackwell, 1992.

Amsden, Alice. *Escape from Empire: The Developing World's Journey through Heaven and Hell.* Cambridge, MA: MIT Press, 2007.

The Rise of "the Rest": Challenges to the West from Late Industrializing Countries. Oxford University Press, 2001.

Anand, Sudhir, Paul Segal and Joseph E. Stiglitz (eds.). *Debates on the Measurement of Global Poverty.* New York: Oxford University Press, 2010.

Anderson, Elizabeth. "Ethical Assumptions in Economic Theory: Some Lessons from the History of Credit and Bankruptcy." *Ethical Theory and Moral Practice* 7 (2004): 347–60.

"What is the Point of Equality?," *Ethics* 109(2) (January 1999): 287–337.

"Ethical Limitations of the Market," in Charles K. Wilber (ed.), *Economics, Ethics and Public Policy*. Lanham, MD: Rowman & Littlefield, 1998, 236 and 239.

"The Ethical Limitations of the Market," *Economics and Philosophy* 6 (1990): 179–205.

"Is Women's Labor a Commodity?," *Philosophy and Public Affairs* 19 (Winter 1990): 71–92.

Andrews, Edmund L. "Report Projects a Worldwide Economic Slide," *New York Times*, March 9, 2009.

Anton, Anatole. "Public Goods as Commonstock," in Anatole Anton, Milton Fisk, and Nancy Holmstrom (eds.), *Not for Sale: In Defense of Public Goods*. Boulder, CO: Westview, 2000.

Antony, Louise. "Naturalized Epistemology, Morality and the Real World," *Canadian Journal of Philosophy* 26 (2000): 103–37.

Armstrong, David and Joseph J. Trento. *America and the Islamic Bomb: The Deadly Compromise*. New York: Random House, 2007.

Arneson, Richard J. "Lockean Self-Ownership: Towards a Demolition," *Political Studies* XXXIX (1991): 36–54.

Arnold, J. E. M. and J. G. Campbell. "Collective Management of Hill Forests in Nepal: The Community Forestry Development Project," *Common Property Resource Management*. Washington, DC: National Academy Press, 1984.

Astell, Mary. "Some Reflections Upon Marriage," in *Women and Men Political Theorists: Enlightened Conversations*, Kristin Waters (ed.). Malden, MA: Blackwell, 2000.

Bain, Peter and Phil Taylor. "Entrapped by the 'Electronic Panopticon'? Worker Resistance in the Call Centre," *New Technology, Work and Employment* 15 (2000): 2–18.

Bales, Kevin. *Disposable People: New Slavery in the Global Economy*. Berkeley, CA: University of California Press, 1999.

Bardan, Pranab and John E. Roemer (eds.). *Market Socialism: The Current Debate*. New York: Oxford University Press, 1993.

Bartky, Sandra. *Femininity and Domination: Studies in the Phenomenology of Oppression*. New York: Routledge, 1990.

Baumol, William J., Robert E. Litan, and Carl J. Schramm. *Good Capitalism, Bad Capitalism, and the Economics of Growth and Prosperity*. New Haven, CT: Yale University Press, 2007.

Bello, Walden. *The Food Wars*. London: Verso, 2009.

"Reforming the WTO is the Wrong Agenda," in Kevin Danaher and Roger Burbach (eds.), *Globalize This! The Battle Against the World Trade Organization and Corporate Rule*. Monroe, ME: Common Courage, 2000.

Beneria, Lourdes. *Gender, Development and Globalization, Economics as if all People Matter*. New York: Routledge, 2003.

Beneria, Lourdes and Savitri Bisnath (eds.). *Global Tensions. Challenges and Opportunities in the World Economy*. New York: Routledge, 2003.

Bennett, H. S. *Life on the English Manor*. Cambridge University Press, 1960.

Bennholdt-Thomsen, Veronika and Maria Mies. *The Subsistence Perspective: Beyond the Globalised Economy*. London: Zed Books, 1999.

Berenson, Alex. "A Year After a Cataclysm, Little Change on Wall St," *New York Times*, September 12, 2009.

Bergmann, Barbara. *The Economic Emergence of Women*, 2nd edn. New York: Palgrave Macmillan, 2005.

Berlin, Isaiah. "Two Concepts of Liberty," in Henry Hardy (ed.), *Liberty*. Oxford University Press, 2002.

Bernstein, Irving. *The Turbulent Years: A History of the American Worker, 1933–1941*. Boston: Houghton Mifflin, 1971.

The Lean Years: A History of the American Worker, 1920–1933. Baltimore: Penguin Books, 1970.

Bhat, P. N. Mari. "Returning a Favor: Reciprocity Between Female Education and Fertility in India," *World Development* 30(10) (October 2002): 1791–803.

Bhattacharjee, Anannya, Sarita Gupta, and Stephanie Luce. "Raising the Floor: The Movement for a Living Wage in Asia," *New Labor Forum* 18(3) (Fall 2009), at: www.asiafloorwage.org/documents/Press/Bhattacharjee%20et%5B1%5Dal.pdf.

"Raising the Floor: The Movement for a Living Wage in Asia," *New Labor Forum* 18 (Summer 2009): 72–82.

Bindman, Jo. "An International Perspective on Slavery in the Sex Industry," in Holmstrom (ed.), *The Socialist-Feminist Project*.

Blau, Francine D. "Gender and Economic Outcomes: The Role of Wage Structure," *Labor* 7 (1993): 73–92.

Blauner, Robert. *Alienation and Freedom: The Factory Worker and His Industry*. University of Chicago Press, 1964.

Bollier, David. *Silent Theft: The Private Plunder of Our Common Wealth*. New York: Routledge, 2002.

Bracking, Sarah. *Money and Power: Great Predators in the Political Economy of Development*. London: Pluto Press, 2009.

Braithwaite, John. *Regulatory Capitalism*. Northampton: Edward Elgar, 2008.

Braverman, Harry. *Labor and Monopoly Capital: The Degradation of Work in the Twentieth Century*. New York: Monthly Review, 1974.

Brenner, Johanna. "On Feminism and Global Justice," *New Politics* New Series IX(2), (34) (Winter 2003): 78–87.

"The Best of Times, the Worst of Times: US Feminism Today," in *Women and the Politics of Class*. New York: Monthly Review Press, 2000.

"Intersections, Locations and Capitalist Class Relations: Intersectionality from a Marxist Perspective," in *Women and the Politics of Class*. New York: Monthly Review Press, 2000.

Brenner, Johanna and Nancy Holmstrom. "Socialist Feminism versus Communitarian Conservatism," in *Women and the Politics of Class*. New York: Monthly Review Press, 2000.

Brenner, Robert. *The Economics of Global Turbulence*. New York: Verso, 2006.

Bright, James R. *Automation and Management*. Boston, MA: Division of Research, Graduate School of Business Administration, Harvard University, 1958.

Broad, Robin with John Cavanaugh. *Plundering Paradise: The Struggle for the Environment in the Philippines*. Berkeley, CA: University of California Press, 1993.

Broder, John and Jad Mouawad. "Energy Firms Find No Unity on Climate Bill," *New York Times*, October 19, 2009.

Brown, Drusilla K., Alan Deardorff, and Robert Stern. "The Effects of Multinational Production on Wages and Working Conditions in Developing Countries," in Robert E. Baldwin and L. Alan Winters (eds.), *Challenges to Globalization: Analyzing the Economics*. University of Chicago Press, 2004.

Buchanan, James M. "The Relevance of Pareto Optimality," *Journal of Conflict Resolution* 6 (1962): 341–54.

Bunkley, Nick and Bill Vlasic. "With Plants Shutting, the SUV Lumbers Near the End of the Line," *New York Times*, December 24, 2008.

Bureau of Labor Statistics. *Occupational Outlook Handbook*, 2010–11 edition, and the *Career Guide to Industries*, 2010–11 edition, Washington, DC.

Callinicos, Alex. *An Anti-Capitalist Manifesto*. Cambridge: Polity, 2003.

Cassidy, John. "The Return of Karl Marx," *The New Yorker*, October 20, 1997.

Cathcart, Rebecca. "Burden of Debt Weighed on Family in Murder-Suicide," *New York Times*, January 29, 2009.

Chandler, Alfred D., Jr., "How High Technology Industries Transformed Work and Life Worldwide from the 1880s to the 1990s," *Capitalism and Society* 1(2) (2006): 1–55.

Chang, Ha-Joon. *The Bad Samaritan: The Myth of Free Trade and the Secret History of Capitalism*. London: Bloomsbury, 2008.

Chen, Martha, Joann Vanek, Francie Lund, and James Heintz. "Progress of the World's Women 2005: Women, Work and Poverty," United Nations Development Fund for Women, 2005.

Chen, Shaohua and Martin Ravallion. "How Have the World's Poorest Fared Since the Early 1980s?," World Bank Policy Research Working Paper No. 3341, June 2004.

Chibber, Vivek. *Locked in Place: State Building and Late Industrialization in India*. Princeton University Press, 2003.

Chomsky, Noam. Interview with Wallace Shawn. *Essays*. Wallace Shawn. Chicago: Haymarket Books, 2009.

Christman, John. *The Myth of Ownership: Toward an Egalitarian Theory of Ownership*. New York: Oxford University Press, 1994.

Church, Jennifer. "Ownership and the Body," in Diana Tietjens Meyers (ed.), *Feminists Rethink the Self*. Boulder, CO: Westview Press, 1997.

Clark, Lorenne M. G. "Women and Locke: Who Owns the Apples in the Garden of Eden?," in Clark Lange and Lynda Lange (eds.), *The Sexism of Social and Political Philosophy*. University of Toronto Press, 1979.

Cohen, G. A. *Self-Ownership, Freedom and Equality*. Cambridge University Press, 1995.

History, Labour and Freedom. Oxford University Press 1988.

Cohen, Morris. "Property and Sovereignty," in Macpherson (ed.), *Property*.

Cohen, Patricia. "Ivory Tower Unswayed by Crashing Economy," *New York Times*, March 5, 2009.

Collins, Patricia Hill. *Black Feminist Thought: Knowledge, Consciousness and the Politics of Empowerment*, 2nd edn. New York: Routledge, 2000.

Combahee River Collective, 1977, in Gloria T. Hull, Patricia Bell Scott and Barbara Smith (eds.), *But Some of Us Were Brave*, Old Westbury, NY: The Feminist Press, 1982.

Conley, Dalton. "America is … # 15?," *The Nation*, March 23, 2009.

Being Black, Living in the Red: Race, Wealth, and Social Policy in America. Berkeley, CA: University of California Press, 1999.

Copelon, Rhonda. "From Privacy to Autonomy: The Conditions for Sexual and Reproductive Freedom," in Marlene Gerber Fried (ed.), *From Abortion to Reproductive Freedom: Transforming a Movement*. Boston, MA: South End Press, 1990.

Cornell, Drucilla. *At the Heart of Freedom*. Princeton University Press, 2000.

Coulson, Margaret, Branka Magas, and Hilary Wainwright. "'The Housewife and Her Labor Under Capitalism' – A Critique," *New Left Review* 89 (January/February 1975): 59–71.

Crowley, Michael. "The 'Death Tax' Scam," *Rolling Stone*, June 11, 2009.

Csikszentmihalyi, Mihaly. *Flow: The Psychology of Optimal Experience*. New York: Harper & Row, 1990.

Cudd, Ann E. "Sporting Metaphors: Competition and the Ethos of Capitalism," *Journal of the Philosophy of Sport* 34 (May 2007): 52–67.

Analyzing Oppression. New York: Oxford University Press, 2006.

"How to Explain Oppression," *Philosophy of the Social Sciences* 35(1) (March 2005): 20–49.

"The Paradox of Liberal Feminism: Choice, Rationality and Oppression," in Amy Baehr (ed.), *Varieties of Feminist Liberalism*. Lanham, MD: Rowman & Littlefield, 2004.

Cummins, Neil. "Marital Fertility and Wealth in Transition Era France, 1750–1850," Paris School of Economics Working Paper No. 2009–16, 2009.

Davies, James B., Susanna Sandström, Anthony Shorrocks, and Edward N. Wolff. "Estimating the Level and Distribution of Global Household Wealth," UN-Wider, Research Paper No. 2007/77, 2007.

Davis, Mike. *Planet of Slums*. London: Verso, 2006.

    The Monster at Our Door: The Global Threat of Avian Flu. New York: New Press, 2005.

    Late Victorian Holocausts: El Niño, Famines and the Making of the Third World. New York: Verso, 2001.

De Waal, Frans. *Good Natured: The Origins of Right and Wrong in Humans and Other Animals*. Cambridge, MA: Harvard University Press, 1996.

Delphy, Christine. *Close to Home: A Materialist Analysis of Women's Oppression*. London: Hutchinson, 1984.

Demsetz, Harold. *From Economic Man to Economic System: Essays on Human Behavior and the Institutions of Capitalism*. New York: Cambridge University Press, 2008.

Deparle, Jason and Robert Gebeloff. "Food Stamp Use Soars Across US, and Stigma Fades," *New York Times*, November 29, 2009.

Devine, Pat. *Democracy and Economic Planning: The Political Economy of a Self-Governing Society*. Cambridge: Polity, 1988.

Diamond, Jared. *Collapse: How Societies Choose to Fail or Succeed*. New York: Viking, 2005.

Dickensen, Donna. *Property, Women and Politics*. New Brunswick, NJ: Rutgers University Press, 1997.

Diener, Ed and Eunkook Suh (eds.). *Culture and Subjective Well Being*. Cambridge, MA: MIT Press, 2000.

Dietz, William H. "Sugar-sweetened Beverages, Milk Intake, and Obesity in Children and Adolescents," *The Journal of Pediatrics* 148 (February 2006): 152–54.

Dobb, Maurice. *Studies in the Development of Capitalism*, revised edition. New York: International Publishers, 1963.

Dominus, Susan. "Connecting Anxious Parents and Educators, at $450 an Hour," *New York Times*, August 18, 2009.

Donner, Wendy. "John Stuart Mill on Education and Democracy," in Nadia Urbinati and Alex Zakaras (eds.), *J. S. Mill's Political Thought*. New York: Cambridge University Press, 2007.

Draper, Hal. *Karl Marx's Theory of Revolution: Vols. 1–5*. New York: Monthly Review Press, 1977–90.

Duhigg, Charles. "Clean Water Laws Neglected, at a Cost in Human Suffering," *New York Times*, September 13, 2009.

Dwyer, Jim. "A Lifesaver Out of Reach, For Want of a Profit," *New York Times*, October 18, 2009.

Eagleton, Terry. *Ideology*. London: Verso, 1991.

Easterlin, Richard A. "How Beneficent is the Market? A Look at the Modern History of Mortality," *European Review of Economic History* 3(3) (1999): 257–94.

Eckholm, Erik. "Last Year's Poverty Rate was Highest in 12 Years," *New York Times*, September 11, 2009.

Ehrenreich, Barbara. *Nickel and Dimed: On (Not) Getting By in America*. New York: Metropolitan Books, 2001.

Ehrenreich, Barbara and Arlie Russell Hochschild (eds.). *Global Woman: Nannies, Maids, and Sex Workers in the New Economy*. New York: Henry Holt, 2002.

Eisenstein, Hester. *Feminism Seduced: How Global Elites Use Women's Labor and Ideas to Exploit the World*. Boulder, CO: Paradigm Publishers, 2009.

Eisenstein, Zillah. "Developing a Theory of Capitalist Patriarchy," *Capitalist Patriarchy and the Case for Socialist Feminism*. New York: Monthly Review Press, 1979.

Elson, Diane. "Market Socialism or the Socialization of the Market?," *New Left Review* 172 (November/December 1988).

Elster, Jon. *Sour Grapes*. Cambridge University Press, 1983.

Elster, Jon and Karl Ove Moene. *Alternatives to Capitalism*. Cambridge University Press, 1989.

Ezorsky, Gertrude. *Freedom in the Workplace?* Ithaca, NY: Cornell University Press, 2007.

Fackler, Martin. "In Japan, New Jobless May Lack Safety Net," *New York Times*, February 8, 2009.

Federici, Silvia. *Caliban and the Witch: Women, the Body and Primitive Accumulation*. Brooklyn, NY: Autonomedia, 2004.

Ferguson, Ann. "Empowerment, Development, and Women's Liberation," in Kathleen B. Jones and Anna G. Jónasdóttir (eds.), *The Political Interests of Gender Revisited: Redoing Theory and Research with a Feminist Face*. Manchester University Press, 2009.

Fernandez-Kelly, Patricia and Diane Wolf. "A Dialogue on Globalization," *Signs* 126 (2001): 1243–249.

Fischler, Stanley I. *Moving Millions: An Inside Look at Mass Transit*. New York: Harper & Row, 1979.

Fisher, William and Thomas Ponniah. *Another World is Possible*. London: Pluto Books, 2003.

Folbre, Nancy. *The Invisible Heart: Economics and Family Values*. New York: New Press, 2002.

Foot, Paul. "Poetry of Protest," *Socialist Review* 55 (July/August 1992): 18–20.

Fraser, Nancy. "Feminism, Capitalism and the Cunning of History," *New Left Review* 56 (March/April 2009).

Friedman, Marilyn. *Autonomy, Gender, Politics*. New York: Oxford University Press, 2003.

Friedman, Milton. *Capitalism and Freedom*. University of Chicago Press, 1962.

Fukuyama, Francis. "The End of History," *National Interest*, Summer 1989.

Galbraith, Kate. "Dark Days for Green Energy," *New York Times*, February 4, 2009.

Gardiner, Jean. "Women's Domestic Labor," *New Left Review* 89 (January/February 1975): 47–57.

Gardner, Howard, Mihaly Csikszentmihalyi, and William Damon. *Good Work: When Excellence and Ethics Meet*. New York: Basic Books, 2002.

Garrett, Laurie. *The Coming Plague: Newly Emerging Diseases in a World Out of Balance*. New York: Penguin, 1995.

Garson, Barbara. *All the Livelong Day: The Meaning and Demeaning of Routine Work*. New York: Penguin, 1994.

   The Electronic Workshop: How Computers Are Transforming the Office of the Future into the Factory of the Past. New York: Simon & Schuster, 1988.

Gasper, Des and Irene van Staveren. "Development as Freedom – And as What Else?," *Feminist Economics* 9 (July/November 2003): 137–61.

Gaus, Gerald F. "Backwards into the Future: Neorepublicanism as a Postsocialist Critique of Market Society," *Social Philosophy and Policy*, 20 (Winter 2003): 59–91.

Gauthier, David. *Morals by Agreement*. Oxford University Press, 1986.

Gibbard, Allan. "What's Morally Special About Free Exchange?," in E. F. Paul, F. D. Miller, Jr., and J. Paul (eds.), *Ethics and Economics*. Oxford University Press, 1985.

Gibson-Graham, J. K. *The End of Capitalism (as we knew it): A Feminist Critique of Political Economy*. Cambridge, MA: Blackwell, 1996.

Glucksmann, Miriam aka Ruth Cavendish. *Women on the Line*. London: Routledge, 2009.

Goldsteen, Raymond L. and John K. Schorr. *Demanding Democracy After Three-Mile Island*. Gainesville, FL: University of Florida Press, 1991.

Goodin, Robert. "Exploiting a Situation and Exploiting a Person," in Andrew Reeve (ed.), *Modern Theories of Exploitation*. London: Sage, 1987.

Gordon, April. *Transforming Capitalism and Patriarchy: Gender and Development in Africa*. Boulder, CO: Lynne Rienner, 1996.

Gough, Ian and John Harrison. "Unproductive Labor and Housework Again," *Bulletin of the Conference of Socialist Economists* IV (February 1975).

Gray, Francine du Plessix. *Soviet Women: Walking the Tightrope*. New York: Doubleday, 1989.

Gray, John. "Hayek on Liberty, Rights and Justice," *Ethics* 92 (October 1981): 73–84.

"On Positive and Negative Liberty," *Political Studies* 28 (1980): 507–26.

Greene, J. Megan. *The Origins of the Developmental State in Taiwan*. Cambridge, MA: Harvard University Press, 2008.

Greenhouse, Steven. "Low-Wage Workers Are Often Cheated, Study Says," *New York Times*, September 2, 2009.

Greider, William. *The Soul of Capitalism: Opening Paths to a Moral Economy*. New York: Simon & Schuster, 2003.

Gundersen, Adolf. *The Environmental Promise of Democratic Deliberation*. Madison, WI: University of Wisconsin Press, 1995.

Hakim, Catherine. *Key Issues in Women's Work*, 2nd edn. London: Glasshouse Press, 2004.

Haoson, Dominique. "Few Safety Nets for Women of Color," Interpress News Service, March 4, 2009.

Hartmann, Heidi. "The Unhappy Marriage of Marxism and Feminism: Toward a More Progressive Union," in Lydia Sargent (ed.), *Women and Revolution*. Cambridge: South End Press, 1981.

Harvey, David. *The New Imperialism*. New York: Oxford University Press, 2005.

Hassoun, Nicole. "Free Trade, Poverty, and Inequality," *The Journal of Moral Philosophy*. forthcoming.

Hayek, Friedrich A. Von. *The Fatal Conceit*. University of Chicago Press, 1988.

The Constitution of Liberty. University of Chicago Press, 1978.

The Road to Serfdom. University of Chicago Press, 1944.

Held, David and Ayse Kaya (eds.). *Global Inequality: Patterns and Explanations*. Cambridge: Polity Press, 2007.

Held, Virginia. "John Locke on Robert Nozick," *Social Research* 43 (Spring 1976): 169–95.

Herbert, Bob. "Safety Nets for the Rich," *New York Times*, October 20, 2009.

Herman, Edward S. and Noam Chomsky. *Manufacturing Consent: The Political Economy of the Mass Media*. New York: Pantheon, 2002.

Hicks, Joe and Grahame Allan, "A Century of Change: Trends in the UK Statistics since 1900," House of Commons Library Research Paper No. 99/111, 1999.

Higgins, Patricia. "The Reactions of Women, with Special Reference to Women Petitioners," in B. Manning (ed.), *Politics, Religion and the English Civil War*. New York: St. Martins Press, 1973.

Hill, Christopher. *Liberty Against the Law*. London: Verso, 1996.

The World Turned Upside Down: Radical Ideas During the English Revolution. Harmondsworth: Penguin Classics, 1972.

Hirschmann, Nancy. *Gender, Class and Freedom in Modern Political Theory*. Princeton University Press, 2008.

The Subject of Liberty: Toward a Feminist Theory of Freedom. Princeton University Press, 2003.

Hochschild, Arlie. *The Managed Heart: Commercialization of Human Feeling*, 2nd edn. Berkeley, CA: University of California Press, 2003.

The Commercialization of Intimate Life. Berkeley, CA: University of California Press, 2003.

Hochschild, Arlie Russell. "Love and Gold," in Ehrenreich and Hochschild (eds.), *Global Woman*.

Holmstrom, Nancy. "Exploitation," in *International Encyclopedia of Ethics*, forthcoming.

(ed.). *The Socialist-Feminist Project: A Contemporary Reader in Theory and Politics*. New York: Monthly Review Press, 2002.

"Review of *Self-Ownership, Freedom and Equality*," *Philosophical Review*, 106 (October 1997): 583–86.

"Humankind(s)," *Biology, Behavior and Society, Canadian Journal of Philosophy* supplementary volume 20 (1994): 69–105.

"Coercion, Exploitation and Labor," *APA Newsletter on Philosophy and Law* 94(1) (Fall 1994): 84–88.

"Exploitation," in Will Kymlicka (ed.), *Justice in Political Philosophy*. Cheltenham: Edward Elgar, 1992.

"A Marxist Theory of Women's Nature," *Ethics* 94 (April 1984): 456–73.

"'Women's Work,' the Family and Capitalism," *Science and Society* XLV (Summer 1981): 186–211.

"Firming Up Soft Determinism," *The Personalist* 58 (1977): 39–51.

Holmstrom, Nancy and Richard Smith. "Their Rationality and Ours," in Anatole Anton and Richard Schmitt (eds.), *Toward a New Socialism*. Lanham, MD: Lexington Books, 2006.

"The Necessity of Gangster Capitalism: Primitive Accumulation in Russia and China," *Monthly Review* (February 2000): 1–15.

Holt-Gimenez, Eric, Raj Patel, and Annie Shattuck. *Food Rebellions! Crisis and the Hunger for Justice*. Oakland, CA: Food First Books, 2009.

International Labor Organization, *Global Wage Report*, 2008–9.

World Employment Report, 2004–5.

Jaggar, Alison (ed.), *Philosophical Topics* (issue devoted to global gender justice) 37(1) (Spring 2009).

"A Feminist Critique of the Alleged Southern Debt," *Hypatia* 17(4) (Fall 2002): 119–42.

Feminist Politics and Human Nature. Totowa, NJ: Rowman & Allanheld, 1983.

Johnson, Chalmers. *The Sorrows of Empire: Militarism, Secrecy and the End of the Republic*. New York: Metropolitan, 2004.

Miti and the Japanese Miracle. Stanford University Press, 1982.

Jónasdóttir, Anna G. "On the Concept of Interest, Women's Interests, and the Limitations of Interest Theory," in Kathleen Jones and Anna G.

Jónasdóttir (eds.), *The Political Interests of Gender: Developing Theory and Research with a Feminist Face*. London: Sage, 1988.

Kabeer, Naila. *The Power to Choose*. New York: Verso, 2002.

Kandiyoti, Deniz. "Bargaining with Patriarchy," in Holmstrom (ed.), *The Socialist-Feminist Project*.

Kaplan, Temma. "The Disappearing Fathers Under Global Capitalism," in Holmstrom (ed.), *The Socialist-Feminist Project*.

Crazy for Democracy: Women in Grassroots Movements. New York: Routledge, 1997.

Kelley, Robin D. G. *Freedom Dreams*. Boston, MA: Beacon Press, 2002.

Kernohan, Andrew. *Liberalism, Equality, and Cultural Oppression*. Cambridge University Press, 1998.

Kirby, Peter. *Child Labour in Britain, 1750–1870*. New York: Palgrave Macmillan, 2003.

Kittay, Eva Feder. *Love's Labor*. New York: Routledge, 1999.

Klein, Naomi. *The Shock Doctrine: The Rise of Disaster Capitalism*. New York: Henry Holt, 2007.

Kozol, Jonathan. *Savage Inequalities*. New York: Crown Publications, 1992.

Kristof, Nicholas. "Where Sweatshops are a Dream," *New York Times*, January 15, 2009.

"In Praise of the Maligned Sweatshop," *New York Times*, June 6, 2006.

Krugman, Paul. Column, *New York Times*, January 5, 2009.

"How Did Economists Get It So Wrong?," *New York Times Magazine*, September 6, 2009.

"Money Can't Buy Happiness. Er, Can It?," *New York Times*, June 1, 1999.

Kruks, Sonia, Rayna Rapp, and Marilyn B. Young (eds.). *Promissory Notes: Women in the Transition to Socialism*. New York: Monthly Review, 1989.

Ladd, Everett Carl and Karlyn H. Bowman. *Attitudes Toward Economic Inequality*. Washington, DC: AEI Press, 1998.

Lan, Pei-Chia. "Among Women: Migrant Domestics and their Taiwanese Employers Across Generations," in Ehrenreich and Hochschild (eds.), *Global Woman*.

Lange, Oscar. "On the Economic Theory of Socialism," in Benjamin Evans Lippincott (ed.), *On the Economic Theory of Socialism*. Minneapolis, MN: University of Minnesota Press, 1938.

Layard, R. *Happiness: Lessons from a New Science*. New York: Penguin Press, 2005.

Le Goff, Jacques. *Time, Work and Culture in the Middle Ages*. Chicago University Press, 1980.

Le Grand, Julian. "Equity versus Efficiency: The Elusive Trade-off," *Ethics* 100 (1990): 554–68.

Le Grand, Julian and Saul Estrin (eds.). *Market Socialism*. Oxford: Clarendon Press, 1989.

Lean, Geoffrey. "Year of the Hungry: 1,000,000,000 Afflicted," *The Independent*, December 28, 2008.

Lehrman, Karen. *The Lipstick Proviso: Women, Sex and Power in the Real World*. New York: Doubleday, 1997.

Leonhardt, David. "Jobless Rate Hits 10.2%, with More Underemployed," *New York Times*, November 7, 2009.

"Scant Progress on Closing Gap in Women's Pay," *New York Times*, December 26, 2006.

Levine, Andrew. *Arguing for Socialism: Theoretical Considerations*. Boston, MA: Routledge & Kegan Paul, 1984.

Linebaugh, Peter. *The Magna Carta Manifesto*. Berkeley, CA: University of California Press, 2008.

Locke, John. *Second Treatise of Government*, C. B. Macpherson (ed.). Indianapolis, IN: Hackett Publishing, 1980.

Longino, Helen. *Science as Social Knowledge: Values and Objectivity in Scientific Inquiry*. Princeton University Press, 1989.

Longworth, Richard C. *Global Squeeze: The Coming Crisis for First World Nations*. Chicago: Contemporary Books, 1998.

Luce, Stephanie and Mark Brenner. "Women and Class: What Has Happened in Forty Years?," *Monthly Review* (July/August, 2006): 80–93.

MacCallum, Gerald C., Jr. "Negative and Positive Freedom," *Philosophical Review* 76 (1967): 312–34.

Maclean, Nancy. "Post-War Women's History: The 'Second Wave' or the End of the Family Wage?," in Jean-Christophe Agnew and Roy Rosensweig (eds.), *A Companion to Post-1945 America*. Malden, MA: Blackwell, 2002.

Macpherson, C. B. *The Rise and Fall of Economic Justice and Other Essays*. New York: Oxford University Press, 1985.

The Life and Times of Liberal Democracy. Oxford University Press, 1978.

(ed.). *Property: Mainstream and Critical Positions*. University of Toronto Press, 1978.

The Political Theory of Possessive Individualism: Hobbes to Locke. Oxford University Press, 1962.

Maines, Rachel P. *The Technology of Orgasm: "Hysteria," the Vibrator, and Women's Sexual Satisfaction*. Baltimore, MD: Johns Hopkins University Press, 1999.

Mander, Jerry and Edward Goldsmith (eds.). *The Case Against the Global Economy and for a Turn Toward the Local*. San Francisco, CA: Sierra Club Books, 1996.

Marx, Karl. *Grundrisse*, trans. Martin Nicolaus. Harmondsworth: Penguin, 1973.

Capital: Vol. III. New York: International Publishers, 1967.

"Wage Labor," in *Economic and Philosophic Manuscripts of 1844*, trans. Martin Mulligan. Moscow: Progress Publishers, 1959.

Capital: Vol. I, trans. Samuel Moore and Edward Aveling. Moscow: Progress Publishers, 1887.

Marx, Karl and Friedrich Engels. *Marx–Engels Reader*, 2nd edn., Robert C. Tucker (ed.). New York: W. W. Norton, 1978.

Mathieu, Nicole-Claude. "When Yielding is Not Consenting," *Gender Issues* 10 (1990): 3–49.

McChesney, Robert. *Rich Media, Poor Democracy: Communication Politics in Dubious Times*. Champaign, IL: University of Illinois Press, 1999.

McKeown, Thomas. *The Modern Rise of Population*. New York: Academic Press, 1976.

McNally, David. *Against the Market: Political Economy, Market Socialism and the Marxist Critique*. New York: Verso, 1993.

Meyers, Chris. "Wrongful Beneficence: Exploitation and Third World Sweatshops," *Journal of Social Philosophy*. 35(3) (2004): 319–33.

Michaels, Walter Benn. *The Trouble with Diversity: How We Learned to Love Identity and Ignore Inequality*. New York: Henry Holt, 2007.

Mihm, Stephen. "Dr. Doom," *New York Times*, August 15, 2008.

Milanovic, Branko. "Global Inequality of Opportunity: How Much of Your Income is Determined by Birth?," World Bank Report, February 2009

Miles, Robert. *Capitalism and Unfree Labor: Anomaly or Necessity?* London: Tavistock, 1987.

Mill, John Stuart. *On Liberty*. London: Longman, Roberts & Green, 1859.

Miller, Judith. "Globalization Widens Rich–Poor Gap, UN Says," *New York Times*, June 29, 1999.

Mills, Charles. "'Ideal Theory' as Ideology," in Peggy DesAutels and Margaret Urban Walker (eds.), *Moral Psychology*. Lanham, MD: Rowman & Littlefield, 2004.

The Racial Contract. Ithaca, NY: Cornell University Press, 1997.

Mishra, Pankaj. "The Myth of the New India," *New York Times*, July 6, 2006.

Moghadam, Valentine M. *Globalizing Women: Transnational Feminist Networks*. Baltimore, MD: Johns Hopkins University Press, 2005.

Molyneux, Maxine. "Mobilization Without Emancipation? Women's Interests, State and Revolution," *Feminist Studies* 11(2) (1985): 227–54. Reprinted as "Conceptualizing Women's Interests," in Holmstrom (ed.), *The Socialist-Feminist Project*.

Monbiot, George. *The Age of Consent: A Manifesto for a New World Order*. London: Flamingo, 2003.

Montgomery, David. "Social Choice in Machine Design: The Case of Automatically Controlled Machine Tools and a Challenge for Labor," *Politics and Society* 3/4 (1978).

Moody, Kim. *Workers in a Lean World*. New York: Verso, 1997.

Moya, Paula M. L. "Post-Modernism, 'Realism,' and the Politics of Identity: Cherrie Moraga and Chicana Feminism," in M. Jacqui Alexander and Chandra Talpade Mohanty (eds.), *Feminist Genealogies, Colonial Legacies, Democratic Futures*. New York: Routledge, 1997.

Multinational Monitor. "A BIG Idea: A Minimum Income Guarantee," interview with Karl Widerquist, May/June 2009.

Narayan, Uma. "Informal Sector Work, Microcredit and Women's Empowerment: A Critical Overview," unpublished, October 18, 2006.

Dislocating Cultures: Identities, Traditions and Third World Feminism. New York: Routledge, 1997.

Noble, David F. *Progress Without People: In Defense of Luddism*. Chicago: Charles H. Kerr, 1993.

Forces of Production: A Social History of Industrial Automation. Oxford University Press, 1986.

Nove, Alec. *The Economics of Feasible Socialism*. London: Routledge, 1983.

Nozick, Robert. *Anarchy, State, and Utopia*. New York: Basic Books, 1974.

Nussbaum, Martha. *Women and Human Development: The Capabilities Approach*. Cambridge University Press, 2000.

Olson, Elizabeth. "'Free Markets Leave Women Worse Off,' Unicef Says," *New York Times*, September 23, 1999.

O'Neill, Onora. "Justice, Gender and International Boundaries," in Martha C. Nussbaum and Amartya Sen (eds.), *The Quality of Life*. New York: Oxford University Press, 1993.

Organization for Economic Cooperation and Development. *OECD Employment Outlook, Statistical Annex*, 2003.

Overton, Richard. "An Arrow Against All Tyrants," in G. E. Aylmer (ed.), *The Levellers in the English Revolution*. London: Thames & Hudson, 1975.

Palast, Greg, Jerrold Oppenheim, and Theo MacGreggor. *Democracy and Regulation: How the Public Can Govern Essential Services*. London: Pluto, 2003.

Pareto, Vilfredo. *Manual of Political Economy*. New York: Austus M. Kelley, 1971.

Parfit, Derek. *Reasons and Persons*. Oxford University Press, 1987.

Patel, Raj. *Stuffed and Starved: The Hidden Battle for the World Food System*. Brooklyn, NY: Melville House Publishing, 2008.

Patel, Raj, Eric Holt-Gimenez, and Annie Shattuck. "Ending Africa's Hunger," *The Nation*, September 21, 2009.

Pateman, Carole. *The Sexual Contract*. Stanford University Press, 1988.

Pateman, Carole and Charles Mills. *Contract and Domination*. Cambridge: Polity, 2007.

Patterson, Orlando. *Freedom in the Making of Western Culture*. New York: Basic Books, 1991.

Perelman, Michael. "Some Economics of Class," *Monthly Review* (July/ August 2006): 18–28.

Perkins, John. *Geopolitics and the Green Revolution: Wheat, Genes and the Cold War.* New York: Oxford University Press, 1997.

Petchesky, Rosalind Pollack. "Human Rights, Reproductive Health and Economic Justice: Why They are Indivisible," in Holmstrom (ed.), *The Socialist-Feminist Project.*

"The Body as Property: A Feminist Re-vision," in Faye D. Ginsburg and Rayna Rapp (eds.), *Conceiving the New World Order: The Global Politics of Reproduction.* Berkeley, CA: University of California Press, 1995.

Pettit, Philip. *A Theory of Freedom: From the Psychology to the Politics of Agency.* New York: Oxford University Press, 2001.

Pincus, Walter and Joby Warrick. "Financial Crisis Called Top Security Threat to US," *Washington Post*, February 13, 2009.

Piper, Adrian M. S. "Higher Order Discrimination," in Amelie Oksenberg Rorty (ed.), *Identity, Character, and Morality.* Cambridge, MA: MIT Press, 2000.

Piven, Frances Fox and Richard A. Cloward. *Poor People's Movements: Why They Succeed and How They Fail.* New York: Random House, 1979.

Pogge, Thomas. *World Poverty and Human Rights: Cosmopolitan Responsibilities and Reforms.* Cambridge: Polity, 2002.

Polanyi, Karl. *The Great Transformation.* Boston, MA: Beacon Press, 1957.

Pope, James Gray, Peter Kellman, and Ed Bruno. "Free Labor Today," *New Labor Forum* (Spring 2007): 8–18.

Porrit, Jonathon. *Capitalism As If the World Matters.* London: Earthscan, 2005.

Potter, Elizabeth. "Locke's Epistemology and Women's Struggles," in Bat-Ami Bar On (ed.), *Modern Engendering: Critical Feminist Readings in Modern Western Philosophy.* Albany, NY: SUNY Press, 1994.

Preis, Art. *Labor's Giant Step: 20 Years of the CIO.* New York: Pioneer Publishers, 1964.

Radin, Margaret Jane. "Market Inalienability," *Harvard Law Review* 100 (1987): 1849–937.

Ramey, Valerie A. "Time Spent in Home Production in Twentieth-Century United States: New Estimates from Old Data," *Journal of Economic History*, 69 (March 2009): 1–47.

Rampell, Catherine. "As Layoffs Surge, Women May Pass Men in Job Force," *New York Times*, February 6, 2009.

Ransom, P. J. G. *The Victorian Railway and How it Evolved.* London: Heinemann, 1990.

Ravaioli, Carla. *Economists and the Environment.* London: Zed Books, 1995.

Rawls, John. *A Theory of Justice.* Cambridge, MA: Harvard University Press, 1971.

Reiman, Jeffrey. "Exploitation, Force and the Moral Assessment of Capitalism: Thoughts on Roemer and Cohen," *Philosophy and Public Affairs* 16 (Winter 1987): 3–41.

Richards, Janet Radcliffe. *The Sceptical Feminist: A Philosophical Inquiry.* Harmondsworth: Penguin, 1980.

Riley, James C. *Rising Life Expectancy: A Global History.* New York: Cambridge University Press, 2001.

Roemer, John. *Free to Lose.* Cambridge, MA: Harvard University Press, 1988.

Rohatyn, Felix. "Saving American Capitalism," *International Herald Tribune,* June 29, 2009.

Roosevelt, Franklin D. *The Public Papers and Addresses of Franklin D. Roosevelt: Vol. XII,* Samuel Rosenman (ed.). New York: Harper, 1950.

Roosevelt, Theodore. "Theodore Roosevelt on Motherhood and the Welfare of the State," *Population and Development Review* 13(1) (March 1987): 141–47.

Rosen, Ellen Israel. *Making Sweatshops: The Globalization of the US Apparel Industry.* Berkeley, CA: University of California Press, 2002.

Rostow, W. W. *The World Economy: History and Prospect.* Austin, TX: University of Texas Press, 1978.

Ryan, Cheyney. "Yours, Mine and Ours: Property Rights and Individual Liberty," *Ethics* 87 (1977): 126–41.

Sachs, Jeffrey. *The End of Poverty: Economic Possibilities for Our Time.* New York: Penguin, 2005.

Sahlins, Marshall. *Stone Age Economics.* New York: Aldine, 1972.

Sample, Ruth. *Exploitation: What it is and Why it's Wrong.* Lanham, MD: Rowman & Littlefield, 2003.

Sandberg, Ake. "Enriching Production: Perspectives on Volvo's Uddevalla Plant as an Alternative to Lean Production," MPRA Paper No. 10785, University Library of Munich Germany, revised 2007.

Sassen, Saskia. "Global Cities and Survival Circuits," in Ehrenreich and Hochschild (eds.), *Global Woman.*

Sayer, Andrew. *The Moral Significance of Class.* Cambridge University Press, 2005.

Schor, Juliet. *The Overspent American.* New York: Basic Books, 1998.

The Overworked American: The Unexpected Decline of Leisure. New York: Basic Books, 1992.

Schwartz, Nelson. "Job Losses Pose a Threat to Stability Worldwide," *New York Times,* February 14, 2009.

Schweickart, David. *After Capitalism.* Lanham, MD: Rowman & Littlefield, 2002.

Against Capitalism. New York: Cambridge University Press, 1993.

Scott, Joan. *Gender and the Politics of History*. New York: Columbia University Press, 1988.

Secombe, Wally. "The Housewife and Her Labor Under Capitalism," *New Left Review* 83 (January 1973): 3–24.

Sen, Amartya. "Capitalism Beyond the Crisis," *New York Times Review of Books*, March 26, 2009.

Development as Freedom. New York: Random House, 1999.

"Gender Inequality and Theories of Justice," in Martha Nussbaum and Jonathon Glover (eds.), *Women, Culture, and Development*. New York: Oxford University Press, 1995.

"Markets and Freedoms," *Oxford Economic Papers* 45 (October 1993): 519–41.

On Ethics and Economics. Oxford: Blackwell, 1987.

Poverty and Famines. Oxford: Clarendon Press, 1981.

Sengupta, Somini. "As Indian Growth Soars, Child Hunger Persists," *New York Times*, March 13, 2009.

"Indian Prosperity Creates Paradox; Many Children are Fat, Even More are Famished," *New York Times*, December 31, 2006.

Sennett, Richard and Jonathan Cobb. *The Hidden Injuries of Class*. New York: W. W. Norton, 1993.

Shanker, Thom. "Despite Slump, US Role as Top Arms Supplier Grows," *The New York Times*, September 7, 2009.

Shawn, Wallace. Interview on *Democracy Now*, Pacifica Radio, November 17, 2009.

Shiva, Vandana. "Why are Indian Farmers Committing Suicide and How Can We Stop This Tragedy?," available at: Voltairenet.org, May 23, 2009.

Silliman, Jael, Marlene Gerber Fried, Loretta Ross, and Elena R. Gutierrez (eds.). *Undivided Rights: Women of Color Organize for Reproductive Justice*. Cambridge: South End, 2004.

Singer, Peter. *The Life You Can Save: Acting Now to End World Poverty*. New York: Random House, 2009.

Skinner, Quentin. "A Third Concept of Liberty," *Proceedings of the British Academy* 117 (2002): 237–68.

Smith, Adam. *The Wealth of Nations*. New York: Modern Library, 1937.

Smith, Richard. "The Eco-suicidal Economics of Adam Smith," *Capitalism Nature Socialism* 19(2) (June 2007): 22–43.

"Capitalism and *Collapse*: Contradictions of Jared Diamond's Market Meliorist Strategy to Save the Humans," *Ecological Economics* 55(2) (November 2005): 294–306.

Steel, Mark. "So Karl Marx Was Right After All," *The Independent*, March 4, 2009.

Stevens, Evelyn P. "Marianismo: The Other Face of Machismo in Latin America," in Anne Minas (ed.), *Gender Basics: Feminist Perspectives on Women and Men*. Belmont, CA: Wadsworth, 1993.

Stiglitz, Joseph. *Freefall: America, Free Markets, and the Sinking of the World Economy*. New York: W. W. Norton, 2010.

"The Contributions of the Economics of Information to Twentieth Century Economics," *The Quarterly Journal of Economics* 115(4) (November 2000): 1441–478.

Whither Socialism? Cambridge, MA: MIT Press, 1994.

Sunstein, Cass. *The Partial Constitution*. Cambridge, MA: Harvard University Press, 1993.

Superson, Anita. "Deformed Desires and Informed Desire Tests," *Hypatia* 20 (Fall 2005): 109–26.

Taylor, Barbara. *Eve and the New Jerusalem: Socialism and Feminism in the Nineteenth Century*. London: Virago Press, 1983.

Teller-Elsberg, Jonathan, James Heintz, and Nancy Folbre. *Field Guide to the U.S. Economy: A Compact and Irreverent Guide to Economic Life in America*. New York: New Press, 2006.

Thaler, Richard. "Psychology of Choice and the Assumptions of Economics," in Alvin E. Roth (ed.), *Laboratory Experimentation in Economics: Six Points of View*. Cambridge University Press, 1987.

Therborn, Gorän. *Between Sex and Power*. London: Routledge, 2004, 293.

Thomas, Janet. "Women and Capitalism: Oppression or Emancipation?," *Comparative Studies in Society and History* 30(3) (July 1988): 534–49.

Thurow, Lester. *The Future of Capitalism: How Today's Economic Forces Shape Tomorrow's World*. New York: Penguin, 1996.

Tilly, Louise. "Gender, Women's History and Social History," *Pasato e Presente* (1989): 20–21.

Tucker, Jonathan B. *Scourge: The Once and Future Threat of Smallpox*. New York: Atlantic Monthly Press, 2001.

Tullock, Gordon. "Inheritance Justified," *Journal of Law and Economics* 13 (1970): 465–74.

Van Parijs, Philippe. *Real Freedom for All: What if Anything can Justify Capitalism?* Oxford: Clarendon Press, 1995.

Varian, Hal R. "Distributive Justice, Welfare Economics, and the Theory of Fairness," *Philosophy and Public Affairs* 4 (1974–75): 223–47.

Varikas, Eleni. "Gender, Experience and Subjectivity: The Tilly–Scott Disagreement," *New Left Review* 211 (May/June, 1995): 89–101.

Veblen, Thorstein. *The Theory of the Leisure Class*. Boston, MA: Houghton Mifflin, 1973.

Visvanathan, Nalini, Lynn Duggan, Laurie Nisonoff, and Nan Wiegersma (eds.). *Women Development and Gender Reader*. London: Zed Books, 1997.

Voronina, Olga. "Soviet Patriarchy Past and Present," trans. Nicole Svobodny and Maude Meisel, *Hypatia* 8 (1993): 97–111.

Wade, Robert. "Global Inequality," *The Economist*, April 28, 2001, 72–74.

Wainwright, Hilary. *Reclaim the State: Experiments in Popular Democracy*. London: Verso, 2003.

Walby, Sylvia. *Patriarchy at Work*. Minneapolis, MN: University of Minnesota Press, 1986.

Waldron, Jeremy. "Property Rights and Welfare Distribution," in R. G. Frey and Christopher Wellman (eds.), *A Companion to Applied Ethics*. Malden, MA: Blackwell, 2003.

 The Right to Private Property. New York: Oxford University Press, 1988.

Walker, John D. "Liberalism, Consent, and the Problem of Adaptive Preferences," *Social Theory and Practice* 21 (Fall, 1995): 457–71.

Warren, Paul. "Self-Ownership, Reciprocity, and Exploitation, or Why Marxists Shouldn't Be Afraid of Robert Nozick," *Canadian Journal of Philosophy* 24 (1994): 33–56.

Weir, David R. "Family Income, Mortality, and Fertility on the Eve of the Demographic Transition: A Case Study of Rosny-Sous-Bois," *Journal of Economic History* 55 (1995): 1–26.

Wertheimer, Alan. *Exploitation*. Princeton University Press, 1996.

Willett, Cynthia. *Irony in the Age of Empire: Comic Perspectives on Democracy and Freedom*. Bloomington, IN: Indiana University Press, 2008.

Williams, Eric. *Capitalism and Slavery*. New York: Capricorn, 1966.

Winstanley, Gerrard. *Winstanley: "The Law of Freedom" and Other Writings*, Christopher Hill (ed.). Harmondsworth: Penguin Classics, 1973.

Wolff, Edward. *Top Heavy: The Increasing Inequality of Wealth in America and What Can Be Done About it*, 2nd edn. New York: New Press, 1996.

Wolff, Robert Paul. *The Poverty of Liberalism*. Cambridge, MA: Harvard University Press, 1968.

Wong, Edward. "China Charges 58 with Covering Up Deadly Mine Blast," *New York Times*, December 1, 2009.

Wood, Ellen Meiksins. *Democracy Against Capitalism: Renewing Historical Materialism*. New York: Cambridge University Press, 1995.

 Peasant-Citizen and Slave: The Foundations of Athenian Democracy. London: Verso, 1988.

Wood, Ellen Meiksins and Neal Wood. *A Trumpet of Sedition*. New York University Press, 1997.

Wright, Erik Olin. *Classes*. London: Verso, 1985.

Xinran. *The Good Women of China: Hidden Voices*. New York: Anchor, 2003.

Young, Iris Marion. *Justice and the Politics of Difference*. Princeton University Press, 1990, ch. 5.

Yunus, Muhammad. *Creating a World Without Poverty*. New York: Public Affairs, 2007.

Zarembka, Joy M. "America's Dirty Work: Migrant Maids and Modern-Day Slavery," in Ehrenreich and Hochschild (eds.), *Global Woman*.

Zimmerman, David. "Coercive Wage Offers," *Philosophy and Public Affairs* 10 (1981): 121–45.

FILMS / MOVIES

Beyond Elections: Redefining Democracy in the Americas, directed by Michael Fox, Progressive Films, 2008.

Crude: The Real Price of Oil, directed by Joe Berlinger, Entendre Films, 2009.

Life and Debt, directed by Stephanie Black, Tuff Gong Pictures Production, 2001.

The Corporation, directed by Mark Achbar, Jennifer Abbott, and Joel Barcan, HelloCoolWorld, 2009.

Who Killed the Electric Car?, directed by Chris Paine, Papercut Films, 2006.

WEBSITES

AAAGRrrr!, at: http://pambazuka.org/en/category/enewsl/53590, accessed July 22, 2010.

Amazon Watch, at: www.AmazonWatch.org, accessed July 23, 2010.

Amnesty International Report 2009. "State of the World's Human Rights, Cuba," at: http://thereport.amnesty.org/en/regions/americas/cuba, accessed August 1, 2009.

   "State of the World's Human Rights, Singapore," at: http://thereport. amnesty.org/en/regions/asia-pacific/singapore, accessed August 1, 2009.

Bell, Beverley and the Other Worlds Collaborative. "Who Says You Can't Change the World: Just Economies on an Unjust Planet," at: www. otherworldsarepossible.org.

Bureau of Labor Statistics, Current Population Survey, at: www.bls.gov/ CPS, accessed July 23, 2010.

Central Intelligence Agency, *CIA World Factbook*, 2008, at: www.cia.gov/ library/publications/the-world-factbook, accessed September 5, 2009.

Charity: Water, at: www.charitywater.org.

Draper, Hal. "The Two Souls of Socialism," Marxists Internet Archives, at: www.marxists.org, accessed July 22, 2010.

Fallon, Peter and Zafiris Tzannatos. "Child Labor: Issues and Directions for the World Bank," the World Bank, 1998, at: http://info.worldbank.org/ etools/docs/library/76309/dc2002/proceedings/pdfpaper/module9pfzt. pdf.

Farmer, Amy, Jill Tiefenthaler, and Amandine Sambira. "The Availability and Distribution of Services for Victims of Domestic Violence in the

US," at: www.waltoncollege.uark.edu/lab/AFarmer/services%20 RR%202004.doc.

Fisk, Donald M. "American Labor in the Twentieth Century," US Bureau of Labor Statistics, at: www.bls.gov/opub/cwc/cm20030124ar02p1. htm#13, accessed August 29, 2009.

Folbre, Nancy. "Welfare for Bankers," *The New York Times Economix Blog*, April 20, 2009, at: http://economix.blogs.nytimes.com/2009/04/20/ welfare-for-bankers.

Gap Minder Foundation. "Gapminder World," at: www.gapminder.org/ gapminder-world/documentation/#gd004, accessed September 5, 2009.

Gini coefficient, at: http://en.wikipedia.org/wiki/Gini_coefficient#Definition.

Haines, M. "Fertility and Mortality in the United States," February 4, 2010, at: http://eh.net/encyclopedia/article/haines.demography.

Human Rights Watch. "Fingers to the Bone: United States Failure to Protect Child Farmworkers," 2000, at: www.hrw.org/en/reports/2000/06/02/ fingers-bone-0.

Kelly, Kevin. "The New Socialism: Global Collectivist Society is Coming Online," at: www.wired.com, accessed May 22, 2009.

Labor Notes at: www.labornotes.org.

London, Kathleen. "The History of Birth Control," *Yale–New Haven Teachers Institute* 6 (1982), published online at: www.yale.edu/ynhti/curriculum/units/1982/6, accessed August 6, 2009.

Maddison, Angus. "World Development and Outlook 1820–2030: Evidence Submitted to the House of Lords," February 20, 2005, at: www.ggdc. net/maddison.

"Historical Statistics for the World Economy: 1–2003 AD," at: www.ggdc. net/maddison.

Mills, Dr. David. "Solar Thermal Electricity as the Primary Replacement for Coal and Oil in the US Generation and Transportation," at: www.ausra. com, accessed July 23, 2010.

Planned Parenthood Federation of America. "History and Success," at: www. plannedparenthood.org/about-us/who-we-are/history-and-successes. htm#Sanger, accessed September 5, 2009.

Rasmussen Poll, April 2009, at: www.rasmussenreports.com.

Stanford, Jim. "The Economics, and Politics, of Auto Workers' Wages," at: www.theglobeandmail.com, accessed April 20, 2009.

United Nations Development Programme (UNDP), Human Development Reports 2009, at: http://hdr.undp.org/en, accessed September 5, 2009.

"Human Development Reports 2007/2008, Statistical Update 2008," at: http://hdr.undp.org/en/statistics.

"Measuring Inequality: Gender-related Development Index (GDI) and Gender Empowerment Measure (GEM)," Human Development Reports

2007/2008, at: http://hdr.undp.org/en/media/HDR_20072008_Tech_Note_1.pdf, accessed September 5, 2009.

"Tracking the Millennium Development Goals," at: http://www.mdg-monitor.org/goal1.cfm.

United Nations Human Development Report 2008, at: http://hdrstats.undp.org/indicators/147.html.

www.hdr.undp.org/publications/papers.cfm

United Nations Millennium Ecosystem Assessment, at: www.millenniumassessment.org.

US Census Bureau, US Census Bureau International Data Base, at: www.census.gov/ipc/www/idb/worldpop.php, accessed August 24, 2009.

War Registers League, February 2010, at: www.warresisters.org.

Whitelegg, John. "Dirty from Cradle to Grave," at: www.worldcarfree.net/resources/freesources/DirtyfromCradletoGrave.rtf.

World Bank. "World Development Indicators Poverty Data," 2009, at: http://siteresources.worldbank.org/DATASTATISTICS/Resources/WDI08supplem, accessed October 5, 2009.

www.aclu.org/workplacerights.

www.CommonDreams.org, accessed May 6, 2009.

Index